IN THE NAME OF

ALLAH

THE ALL-COMPASSIONATE, ALL-MERCIFUL

BELIEF IN ALLAH

- Title: BELIEF IN ALLAH
- Author: ‘Umar S. al-Ashqar
- Translated from Arabic edition 10 (1995)
- English Edition 1 (2002)
- English Edition 3 (2005)
- Translator: Nasiruddin al-Khattab
- Editor: Huda Khattab
- Layout: IIPH, Riyadh, Saudi Arabia
- Cover Designer: Haroon Vicente Pascual, Arlington, U.S.A.

ISLAMIC CREED SERIES 1

BELIEF IN ALLAH

In the Light of the Qur'an and Sunnah

‘Umar S. al-Ashqar

Translated by:
Nasiruddin al-Khattab

INTERNATIONAL ISLAMIC PUBLISHING HOUSE

King Fahd National Library Cataloging-in-Publication Data

Al-Ashqar, Umar S.

Belief in Allah in the light of the Qur'an and Sunnah. / Umar S. al-Ashqar ; translated by Nasiruddin al-Khattab - 3rd ed.,- Riyadh , 2005

...p ; 22 cm ,- **(Islamic creed series ; 1)**

1- Faith (Islamic creed) I-Nasiruddin al-Khattab (trans.)
II-Title III-Series

243 dc 1424/2957

Legal Deposit no. **1424/2957**
ISBN Hard Cover: **9960-850-38-2**
ISBN Soft Cover: **9960-672-92-1**

International Islamic Publishing House (IIPH)
P.O.Box 55195 Riyadh 11534, Saudi Arabia
Tel: 966 1 4650818 - 4647213 - Fax: 4633489
E-Mail: iiph@iiph.com.sa . www.iiph.com.sa

Please take part in this noble work by conveying your comments to ***IIPH*** *through e-mail, fax or postal-mail address.*

CONTENTS

CHAPTER TWO

PUBLISHER'S NOTE

All Praise is due to Allah, the Exalted, Lord of the universe. Blessings and peace be upon the last of the prophets and messengers, Muhammad son of 'Abdullah, his family, Companions and those who follow his footsteps till the end of time.

"Belief in Allah", the One, the Only, the Supreme, is the very core of the Islamic Creed. All aspects of Islamic life, socio-economical, political, international relations, etc., revolve around the belief in One God, Allah.

Dr. Al-Ashqar dealt with this subject at length, and augmented his book with all evidence available to him, but primarily from the basic fundamental sources - the Qur'an and the Sunnah of the last Messenger (Blessings and Peace be upon him). Professor Al-Ashqar discussed all aspects of the concept: proofs of existence, definition, deviations, theo-philosophical schools, impacts, etc.

We feel blessed to be able to publish this book in a number of languages. This English edition, we believe, is an instrumental guide to all readers of English who seek enlightenment. May Allah accept this work and reward all those associated with its production.

Muhammad ibn 'Abdul-Muhsin Al-Tuwaijri

General Manager
International Islamic Publishing House, IIPH
Riyadh, Saudi Arabia

TRANSLATOR'S FOREWORD

The existence of a Creator or Supreme Being is a matter which, until recent centuries, has never been disputed. The first man on earth — Adam — believed in and had the right concept of the Creator. Even though mankind subsequently slid into *shirk* and idolatry, almost all civilizations and cultures believed in a Supreme Being or Creator.

But when mankind went astray, their concept of this Supreme Being became distorted. They attributed partners or rivals to Him, or they thought of Him in human terms, or they ascribed evil actions and characteristics to Him.

Modern times brought a new phenomenon — the denial of God's existence altogether. The bitter struggle between science and the Church ended with the scientists prevailing. They then proceeded to attack the very foundations of the Church, seeking to prove that God had never existed at all.

Yet science also points to the existence of the Creator. Those who ponder the universe and study the details of natural phenomena cannot but conclude that this is the work of an Almighty Creator; it did not happen by chance. The more one ponders the signs in creation, the more one comes to understand the attributes of the Creator — wisdom, power, mercy... Thus Dr. 'Umar al-Ashqar devotes a large section of this book to an examination of natural phenomena, as the Qur'an urges us to do, and notes how they point to the existence of the Creator.

In this book, Dr. 'Umar al-Ashqar takes us on a journey of discovery, through poetry, philosophy and science, to the Qur'an and Sunnah, the Revelation through which the Creator, Allah (ﷻ), has revealed

Himself to mankind. He explains the importance of understanding the attributes of Allah in the light of the Qur'an and Sunnah and the way in which these texts were understood by the *salaf* (the pious predecessors); we should not try to twist the meanings to suit philosophical principles, human ideas or other whims. He contrasts the pure Islamic *'aqeedah* (creed) with human deviations within and without the Muslim world, and affirms the principle which lies at the heart of Islamic belief and practice, viz. *Tawḥeed* or the absolute Oneness of the Divine.

May Allah (ﷻ), reward the author for his presentation of the Islamic belief in the Creator. May He cause this book to bring a deeper understanding of *Tawḥeed* to English-speaking readers and may He keep us on the Straight Path of pure belief which leads to Paradise. May Allah bless our Prophet Muhammad (ﷺ) and his family and Companions, and grant them peace.

Naṣiruddin al-Khaṭṭab

PREFACE TO THE NEW, REVISED EDITION

Praise be to Allah (ﷻ), the One and Only God, the Sustainer of the heavens and the earth, Who has guided us to His perfect religion and His straight path. I send blessings upon His chosen one, the Seal of His Prophets and Messengers, Muhammad (ﷺ), and upon his righteous family and Companions, and upon those who follow them in truth until the Day of Judgement.

I started to write this series on *'aqeedah* (creed) in the light of the Qur'an and Sunnah approximately fifteen years ago, and I only completed it a few years ago. Allah decreed that this series should become popular worldwide, and that it should be studied and be a source of benefit for seekers of knowledge in various lands. All of this is from the grace and bounty of Allah alone, for He is the One Who guided me to write it and He is the One Who blessed me by enabling me to complete it. He is the One Who caused it to be accepted by His slaves, so to Him alone be praise and blessings. I ask Him to keep the reward with Him for the Day when I meet Him.

Since I completed this series, I have been hoping to review it, especially the earliest parts of it, but I was prevented from fulfilling this hope by other work commitments, and by ill-health. But in recent months I had some spare time which I was able to make the most of by reviewing what I had written. Hence this new, revised edition, with additional material in the first three chapters. I hope that I will be able to review the rest of the series in the coming days, by the help of and strength of Allah.

I have not changed the main ideas of this book, but sought to verify the texts quoted, attributing them to their proper sources. I have changed the order in which some topics appear, and expanded some passages where the material required further explanation or further evidence to support an idea. I also shortened some passages and added to others, in a very few places.

Changing and altering and improving what a person has written is all part of human nature. Allah, the All-Glorious, has decreed that no writing should be perfect apart from His Book.

Praise be to Allah, the Lord of the Worlds.

'Umar Sulaymaan 'Abdullah al-Ashqar

College of Shari'ah — Jordan University

PREFACE TO THE FIRST EDITION

Praise be to Allah (ﷻ). We praise Him and seek His help, forgiveness and guidance. We repent to Him, and we seek refuge in Him from the evils of our own selves and from our evil actions. Whomsoever Allah guides, none can lead him astray, and whomsoever Allah sends astray, none can guide him. I bear witness that there is no god except Allah alone, with no partner or associate, and I bear witness that Muhammad (ﷺ) is His slave and Messenger.

This book is about Islamic *'aqeedah* (creed), and I ask Allah to make it of benefit to its author, readers and publisher. May He make this effort sincerely for His sake alone, and may He keep it (its reward) with Him for the Day when I meet Him, for He is the All-Hearing Who answers prayers.

The title of this book is significant. It is a book about the Islamic creed (*'aqeedah*), based on the two sources of Islam, the Book of Allah and the Sunnah of His Messenger. These two sources are those on which the *'aqeedah* of the first generation of this ummah was built.

I do not think that anyone will disagree that the *'aqeedah* of those men was the pure *'aqeedah*, as pure as the water of the sea when it is undisturbed by the winds, and as strong as the mighty mountains, the most trustworthy handhold. Through those who believed in this creed (*'aqeedah*), Allah (ﷻ), changed the course of human history. Shall we be blamed if we trace this *'aqeedah* back to its source, the well from which the righteous forebears of this ummah drank?

Many people claim that they refer to the Qur'an and Sunnah, paying lip-service to them in their *khuṭbahs* (speeches/sermons) and writings, but they go against them when they quote evidence and seek guidance elsewhere.

So we see them giving priority to the views of men over the texts of the Qur'an and *aḥaadeeth*. We see them seeking guidance other than that of Islam concerning conduct and dealings with others. This is why I took the time in my Introduction to this book to refer to these two sources, the Qur'an and the *ṣaḥeeḥ* (sound and authentic) Sunnah, concerning *'aqeedah* (creed) and shari'ah (Islamic law), and to discuss the specious arguments of those who want to ignore the Sunnah.

The Introduction also includes other topics, such as the definition of *'aqeedah*, its position in relation to shari'ah and *eemaan* (faith) and the ruling on one who denies *'aqeedah* or one of its basic principles. I also explore in more detail the confusion of ancient and modern groups who denounce people as *kaafir* (disbeleiver) on the grounds of sins alone.

I did not omit in the Introduction to describe the Qur'anic methodology of explaining *'aqeedah* which was brought by Islam, and to show how this methodology differs from the methodology of philosophy and theology (*'ilm al-kalaam*) which brought such great disasters to the ummah. I hope that I have succeeded in defining the difference between the two methodologies with regard to sources, methods and ways, how they quote evidence and in their consequences.

Through this discussion, the uniqueness and distinguishing features of the Qur'anic methodology will become clear.

In the chapter on belief in Allah, you will find evidence that proves the existence of Allah. I also discussed the specious arguments of the atheists and refuted those who say that the universe came into existence accidentally, or that it was made by "nature."

Following on from that, I shed light on the two ways in which we learn about our Lord, which are the visible signs and the written signs. I sought to discuss this in the light of the texts of the Qur'an and *aḥaadeeth* of the Prophet (ﷺ). These topics form the main issue of this book.

Because this issue is of the utmost importance, and is the main reason for the division of the ummah, I found that I had no other option but to discuss the principles in the light of which the texts which speak of the Names and Attributes of Allah are to be interpreted, and the guidelines which explain this topic, so as to refute the arguments of those whose interpretation of these *aayaat* (verses) was not in accordance with the Qur'anic methodology.

Finally, I discussed the issue of *Tawḥeed* or the belief in the oneness of Allah: the concept, and how to achieve this belief, under the heading of *Laa ilaaha illa-Allah*. I explained the meaning and conditions of *Tawḥeed*, as well as that which contradicts and negates *Tawḥeed*, namely *shirk* (polytheism).

Then I turned my attention to the history of *'aqeedah* (creed), refuting the theory that *'aqeedah* (belief in Allah) is something which is evolved.

I sought the help of whatever books, ancient and modern, that came my way, some of which I mentioned at the end of this book. My selection of books was dictated by the methodology indicated by the titles of the books.

This book may please some people and anger others. Allah knows that the good pleasure of my Lord was the goal I kept before me as I wrote. That does not mean that everything in this book is correct, for the pen may slip and the mind may wander and lose its focus. No one is infallible except *Al-Muṣṭafaa* (ﷺ). So long as there is life left in me, I recant any mistakes that I may have made which go against that which came from Allah, the Almighty, and from His Messenger. If Allah takes my soul before I am able to correct the mistakes, then I say the same as Imam ash-Shaafa'i (may Allah have mercy on him) said: "If a hadith is *ṣaḥeeḥ* (sound), then that is my *madhhab* (school of thought - my way). If you see that what I said goes against what the Messenger of Allah said, then cast my view aside."

We will publish other works in this series, dealing with other principles of *'aqeedah* in the same manner, *Insha Allah* (Allah Willing). I ask Allah (ﷻ), the All-Glorious, to help me say and do the right thing. There is no power and no strength except with Allah, the Exalted.

'Umar Sulaymaan 'Abdullah al-Ashqar

INTRODUCTION

1- *'AQEEDAH*: DEFINITION AND EXPLANATION

1) *'Aqeedah*: Meaning and Usage

The word *'aqeedah* and related words are constantly repeated by people in their everyday conversations. So we hear them saying "*Ana a'taqid kadha* (I believe such and such)," "*Foolaan 'aqeedatuhu ḥasanah* (So and so's belief is sound)," "The Islamic *'aqeedah* is the strongest cause for the great Islamic victories in every time and place," "The war between us and the Jews is in fact an ideological war (*ḥarb 'aqaa'idiyah*)" and so on.

What do people mean by the word *'aqeedah* (faith)? What does this word mean in Arabic? What is the concept of *'aqeedah* (faith) in Islam?

'Aqaa'id (plural of *'aqeedah*) are the things which people's hearts affirm and believe in, the things that they accept (as true). These are matters which are held as certain beliefs, with no taint of doubt.[1]

'Aqd al-ḥabl (tying the rope) means tying one part to another part, as opposed to untying it. In Arabic, the meanings of the word *'aqd* revolve around ideas of adherence, certainty and affirmation. There is *aayah* (verse) in the Qur'an:

---

[1] *Risaalat al-'Aqaa'id* by *Shaykh* Ḥasan al-Banna. See *Majmoo' ar-Rasaa'il*, 429. The Muslim scholars of earlier and recent times have discussed the issues of this branch of knowledge under the heading of *Al-'Aqaa'id*, although the word *'aqeedah* is not mentioned in the Book of Allah or in the Sunnah of His Messenger (ﷺ).

﴿ لَا يُؤَاخِذُكُمُ ٱللَّهُ بِٱللَّغْوِ فِىٓ أَيْمَـٰنِكُمْ وَلَـٰكِن يُؤَاخِذُكُم بِمَا عَقَّدتُّمُ ٱلْأَيْمَـٰنَ... ﴿٨٩﴾ ﴾

﴾Allah will not punish you for what is unintentional in your oaths, but He will punish you for your deliberate oaths [*'aqqadtum*];...﴿ *(Qur'an 5: 89)*

A deliberate oath is one in which there is resolve and determination in the heart, unlike an unintentional oath which may be spoken of without any intention.

'Uqood refers to the strongest of covenants, as when Allah (ﷻ), says:

﴿ يَـٰٓأَيُّهَا ٱلَّذِينَ ءَامَنُوٓا۟ أَوْفُوا۟ بِٱلْعُقُودِ ... ﴿١﴾ ﴾

﴾O' you who believe! Fulfil [your] obligations [*awfoo bi'l-'uqood*]...﴿ *(Qur'an 5: 1)*

The Arabs say "*a'taqada ash-shay'u*" when a thing becomes solid and strong.[2]

In Islam, *'aqeedah* (belief) is the counterpart of shari'ah, because Islam is composed of both *'aqeedah* and shari'ah. Shari'ah means the practical duties enjoined by Islam, about acts of worship and dealings with others.

2) *'Aqeedah* is a Matter of Knowledge in the Heart

'Aqeedah is not a practical matter, but a matter of knowledge which the Muslim is obliged to believe in his heart, because Allah has told him about these matters in His Book or through the Revelation to His Messenger (ﷺ).

The basic principles of the *'aqeedah* Allah commands us to believe in are mentioned in the *aayah* (verse):

---

[2] *Lisaan al-'Arab*, 2/836, listing of words derived from the root *'aqada.*

﴿ ءَامَنَ ٱلرَّسُولُ بِمَآ أُنزِلَ إِلَيۡهِ مِن رَّبِّهِۦ وَٱلۡمُؤۡمِنُونَۚ كُلٌّ ءَامَنَ بِٱللَّهِ وَمَلَٰٓئِكَتِهِۦ وَكُتُبِهِۦ وَرُسُلِهِۦ لَا نُفَرِّقُ بَيۡنَ أَحَدٖ مِّن رُّسُلِهِۦۚ وَقَالُواْ سَمِعۡنَا وَأَطَعۡنَاۖ غُفۡرَانَكَ رَبَّنَا وَإِلَيۡكَ ٱلۡمَصِيرُ ﴿٢٨٥﴾ ﴾

﴾The Messenger [Muhammad] believes in what has been sent down to him from his Lord, and [so do] the believers. Each one believes in Allah, His Angels, His Books, and His Messengers. [They say], 'We make no distinction between one another of His Messengers' - and they say, 'We hear, and we obey. [We seek] Your forgiveness, our Lord, and to You is the return [of all].'﴿
(Qur'an 2: 285)

The Prophet (ﷺ) defined this belief in the famous hadith of Jibreel (Gabriel) (عليه السلام) (may Allah's peace be upon him), in which he (ﷺ) said:

"*Eemaan* (faith) is to believe in Allah, His angels, His Books, the Meeting with Him and His Messengers, and to believe in the final Resurrection."[3]

So *'aqeedah* in Islam refers to those matters of knowledge which have been transmitted in authentic reports from Allah and His Messenger, and which the Muslim must believe in with all his heart, believing in what Allah and His Messenger say.

3) *'Aqeedah* means Certain Belief, with no Room for Doubt

In order for these principles to form *'aqeedah*, we must believe in them firmly, with no room for doubt. If there is any element of doubt, then they are merely speculation, not *'aqeedah* (belief). "*Al-Mu'jam al-Waseeṭ*" defines *'aqeedah* as a belief in which the one who holds

[3] Bukhari. See *Ṣaḥeeḥ al-Bukhari bi Sharḥihi Fatḥ al-Baari*, 1/114; Muslim, 1/39, hadith no. 5. This version is narrated by Muslim.

that belief will not entertain any doubt whatsoever."[4] Evidence (*daleel*) for that is found in the Qur'an:

﴿ إِنَّمَا ٱلْمُؤْمِنُونَ ٱلَّذِينَ ءَامَنُوا۟ بِٱللَّهِ وَرَسُولِهِۦ ثُمَّ لَمْ يَرْتَابُوا۟ ... ﴿١٥﴾ ﴾

﴿Only those are the believers who have believed in Allah and His Messenger, and afterward doubt not...﴾ *(Qur'an 49: 15)*

﴿ الٓمٓ ﴿١﴾ ذَٰلِكَ ٱلْكِتَٰبُ لَا رَيْبَ فِيهِ ... ﴿٢﴾ ﴾

﴿*Alif-Laam-Meem*..This is the Book [the Qur'an], whereof there is no doubt.﴾ *(Qur'an 2: 1-2)*

﴿ رَبَّنَآ إِنَّكَ جَامِعُ ٱلنَّاسِ لِيَوْمٍ لَّا رَيْبَ فِيهِ ... ﴿٩﴾ ﴾

﴿'Our Lord! Verily, it is You Who will gather mankind together on the Day about which there is no doubt...'﴾ *(Qur'an 3: 9)*

Allah condemned the *mushrikeen* (polytheists) who were filled with doubt:

﴿ ... وَٱرْتَابَتْ قُلُوبُهُمْ فَهُمْ فِى رَيْبِهِمْ يَتَرَدَّدُونَ ﴿٤٥﴾ ﴾

﴿...There hearts are in such doubt that they even waver in their doubt.﴾ *(Qur'an 9: 45)*

4) The Issues of *'Aqeedah* are Invisible

It may be noted that the issues which we are required to believe in are unseen matters, not visible, tangible things. This is what Allah referred to when He praised the believers:

﴿ ٱلَّذِينَ يُؤْمِنُونَ بِٱلْغَيْبِ ... ﴿٣﴾ ﴾

[4] *Al-Mu'jam al-Waseet*, 2/614.

﴾Who believe in the *Ghayb*[5]...﴿ *(Qur'an 2: 3)*

Allah is unseen, as are His angels and the Last Day. With regard to His Books and Messengers, one might think that they are visible, but what is referred to here is the belief that they come from Allah, i.e., that the Messengers were sent by Allah and that the Books were revealed by Allah, which is the matter of the unseen.

5) Correct *'Aqeedah* and False *'Aqeedah*

'Aqeedah (belief) is not exclusive to Islam. The adherents of religions and schools of thought inevitably have beliefs according to which they run their lives. This applies to individuals just as it applies to societies. From the beginning of the creation until the Day (of Judgement), until the time when Allah will inherit the earth and everything on it. Beliefs are divided into two kinds:

a) The correct *'aqeedah*: It is composed of the set of beliefs brought by the noble Messengers. This is the one *'aqeedah*, because it was sent down by the All-Knowing, All-Aware (Allah); it cannot be imagined that it differs from one Messenger to another, or from one time to another.

b) False beliefs: They are very many indeed. Their falseness stems from the fact that they are the product of human thought and intellect. No matter how great mankind may become, their knowledge is (and will remain) limited and is (and will continue to be) influenced by the

---

[5] *Al-Ghayb*: Literally means a thing not seen. But this word includes vast meanings: Belief in Allah, Angels, Holy Books, Allah's Messengers, Day of Resurrection and *Al-Qadar* (Divine Pre-Ordainments). It also includes what Allah and His Messenger informed about the knowledge of the matters of past, present, and future, e.g., news about the creation of the heavens and earth, botanical and zoological life, the news about the nations of the past, and about Paradise and Hell. (Footnote from *Interpretation of the Meanings of the Noble Qur'an* by Dr. Muhammad Muḥsin Khan and Dr. Muhammad Taqi-ud-Din al-Hilali).

customs, traditions and thoughts that surround them.

There are also false beliefs which are the result of distortion, changes and alteration, as is the case with the Jewish and Christian beliefs at the present time. They were distorted a long time ago, and were corrupted as a result of this distortion, even though each of them was originally a sound *'aqeedah*.

Where is the true *'aqeedah* today?

The true *'aqeedah* today is not found anywhere except in the religion of Islam, because this is the protected religion which Allah (ﷻ), has guaranteed to protect.

﴿ إِنَّا نَحْنُ نَزَّلْنَا ٱلذِّكْرَ وَإِنَّا لَهُۥ لَحَٰفِظُونَ ﴿٩﴾ ﴾

﴿Verily, We, it is We Who have sent down the *Dhikr* [i.e. the Qur'an] and surely, We will guard it [from corruption].﴾ *(Qur'an 15: 9)*

The beliefs of other religions, even though they may contain some grains of truth here and there, do not present a clear image of the truth.

Whoever wants to know the true, correct *'aqeedah* will not find it in Judaism or in Christianity, or in the words of the philosophers. He will only find it in Islam, in the original sources of the faith: the Qur'an and Sunnah, pure and clear and shining, which convince man's mind with evidence and proof, and fill the heart with *eemaan*, certainty, light and life.

﴿ وَكَذَٰلِكَ أَوْحَيْنَآ إِلَيْكَ رُوحًا مِّنْ أَمْرِنَاۚ مَا كُنتَ تَدْرِى مَا ٱلْكِتَٰبُ وَلَا ٱلْإِيمَٰنُ وَلَٰكِن جَعَلْنَٰهُ نُورًا نَّهْدِى بِهِۦ مَن نَّشَآءُ مِنْ عِبَادِنَاۚ ... ﴿٥٢﴾ ﴾

﴿And thus We have sent to you [O' Muhammad] *Rooḥ* [a Revelation, and a Mercy] of Our Command. You knew not what is the Book, nor what is Faith? But We have made it [this Qur'an] a light wherewith We guide whosoever of Our slaves We will...﴾ *(Qur'an 42: 52)*

6) The Importance and Necessity of Islamic *'Aqeedah*

The Islamic *'aqeedah* is as essential for man as water and air. Without this *'aqeedah* he is lost and confused. The Islamic *'aqeedah* is the only one which can answer the questions that have always preoccupied man and still preoccupy human thought and cause frustration: where did I come from? Where did the universe come from? Who is the Creator? What are His attributes and names? Why did He create us and the universe? What is our role in this universe? What is our relationship to the Creator who created us? Are there other, invisible worlds beyond the world that we can see? Are there other intelligent beings apart from man? Is there another life after this life? If the answer is positive, what is that other life like?

There is no other belief today, apart from the *'aqeedah* of Islam, that can answer these questions in a true and convincing way. Everyone who does not know or believe in this *'aqeedah* is like that miserable poet[6] who knows nothing of it. He says:

I came, I know not from whence, but I came
I saw before me a path, so I followed it
And I shall continue to tread this path, whether I like it or not
Where did I come from? How did I find this path?

I know not

Am I new or ancient in this universe?
Am I free, or a prisoner in chains?

---

[6] His name is Eeliya Abu Maaḍi; the couplets quoted come from his lengthy poem entitled *Aṭ-Ṭalaasim* (mysteries), from his collection of poems entitled *Al-Jadaawil* (streams), Pp. 106.

Am I controlling my own fate in this life, or am I controlled?
How I wish I knew, but

I know not

My path, what is my path? Is it long or short?
Am I ascending, or descending?
Am I running through this life, or is it life that is running?
Or are we both standing still, whilst time runs?

I know not

I wonder, when I was in that unseen, secure world,
Did I know that I was hidden there
And that I would emerge and come into being?
Or, I wonder, did I not know a thing?

I know not

I wonder, before I became a complete human being,
Was I non-existent, or was I something possible, or was I something?
Is there an answer to this mystery? Or will I remain forever
Not knowing... why I don't know?

I know not

What confusion is this! What anxiety this uncertainty brings to human souls! Do the children of this generation, who have missed out on knowledge of the "great universal facts" without which their lives cannot be sound and healthy, deserve to suffer these worries which fill their hearts and cause pain and complexes? Compare their situation to that of the Muslim who knows for certain all of these facts, and through them finds comfort and peace of mind. So he travels on a straight path towards a definite goal whose features are known.

Listen to this miserable poet speaking about death and one's ultimate fate:

If death is a punishment, what sin can the pure soul commit?
If it is a reward, what blessings does the promiscuous soul deserve?
If there is no reward or loss in it,
Then what is the point of calling things sinful or righteous?

I know not

If death is a kind of sleep after being awake,
Why do we not stay awake?
Why does a man not know when he is to depart?
When will the secret be revealed so that he will know?

I know not

If death is a kind of sleep to allow man to relax
And it is a setting free rather than an imprisonment, a beginning rather than an end,
Then why do I not love this sleep and long for this?
Why are souls so afraid of it?

I know not

After the grave, after death, will there be any resurrection
And life, and eternity, or only final oblivion?
Is what people say true or false?
Is it true that some people know?

I know not

If I am resurrected after death, physically and spiritually,
I wonder, will I be resurrected in part, or in total?
I wonder, will I be resurrected as a child, or as an adult?
Then will I know myself after I am resurrected?

I know not

He does not know what his ultimate destiny will be, and man's ultimate fate concerns him. He wants to be reassured about that destiny. We see the poet's pain, because he does not know where his ultimate destiny lies and what will become of him. He is misguided from the truth, his heart is filled with misery and laden with worry and grief. His wonderings have exhausted him. How many people there are in this world who are like this misguided, miserable poet! Some of them are able to express their misery and confusion, whilst others feel and suffer, but their thoughts remain trapped in their miserable souls.

"I know not," is the response to these eternal questions. These are not the words of this poet alone. Socrates, the thinker who is viewed as one of the giants of philosophy, clearly stated, "The thing that I still do not know about is the fact that I do not know."[7] Indeed, scepticism/agnosticism (in Arabic, *laa adriyah*, lit. "not knowing") is an ancient school of philosophical thought.

Only through the guidance of Islam does man learn where he came from, where he is going, why the universe exists, and what his role is in this universe. He knows that in truth, and there is a great difference between those who know and those who do not know:

﴿ أَفَمَن يَمْشِى مُكِبًّا عَلَىٰ وَجْهِهِۦٓ أَهْدَىٰٓ أَمَّن يَمْشِى سَوِيًّا عَلَىٰ صِرَٰطٍ مُّسْتَقِيمٍ ﴿٢٢﴾ ﴾

﴾Is he who walks prone [without seeing] on his face, more rightly guided, or he who [sees and] walks upright on the Straight Way [i.e. Islamic Monotheism]?﴿

(Qur'an 67: 22)

[7] *Ad-Deen* by Ad-Darraaz, 69.

2 - THE RELATIONSHIP BETWEEN *'AQEEDAH* AND *EEMAAN*, AND SHARI'AH

1) The Relationship Between *'Aqeedah* and *Eemaan*

In the Qur'an, Allah, the Exalted, praises *eemaan* (faith) and the people of *eemaan*, in *aayaat* (verses) such as the following:

﴿ قَدْ أَفْلَحَ ٱلْمُؤْمِنُونَ ۝١ ﴾

﴾Successful indeed are the believers.﴿ *(Qur'an 23: 1)*

﴿ أُوْلَٰٓئِكَ عَلَىٰ هُدًى مِّن رَّبِّهِمْ ۖ وَأُوْلَٰٓئِكَ هُمُ ٱلْمُفْلِحُونَ ۝٥ ﴾

﴾They are on [true] guidance from their Lord, and they are the successful.﴿ *(Qur'an 2: 5)*

Allah (ﷻ), promised them Paradise:

﴿ أُوْلَٰٓئِكَ هُمُ ٱلْوَٰرِثُونَ ۝١٠ ٱلَّذِينَ يَرِثُونَ ٱلْفِرْدَوْسَ هُمْ فِيهَا خَٰلِدُونَ ۝١١ ﴾

﴾These are indeed the inheritors, who shall inherit the *Firdaus* [Paradise]. They shall dwell therein forever.﴿ *(Qur'an 23: 10-11)*

The *eemaan* (faith) for which Allah praised people was not only *'aqeedah* (belief). *'Aqeedah* formed the foundation and basis of *eemaan* (firm belief). So *eemaan* is the *'aqeedah* which is established firmly in the heart, clings to it and never departs from it. It is verbally declared and pronounced by the believer in whose heart this *'aqeedah* takes firm roots. His belief and declaration are confirmed by his actions conforming to the dictates of that *'aqeedah*.

Belief that takes roots in the heart but has no visible manifestation is an empty and cold belief that does not deserve to be called *'aqeedah*. We see many people who know the truth, but they do not abide by it or live their lives in accordance with it. They may even resist the truth which they believe to be true. *Iblees* (Satan) knows the great universal truths with certainty, he knows Allah, and the truth, the Messengers and Books, but he devoted himself to opposing the truth even after full knowledge.

Pharaoh (Fir'awn) was certain that the miracles brought by Moosa (Moses) (ﷺ) (May peace be upon him) were indeed from Allah, but he denied them out of stubborn pride and arrogance, as Allah the Exalted, tells us about him and his people:

﴿ وَجَحَدُوا۟ بِهَا وَٱسْتَيْقَنَتْهَآ أَنفُسُهُمْ ظُلْمًا وَعُلُوًّا ... ﴿١٤﴾ ﴾

﴾And they belied them [those *Ayaat*] wrongfully and arrogantly, though their ownselves were convinced thereof...﴿ *(Qur'an 27: 14)*

Moosa (Moses) (ﷺ) had addressed Pharaoh, saying:

﴿ قَالَ لَقَدْ عَلِمْتَ مَآ أَنزَلَ هَٰٓؤُلَآءِ إِلَّا رَبُّ ٱلسَّمَٰوَٰتِ وَٱلْأَرْضِ بَصَآئِرَ ... ﴿١٠٢﴾ ﴾

﴾Verily, you know that these signs have been sent down by none but the Lord of the heavens and the earth [as clear evidences, i.e. proofs of Allah's Oneness and His Omnipotence]...﴿ *(Qur'an 17: 102)*

The People of the Book know that Muhammad (ﷺ) is a Messenger sent by his Lord:

﴿ ٱلَّذِينَ ءَاتَيْنَٰهُمُ ٱلْكِتَٰبَ يَعْرِفُونَهُۥ كَمَا يَعْرِفُونَ أَبْنَآءَهُمْ ... ﴿١٤٦﴾ ﴾

﴾Those to whom We gave the Scripture [Jews and Christians] recognize him [Muhammad] as they recognize their sons...﴿ *(Qur'an 2: 146)*

— but they do not admit that.

Listen to what Abu Ṭaalib said to the Messenger (ﷺ) as his excuse for not believing: "I know that the religion of Muhammad is one of the best religions in the world, were it not for the fear of blame and slander, you would see me acknowledging that openly."

So *eemaan* does not mean only acknowledging that Allah, the All-High, exists, or knowledge that a person admits not because of superiority complex, or refuses to abide by its rulings. *Eemaan* means *'aqeedah* (belief) that a person accepts in his heart and affirms by his tongue, and he accepts and always adheres to the way laid down by Allah (ﷻ).

Hence the scholars of the *salaf* (Pious Predecessors) said: "*Eemaan* means belief in the heart, words on the tongue (declaration) and striving to implement its pillars."[8]

2) The Relationship Between *'Aqeedah* and Shari'ah

As we have mentioned above, there are two conditions of faith: *'aqeedah* which is deeply rooted in the heart, and deeds which manifest themselves in a person's actions. If either of these two essential components is missing, eemaan is lost or becomes unbalanced. Hence the connection between these two elements is very important.

Eemaan is like a good, strong tree that is firmly rooted in good soil with its branches reaching up into the sky, bearing abundant fruit,

---

[8] This is the general view of the *salaf*, including the three Imams Aḥmad, Maalik and Ash-Shaafa'i. Imam Abu Ḥaneefah said that *eemaan* was belief and words (declaration), and that actions were one of the requirements of faith, but not included in it.

Another group is of the view that *eemaan* was only belief, even if it was not accompanied by words and actions. This is the view of the *Jahamiyah* and the *Ash'ariyah*. The *Karaamiyah* thought that *eemaan* was only words; the refutation of their view may be seen in the text we have referred to.

producing its fruit for everyone by the grace of its Lord. Thus *eemaan* is the tree; *'aqeedah* is rooted deeply in the heart, and its trunk, branches and fruits are deeds and actions.

Undoubtedly if the roots are removed or turn rotten or dried up, they will no longer exist. Similarly, *eemaan* will no longer exist if *'aqeedah* is taken away. If the trunk or branches are cut off, or some of them are cut off, the tree will weaken, and may die altogether, because the presence of branches and leaves are essential to the tree's continued existence. Similarly, if deeds are neglected, in part or in whole, then *eemaan* will be reduced or destroyed.

3) Paying Attention to Deeds

It is incumbent on us to pay attention to the deeds that Allah (سبحانه وتعالى), has enjoined upon us as obligatory duties, or that He has encouraged us to do, and to abstain from the deeds that He has forbidden us to do, because this is a part of *eemaan*. Doing the deeds that are forbidden — even if it is only a little — detracts from *eemaan* proportionately.

Hence those who undermine the importance of implementing and adhering to the Sunnah of the Prophet should be aware of their dangerous attitude. Some of them may overstep the mark and describe some issues of Sunnah or Islamic religion as unimportant or insignificant. We ask Allah to forgive these people, for all of the religion is important and nothing in it is insignificant, although matters may vary in their degree of importance.

What we say should not be taken as meaning that we do not pay attention to the priorities in knowledge, actions and in calling people to Allah. This is a matter which should be well known and established. But what we are denouncing here is negligence of minor issues and condemnation of those who pay attention to both minor and major issues in Islam and the Sunnah of the Chosen Prophet (صلى الله عليه وسلم).

How deeply moved I am when I think of 'Umar's attitude after he had been stabbed, and a young man came to see him and spoke kindly to him. When the young man turned to leave, his *izaar* (lower garment) was trailing on the ground. 'Umar (رضي الله عنه) (may Allah be pleased with him) called him and said to him: "O son of my brother, lift up your garment, for that is cleaner for your garment and more pleasing to your Lord."[9] His approaching death did not prevent him from telling that man about a matter which many people nowadays regard as insignificant and as something which we should not pay attention to.

3 - *EEMAAN* AND *KUFR*

1) Ruling on Rejection of *'Aqeedah*

He who rejects *'aqeedah* altogether, such as the communists who deny the existence of Allah, reject the Messengers and the Books, and do not believe in the Hereafter and reward and punishment, or who denies part of the *'aqeedah*, is a *kaafir* (disbeliever) and is not a Muslim. He should be told that the Islamic *'aqeedah* can never be accepted in part, because the whole is so strongly interconnected.

Belief in Allah requires that one believe also in the angels, the Books, the Messengers and the Last Day. Belief in the Books requires that one believe in all the other basic principles of faith (*uṣool al-eemaan*). Belief in the Messenger (ﷺ) means that one believes and accepts all that he brought... Hence Allah considers the person who believes in one principle and denies another as being a *kaafir*.

Allah (سبحانه وتعالى), the All-Glorious, says:

---

[9] Bukhari in his *Ṣaḥeeḥ*. See *Ṣaḥeeḥ al-Bukhari bi Sharḥihi Fatḥ al-Baari*, 7/60, hadith no. 3700.

﴿ إِنَّ ٱلَّذِينَ يَكۡفُرُونَ بِٱللَّهِ وَرُسُلِهِۦ وَيُرِيدُونَ أَن يُفَرِّقُواْ بَيۡنَ ٱللَّهِ وَرُسُلِهِۦ وَيَقُولُونَ نُؤۡمِنُ بِبَعۡضٖ وَنَكۡفُرُ بِبَعۡضٖ وَيُرِيدُونَ أَن يَتَّخِذُواْ بَيۡنَ ذَٰلِكَ سَبِيلًا ﴿١٥٠﴾ أُوْلَٰٓئِكَ هُمُ ٱلۡكَٰفِرُونَ حَقّٗاۚ ... ﴿١٥١﴾ ﴾

﴾Verily, those who disbelieve in Allah and His Messengers and wish to make distinction between Allah and His Messengers [by believing in Allah and disbelieving in His Messengers] saying, "We believe in some but reject others," and wish to adopt a way in between. They are in truth disbelievers...﴿

(Qur'an 4: 150-151)

Disbelieving in some of the minor issues of *'aqeedah* which have been proven definitively in the Qur'an or Sunnah is also counted as *kufr* (disbelief), such as denying one of the Messengers or one of the Angels.

2) Actions and Words Which are Counted as *Kufr* (Disbelief)

Kufr does not consist only of denying basic principles of *'aqeedah*. There are certain actions which, if done, are also *kufr*. They may be summed up in one phrase: "worshipping others besides Allah." Worship is the right of Allah alone, and directing worship to anyone or anything other than Allah is *shirk* (polytheism), such as praying to anything other than Allah, offering sacrifice to anything other than Allah, calling upon anything or anyone other than Allah etc.

A man may become a *kaafir* (disbeliever) by uttering words which insult the Creator, Glorified and Exalted be He, or Islam, or the Prophet, or words which make fun of Islam, or which give preference to misguided principles such as communism or Buddhism, or deviant religions such as Judaism or Christianity over Islam, or which accuse Islam of being imperfect, backward and reactionary.

3) Attitude Towards the *Kuffaar* (Disbelievers)

The Muslim should regard the *kuffaar* as enemies and hate them because of their *kufr*, just as he hates their *kufr* (disbelief) itself. He should oppose this falsehood and its followers by speaking out clearly, and by calling them to the truth. He should explain to them their misguided state, and show them the truth, explaining it to them clearly and confidently. Even though we hate the disbelievers, we want them to be guided and we hope that they will be.

There are rulings concerning the *kuffaar* which are explained in the books of *fiqh* (Islamic jurisprudence). For example, we do not let them marry Muslim women, we do not marry any of their women except those of the People of the Book, and we do not wash their dead or pray for them...

4) The *Kaafir* before Allah

The person who hears of Islam, and knowingly rejects it is a *kaafir* (disbeliever) who will abide in the Hell-Fire forever, for he will have no excuse on the Day of Resurrection.

Those who do not hear of Islam for whatever reason, such as living in remote areas or because they have lost their hearing and sight, or because Islam reached them when they were too old to understand, will not be punished on the Day of Resurrection until they have been tried and tested, because the proof did not reach them. Allah, the Almighty, says:

﴿... وَمَا كُنَّا مُعَذِّبِينَ حَتَّىٰ نَبْعَثَ رَسُولًا ﴿١٥﴾﴾

﴾...And We never punish until We have sent a Messenger [to give warning].﴿ *(Qur'an 17: 15)*

The evidence that they will be tested is the hadith narrated by Al-Aswad ibn Saree', who said: "The Messenger of Allah (ﷺ) said:

> "There are four who will be tested on the Day of Resurrection: the deaf man who could not hear anything; the imbecile; the senile old man; and the man who died during the *fatarah* (interval between two Prophets, when no Message reached him). The deaf man will say, "O Lord, Islam came and I did not hear anything." The imbecile will say, "O Lord, Islam came but the young boys were pelting me with camel dung." The senile old man will say, "O Lord, Islam came and I did not hear anything." The man who died during the *fatarah* will say, "O Lord, no Messenger came to me." Then Allah will take their pledge to obey Him, and He will send word to them to enter the fire. By the One in Whose hand is the soul of Muhammad, if they enter it, it will be cool and safe for them."[10]

5) Neglecting Obligatory Duties and Committing Prohibited Actions

i) The attitude of the *salaf* towards those who commit major sins

Undoubtedly, if a person neglects the duties that Allah has enjoined upon him, such as paying zakah, fasting, performing Ḥajj and honouring one's parents, or does *ḥaraam* (forbidden) things such as committing adultery (*zina*), engaging in usury or interest (*riba*) or consuming orphans' property, his faith is distorted and is lacking in proportion to the duties neglected or sins committed. But is he to be regarded as a *kaafir* - disbeliever - simply because he has neglected those duties or committed those *ḥaraam* actions, so long as he does not deny the former or claim that the latter is *ḥalaal* (legal)?

---

[10] Aḥmad in his *Musnad*, and classed as *ṣaḥeeḥ* by Al-Bayhaqi. See Ibn Katheer in his *tafseer* of the *aayah* of *Al-Israa'* 15.

The texts that we have before us teach us that the Muslim does not become a *kaafir* by committing sins or by neglecting obligatory duties, but this does detract from his faith and his case rests with Allah - if He wills, He will forgive him, and if He wills, He will punish him. Among the texts which state that clearly is the *aayah* (verse):

﴿ إِنَّ ٱللَّهَ لَا يَغۡفِرُ أَن يُشۡرَكَ بِهِۦ وَيَغۡفِرُ مَا دُونَ ذَٰلِكَ لِمَن يَشَآءُۚ... ﴿٤٨﴾ ﴾

﴿Verily, Allah forgives not that partners should be set up with Him [in worship], but He forgives except that [anything else] to whom He wills;...﴾ *(Qur'an 4: 48)*

The only sin that He will not forgive is *shirk*. In the case of every lesser sin, it is up to Allah: if He wills, He will forgive, and if He wills, He will punish.

There are also *aḥaadeeth* which clearly state the same thing that is indicated in this *aayah*. According to a hadith *qudsi*:[11]

> "O son of Adam, if you were to come to me with an earthful of sin, then you were to meet Me not associating anything in worship with Me, I would come to you with an earthful of forgiveness."[12]

According to another hadith *qudsi*:

> "Whoever meets Me with an earthful of sin, but does not associate anyone in worship with Me, I will meet him with forgiveness equal to it."[13]

---

[11] The inspired words of Allah conveyed by the Prophet in his words.

[12] Tirmidhi in his *Sunan*, 4/49, hadith no. 3540. He said: this is a *ghareeb* hadith which we know only with this isnad. See *Ṣaḥeeḥ Sunan at-Tirmidhi* by Al-Albaani, 3/175, hadith no. 2805.

[13] Muslim, 4/2068, hadith no. 2687.

It is reported that 'Utbaan ibn Maalik stated: "The Messenger of Allah (ﷺ) said:

> 'Allah has forbidden for the Fire all those who say *Laa ilaaha illa-Allah* seeking thereby the Face of Allah.'"[14]

It is reported from Jaabir that the Messenger of Allah (ﷺ) said:

> "Whoever dies not associating anything with Allah will enter Paradise."[15]

In the hadith about intercession, it is reported that Allah (سبحانه وتعالى) said:

> "By My Glory, My Majesty, My Pride and My Might, I will bring forth from it (Hell) those who say *Laa ilaaha illa-Allah.*"[16]

It is reported from Abu Sa'eed al-Khudri that the Messenger of Allah (ﷺ) said:

> "The people of Paradise will enter Paradise, and the people of Hell will enter Hell, then Allah, will say: 'Bring forth everyone in whose heart was faith the weight of a grain of mustard seed.'"[17]

Abu Sufyaan said: "I lived near Jaabir ibn 'Abdullah in Makkah for six months. A man asked him, 'Do you call any of the people of the *Qiblah* (i.e., Muslims) a *kaafir*?' He said, 'Allah forbid!' He asked, 'Do you call anybody a *mushrik*?' He said, 'No.'"[18]

---

[14] Bukhari, 1/519, hadith no. 425.

[15] Muslim, 1/94, hadith no. 94.

[16] Bukhari, 13/474

[17] Bukhari, 1/72, hadith no. 22

[18] Abu 'Ubayd al-Qaasim ibn Salaam in his book *Al-Eemaan*, edited by *Shaykh* Naṣiruddin al-Albaani, Pp. 98. The editor said, its isnad is *ṣaḥeeḥ* according to the conditions of Muslim. Abu Sufyaan, the narrator of the hadith was a *Taabi'ee.*

These texts led prominent scholars among the *salaf* of this ummah to say of the one who commits sins and neglects obligatory duties: "He is a believer because of his faith but a *faasiq* (sinner) because of his sin." They attributed faith to him, but it was not the perfect faith that is the rightful attribute of those who do acts of obedience and refrain from committing sin. His faith is impaired because of his wrongs (*fisq*) and because of the sin that he has committed.

ii) The *khawaarij* who denounced people as *kaafir* because of their sins

In contrast to these (the *salaf*), there was another group who accused people of *kufr* if they fell short in any obligatory duty, or if they committed any *ḥaraam* actions. We still see many people hastening to condemn people as *kaafir* in a similar manner. The first group to adopt this approach was the *Khawaarij*, a group who emerged (*kharaja*) from the army of 'Ali ibn Abi Ṭaalib (رضي الله عنه) after the appointed arbitrators, Abu Moosa al-Ash'ari and 'Amr ibn al-'Aaṣ, had failed to end the dispute that was raging among the Muslims under the leadership of 'Ali and Mu'aawiyah.

The *Khawaarij* claimed that appointing men as arbitrators was a mistake according to shari'ah, and they regarded it as *kufr*. They viewed as *kuffaar* all the Muslims who had agreed to that, and testified that they themselves turned to be disbelievers. [Because they had initially agreed to the arbitration — Translator]. They then entered the pale of Islam afresh. They demanded that 'Ali should also accept that he committed *kufr* by agreeing to the arbitration (and pronounce *shahadah* afresh) as a precondition for their returning to the ranks of his army. 'Ali (رضي الله عنه) (may Allah be pleased with him) disputed with them, and sent to them the great scholar of this ummah, Ibn 'Abbaas, who established proof against them and refuted their point of view. A few thousand of them came back (to the army and to Islam), but two thousand persisted in following their opinion and fought ‘Ali, who defeated them and finished them off. But their thinking spread, and was adopted by many people after them. This idea of denouncing others as *kaafir* still emerges from time to time, and it has resurfaced in our own times.

The evidence quoted by the *khawaarij* for denouncing as *kaafir* those who commit major sins

The *Khawaarij* [19] claim that the one who commits a major sin is a *kaafir* and is no longer Muslim, and his blood and wealth are *halaal* [lawful (i.e., he may be killed and his wealth seized by the Muslims)]. They say that he will abide in Hell forever. They quote in support of their view; evidence, which they thought, proved their case, such as the following:

a) They said, “You agree with us that deeds are part of faith, because *eemaan* is composed of belief, words and deeds. If one part of faith, such as actions, is missing, then the whole of *eemaan* is absent.”

b) They quoted as evidence the fact that Allah describes some sins as *fisq*, as in the *aayah* (verse):

﴿ ... إِن جَآءَكُمْ فَاسِقٌۢ بِنَبَإٍ فَتَبَيَّنُوٓا۟ ... ﴿٦﴾ ﴾

﴿...If a *Faasiq* [liar - evil person] comes to you with any news, verify it...﴾ *(Qur’an 49: 6)*

The word *faasiq* here is applied to a liar, which is quite obvious to anyone who looks at the context of the *aayah*.

The Prophet (ﷺ) said:

---

[19] There is another group, the *Mu‘tazilah*, who are the followers of Waaṣil ibn ‘Aṭaa’, who said that the one who commits a major sin is neither a believer nor a *kaafir*, but is in a position between *kufr* and *eemaan*, but in the Hereafter he will be doomed to eternity in Hell.

"For a believer to trade insults with another is *fusooq* (evil)."[20]

And they said that Allah called some sins, such as consuming orphans' wealth, *ẓulm*:

﴿إِنَّ ٱلَّذِينَ يَأْكُلُونَ أَمْوَٰلَ ٱلْيَتَـٰمَىٰ ظُلْمًا إِنَّمَا يَأْكُلُونَ فِى بُطُونِهِمْ نَارًا ... ﴿١٠﴾﴾

﴿Verily, those who unjustly [*ẓulman*] eat up the property of orphans, they eat up only fire into their bellies,...﴾ *(Qur'an 4: 10)*

And He (ﷻ), calls the one who evicts a widow from her marital home during the time of her *'iddah*, a *ẓaalim*, because he transgresses the limits set by Allah (ﷻ):

﴿... وَٱتَّقُوا۟ ٱللَّهَ رَبَّكُمْ ۖ لَا تُخْرِجُوهُنَّ مِنۢ بُيُوتِهِنَّ وَلَا يَخْرُجْنَ إِلَّآ أَن يَأْتِينَ بِفَـٰحِشَةٍ مُّبَيِّنَةٍ ۚ وَتِلْكَ حُدُودُ ٱللَّهِ ۚ وَمَن يَتَعَدَّ حُدُودَ ٱللَّهِ فَقَدْ ظَلَمَ نَفْسَهُۥ ... ﴿١﴾﴾

﴿...And fear Allah your Lord [O' Muslims]. And turn them not out of their [husband's] homes nor shall they [themselves] leave, except in case they are guilty of some open illegal sexual intercourse. And those are the set limits of Allah. And whosoever transgresses the set limits of Allah, then indeed he has wronged himself...﴾ *(Qur'an 65: 1)*

They said, these sins are *fisq* and *ẓulm*, and the *faasiqoon* and *ẓaalimoon* are *kaafir* as the Qur'an says:

﴿... وَٱلْكَـٰفِرُونَ هُمُ ٱلظَّـٰلِمُونَ ﴿٢٥٤﴾﴾

---

[20] Muslim, 1/80, hadith no. 64.

﴿...And it is the disbelievers who are the *Ẓaalimoon* [wrongdoers].﴾ *(Qur'an 2: 254)*

﴿ ... وَمَن كَفَرَ بَعْدَ ذَٰلِكَ فَأُوْلَٰٓئِكَ هُمُ ٱلْفَٰسِقُونَ ﴿٥٥﴾ ﴾

﴿...But whoever disbelieved after this, they are the *Faasiqoon* [rebellious, disobedient to Allah].﴾
(Qur'an 24: 55)

And they said: the texts indicate that those who commit sins are not believers, for example, the report narrated by Muslim which says that the Prophet (ﷺ) said:

"The one who commits *zina* is not a believer at the time when he is committing *zina*, and the one who steals is not a believer at the time when he is stealing, and the one who drinks wine is not a believer at the time when he is drinking."[21]

And he (ﷺ) said:

"No one who believes in Allah and His Messenger can hate the *Anṣaar*"[22]

And:

"By the One in Whose hand is my soul, you will not enter Paradise until you believe, and you will not believe until you love one another."[23]

c) They said: the Messenger (ﷺ) disowned those who committed certain sins, such as when he said:

---

[21] Muslim, 1/76, hadith no. 57.

[22] Ibid, 1/86.

[23] Ibid, 1/74, hadith no. 54.

> "Whoever bears arms against us is not one of us, and whoever deceives us is not one of us."[24]

And, according to another hadith:

> "Whoever cheats is not one of us."[25]

According to a hadith narrated by Bukhari and Muslim from Abu Hurayrah (رضي الله عنه), the Messenger of Allah (ﷺ) said:

> "By Allah, he does not believe; by Allah, he does not believe; by Allah, he does not believe." They said, "Who, O' Messenger of Allah?" He said, "The one from whose annoyance his neighbour is not safe."[26]

d) They said: some sins were described as *kufr*, as when Allah (سبحانه وتعالى), said:

﴿...وَلِلَّهِ عَلَى ٱلنَّاسِ حِجُّ ٱلْبَيْتِ مَنِ ٱسْتَطَاعَ إِلَيْهِ سَبِيلًا ۚ وَمَن كَفَرَ فَإِنَّ ٱللَّهَ غَنِىٌّ عَنِ ٱلْعَـٰلَمِينَ ﴿٩٧﴾﴾

> ﴿...And Ḥajj [pilgrimage to Makkah] to the House [Ka'bah] is a duty that mankind owes to Allah, those who can afford the expenses [for one's conveyance, provision and residence]; and whoever disbelieves [i.e. denies Ḥajj (pilgrimage to Makkah), then he is a disbeliever of Allah], then Allah stands not in need of any of the *'Aalameen* [mankind, jinn and all that exist].﴾ *(Qur'an 3: 97)*

And the Messenger (ﷺ) said:

> "Do not go back to *kufr* after I am gone by killing one

---

[24] Muslim, 1/99, hadith no. 101.

[25] Ibid, 1/101, hadith no. 102.

[26] *Mishkaat al-Maṣabeeḥ*, 2/607, hadith no. 4962.

another."[27] And: "If a man denounces his brother as a *kaafir*, it will be the case that one of them is a *kaafir*."[28]

Refutation of the evidences quoted by the *khawaarij*

These are the evidences which they referred to, for their labelling as *kaafir* those who commit sins. We will strive to point out where they went wrong in using these texts as evidences:

a) With regard to their point that deeds are included in the components of *eemaan*, we do not deny this. But where they went wrong is when they counted deeds as a condition of faith. The correct view is that this is not so. If deeds are lacking, this impairs the required perfection of faith, i.e., if deeds are lacking then faith is also lacking in part, and it remains imperfect. This is like a man whose hand or foot has been cut off, or whose eye has been taken out, or his ear has been cut off. He is still a human being and is still alive. But if he is cut in two or his head is cut off, or his heart is torn out, then he is like a person whose faith is removed. If the hand, foot or eye is removed, this is like a person who neglects some obligatory duties or does some *ḥaraam* (forbidden) actions. When the head or heart is removed, is like the *'aqeedah* is taken away.

b) Their explanation of *fisq* and *ẓulm* being *kufr* is a misunderstanding. The meaning of *fisq* is to disobey Allah (ﷻ), and all acts of disobedience towar ds Allah are not on the same level. They may entail *kufr*, or they may not. A person who denies the angels disobeys Allah in a manner that constitutes *kufr*, whilst a person who drinks wine disobeys Allah in a manner that is sinful, but does not constitute *kufr*.

Ẓulm also varies in degree; it may take an extreme form that reaches the level of *kufr*, or it may be of a lesser degree than that.

---

[27] Muslim, 1/82, hadith no. 65.

[28] Ibid, 1/79, hadith no. 79.

We may picture this if we draw a large circle in the middle of which is a smaller circle. The large circle represents *ẓulm* and *fisq*, and the smaller circle represents *kufr*, so *kufr* is included in *ẓulm* and *fisq*, because they are broader in meaning than *kufr*, but some kinds of *ẓulm* and *fisq* are not *kufr*.

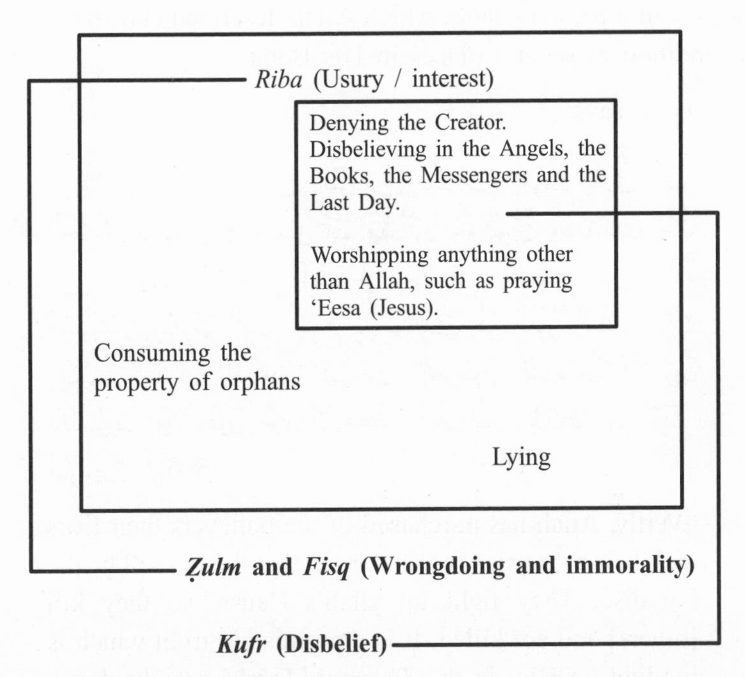

What indicates that *fisq* may not be *kufr* is the hadith of the Prophet (ﷺ), in which he said:

> "Slandering a Muslim is *fusooq*, and killing him is *kufr*."[29]

The Messenger distinguished between the two, even though what is meant by *kufr* in this hadith is not the kind of *kufr* which puts a person beyond the pale of Islam.

---

[29] Muslim, 1/80, hadith no. 64.

The texts which they quote to support their view that faith is cancelled out by sins, or that the Messenger (ﷺ) disowned people who committed sins, or that the person who commits a certain sin is a *kaafir*, do not mean that faith is taken away by sins or that sin implies that a person is a *kaafir*. But sins do detract from the perfection and sincerity of a person's faith, which Allah described and stated was a precondition in several places in His Book.

Allah (سبحانه وتعالى), says:

﴿ ۞ إِنَّ ٱللَّهَ ٱشۡتَرَىٰ مِنَ ٱلۡمُؤۡمِنِينَ أَنفُسَهُمۡ وَأَمۡوَٰلَهُم بِأَنَّ لَهُمُ
ٱلۡجَنَّةَۚ يُقَٰتِلُونَ فِي سَبِيلِ ٱللَّهِ فَيَقۡتُلُونَ وَيُقۡتَلُونَۖ وَعۡدًا عَلَيۡهِ حَقّٗا
فِي ٱلتَّوۡرَىٰةِ وَٱلۡإِنجِيلِ وَٱلۡقُرۡءَانِۚ وَمَنۡ أَوۡفَىٰ بِعَهۡدِهِۦ مِنَ ٱللَّهِۚ
فَٱسۡتَبۡشِرُواْ بِبَيۡعِكُمُ ٱلَّذِي بَايَعۡتُم بِهِۦۚ وَذَٰلِكَ هُوَ ٱلۡفَوۡزُ ٱلۡعَظِيمُ ١١١
ٱلتَّٰٓئِبُونَ ٱلۡعَٰبِدُونَ ٱلۡحَٰمِدُونَ ٱلسَّٰٓئِحُونَ ٱلرَّٰكِعُونَ ٱلسَّٰجِدُونَ ٱلۡأٓمِرُونَ
بِٱلۡمَعۡرُوفِ وَٱلنَّاهُونَ عَنِ ٱلۡمُنكَرِ وَٱلۡحَٰفِظُونَ لِحُدُودِ ٱللَّهِۗ وَبَشِّرِ
ٱلۡمُؤۡمِنِينَ ١١٢ ﴾

﴾Verily, Allah has purchased of the believers their lives and their properties for [the price] that theirs shall be the Paradise. They fight in Allah's Cause, so they kill [others] and are killed. It is a promise in truth which is binding on Him in the *Tawraat* [Torah] and the *Injeel* [Gospel] and the Qur'an. And who is truer to his covenant than Allah? Then rejoice in the bargain which you have concluded. That is the supreme success. [The believers whose lives Allah has purchased are] those who turn to Allah in repentance [from polytheism and hypocrisy], who worship [Him], who praise [Him], who fast [or go out in Allah's Cause], who bow down [in prayer], who prostrate themselves [in prayer], who enjoin [on people] *Al-Ma'roof* and forbid [people] from

Al-Munkar, and who observe the limits set by Allah. And give glad tidings to the believers."﴾

(Qur'an 9: 111-112)

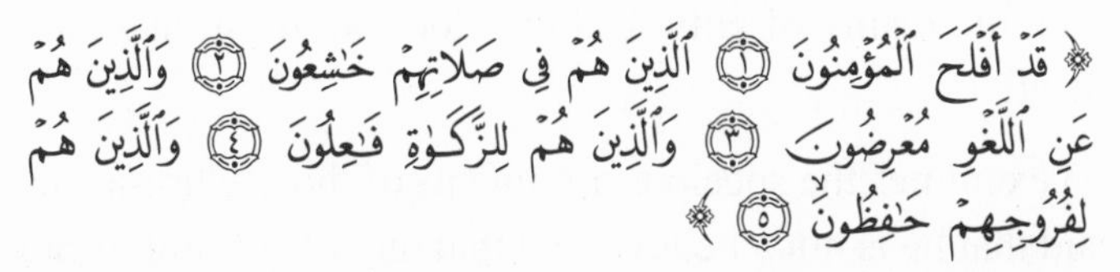

﴿Successful indeed are the believers. Those who offer their *ṣalaah* [prayers] with all solemnity and full submissiveness. And those who turn away from *Al-Laghw* [dirty, false, evil vain talk, falsehood, and all that Allah has forbidden]. And those who pay the Zakah. And those who guard their chastity [i.e. private parts, from illegal sexual acts].﴾ *(Qur'an 23: 1-5)*

﴿ إِنَّمَا الْمُؤْمِنُونَ الَّذِينَ إِذَا ذُكِرَ اللَّهُ وَجِلَتْ قُلُوبُهُمْ وَإِذَا تُلِيَتْ عَلَيْهِمْ آيَاتُهُ زَادَتْهُمْ إِيمَانًا وَعَلَىٰ رَبِّهِمْ يَتَوَكَّلُونَ ﴿٢﴾ الَّذِينَ يُقِيمُونَ الصَّلَاةَ وَمِمَّا رَزَقْنَاهُمْ يُنفِقُونَ ﴿٣﴾ ﴾

﴿The believers are only those who, when Allah is mentioned, feel a fear in their hearts and when His *aayaat* [verses] [this Qur'an] are recited unto them, they [i.e. the *Aayaat*] increase their Faith; and they put their trust in their Lord [Alone]; Who perform *Aṣ-Ṣalaah* [*Iqaamat-aṣ-Ṣalaah*] and spend out of that We have provided them.﴾ *(Qur'an 8: 2-3)*

After quoting these *aayaat*, Abu 'Ubayd al-Qaasim ibn Sallaam[30] said: "These *aayaat* explain the obligations that Islam has enjoined upon its followers, and prohibited all kinds of sin." The *aḥaadeeth* of

[30] These quotations are taken from the book *Al-Eemaan* by Abu 'Ubayd, a collection of his four treatises edited by *Shaykh* Naṣiruddeen al-Albaani, Pp. 90-96.

the Sunnah describe the features of *eemaan*. When sins are mixed with faith, it may be said that this is not what Allah has enjoined upon the believers, and these are not the signs by which faith is known, i.e., this is not the reality of faith. But this does not mean that there is no faith at all."

He then examines the specious arguments of those who say, how can it be said that he is not a believer but that the title of faith is not taken away from him? He explains this by pointing out that this is the way the Arabs speak: they deny that a deed has been done if it had not been done properly. The Qur'an was revealed in the language of the Arabs using the stylistic devices of their language. "In the language of the Arabs, about which we know a great deal, it is not uncommon to deny a deed if the person who did it failed to do it properly. Do you not see that if a worker does not do his job properly, they will say to him, 'You haven't done anything'? The intention here is to deny the quality, not to deny the work itself. In their view, the job is done nominally but not properly."

He explained that the Arabs may speak in an even harsher tone, such as when a son disobeys his father and annoys him to the extent that the father may say, 'He is not a son' — although they know that he is his son, born from his loins. A similar thing may be said concerning a brother, wife or slave.

Then he explained that these texts which deny faith were narrated in a similar fashion. He said: "The same applies to these sins for which faith is denied, because what cancelled out the reality of faith is not complying with the rulings which are attributes of *eemaan*. But a person's classification remains as it was, and he is not described as being anything other than a believer, and the rulings which apply to believers remain intact in his case."

He quoted the *aayah* (verse) from *Soorah Aal 'Imraan* (the third chapter of the Qur'an) which states that Allah took a covenant from those who had been given the Scripture, that they would make it [the news of the coming of Prophet Muhammad (ﷺ)] known and clear to mankind, and not to hide it, but they threw it away behind their backs, yet despite that they are still described as People of the Book in other *aayaat*, and it is permissible for us to eat their meat and marry their women. Then he said: "In the rulings and in name they are still described as People of the Book, although in reality they have departed from it."

And he narrated the hadith of the man who prayed badly, which was narrated by the two *Shaykhs* (Bukhari and Muslim), in which the Messenger (ﷺ) said:

> "Go back and pray, for you have not prayed,"[31]

— more than once. Although the man had prayed each time, it was a nominal prayer only, and was not a prayer as it should be.

What is meant by the texts in which the Messenger of Allah (ﷺ) disowned those who commit sins

Abu 'Ubayd stated: "This disowning does not mean that they no longer have anything to do with the Messenger of Allah (ﷺ) and his religion. But in our opinion he is not one of those who obey the Messenger or follow his example or adhere to his laws (as required)."

What is meant by the texts which state that some sins imply *kufr* and *shirk*

"With regard to the texts which state that some sins imply *kufr* and *shirk*, the way we understand them is not that those people become *kaafir* (disbelievers) and *mushrikeen* (polythiests) in such a way that

[31] Bukhari, 2/277, hadith no. 793; Muslim, 1/298, hadith no. 397.

they no longer have any *eemaan* at all. Rather, the way in which they are to be interpreted is that these sins are akin to the characteristics and ways of the *kuffaar* and *mushrikeen*. We find a similar amount of reports of these two types as we do of reports of the first two types."

He explaines that what is meant by the sins which are called *kufr* and *shirk* is "the characteristics of the *mushrikeen* and their names, ways, words and rulings, etc."

In support of this view, he quoted the comment of Ibn 'Abbaas (رضي الله عنه) in his *tafseer* of the *aayah*,

﴿... وَمَن لَّمْ يَحْكُم بِمَآ أَنزَلَ ٱللَّهُ فَأُوْلَـٰٓئِكَ هُمُ ٱلْكَـٰفِرُونَ ﴿٤٤﴾﴾

> ﴿...And whosoever does not judge by what Allah has revealed, such are the *kaafiroon* [i.e. disbelievers - of a lesser degree as they do not act on Allah's Laws].﴾
>
> *(Qur'an 5: 44)*

Ibn 'Abbaas (رضي الله عنه) said: "This is not (the kind of) *kufr* that puts a person beyond the pale of Islam." 'Aṭaa' said: "It is a lesser form of *kufr*." Concerning the report narrated from Ibn 'Abbaas, the editor of the book said: "This is narrated by Al-Ḥaakim in *Al-Mustadrak* via Ṭaawoos, and he and Adh-Dhahabi classed it as *ṣaḥeeḥ*."[32]

Although judging by other than that which Allah has revealed is called *kufr*, it does not put a person beyond the pale of Islam. *Eemaan* is still present in this case, even though it is mixed with this sin. What is meant is that judging by other than that which Allah has revealed is the way of the *kuffaar* (disbelievers). Have you not heard the words of Allah (سبحانه وتعالى):

﴿أَفَحُكْمَ ٱلْجَـٰهِلِيَّةِ يَبْغُونَ... ﴿٥٠﴾﴾

---

[32] *Kitaab al-Eemaan* by Abu 'Ubayd al-Qaasim ibn Sallaam, Pp. 94. Published in the anthology of Four Desertations - *Arba' Rasaa'il*.

﴿Do they then seek the judgement of [the days of] Ignorance?...﴾ *(Qur'an 5: 50)*

Then he says: the way in which this was interpreted by the scholars of *Tafseer* is that whoever judges by other than that which Allah has revealed - and he is a Muslim - becomes thereby like the people of the *Jaahiliyah*, for it is to be understood that this is how the people of the *Jaahiliyah* used to judge. This is like the hadith:

"Three things belong to the *Jaahiliyah*: slandering people's lineage, wailing over the dead, and astrology." (This is) a *ṣaḥeeḥ* (authentic) ḥadith.[33]

Similarly there is a hadith that reads:

"The signs of the hypocrite are three: when he speaks, he lies; when he makes a promise, he breaks it; when he is entrusted with something, he betrays that trust."[34]

Abu 'Ubayd said:

"These reports are not to be interpreted as meaning that the one who commits sin is to be labelled as belonging to the people of *Jaahiliyah*, a *kaafir* (disbeliever) or a hypocrite, when he believes in Allah and the Message sent by Him, and he fulfils the obligatory duties. What these reports mean is that these sins are part of the actions of the *kuffaar* (disbelievers) which are forbidden in the Qur'an and Sunnah, so that the Muslims can avoid these things and steer clear of them, and not imitate the *kuffaar* in any of their attitudes or ways."

---

[33] *Ṣaḥeeḥ al-Jaami' aṣ-Ṣagheer*, 1/583, hadith no. 3039, where the wording is: "Three actions of the people of the *Jaahiliyah* which the people of Islam will not manage to avoid: seeking rain through the stars (astrology), slandering people's lineage, and wailing over the dead." He attributed it to Bukhari in *At-Taareekh*, and to Aṭ-Ṭabaraani in *Al-Kabeer*, and Aḥmad in *Al-Musnad*, and Ibn Ḥibbaan in his *ṣaḥeeḥ*.

[34] Bukhari, 1/89, hadith no. 33; Muslim, 1/78, hadith no. 59.

He quoted the hadith:

> "If a woman puts on perfume then passes by people who can detect her fragrance, she is a *zaaniyah* (adulteress)."[35] Is this the kind of *zina* which incurs the prescribed punishment (*ḥadd*)?

Perhaps what Abu 'Ubayd al-Qaasim ibn Sallaam meant when he said that "judging by other than that which Allah revealed is not *kufr* that puts a person beyond the pale of Islam" was when a *qaaḍi* (Muslim judge) judges a particular case according to his own whims and desires, although he usually judges in accordance with the rulings of Allah.

With regard to ruling by the laws of the disbelievers, and applying them by force to the Islamic peoples, and opposing and fighting all those who call for the application of Islam - this is nothing to do with Islam.

﴿ فَلَا وَرَبِّكَ لَا يُؤْمِنُونَ حَتَّىٰ يُحَكِّمُوكَ فِيمَا شَجَرَ بَيْنَهُمْ ثُمَّ لَا يَجِدُوا فِي أَنفُسِهِمْ حَرَجًا مِّمَّا قَضَيْتَ وَيُسَلِّمُوا تَسْلِيمًا ﴿٦٥﴾ ﴾

> ﴾But no, by your Lord, they can have no Faith, until they make you [O' Muhammad] judge in all disputes between them, and find in themselves no resistance against your decisions, and accept [them] with full submission.﴿
>
> *(Qur'an 4: 65)*

---

[35] The editor of *Kitaab al-Eemaan* (p. 96) said: (this is a) *ṣaḥeeḥ* hadith, narrated by Ibn Khuzaymah, Ibn Ḥibbaan and Al-Ḥaakim in their *Ṣaḥeeḥs*, from Abu Moosa al-Ash'ari and attributed to the Prophet (ﷺ), where the wording is, "Any woman who puts on perfume and passes by people so that they can smell its fragrance, is a *zaaniyah*, and every eye is *zaaniyah*." A similar report is narrated by Abu Dawood and Tirmidhi, who classed it as *ṣaḥeeḥ*.

iii) Those who say that the person who commits major sins has perfect faith

The *Khawaarij* went to one extreme, by misinterpreting the texts which say that a person who commits a major sin has distorted and diminished his faith. They did not understand the texts which state that his faith, nevertheless does not disappear in totality. In contrast to the *Khawaarij*, there is another group[36] which claimed that the faith of a person who commits a major sin is still intact. They said, "Sin does not have any harmful effect so long as a person believes." They said that *eemaan* was belief in the heart and words spoken by the tongue, and that actions had nothing to do with *eemaan*. They said that faith in the heart was something which did not differ from one person to another, and they quoted as evidence the texts which indicate that those who commit major sins are still believers and will enter Paradise.

Their view is refuted by the fact that many reports state that deeds are considered to be a part of faith, such as the hadith of the Prophet (ﷺ):

> "*Eemaan* has seventy-odd or sixty-odd branches, the best of which is saying *Laa ilaaha illa-Allaah*, and the least of which is removing something harmful off the road. And modesty is a branch of faith."[37]

Their view is also refuted by texts which contain warnings, such as the hadith of the Prophet (ﷺ):

> "An adulterer is not a believer at the time when he is committing adultery; a thief is not a believer at the time when he is stealing; a drinker of wine is not a believer at

---

[36] This group is known as *Al-Murji'ah* because they separated [*arjaru*] actions from *eemaan*, and regarded them as less important.

[37] Bukhari, 1/51, hadith no. 9; Muslim, 1/63, hadith no. 35. This version is narrated by Muslim.

the time when he is drinking."[38]

Both of the groups went astray. The first group, which denounces people as *kaafir*, causes people to despair of the mercy of Allah, whilst the second group encourages people to commit sins. The *salaf* of this ummah trod a middle path between these two extremes, stating that those who committed major sins were still believers in this world, although their faith was imperfect; as for the Hereafter, their case rests with Allah (ﷻ): if He wills, He will punish them and if He wills, He will forgive them.

4 - *'AQEEDAH* VS. PHILOSOPHY AND *'ILM AL-KALAAM*

1) The Difference Between Islamic *'Aqeedah* and Philosophy and *'Ilm al-Kalaam*

Philosophy deals with the exact same topics that religion deals with, for the philosophers claim that their research is aimed at discovering the origins and purpose of the universe, and discovering the ways of attaining human happiness in the short term and the long term. These form the two components of the discipline of philosophy, the theoretical and the practical, which are also the topics addressed by religion.[39] Yet, despite all this, I say that there is immense difference between religion and philosophy. They differ with regard to their origins and sources, their methodology and way, the extent of their prevalence and influence, in their styles and methods of deriving evidence, and in the effects that each of them have. We will endeavour to explain all of this so as to remove any confusion of religion with philosophy.

---

[38] Bukhari and Muslim; details have been given above.

[39] Darraaz, *Ad-Deen*, 59, 60.

i) Origins and sources

Philosophy, in all its guises, is a "human endeavour" which is subject to all the restrictions, limitations and slow progress towards an unknown objective that are inherent in human nature. It is subject to the human potential for change, and the human alternation between guidance and misguidance, between approaching perfection and straying far from that goal.

Hence the prominent philosophers were not able to rid themselves of the influence of their environment, so their concepts and beliefs reflected their surroundings.[40]

In all his works, Plato, for example, repeats the myths which were prevalent at his time, and he even produces myths of his own as part of his ideas and beliefs. Indeed, many of his beliefs and ideas are myths in themselves.

Listen to what Al-'Aqqaad says about Plato: "The idolatrous environment in which Plato lived overwhelmed his thoughts, because of the customs of his society and the effect of his surroundings. So he included in his beliefs the idea of gods and demi-gods which have no place in the monotheistic religions."[41]

Then Al-'Aqqaad discusses Plato's point of view concerning the universe, using Plato's theory of the universe to prove the point that is quoted above: "According to Plato, the universe consists of two opposing levels, the level of absolute reason, and the level of the primordial matter. All power comes from absolute reason, and all incapability comes from the primordial matter. In between, there are beings on various levels; higher status is determined by the extent to which they are influenced by reason, and lower levels by how much

---

[40] Darraaz, *Ad-Deen*, 73.

[41] Al-'Aqqaad, *Kitaab-Allah*, 129.

they take from the primordial matter. Some of these intermediate beings are gods, some are demi-gods, and some are human beings."[42]

The reason why Plato accepted the idea of these intermediate gods is, as Al-'Aqqaad says, because "he wanted to explain thereby the reason why evil, imperfection and pain exist in this world. For absolute reason is perfect and is not limited by time or place, and produces nothing but good and virtue. So these intermediate gods are taking care of creation because they exist between the all-powerful God and the incapable primordial matter. Hence imperfection, evil and pain stem from these intermediaries between the two extremes."[43]

It is also well-known that Plato believed in the idea of transmigration of souls.

This is philosophy as described from its own sources.

The Islamic *'aqeedah*, on the other hand, is a Revelation (*Waḥy*) from Allah (ﷻ), and has all the Divine qualities of unalterable truth whose words cannot be changed, and decisive truth which falsehood cannot approach from before it or behind it *(cf. Qur'an 41: 42)*. Furthermore, it is a great blessing which comes to people without any effort on their part, bestowing its light upon them in a very short period, like the blinking of an eye.[44]

ii) Methodology and way[45]

The philosophical methodology differs from its Islamic counterpart from the beginning to the end. Many philosophers begin by studying

---

[42] Al-'Aqqaad, *Kitaab-Allah*, 129.

[43] Ibid.

[44] Darraaz, *Ad-Deen*, 73.

[45] *Majmoo' al-Fataawa Shaykh al-Islam*, 2/1, 25. He (Ibn Taymiya) has mentioned this and we have only summarized it.

the human psyche, making this their basis and starting point. So when they speak of their understanding of knowledge, they say that sometimes it is empirical (based on experience), sometimes it is rational (based on reason), and sometimes it is both.

They made the empirical, natural and other sciences the basis without which knowledge cannot be acquired, then they claimed that in this manner they could understand matters which were close to them, in the realms of nature, mathematics and ethics. They made these three the foundations on which all sciences are built. Thus they are also represented in the bases of *'ilm al-kalaam* (scholasticism), where it is said that one is half of two, the body cannot be in two places at once, and that two opposites, such as black and white, cannot be joined.

Many of these people do not consider ethical matters, such as justice and chastity, as being part of the basic principles; rather they see them as minor issues for which support and evidence are required.

Many philosophical writers start with logic, then empirical science and mathematics, then they move on to knowledge of the Divine. So you find that writers on *'ilm al-kalaam* follow the same principles when examining, studying and deriving evidence, which is like logic, then they move on to discuss, how the universe is created, and strive to prove the existence of the Creator. Some of them divide knowledge into that which exists and that which does not, and sub-categories thereof, as the philosopher when he starts to seek knowledge of the Divine.

Most philosophers speak in depth about matters of nature or instinct, they then discuss the stars and planets, then those among them who study the matter of divinity start to speak about the "One - Who - must - exist" (i.e., Allah), and about reasons and human nature. Some of them try to prove the existence of the "One - Who - must - exist" on the basis that this universe has to have the "One - Who - must - exist".

The aim of those scholars of *'ilm al-kalaam* (scholasticism) who affirm *Tawḥeed* in their books is to prove the Oneness of the Creator, and that He has no partner or associate. They think that this is what is meant by the phrase *Laa ilaaha illa-Allah* (there is no god except Allah).

This methodology of philosophy and *'ilm al-kalaam* may keep the researcher busy for a lifetime, without ever reaching any conclusions. Whatever he learns from it is still accompanied by doubts which forestall any kind of certainty. Thus the researcher is beset by confusion.

The Qur'anic methodology, on the other hand, makes the call to worship Allah Alone, with no partner or associate, the starting point of its message and the message of all the Messengers:

﴿ وَمَآ أَرْسَلْنَا مِن قَبْلِكَ مِن رَّسُولٍ إِلَّا نُوحِىٓ إِلَيْهِ أَنَّهُۥ لَآ إِلَٰهَ إِلَّآ أَنَا۠ فَٱعْبُدُونِ ﴿٢٥﴾ ﴾

﴾And We did not send any Messenger before you [O' Muhammad] but We revealed to him [saying]: *Laa ilaaha illa Ana* [none has the right to be worshipped but I (Allah)], so worship Me [Alone and none else].﴿

(Qur'an 21: 25)

Every Messenger first of all asked his people to worship Allah (ﷻ), Alone:

﴿ ... يَٰقَوْمِ ٱعْبُدُوا۟ ٱللَّهَ مَا لَكُم مِّنْ إِلَٰهٍ غَيْرُهُۥٓ ... ﴿٢٣﴾ ﴾

﴾...O' my people! Worship Allah! You have no other *Ilaah* [God] but Him...﴿ *(Qur'an 23: 23)*

He asked them to worship Him (Allah) with their hearts, with their tongues and with their physical faculties; the worship of Allah implies that one knows Him and remembers Him.

According to this methodology, the foundation of knowledge is knowledge of Allah (ﷻ), not empirical knowledge. For Allah is the First, Who created all that exists, and the Last, to Whom all of creation will return. He is the all-encompassing principle; knowledge of Him is the basis of all knowledge, remembrance of Him is the basis of all remembrance, and striving for His sake is the basis of all effort.

From the knowledge of Allah stem all other kinds of knowledge. From the worship of Him and seeking Him alone stem all kinds of good objectives. By worshipping Him and seeking His help, the heart is protected, for it has taken refuge in the trustworthy support and is clinging to guidance and certain proof. So it is always increasing either in knowledge and *eemaan*, or in safety from ignorance and disbelief. For learning by the help of Allah is the greatest means of learning about Allah and about life and other things, and about the human psyche.

Ibn Abi Ḥaatim said: "We learned about everything by the help of Allah." Ibn 'Abbaas was asked, "How did you come to know about your Lord?" He said, "Whoever tries to understand his religion by analogy will remain confused throughout his life, wandering and deviating from the right way. We learned about Allah (ﷻ), from the way He described Himself and from the attributes of which He told us."

When the Messenger (ﷺ) sent Mu'aadh to Yemen to call the people to Allah, he told him that he would come to some of the People of the Book. He (the Prophet) advised him that the first thing to which he should call them should be the worship of Allah Alone. If they acknowledged that, then he was to call them to do the obligatory duties. He did not tell him to call them first to doubt or to examine things anew, as is the way of some philosophers and scholastics.

Therefore Bukhari started his book with the foundation on which knowledge and *eemaan* are built, that is, the Revelation. So he started with the chapter entitled "The beginning of the Revelation," in which he described how knowledge and *eemaan* were revealed to the Prophet (ﷺ). Then he followed this with the "Book of Faith (*eemaan*)," which implies acceptance of what the Prophet brought. This is followed by the chapter "Book of Knowledge" wherein he explains what the Prophet (ﷺ) brought. So he organized his book in a manner which is indicative of his knowledge and wisdom, may Allah have mercy on him.

When Allah (ﷻ) resurrects mankind, He will not ask them about the empirical sciences, or logic and natural sciences; rather He will ask them whether or not they responded to His Messengers.

﴿... كُلَّمَآ أُلْقِىَ فِيهَا فَوْجٌ سَأَلَهُمْ خَزَنَتُهَآ أَلَمْ يَأْتِكُمْ نَذِيرٌ ۝٨ قَالُوا۟ بَلَىٰ قَدْ جَآءَنَا نَذِيرٌ فَكَذَّبْنَا وَقُلْنَا مَا نَزَّلَ ٱللَّهُ مِن شَىْءٍ إِنْ أَنتُمْ إِلَّا فِى ضَلَٰلٍ كَبِيرٍ ۝٩ وَقَالُوا۟ لَوْ كُنَّا نَسْمَعُ أَوْ نَعْقِلُ مَا كُنَّا فِىٓ أَصْحَٰبِ ٱلسَّعِيرِ ۝١٠ فَٱعْتَرَفُوا۟ بِذَنۢبِهِمْ فَسُحْقًا لِّأَصْحَٰبِ ٱلسَّعِيرِ ۝١١﴾

> ﴾...Every time a group is cast therein [into Hell], its keeper will ask: 'Did no warner come to you?' They will say: 'Yes, indeed a warner did come to us, but we belied him and said: 'Allah never sent down anything [of Revelation]; you are only in great error." And they will say: 'Had we but listened or used our intelligence, we would not have been among the dwellers of the blazing Fire!' Then they will confess their sin. So, away with the dwellers of the blazing Fire!﴿ *(Qur'an 67: 8-11)*

Evidence can only be established against mankind by sending Messengers:

﴿... وَمَا كُنَّا مُعَذِّبِينَ حَتَّىٰ نَبْعَثَ رَسُولًا ۝١٥﴾

﴿...And We never punish until We have sent a Messenger [to give warning].﴾ *(Qur'an 17: 15)*

Just as the call to worship Allah (ﷻ) is the starting point in the Qur'anic methodology, and knowledge of Allah is the basis from which stem all other kinds of knowledge, the final point, too, is the worship of Allah, which includes knowing Him and affirming His Oneness (*Tawḥeed*). Affirming the oneness of the Creator, which is the ultimate aim of the Islamic philosophers, is only a part of the Qur'anic methodology; despite its importance, it is not sufficient merely to state that. Hence the *mushrikeen* — the polytheists — whom the Messenger (ﷺ) fought did not benefit from their affirmation of that.

﴿ وَلَئِن سَأَلْتَهُم مَّنْ خَلَقَ ٱلسَّمَٰوَٰتِ وَٱلْأَرْضَ لَيَقُولُنَّ ٱللَّهُ ... ﴿٢٥﴾ ﴾

﴿And if you [O' Muhammad] ask them: 'Who has created the heavens and the earth,' they will certainly say: 'Allah'...﴾ *(Qur'an 31: 25)*

﴿ قُلْ مَن رَّبُّ ٱلسَّمَٰوَٰتِ ٱلسَّبْعِ وَرَبُّ ٱلْعَرْشِ ٱلْعَظِيمِ ﴿٨٦﴾ سَيَقُولُونَ لِلَّهِ ... ﴿٨٧﴾ ﴾

﴿Say: 'Who is [the] Lord of the seven heavens, and [the] Lord of the Great Throne?' They will say: 'Allah'...﴾ *(Qur'an 23: 86-87)*

But the philosophers who examined the human mind and psyche have gotten nowhere in this vast and endless field. You find sufficient evidence of that in the fact that the immense scientific progress of the modern age has not revealed to us the true nature of the human psyche. "Mankind has made huge efforts to discover his psyche, but despite the fact that we possess a huge treasure of observations made by philosophers, scientists, poets and spiritual leaders of all times, we can only understand a specific aspect of ourselves, but not man as a whole... We know that man is composed of different parts, but even these parts are known to us only through our limited means. Each one of us is formed from his physical parts, in the midst of which is an unknown reality.

The fact remains that our ignorance is almost total, and the deepest questions about mankind remain unanswered, because unlimited areas in our inner selves are still unknown."[46]

If this is the knowledge gained through the twentieth century research, how can the human psyche be the basis from which other kinds of knowledge stem? With regard to the knowledge of whatever lies beyond the natural world, philosophy has clearly gone far astray.

iii) Forceful impact

'Aqeedah — creed/belief, is distinguished by its great power over the souls of its followers. Philosophy has no hope of reaching such a level of influence, or else it would reach an inappropriate high position and contradict itself. The reason for that is that philosophy looks for knowledge and truth within the framework of human ability. The philosophers deal with whatever they have discovered about the aspects of that truth. The philosopher is the one who knows the shortcomings of the human mind, and anything that is human, lack perfection. Hence academic tolerance and modesty are among the most prominent features. Socrates, with his great standing among philosophers, said, "The thing that I still know so well is that I do not know anything."

But the follower of *'aqeedah* — creed/belief sees that the *'aqeedah* to which he holds fast has its origins with the One Who knows the secrets of creation and Who encompasses all things with His knowledge. So *'aqeedah* gives a true and clear image of reality.

---

[46] *Al-'Ilm yad'oo ila'l-eemaan.*

'Aqeedah demands commitment, humility and submission, and does not accept any argument or contradiction when it comes to its rulings. Indeed, it does not allow any room for discussion or re-examination of itself. If a person does that with regard to some issue, then as far as that issue is concerned, he becomes like a philosopher and not a religious person, until he reaches a stage of conviction to which he adheres. At that point no compromise can be accepted and he cannot free himself from the obligations that are required. Then it becomes a belief to which he demonstrates an extraordinary devotion to the extent that he does not care if he sacrifices himself for its sake. We hardly ever see any other kind of idea having such a hold over its followers, be it academic, political or otherwise.

Shaykh Muhammad 'Abdullah Darraaz explained the mystery behind this phenomenon when he said: "The mystery behind this phenomenon — the distinctive power wielded by *'aqeedah*, which distinguishes it from philosophy — is represented by the difference between the essence of knowledge and the essence of *eemaan*, and the difference between conviction that is based on reason and conviction that is based on faith. A person may understand the meaning of hunger and thirst without feeling their pain, and he may understand the meaning of love and desire without actually feeling them. He may understand the effect of a brilliant piece of art, the techniques involved and the fine details of the piece, without truly appreciating it or liking it.

These different types of knowledge are learned through the senses, or by thought, or by instinct. One notices them as something that is detached from the soul or something that passes by (it) and touches it in a superficial way leaving some impression, but without sinking deeply into it or affecting its behaviour. Every person whose ideas and principles are formed in this manner has no faith at all.

Eemaan — creed/belief is knowledge which reverberates deep in the conscience, so that the heart does not feel any hesitation concerning it, rather filled with the comfort of certainty. *Eemaan* has to do with feelings and conscience which take an idea from the level of reason into the depths of the heart, as if the idea is food and drink which nourish the soul. Thus the idea becomes one of the elements in its life, and *eemaan* changes the idea into a vital driving force which lets nothing stand in its way.

This is the difference between religion and philosophy. The aim of philosophy is knowledge, and the aim of religion is *eemaan*. The goal of philosophy is dry knowledge which takes a lifeless form, whilst the goal of religion is an energetic soul and vital power.

Darraaz notes that philosophy focuses on just one aspect of the soul, whilst religion takes control of the soul in its entirety. Philosophy observes, analyzes and draws conclusions; it seeks to dissect reality and kill its spirit, then it tries to put the pieces back together in an artificial manner so that it may be understood by reason. Philosophy, therefore, leaves the impression that the soul is a dry, empty shell. Religion, on the other hand, is an cantillation that gives a full picture of reality, penetrating deep beneath the surface of the heart, so that the soul gives its all to it and surrenders its reins to it.

Here Darraaz illustrates the subtle difference between philosophy and religion. He notes that the aim of philosophy is theoretical even in its practical aspect, whereas the aim of religion is practical even in its theoretical aspect. The ultimate aim of philosophy is to show us what is true and good, and where it is to be found; after that, it is not concerned with our attitude towards the truth and good that it has defined. Religion, on the other hand, tells us what is true, not only so that we may know it, but so that we may believe in it, love it and venerate it, and it tells us what is obligatory so that we may do it and perfect our souls by doing so.

In order to make the matter even clearer, he compares the practical effects of religion and philosophy. Darraaz explains that religion draws man's attention to His Creator so that He may know Him and turn to Him, loving Him and glorifying Him, whereas the aim of philosophy is merely to point out the knowledge which makes the connection between cause and effect.

He explains that religious belief (*'aqeedah*) has an influence on society, motivating the believer to achieve its aims and propagate its message, whereas philosophy is not concerned with spreading its message; on the contrary philosophers may even keep it from others and take philosophy as a monopoly which they keep to themselves.

iv) Style [47]

Islamic *'aqeedah* has a distinct, dynamic and rhythmic style, a direct approach that touches upon universal realities that cannot be put into words, though can be evoked by words and phrases. It is distinguished by the fact that it addresses all aspects of the human condition, motivating all its potentials and faculties; it does not address itself solely to the rational aspect of humanity.

Philosophy, on the other hand, takes a different approach, whereby it seeks to contain universal reality in phrases, although the kind of reality which it seeks to deal with cannot be moulded into mere words. Moreover, the essential aspects of these realities are, by their very nature, far beyond the arena in which the human intellect usually operates. The inevitable result is that philosophy turns out to be unduly complex, confused and dry. Therefore, Islamic *'aqeedah* should not be discussed in the philosophical manner, because this will kill it and extinguish its light, and confine it to just one aspect of the human condition.

---

[47] Sayyid Quṭb, *Khaṣaa'iṣ at-Taṣawwur al-Islami*, Pp. 16.

From this point we may note the complexity, dryness, shortcomings and deviation that exist in all attempts to discuss *'aqeedah* in this manner which is alien to its nature. The Qur'anic way of explaining the Islamic *'aqeedah* is characterized by simplicity and clarity which make it possible for all people to grasp, regardless of the level of their understanding. So each person absorbs it according to his own ability to understand and believe. This is in contrast to the complex style of philosophy which is filled with jargon which is understood by very few.

v) Deduction method

The way in which the Qur'an gives evidence is different from the manner in which philosophy and *'ilm al-kalaam* give evidence. We may make this distinction clearer by mentioning the following points:

a) The Qur'an points to the evidence of visible signs in the universe which indicate the Oneness of the Creator. Philosophy and *'ilm al-kalaam* do likewise, but the Qur'anic approach differs from the philosophical approach. The Qur'an refers to the same signs which inevitably lead to knowledge of their Creator, just as knowing the rays of the sun inevitably leads one to know that the sun exists, with no need for creating analogies as the philosophers do in order to prove that the universe is a created entity.

Knowing that this universe was created by and is subject to Allah is something instinctive. There is no need to produce evidence and to establish proof. Man knows instinctively that this universe which he sees is in need of its Creator, and that it is subject to and controlled by Him. This does not need the analogies which the philosophers produce to prove that the universe is a created entity and that there is a Creator. Allah (ﷻ), says:

﴿ أَوَلَمْ يَرَ ٱلَّذِينَ كَفَرُوٓا۟ أَنَّ ٱلسَّمَٰوَٰتِ وَٱلْأَرْضَ كَانَتَا رَتْقًا فَفَتَقْنَٰهُمَا ۖ وَجَعَلْنَا مِنَ ٱلْمَآءِ كُلَّ شَىْءٍ حَىٍّ ۖ أَفَلَا يُؤْمِنُونَ ﴿٣٠﴾ وَجَعَلْنَا فِى ٱلْأَرْضِ رَوَٰسِىَ أَن تَمِيدَ بِهِمْ وَجَعَلْنَا فِيهَا فِجَاجًا سُبُلًا لَّعَلَّهُمْ يَهْتَدُونَ ﴿٣١﴾ وَجَعَلْنَا ٱلسَّمَآءَ سَقْفًا مَّحْفُوظًا ۖ وَهُمْ عَنْ ءَايَٰتِهَا مُعْرِضُونَ ﴿٣٢﴾ وَهُوَ ٱلَّذِى خَلَقَ ٱلَّيْلَ وَٱلنَّهَارَ وَٱلشَّمْسَ وَٱلْقَمَرَ ۖ كُلٌّ فِى فَلَكٍ يَسْبَحُونَ ﴿٣٣﴾ ﴾

﴿Have not those who disbelieve known that the heavens and the earth were joined together as one united piece, then We parted them? And We have made from water every living thing. Will they not then believe? And We have placed on the earth firm mountains, lest it should shake with them, and We placed therein broad highways for them to pass through, that they may be guided. And We have made the heaven a roof, safe and well-guarded. Yet they turn away from its signs [i.e. sun, moon, winds, clouds]. And He it is Who has created the night and the day, and the sun and the moon, each in an orbit floating.﴾ *(Qur'an 21: 30-33)*

b) The rational evidence[48] which the Qur'an gives is befitting to the majesty and perfection of Allah (ﷻ). The Qur'an does not use analogies which apply to absolutely everything when it speaks of

[48] Many scholars of *'ilm al-kalaam* and philosophers make the mistake of thinking that the Qur'an and Sunnah are merely narrative (as opposed to analytical - Translator), and that they do not discuss rational evidence. The truth of the matter is that the Qur'an explains evidence as needed to impart knowledge of Allah and His Oneness in a manner which none of them are able to do. The ultimate aim of the scholars of *'ilm al-kalaam* has been explained by the Qur'an briefly and in the best manner, such as the parables given by Allah (ﷻ), in His Book, of which He says:
﴿And indeed We have put forth every kind of example in this Qur'an, for mankind.﴾ *(Qur'an 18: 54)*.
The examples given are rational analogies.

Allah (ﷻ), for this would imply that the Creator and His creation are equal. Rather, it uses the analogy of "more so" when it speaks of Allah, which means that if there is any attribute of perfection which may be applied to any mortal creation, it is more befitting for the Creator to be described in this manner, because He is the One Who has bestowed that perfection upon His creation. If He did not have that attribute of perfection, then that would imply that there was something in His creation that was more perfect than He — which is impossible.

Allah (ﷻ), says:

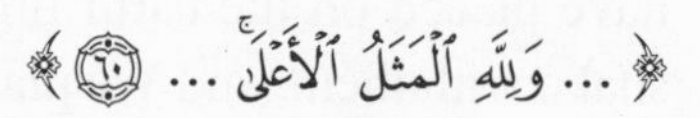

﴾...And for Allah is the highest description...﴿

(Qur'an 16: 60)

Every shortcoming which the created being does not have, then it is more befitting for the Creator to be free of it.

c) We may also note that the rational evidence given by the Qur'an points to the truth in the most eloquent and concise manner, whilst much of the rational evidence presented by the philosophers and scholars of *'ilm al-kalaam* is not strong. If the evidence used to prove the truth is weak, then this leads to doubt, confusion and frustration concerning the truth, and may even lead to a rejection of the truth, because it becomes easy for opponents to expose the shortcomings of the evidence. If they refute the evidence, then they refute the truth, although the truth is strong in and of itself, and the weakness exists in the evidence (and not in the truth itself). For this reason we see that the scholars of *'ilm al-kalaam* are the people who shift most frequently from one opinion to another; they may affirm one opinion on one occasion, and its opposite on another, and they may even denounce as *kaafir* people who hold an opinion which they themselves have stated on another occasion. This is in contrast to the evidence of the Qur'an and Sunnah, whose followers adhere to what they say and are not confused about it.[49]

d) We may note that some of the evidences used by the scholars of *'ilm al-kalaam* are ineffective and sometimes even false, because it implies rejecting the truth which is established by the Qur'an and Sunnah.

They rejected the texts which state that Allah is in heaven (sky), because they claimed that Allah cannot be in a particular direction, because that would mean limiting Him. But the texts clearly state that He is in heaven. Their mistake was in thinking that His being in heaven means that He is contained. They also erred when they tried to apply human analogies to the Divine nature.

vi) Results

Another difference is that the Qur'an gives details about *eemaan*, as Jundub ibn 'Abdullah said, "We learnt about *eemaan*, then we learnt the Qur'an, then our *eemaan* increased."

The Qur'an describes for us our Lord, and tells us that He has a Face and Hand, and He can hear and see. It recounts for us His Names and Attributes, telling us that He is *Ar-Raḥmaan* (the Most Beneficent), *Ar-Raḥeem* (the Most Merciful), *Al-Malik* (the King), *Al-Quddoos* (the Holy), *As-Salaam* (the One Free from all defects), *Al-Mu'min* (the Giver of security), *Al-Muhaymin* (the Watcher over His creatures), *Al-'Azeez* (the Almighty), *Al-Jabbaar* (the Compeller)... It tells us of His deeds and creations, and describes for us the Resurrection and its terrors, as well as Paradise and Hell, as if we can see them.

But in the case of *'ilm al-kalaam*, the most that it tells us is the briefest of descriptions, without any details at all.

---

[49] *Majmoo' al-Fataawa*: Ibn Taymiya 4/50.

No Meeting-Point

There is no meeting point between religion and philosophy, because they are two different methodologies, from beginning to end, in their ways and styles, in the influence they wield, and - above all - in their origins and sources.

Islam does not need anything else to complete or perfect it, because it has been made perfect by the All-Knowing, All-Aware:

﴿... ٱلْيَوْمَ أَكْمَلْتُ لَكُمْ دِينَكُمْ وَأَتْمَمْتُ عَلَيْكُمْ نِعْمَتِى ... ﴿٣﴾﴾

﴾...This day, I have perfected your religion for you, [and] completed My Favour upon you...﴿ *(Qur'an 5: 3)*

We do not need to reconcile Islam to philosophy, or Islam to Judaism or Christianity, or Islam to communism or socialism. Islam is true, and there is no falsehood in it.

﴿لَّا يَأْتِيهِ ٱلْبَٰطِلُ مِنۢ بَيْنِ يَدَيْهِ وَلَا مِنْ خَلْفِهِۦ ... ﴿٤٢﴾﴾

﴾Falsehood cannot come to it from before it or behind it...﴿ *(Qur'an 41:42)*

Anything else is either falsehood, or truth mixed with falsehood. Islam did not come to be ruled by people's ideas; rather it came to dominate life and living beings and to correct whatever beliefs and ideas are crooked.

We must keep our *'aqeedah* and shari'ah distinct and pure, as our Lord wants us to do:

﴿... قَد تَّبَيَّنَ ٱلرُّشْدُ مِنَ ٱلْغَىِّ ... ﴿٢٥٦﴾﴾

﴾...Verily, the Right Path has become distinct from the wrong path...﴿ *(Qur'an 2: 256)*

If it is mixed with something else, this leads to the confusion which Allah (ﷻ) condemned in the case of the People of the Book (the Jews and the Christians):

﴿ يَٰٓأَهۡلَ ٱلۡكِتَٰبِ لِمَ تَلۡبِسُونَ ٱلۡحَقَّ بِٱلۡبَٰطِلِ ... ﴿٧١﴾ ﴾

﴾O' people of the Scripture [Jews and Christians]: 'Why do you mix truth with falsehood...?'﴿ *(Qur'an 3: 71)*

2) The Attitude of the Scholars Towards Philosophy

Muslim scholars resisted the trend towards mixing matters of *'aqeedah* — belief — with philosophy and *'ilm al-kalaam*, which was started by those who were known as the "philosophers of Islam," such as Ibn Seena (Avicenna), and they fought those who were influenced by these philosophies.

The great scholars were of two types: one group was composed of those who noted the danger of this idea from the start and resisted this trend from the outset, such as Imam Aḥmad and Imam ash-Shaafa'i (may Allah have mercy on him). Shaafa'i said: "My ruling concerning the scholars of *'ilm al-kalaam* is that they should be beaten with palm-branches and shoes, and paraded before the tribes and clans, and it should be announced that this is the punishment of those who forsake the Qur'an and Sunnah and turn to *'ilm al-kalaam*."

The other group is composed of scholars who followed in the footsteps of the philosophers and were exhausted by their methods, but they did not realize what was happening until the sunset of their years, when they were filled with regret at the time when it was too late. They were left with nothing but grief and sorrow, and could do no more than ask Allah for forgiveness and warn those who came after them against following the mistaken path that they trod.

Among this group was Muhammad ibn 'Umar ar-Raazi, who said in his book *Aqsaam al-Ladhdhaat*:[50]

"The most that reason can achieve is a dead end, and the ultimate result of people's striving is misguidance.
Our souls are alienated in our bodies, and all that we get from this world is harm and annoyance.
We have not gained anything from our lifelong search apart from a collection of what the philosophers said.
How often have we seen men and nations, but they have all vanished quickly and disappeared.
How many mountains have men climbed, but the men have gone and the mountains remain."
Ar-Raazi said:

"I examined the various *kalaami* and philosophical schools of thought, and I realized that they have nothing to offer to one who is sick, and they cannot quench a man's thirst (for knowledge)." He came back to the Qur'anic methodology, and gave an example of the Qur'anic methodology concerning the Divine attributes: "I saw that the best way is the way of the Qur'an. Read where it confirms the attributes of Allah (سبحانه وتعالى):

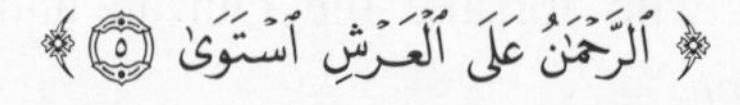

﴾The Most Gracious [Allah] rose over [*Istawaa*] the [Mighty] Throne [in a manner that suits His Majesty].﴿
(Qur'an 20: 5)

﴿ ... إِلَيْهِ يَصْعَدُ ٱلْكَلِمُ ٱلطَّيِّبُ ... ﴿١٠﴾ ﴾

---

[50] Ibn al-Qayyim, *Aṣ-Ṣawaa'iq al-Mursalah*, Pp. 7; Ar-Raazi, *I'tiqaadaat firaq al-Muslimeen*, Pp. 23.

﴾...To Him ascend [all] the goodly words...﴿ *(Qur'an 35: 10)*

And read where it denies things with regard to His attributes:

﴾... لَيْسَ كَمِثْلِهِۦ شَىْءٌ ... ﴿١١﴾﴿

﴾...There is nothing like Him...﴿ *(Qur'an 42: 11)*

﴾... وَلَا يُحِيطُونَ بِهِۦ عِلْمًا ﴿١١٠﴾﴿

﴾...But they will never compass anything of His Knowledge.﴿ *(Qur'an 20: 110)*."

Then he said: "Whoever goes through the same experience as I have will know what I know."[51]

Ash-Shahrastaani said the same thing, noting that after spending a long time studying with the philosophers and scholars of *'ilm al-kalaam*, he found nothing but confusion and regret, as he says:[52]

"All my life, I went around all the schools of philosophy, studying all of those schools. And I never saw anything but people resting their chins on their hands or gnashing their teeth in regret."

Al-Juwayni, one of the most prominent students of Islamic philosophy (*'ilm al-kalaam*), warned against studying this: "O' my friends, do not study *'ilm al-kalaam*. Had I known what *'ilm al-kalaam* would do to me, I would not have studied it."[53]

When he was dying, he said in regret and sorrow: "I threw myself into a vast ocean, and forsook the people of Islam and their knowledge. I indulged in that which they had warned me against, and

---

[51] *Shaykh al-Islam* Ibn Taymiyah, *Al-Fatwa al-Ḥamawiyah al-Kubra*, Pp. 7.

[52] Ash-Shahrastaani, *Nihaayat al-Iqdaam fi 'Ilm al-Kalaam*, Pp. 3.

[53] *Majmoo' al-Fataawa Shaykh al-Islam Ibn Taymiyah*; see *Al-Fatwa al-Ḥamawiyah al-Kubra*, Pp. 7.

now if Allah does not shower me with His mercy, then woe to Ibn al-Juwayni. 'Here I am, dying on the *'aqeedah* of my mother,' or he said, 'on the *'aqeedah* of old women (i.e., simple *'aqeedah*).'"

Abu Ḥaamid al-Ghazaali (may Allah have mercy on him) was one of those who spent a long time examining and studying *'ilm al-kalaam*, moving from one group to another, until at the end of his life he was hesitant and confused about philosophical matters. He wrote a book entitled *Iljaam al-'Awaam 'an 'Ilm al-Kalaam* (Preventing the masses from studying *'Ilm al-Kalaam* — Islamic philosophy i.e., Scholasticism). He regarded it as *ḥaraam* to study philosophy except in certain circumstances: "The truth is that *'ilm al-kalaam* is *ḥaraam* except for two types of people."

At the end of his life, he turned away from the study of *'ilm al-kalaam* and turned to the *aḥaadeeth* of the Messenger (ﷺ), and he died with a copy of *Ṣaḥeeḥ al-Bukhari* on his chest.

Abu'l-Ḥasan al-Ash'ari grew up as a *Mu'tazili*, and remained such for forty years, then he turned his back on that and stated clearly that the *Mu'tazilah* were misguided, and he refuted them in unequivocal terms.[54]

Later there emerged a group which followed the correct methodology, but they studied the work of the philosophers in order to know its weak points and refute them according to the Qur'anic methodology. They fought them with their own weapon, pointing out what was wrong with it. The leader and standard-bearer of this group was *Shaykh al-Islam* Ibn Taymiyah (may Allah have mercy on him).

---

[54] See our book, *Mu'taqad al-Imam Abi'l-Ḥasan al-Ash'ari wa Manhajuhu.*

3) Comparison Between Man of Thought (Philosophy) and Man of *'Aqeedah*

Before closing this topic, I would like to say that we need men of *'aqeedah*, not men of philosophy. We need people who can deal with the ailments and problems of this ummah, and philosophers cannot do that.

Professor Aḥmad Ameen (may Allah have mercy on him) made a comparison between man of philosophy and man of *'aqeedah*, and the respective effect on life.

"There is a great difference between holding an opinion and believing in something. If you have an opinion, it simply becomes part of the information that you have retained; but if you believe in it, it flows with your blood and sinks deep into your heart and mind."

The philosopher who has an opinion and an idea says, "I think that this is correct but in reality it may be wrong; this is what the evidence points to today, but tomorrow the evidence may point to the opposite; I may be wrong about this or I may be right."

But the one who follows *'aqeedah* — creed — is definite and certain; he has no doubts and does not engage in speculation. His *'aqeedah* is true and does not change, and it will still be true tomorrow. It is no longer subject to evidence. It is above doubts and conjecture.

The one who holds an inference and thinking — opinion — is emotionally cool and unenthusiastic. If what he thinks is proven to be true, he merely smiles in a restrained manner, and if it is not proven to be true, it doesn't matter, for he has already taken the precaution of noting that whilst he believes his opinion to be correct, it may be wrong, and that another person's opinion, which he believes to be mistaken, may be right. But the one who follows *'aqeedah* is warm and enthusiastic, and does not feel content unless his *'aqeedah* is fulfilled.

The one who has philosophical opinion may easily change his mind and adopt new ideas, because he only follows evidence, or his own interests when they come in the form of evidence. But the best way to describe the one who follows *'aqeedah* is the way in which the Messenger (ﷺ) described:

> "If the sun were to be placed in my right hand and the moon in my left, to make me forsake that which I have brought, I would not do so."[55]

Mere opinion is like a dead body; it is lifeless unless it is infused with the breath of *'aqeedah*. Mere opinion is like a dark cave which remains unlit unless *'aqeedah* shines its rays into it. Mere opinion is like a stagnant pond in which mosquitoes lay their eggs. *'Aqeedah*, on the other hand, is like a vast ocean where insignificant insects are not allowed to multiply.

Mere opinion is an unformed nebula, whilst *'aqeedah* is a brightly shining star.

Mere opinion creates problems and obstacles, pays attention to physical desire, creates doubts and fosters hesitation, whilst *'aqeedah* pays no heed to danger, causes mountains to tremble, changes the course of history, wipes out doubt and hesitation, and engenders strength and certainty; it permits nothing but the fulfilment of the aims of the soul.[56]

---

[55] This is a *ḍa'eef* (weak) hadith which is narrated by Aṭ-Ṭabari in his *Taareekh* (2/326) and by Al-Bayhaqi in *Dalaa'il an-Nubuwwah* (2/187), from Ibn Isḥaaq. Its isnad is *munqaṭi'* (broken). See *As-Seerah an-Nabawiyah* by Ibn Hishaam, 1/330.

[56] Aḥmad Ameen, *Fayḍ al-Khaaṭir*, quoting from Al-Qaraḍaawi's, *Al-Eemaan wa'l-Ḥayaat*, Pp. 22.

5 - SCHOLARS' METHODOLOGY IN AFFIRMING *'AQEEDAH*[57]

Do we believe in the torment of the grave, the Cistern, the Balance and other matters of *'aqeedah*? What makes us believe in that or deny it?

a) The scholars of the righteous predecessors - *Salaf* - believed that it is obligatory for us to believe in everything that Allah or His Messenger (ﷺ) have told us, and in what has reached us via a *ṣaḥeeḥ* isnad. They did not distinguish between *mutawaatir* reports and *aaḥaad* reports[58] as long as they were *ṣaḥeeḥ* (sound), and they used both (types of report) to prove matters of *'aqeedah*, without distinguishing between them.

Their basis for doing so was the general evidence which commands us to believe all that Allah (ﷻ) and His Messenger (ﷺ) tell us, and to obey them in all that they command, as in the *aayaat* (verses):

﴿وَمَا كَانَ لِمُؤْمِنٍ وَلَا مُؤْمِنَةٍ إِذَا قَضَى ٱللَّهُ وَرَسُولُهُۥٓ أَمْرًا أَن يَكُونَ لَهُمُ ٱلْخِيَرَةُ مِنْ أَمْرِهِمْ ... ﴿٣٦﴾﴾

﴿It is not for a believer, man or woman, when Allah and His Messenger have decreed a matter that they should have any option in their decision...﴾ *(Qur'an 33: 36)*

﴿قُلْ أَطِيعُوا۟ ٱللَّهَ وَٱلرَّسُولَ ... ﴿٣٢﴾﴾

﴿Say [O' Muhammad]: "Obey Allah and the Messenger [Muhammad]..."﴾ *(Qur'an 3: 32)*

---

[57] See our book *Aṣl al-I'tiqaad*, in which this is discussed in detail.

[58] A *mutawaatir* hadith is one which is narrated by such a large number from the beginning of the isnad to the end that it would be impossible for them all to agree upon a lie. *Aaḥaad* reports are any that do not reach the degree of *mutawaatir*.

b) A group that lacked the knowledge of differentiating between sound and weak *aḥaadeeth* argued using *mawḍoo'* (fabricated) and *ḍa'eef* (weak) *aḥaadeeth* as evidences.[59] For example, the hadith:

> "I reached my Lord on the night on which I was taken up to the heavens, and I saw my Lord, and between Him and me there was a visible barrier. I saw everything of Him, I saw even a crown adorned with pearls." - This is a *mawḍoo'* hadith.[60]

The hadith,

> "Verily Allah sits on an arch between Paradise and Hell."[61] - This is *ḍa'eef.*

It is essential to examine *aḥaadeeth* before using them as evidence, whether they have to do with *'aqeedah* or *aḥkaam* (rulings), otherwise the result will be the attribution to the religion of Allah of things that are not a part of it, and we will affirm matters of belief that are false.

Those who try to prove beliefs by using fabricated and weak *aḥaadeeth* are like those who try to use myths, dreams and legends as evidence.

c) A third group refused to use the transmitted reports, i.e., the texts of the Qur'an and *aḥaadeeth*, as evidence in proving matters of *'aqeedah*. They claimed that "the transmitted evidence did not reach the level of certainty that would inspire in us the required level of faith, so *'aqeedah* cannot be confirmed thereby."[62] They explained

---

[59] *Mawḍoo'* (fabricated) means false, i.e. a hadith in which the isnad contains liars. *ḍa'eef* (weak) means a hadith which does not fulfil the conditions of being *ṣaḥeeḥ* (sound).

[60] Ash-Shawkaani, *Al-Fawaa'id al-Majmoo'ah fi'l-Aḥaadeeth al-Mawḍoo'ah*, 441.

[61] Ibid, 448.

[62] Shaltoot: *Al-Islam 'Aqeedah wa Sharee'ah*, Pp. 53.

why it does not reach the level of certainty by saying that "in the case of the transmitted evidence there is too much scope for too many things that would prevent this level of certainty."[63]

This view is clearly nonsense, and no great effort is required to refute it because it contradicts the consensus (*ijmaa'*) of the ummah. If there is too much room for doubt with regard to the texts, then how about what people say? How come issues of faith cannot be proven by what Allah and His Messenge said? Glory be to You (O' Allah)! This is a great lie *(cf. Qur'an 24: 16).*

d) A fourth group rejected the idea of using *ṣaḥeeḥ aaḥaad aḥaadeeth* as evidence in matters of *'aqeedah*. They refer only to the Qur'an and the *mutawaatir aḥaadeeth*, and they do not prove *'aqeedah* from the Qur'an and *mutawaatir aḥaadeeth* except when the text had a definitive meaning.[64] If a text does not have a definitive meaning, then in their view it is not permissible to use it as evidence.

This was the view of the scholars of *'ilm al-kalaam* in the past. Some scholars of *uṣool* followed them. This idea is widespread in our own time, to the extent that the truth has almost been forgotten and people regard as strange those who follow it. The scholars of the past and the present have always explained how corrupt and dangerous this view is, and refuted the specious arguments of its proponents.

---

[63] Shaltoot: *Al-Islam 'Aqeedah wa Sharee'ah*, p. 53.

[64] By definitive evidence they mean, the Qur'an and *mutawaatir aḥaadeeth*.

By definitive evidence, they meant that the text should not have a second possible meaning, or be open to interpretation. Thus they rejected the texts which state that the believers will see their Lord on the Day of Resurrection. With regard to the *aḥaadeeth*, even if they were definitive in meaning, they still claimed that they were *aaḥaad aḥaadeeth*. With regard to the texts of the Qur'an, they are not definitive in meaning and they interpreted them differently. (See *Shaykh* Shaltoot's denial that people will see their *Rabb*, in his book *Al-Islam 'Aqeedah wa Sharee'ah*, Pp. 57)

Explanation of Their Specious Arguments [65]

We have noted that their argument is based on the claim that the reports used as evidence regarding matters of *'aqeedah* should reach the level of certainty, and that if the meanings of the *aaḥaad aḥaadeeth*, the texts of the Qur'an and the *mutawaatir aḥaadeeth* are not definitive, then they do not reach that level of certainty; rather they are conjecture, and conjecture cannot be used as evidence with regard to these matters because Allah (ﷻ) says:

﴿... إِن يَتَّبِعُونَ إِلَّا ٱلظَّنَّ وَمَا تَهْوَى ٱلْأَنفُسُ ... ﴿٢٣﴾﴾

﴿...They follow but a guess and that which they themselves desire,...﴾ *(Qur'an 53: 23)*

And:

﴿... إِن يَتَّبِعُونَ إِلَّا ٱلظَّنَّ وَإِنَّ ٱلظَّنَّ لَا يُغْنِى مِنَ ٱلْحَقِّ شَيْـًٔا ﴿٢٨﴾﴾

﴿...They follow but a guess, and verily, guess is no substitute for the truth.﴾ *(Qur'an 53: 28)*

And there are other *aayaat* (verses) in which Allah (ﷻ), condemns the *mushrikeen* (idolaters) for following conjecture.

Their use of these and similar *aayaat* as evidence may be rejected, because the kind of conjecture or guess referred to in the *aayaat* is not the conjecture that they are referring to. The texts that they refuse to accept as evidence concerning matters of *'aqeedah* reached a level of high probability, whereas the conjecture which Allah condemns in the *aayah*: ﴿...They follow but a guess,...﴾ *(Qur'an 53: 23)* is the kind of doubt which is mere speculation and conjecture, but in *An-*

---

[65] See *Al-Ḥadeeth Ḥujjah bi Nafsihi* and *Wujoob al-Akhdh bi Aḥaadeeth al-Aaḥaad fi'l-'Aqaa'id wa'l-Aḥkaam*, by *Shaykh* Naaṣiruddeen al-Albaani, and our book *Aṣl al-I'tiqaad*.

Nihaayah, Al-Lisaan and other Arabic dictionaries it is stated that *ẓann* (translated as "guess" in the *aayah* quoted above) refers to "when you have doubts about something but you accept it and judge according to it."

This is the *ẓann* or guess which Allah condemned on the part of the *mushrikeen*. What supports this view is the fact that Allah (ﷻ), said concerning them:

﴿... إِن يَتَّبِعُونَ إِلَّا ٱلظَّنَّ وَإِنْ هُمْ إِلَّا يَخْرُصُونَ ﴿١١٦﴾﴾

﴾...They follow nothing but conjectures, and they do nothing but lie.﴿ *(Qur'an 6: 116)*

So *ẓann* refers to conjecture which is mere speculation and guessing. If the *ẓann* for which the *mushrikeen* were condemned was high probability, then it would not be permitted to use the Qur'an and *aḥaadeeth* as evidence for rulings either, because Allah condemned the *mushrikeen* (idolaters) for following any kind of *ẓann* whatsoever. He did not condemn only *ẓann* in the case of beliefs and ignore the matter of rulings; in some *aayaat* (verses) He explains that the *ẓann* for which the *mushrikeen* are to be condemned includes their ideas about rulings too. Here is what Allah (ﷻ) says, on this matter:

﴿سَيَقُولُ ٱلَّذِينَ أَشْرَكُوا۟ لَوْ شَآءَ ٱللَّهُ مَآ أَشْرَكْنَا وَلَآ ءَابَآؤُنَا ... ﴿١٤٨﴾﴾

﴾Those who took partners [in worship] with Allah will say: 'If Allah had willed, we would not have taken partners [in worship] with Him, nor would our fathers...'﴿ *(Qur'an 6: 148)*

— this refers to belief or *'aqeedah*;

﴿... وَلَا حَرَّمْنَا مِن شَىْءٍ ... ﴿١٤٨﴾﴾

﴾...And we would not have forbidden anything [against His Will]...﴿ *(Qur'an 6: 148)*

— this refers to rulings or *ḥukm.*

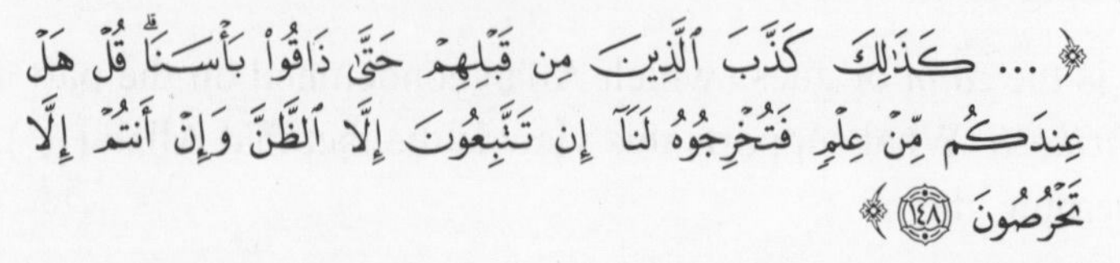

﴾...Likewise belied those who were before them, [they argued falsely with Allah's Messengers], till they tasted Our Wrath. Say: 'Have you any knowledge [proof] that you can produce before us? Verily, you follow nothing but guess and you do nothing but lie.'﴿ *(Qur'an 6: 148)*

We do not accept what they say about the *aaḥaad aḥaadeeth* not reaching the level of certainty. They do indeed reach that level. Ṣiddeeq Ḥasan Khan said: "The dispute is with regard to *aaḥaad* reports for which there is no corroborating evidence and whether they constitute conjecture or certainty. In the case of *aaḥaad* reports for which there is corroborating evidence, there is no such dispute.

There is no dispute concerning *aaḥaad* reports where there is consensus (*ijmaa'*) that they should be acted upon, because this (*ijmaa'*) takes them to the level of certainty as it brings them to a point where they are known to be true. The same applies to *aaḥaad* reports which are accepted by the ummah, and followed according to the apparent meaning or an interpretation of their meaning, as is the case with the *aḥaadeeth* in the Two *Ṣaḥeeḥs* of Bukhari and Muslim."

Al-'Allaamah as-Safaareeni said in *Lawaami' al-Anwaar al-Bahiyah*:

"If an *aaḥaad* report is well-known and widely accepted, suggests certainty, as is narrated by 'Allaamah ibn Mufliḥ and others from Ibn Isḥaaq al-Asfaraayini and Ibn Foorak. It is also said that this brings it up to the level of being definite (definitely *ṣaḥeeḥ*)."

Then he mentioned the view that if an *aaḥaad* report is not well known and widely accepted, this brings it to the level of probability (not certainty), because there is the possibility of confusion and error. But it is narrated that Imam al-Muwaffaq (Ibn Qudaamah), Ibn Ḥamdaan and Aṭ-Ṭoofi concluded that such reports should reach the level of certainty if there is corroborating evidence.

Al-'Allaamah 'Alaa' ad-Deen 'Ali ibn Sulaymaan al-Mirdaawi said in *Sharḥ at-Taḥreer*:

"This is a stronger, clear opinion and is correct." He explained that corroborating evidence means "that one feels at ease with the *aaḥaad* reports just as one feels at ease with the *mutawaatir* reports, or something similar to that, to the extent that one has no doubts at all."

He also stated that *aaḥaad* reports which are not well known and widely accepted may reach the level of certainty if it is narrated by one of the Imams whose scholarly pre-eminence and precise knowledge of *aḥaadeeth* is agreed upon.

He narrated from Al-Qaaḍi Abu Ya'laa, "This is the correct view (the view of the Ḥanbalis). Abu'l-Khaṭṭaab said, this is the apparent meaning of our companions' view."

As-Safaareeni mentioned that this was the view adopted by Ibn al-Zaa'ooni and Imam Taqiuddeen ibn Taymiya, then he said that this was the opinion of "the *uṣooliyeen* among the companions of Abu Ḥaneefah, Ash-Shaafa'i and Aḥmad — may Allah have mercy on them all — (who said that) if an *aaḥaad* report is accepted and followed by the ummah, then it reaches the level of certainty."

Then he stated that those among the followers of the *Aimmah* (Imams)[66] who opposed this view were very few, and they were influenced by the scholars of *'ilm al-kalaam*. He said that among those who said that *aaḥaad* reports reach the level of certainty were "Abu Isḥaaq and Abu aṭ-Ṭayyib. This has been mentioned by 'Abdul Wahhaab and his colleagues among the Maalikis, and by As-Sarkhasi and his colleagues among the Ḥanafis." He said: "This is the view of most of the *fuqahaa'*, scholars of hadith, the *salaf* and most of the Ash'aris and others."

Ibn aṣ-Ṣalaaḥ said: "What is narrated by Bukhari and Muslim reaches the level of certainty, contrary to the opinion of those who deny that on the basis that it only reaches the level of probability. But they explain that the ummah has widely accepted these *aḥaadeeth* because they have to act upon a hadith even if it reaches the level of probability only. He said: 'but *aḥaadeeth* which only reach the level of probability may be wrong.'"

Ibn aṣ-Ṣalaaḥ said: "I used to favour this view and thought that it was valid, then it became clear to me that what we referred to first was the correct view, because it is thought to be correct by one who is infallible and whose thoughts cannot be wrong, for the ummah (Muslim community) in its consensus is infallible and is protected from error." Ibn aṣ-Ṣalaaḥ meant that the ummah had agreed unanimously that the *aḥaadeeth* of Bukhari and Muslim are authentic.

As-Safaareeni said: "When Ibn Katheer examined the view of Ibn aṣ-Ṣalaaḥ that what is narrated in *Aṣ-Ṣaḥeeḥayn*[67] is definitely correct, he said: 'I agree with what Ibn aṣ-Ṣalaaḥ stated and pointed out.'"

---

[66] The founders of the schools of Islamic jurisprudence - Abu Ḥaneefa, Maalik, Shafi'i, and Aḥmad ibn Ḥanbal (may Allah be merciful to them all).

[67] The two collections of sound *aḥaadeeth* - Bukhari and Muslim.

Then he mentioned that Ibn Katheer saw some written statements of his *shaykh*, Ibn Taymiyah, the conclusion of which was that he stated that the *aḥaadeeth* which were well known and widely accepted by the ummah and transmitted from many scholars were definitely sound. After mentioning some of their names, he (i.e., Ibn Taymiyah) said: "This is the view of all the scholars of hadith and most of the *salaf*."[68]

The correct view is that the *ṣaḥeeḥ aaḥaad aḥaadeeth* reach the level of certainty if they are supported by corroborating evidence, as we have narrated from a group of scholars. The *aḥaadeeth* which were transmitted in the books of Sunnah and classed as *ṣaḥeeḥ* (sound) by the scholars, with no doubts about their soundness and authenticity expressed by any of the scholars, reach the level of certainty by the consensus of the ummah that they are *ṣaḥeeḥ*. This includes those *aḥaadeeth* which were agreed upon by the two authors of the *ṣaḥeeḥs* (i.e., Bukhari and Muslim), or which were narrated in either of the *ṣaḥeeḥayn*, and about which no doubts were expressed by any scholars. The same applies to any other reports which are well known and widely accepted or have been narrated by one of the major celebrated scholars such as Maalik from Naafi' from Ibn 'Umar.

In conclusion: the Sunni scholars accept the *ṣaḥeeḥ aaḥaad aḥaadeeth* concerning both *'aqeedah* and *aḥkaam*, without differentiating between the two. This is indicated by the fact that the *aaimmah* (Imams) of the *Ahl as-Sunnah*, such as Maalik, Aḥmad, Bukhari, Muslim, Abu Dawood, Tirmdhi, Nasaa'i, Ad-Daarimi and others, narrated in their compilations *aḥaadeeth* which speak of *'aqeedah*, and that there are few *mutawaatir* reports among them. If they did not believe that such reports could be used as evidence, they would not have bothered to narrate them, examine them and record

---

[68] *Lawaami' al-Anwaar al-Bahiyah*, Pp. 17.

them. Whoever narrates anything other than that from them is lying about them, and it is not the issue whether the *aaḥaad* reports reached the level of high probability or certainty.

Those who say that these reports do not reach the level of certainty say that they can be accepted with regard to *'aqeedah* if they are proven sound. Even if they only reach the level of probability (in the view of some scholars), this does not mean that they are to be rejected if they talk about *'aqeedah*.

Ibn 'Abdul Barr (may Allah have mercy on him), although he suggested that the *aaḥaad* reports do not reach the level of certainty, still believed that they should be accepted concerning matters of *'aqeedah*, just as they should be accepted concerning rulings (*aḥkaam*). He attributed this view to *Ahl as-Sunnah*.[69]

Texts Which Indicate that *Aaḥaad* Reports are Sound Enough to be Used as Evidence

Many texts indicate that we should accept the *aaḥaad aḥaadeeth* as evidence in proving matters of *'aqeedah*. Examples include the following:

a) The *aayah* (verse):

﴿ ۞ وَمَا كَانَ ٱلْمُؤْمِنُونَ لِيَنفِرُوا۟ كَآفَّةً ۚ فَلَوْلَا نَفَرَ مِن كُلِّ فِرْقَةٍ مِّنْهُمْ طَآئِفَةٌ لِّيَتَفَقَّهُوا۟ فِى ٱلدِّينِ وَلِيُنذِرُوا۟ قَوْمَهُمْ إِذَا رَجَعُوٓا۟ إِلَيْهِمْ لَعَلَّهُمْ يَحْذَرُونَ ﴿١٢٢﴾ ﴾

﴿And it is not [proper] for the believers to go out to fight [Jihad] all together. Of every troop of them, a party only should go forth, that they [who are left behind] may get instructions in [Islamic] religion, and that they may warn

[69] Ibn 'Abdul Barr, *At-Tamheed*, 1/7.

their people when they return to them, so that they may beware [of evil].﴾ *(Qur'an 9: 122)*

This *aayah* (verse) urges the tribes, clans and people of various regions who are believers to send forth a party to get instruction in their religion, then they should go back to their people and warn them. The Arabic word *ṭaa'ifah* (translated here as "a party") may apply to one or more persons. Getting instruction in religion includes both *'aqeedah* (belief) and *aḥkaam* (rulings); indeed, understanding of *'aqeedah* is more important than understanding the *aḥkaam*. Hence Imam Abu Ḥaneefah (may Allah have mercy on him) wrote a small book about *'aqeedah* entitled: *Al-Fiqh al-Akbar* (The Great *Fiqh*). This *aayah* (verse) clearly indicates that we should accept the *aaḥaad* reports as evidence with regard to matters of *'aqeedah*, otherwise it would not be permissible for the *ṭaa'ifah* (a party of one or more persons) to warn the people.

b) The *aayah* (verse):

﴿ يَٰٓأَيُّهَا ٱلَّذِينَ ءَامَنُوٓاْ إِن جَآءَكُمۡ فَاسِقُۢ بِنَبَإٖ فَتَبَيَّنُوٓاْ ... ٦ ﴾

﴾O' you who believe! If a *Faasiq* [liar - evil person] comes to you with any news, verify it...﴾ *(Qur'an 49: 6)*

This proves that if one who is not a *faasiq* (liar) and is reliable and honest brings some information, then evidence has been established and it does not have to be checked; on the contrary, it is to be accepted straight away.

c) The Sunnah explains the *aayah*:

﴿ ... فَلَوۡلَا نَفَرَ مِن كُلِّ فِرۡقَةٖ مِّنۡهُمۡ طَآئِفَةٞ ... ١٢٢ ﴾

﴾...Of every troop of them, a party only should go forth...﴾ *(Qur'an 9: 122).*

Bukhari narrated in his *ṣaḥeeḥ* that Maalik ibn al-Ḥuwayrith said:

> "We came to the Prophet (ﷺ) and we were young men, close in age. We stayed with him for twenty days, and the Messenger of Allah was merciful and kind. When he sensed that we were missing our families, he asked us who we had left behind, and we told him. He said, 'Go back to your families and stay with them, and teach them and instruct them, and pray as you have seen me praying.'"[70]

He commanded each of these young men to teach their respective family members, and teaching includes *'aqeedah*; indeed, *'aqeedah* is the first thing to be included in teaching. If *aaḥaad* reports cannot be used in establishing *'aqeedah*, there would have been no sense in this instruction to these young men.

d) In *Ṣaḥeeḥ al-Bukhari* and *Ṣaḥeeḥ Muslim* it is also reported that the people of Yemen came to the Messenger of Allah (ﷺ) and said:

> "Send with us a man who can teach us the Sunnah and Islam." He (the Prophet) took the hand of Abu 'Ubaydah and said, "This is the trustee of this ummah."[71]

If evidence could not be established by the report of one man, the Messenger (ﷺ) would not have sent Abu 'Ubaydah to them on his own. The same could be said of other occasions when he (ﷺ) sent others of his *ṣaḥaabah* (Companions) to various lands, such as when he sent 'Ali ibn Abi Ṭaalib, Mu'aadh ibn Jabal and Abu Moosa al-Ash'ari (may Allah be pleased with them all). Their *aḥaadeeth* are recorded in *ṣaḥeeḥayn* and elsewhere.

---

[70] Bukhari, 2/110, hadith no. 627; Muslim, 1/465, hadith no. 674. This version is narrated by Bukhari.

[71] Muslim, 4/1888, hadith no. 2419. The hadith in Bukhari states that he sent him to the people of Najraan. Bukhari, 7/93, hadith no. 3745; 13/232, hadith no. 7254.

Undoubtedly what these men taught included *'aqeedah*. If they could not have established proof of *'aqeedah* and left the people with no excuse, the Messenger of Allah (ﷺ) would not have sent them individually.

Imam ash-Shaafa'i (may Allah have mercy on him) said in his book *Ar-Risaalah*: "When he sent someone, then evidence was established for or against the people to whom he was sent by their knowing that what he told them was from the Messenger of Allah (ﷺ)."[72]

Refuting the Argument of those Who say that *Aaḥaad Aḥaadeeth* cannot be Used as Proof with Regard to *'Aqeedah*

The scholars refuted those who do not accept *aaḥaad aḥaadeeth* as proof concerning matters of *'aqeedah* on several points, such as:

a) The view that *aaḥaad aḥaadeeth* cannot be used to prove matters of *'aqeedah* is an innovated and invented opinion which has no basis in shari'ah. Every such opinion is to be rejected.

b) This opinion of theirs (that *aaḥaad aḥaadeeth* cannot be used as evidence) is in itself *'aqeedah* (a belief). According to their own methodology, this belief requires definitive proof that it is forbidden to use the *aaḥaad aḥaadeeth* as evidence concerning *'aqeedah*, and there is no such evidence.

c) If there was any definitive proof that *aaḥaad aḥaadeeth* cannot be used to prove matters of *'aqeedah*, the Companions (*ṣaḥaabah*) would have known this and would have stated it clearly, as would those of the righteous predecessors (*salaf*) who came after them.

d) This view is contrary to the methodology followed by the *ṣaḥaabah*, one of whom would accept what another told him from the Messenger (ﷺ) and would be certain about it. They would not

[72] Ash-Shaafa'i: *Ar-Risaalah*, Pp. 412.

reject what their brother told them on the grounds that the hadith that he was transmitting was an *aaḥaad* hadith.

e) The evidence which indicates that it is obligatory to accept the evidence of the Qur'an and Sunnah refers to both *'aqeedah* and *aḥkaam*. There is nothing to support the idea of this evidence being acceptable only in the case of *aḥkaam* and not *'aqeedah* if the reports are *aaḥaad*.

f) Allah (ﷻ), commanded His Messenger to convey the Message clearly. It is known that a clear message is the one in which proof is established so that what is being conveyed may be made known. If an *aaḥaad* report was not sufficient for the establishment of knowledge, then the message has not been conveyed. Proof can only be established when it reaches the level of certainty.

g) The conclusion of this opinion is that we should not follow the *aaḥaad* reports with regard to *'aqeedah* at all, after the time of the *ṣaḥaabah* (Companions) who heard them directly from the Prophet himself - because until they were compiled in written form, the *aḥaadeeth* were only conveyed as *aaḥaad* reports, and those people whom the *aḥaadeeth* reached as *mutawaatir* reports were few, and even fewer than a few. Even when those who did hear *mutawaatir* reports conveyed them to others, a given *mutawaatir* report would still not reach the level of certainty, because when this one person narrated it, it was an *aaḥaad* report.

h) This view implies that we should not follow the *aaḥaad aḥaadeeth* which speak of *'aqeedah* or actions, because if we reject them in the case of *'aqeedah*, how can we accept them in the case of *aḥkaam*?

i) The *uṣooliyeen* did not agree on this view - as *Shaykh* Shaltoot claims. Imam Maalik, Ash-Shaafa'i, the companions of Abu Ḥaneefah, and Dawood ibn 'Ali and his companions such as Ibn Ḥazm, stated that *aaḥaad* reports reach the level of certainty. This was also stated by Al-Ḥusayn ibn ‘Ali al-Karaabeesi, Al-Ḥaarith ibn Asad al-Muḥaasibi and Al-Qaaḍi Abu Ya‘la among the Ḥanbalis.

Beliefs Which are Proven by the *Aḥaadeeth*

Before concluding this discussion, we will list the beliefs which are proven as per *ṣaheeḥ aḥaadeeth* (hadiths):

a) The Prophethood of Adam (ﷺ) (Peace be upon him) and other Prophets whose Prophethood is not confirmed in the Qur'an.

b) The superiority of our Prophet Muhammad (ﷺ) over all other Prophets and Messengers.

c) His major intercession in the arena of gathering (on the Day of Judgement).

d) His intercession for members of his ummah who commit major sins.

e) One of his (ﷺ) miracles apart from the Qur'an, is the splitting of the moon. Although this is mentioned in the Qur'an, they interpret it in a manner that contradicts the *ṣaheeḥ aḥaadeeth* which clearly state that the moon was split.

f) The *aḥaadeeth* which speak of the beginning of creation; the attributes of the angels and jinn; Paradise and Hell, and the fact that they are both created; and the fact that the Black Stone came from Paradise.

g) Many of the unique attributes of the Prophet (ﷺ), which As-Suyooṭi compiled in his book *Al-Khaṣaa'iṣ al-Kubra*, such as the fact that he entered Paradise and saw its people and what has been prepared for the pious there, and the fact that his *qareen* (jinn companion) became Muslim.

h) Definitive statements that the ten who were given the glad tidings of Paradise (*Al-‘Asharah al-Mubashsharah*) are indeed among the people of Paradise.

i) Belief in the questioning of *Munkar* and *Nakeer* in the grave.

j) Belief in the torment of the grave.

k) Belief in the squeezing or compression of the grave.

l) Belief in the double-panned Balance (in which people's deeds will be weighed) on the Day of Resurrection.

m) Belief in *Aṣ-Ṣiraaṭ* (a bridge that crosses Hell).

n) Belief in the Cistern of the Prophet (ﷺ), and that whoever drinks from it will never experience or suffer from thirst again.

o) That seventy thousand of his (ﷺ) ummah will enter Paradise without being brought to account.

p) Belief in everything that has been narrated in *ṣaḥeeḥ aḥaadeeth* about the resurrection and gathering (for Judgement) that has not been mentioned in the Qur'an.

q) Belief in the Divine Will and Predestination (*Al-Qaḍaa' wa'l-Qadar*), both good and bad, and that Allah (ﷻ), has written (decreed) for each person whether he is blessed (destined for Paradise) or doomed (destined for Hell), what his provision will be and how long he will live.

r) Belief in the Pen which has written all things.

s) Belief that those (Muslims) who commit major sins will not remain in Hell forever.

t) Belief that the souls of the *shuhadaa'* (martyrs for the cause of Allah) are in the forms of green birds in Paradise.

u) Belief that Allah has forbidden the earth to consume the bodies of the Prophets.

v) Belief that Allah has angels who travel about, conveying the *salaams* (greetings of peace) of his ummah to the Prophet (ﷺ).

w) Belief in all the signs of the Hour such as the appearance of the Mahdi, the descent of 'Eesa (Jesus) (عليه السلام), the emergence of the *Dajjaal* (Pseudo-Christ), etc.

Not all the evidence for these beliefs is in *aaḥaad aḥaadeeth*; some of them are proven by *mutawaatir aḥaadeeth*. But these people who do not know the *mutawaatir* Sunnah and do not distinguish between *mutawaatir* and *aaḥaad* reports may reject all or most of these beliefs. Otherwise, the *aḥaadeeth* about the emergence of the *Dajjaal*, the appearance of the Mahdi and the descent of 'Eesa ibn Maryam (عليه السلام) are *mutawaatir aḥaadeeth* as the scholars of hadith have stated clearly.

What is even worse is that they deny the beliefs which are narrated in the *mutawaatir aḥaadeeth*, and even those that are narrated in the Qur'an, on the basis that the meaning of these texts is not definitive as mentioned above. We have already referred to the view of *Shaykh* Shaltoot. Hence they did not believe that people will see their Lord on the Day of Resurrection, even though the Qur'an states this quite clearly:

﴾Some faces that Day shall be *Naaḍirah* [shining and radiant]. Looking at their Lord [Allah].﴿

(Qur'an 75: 22-23)

And the *aḥaadeeth* which mention that also reach the degree of being *mutawaatir*.

Abu'l-Ḥasan al-Ash'ari launched an attack against the *Mu'tazilah* because of their rejection of the texts of the Qur'an and Sunnah, which was in imitation of their leaders. He (may Allah have mercy on him) said: "Those among the *Mu'tazilah* and *Qadariyah* who deviate from the truth have been led by their desires to imitate their leaders and predecessors. They interpret the Qur'an according to their leaders' opinions in a way for which they have no authority from Allah, they did not transmit any report from the Messenger of the Lord of the Worlds, or from the earlier generations. They contradicted the reports of the *ṣaḥaabah* from the Prophet of Allah (ﷺ) concerning the people seeing Allah with their own eyes, although reports on this came from various sources and the reports reach the level of being *mutawaatir*, coming one after another. They denied that the Prophet (ﷺ) will intercede for sinners, and rejected the reports from the earlier generations concerning that. They denied the torment of the grave, and that the *kuffaar* — disbelievers — will be punished in their graves."[73]

Elsewhere, Abu'l-Ḥasan said: "The *Mu'tazilah* denied the Cistern, and the *Mu'tazilah* denied the torment of the grave."[74]

Abu'l-Ḥasan said in *Maqaalaat al-Islamiyeen*: "They differed concerning the torment of the grave. Some denied it and some affirmed it. These were the *Mu'tazilah* and *Khawaarij*."[75]

He also said in his *Maqaalaat* (articles):

"They differed concerning the intercession of the Messenger of Allah (ﷺ) and whether he would intercede for those who had committed major sins. The *Mu'tazilah* denied that and said that it would not happen."[76]

---

73 *Al-Ibaanah 'an Uṣool ad-Diyaanah*, Pp. 6.

74 Ibid., Pp. 75.

75 *Maqaalaat al-Islamiyeen*, Pp. 340.

76 Ibid, Pp. 340.

He also mentioned in several places in his *Maqaalaat* (articles) that the *Mu'tazilah* denied that Allah has an Eye and a Hand, and they denied that people will see Him with their own eyes and that He will come on the Day of Resurrection and that He comes down to the lowest heaven. They believed that the *fussaaq* (evildoers among the Muslims) will remain in Hell forever, and they held other beliefs which contradict the *ṣaḥeeḥ mutawaatir aḥaadeeth* and even the texts of the Qur'an.[77]

Whoever denies these beliefs which were reported in *ṣaḥeeḥ aḥaadeeth* is following the path of the *Mu'tazilah*, not the path of the Sunnis (*Ahl as-Sunnah*).

I have seen people of earlier and later generations stating that all the Signs of the Hour are narrated in *aaḥaad aḥaadeeth*, so they reject them on that basis, and those that they think are *mutawaatir* they misinterpret.

Ruling on Those who Deny that Which has been Proven in *Aaḥaad* Reports

Safaareeni narrated from Isḥaaq ibn Raahawayh the view that those who reject the *aaḥaad* reports are *kaafir* (disbelievers). The correct view is that they are not *kaafir*. It seems that those who said that they are *kaafir* were thinking of the *aḥaadeeth* which are unanimously accepted by the ummah as being *ṣaḥeeḥ* (sound).

Although we do not say that they are *kaafir*, we do say that those who reject the *ṣaḥeeḥ aḥaadeeth* of the Messenger (ﷺ) and do not use them to prove matters of *'aqeedah* (belief) are clearly mistaken, and there is the fear that they may become misguided because of their rejection of these *aḥaadeeth*, and Allah may punish them by sending them astray:

---

[77] *Maqaalaat al-Islamiyeen*, Pp. 157, 216, 195, 474.

﴿ ... فَلْيَحْذَرِ ٱلَّذِينَ يُخَالِفُونَ عَنْ أَمْرِهِۦٓ أَن تُصِيبَهُمْ فِتْنَةٌ أَوْ يُصِيبَهُمْ عَذَابٌ أَلِيمٌ ﴿٦٣﴾ ﴾

﴾...And let those who oppose the Messenger's [Muhammad's] commandment [i.e. his Sunnah legal ways, orders, acts of worship, statements] [among the sects] beware, lest some *Fitnah* [disbelief, trials, afflictions, earthquakes, killing, overpowered by a tyrant] should befall them or a painful torment be inflicted on them.﴿ *(Qur'an 24: 63)*

The Correct Methodology

In this study we are adhering to what is stated in the Qur'an and Sunnah. Hence we must examine *'aqeedah* according to the methodology used in the Qur'an and Sunnah, and not go beyond this methodology. This is the way which revived the hearts of the earliest generations of this ummah.

This is the only way in which the ummah in its modern stage can reform itself. Imam Maalik — the Imam and scholar of Madeenah — spoke the truth when he said: "The last (generations) of this ummah will not be reformed by anything other than that which reformed its first (generations)."

We have already seen how the Qur'anic methodology is distinct from philosophy in the way it discusses and confirms different issues of religion and belief. This distinction means that we must use the Qur'anic methodology and none other.

A matter which must be clarified: How can we use the Qur'an to address those who do not believe in it?

Some of those who have some commitment to Islam say: How can we present the Qur'an to those who do not believe in Allah? We have to address people nowadays with the logic of modern material, science and rational evidence, then if they are convinced of Islam, we will address them with the Qur'an.

We say to these people: We ask you by Allah, how did Allah command His Messenger to warn with the Qur'an the *kuffaar* who disbelieved in Allah, the Qur'an and the Messenger?

﴿... وَأُوحِيَ إِلَيَّ هَٰذَا ٱلْقُرْءَانُ لِأُنذِرَكُم بِهِۦ وَمَنۢ بَلَغَ ... ﴿١٩﴾﴾

> ﴿...This Qur'an has been revealed to me that I may therewith warn you and whomsoever it may reach...﴾
>
> *(Qur'an 6: 19)*

How did He command him to recite this Qur'an to them? Did he not recite it to these stubborn disbelievers, and it moved them and stirred their hearts?

What effect did the verses of the Qur'an have on Umayyah ibn Khalaf and Al-Waleed ibn 'Utbah, and others, despite their extreme *kufr* (disbelief) and stubborn enmity?

It could be said that nowadays the Qur'an is recited in all places and is even broadcast from London and Washington, yet the followers of Islam who recite the Qur'an do not believe in what it says.

The response to these people is that the Arabs of the past would listen to what was recited to them and it would penetrate to the depths of their being, because they were Arabs who understood the meanings of the *aayaat* (verses), and there was no barrier between them and the words.

But nowadays there are barriers between the people and the Qur'an, some of which have to do with language, and others have to do with the doubts that fill people's minds and have virtually become unquestionable facts.

So the bearers of the Qur'an nowadays have to explain the Qur'an in a language that the people can understand. They have to put the people in touch with the Qur'an, and the Qur'an in touch with the people, by explaining its meanings to them, and renewing the meanings of this Book in their hearts, so that once again they will appreciate it and feel it... and its meanings will reach those who disbelieve it and deny it in this way. Thus the call will be given and it will leave no person with any excuse.

We have already explained that the Qur'an contains evidence which addresses the mind and the heart; it is not merely telling stories or giving information.

A Dubious Call: Bringing Religions Together

This is the right way: explaining the methodology which Allah has showed us in order to establish faith in people's hearts and to adhere to it ourselves when calling, leading and teaching people.

The enemies of Allah and those among this ummah who have been deceived are trying to distort this methodology, by calling for all religions to come together. They have held conferences and seminars for this purpose.

Those Muslims who attended these conferences have made a big mistake, because they agreed to make Islam subject to examination at the same level as Judaism and Christianity.

We say that these people had an excuse if they went there in order to say to others what the Qur'an says:

﴿ قُلْ يَـٰٓأَهْلَ ٱلْكِتَـٰبِ تَعَالَوْا۟ إِلَىٰ كَلِمَةٍ سَوَآءٍۭ بَيْنَنَا وَبَيْنَكُمْ أَلَّا نَعْبُدَ إِلَّا ٱللَّهَ وَلَا نُشْرِكَ بِهِۦ شَيْـًٔا وَلَا يَتَّخِذَ بَعْضُنَا بَعْضًا أَرْبَابًا مِّن دُونِ ٱللَّهِ ۚ فَإِن تَوَلَّوْا۟ فَقُولُوا۟ ٱشْهَدُوا۟ بِأَنَّا مُسْلِمُونَ ﴿٦٤﴾ ﴾

﴿Say [O' Muhammad]: 'O' people of the Scripture [Jews

> and Christians]: Come to a word that is just between us and you, that we worship none but Allah [Alone], and that we associate no partners with Him, and that none of us shall take others as lords besides Allah.' Then, if they turn away, say: 'Bear witness that we are Muslims.'﴿
> *(Qur'an 3: 64)*

They should explain the falsehood of these (other religions) in a way that is better, and show them the true religion, and establish proof against them, rather than pursuing friendship and turning a blind eye to their falsehood for the sake of being friendly.

Those who mix Islam with other religions, ways of thinking and philosophies make a mistake when they claim that they are trying to reconcile the texts of the Qur'an to the beliefs of those other people in order to meet others halfway. Their claim is a lie and they have gone astray in their methodology. Islam is the religion of Allah which controls life and living beings. It does not need to be reconciled with anything else. Other beliefs contain truth and falsehood, but Islam is entirely true, and our mission is to keep the Book of our Lord and His religion distinct.

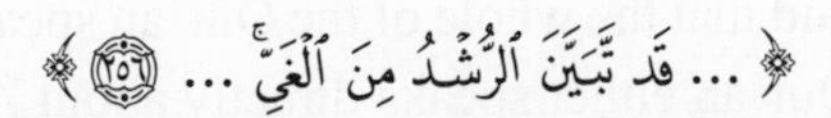

> ﴾...Verily, the Right Path has become distinct from the wrong path...﴿
> *(Qur'an 2: 256)*

— so that people may resort to it and find it pure and not mixed with anything else.

Allah (ﷻ), has condemned this type of people who want to mix Islam with other religions and meet others halfway on the basis of reconciliation. He tells us that this is the action of the *munaafiqeen* (hypocrites):

﴿ وَإِذَا قِيلَ لَهُمْ تَعَالَوْاْ إِلَىٰ مَآ أَنزَلَ ٱللَّهُ وَإِلَى ٱلرَّسُولِ رَأَيْتَ ٱلْمُنَٰفِقِينَ يَصُدُّونَ عَنكَ صُدُودًا ﴿٦١﴾ فَكَيْفَ إِذَآ أَصَٰبَتْهُم مُّصِيبَةٌۢ بِمَا قَدَّمَتْ أَيْدِيهِمْ ثُمَّ جَآءُوكَ يَحْلِفُونَ بِٱللَّهِ إِنْ أَرَدْنَآ إِلَّآ إِحْسَٰنًا وَتَوْفِيقًا ﴿٦٢﴾ ﴾

﴿And when it is said to them: 'Come to what Allah has sent down and to the Messenger [Muhammad],' you [Muhammad] see the hypocrites turn away from you [Muhammad] with aversion. How then, when a catastrophe befalls them because of what their hands have sent forth, they come to you swearing by Allah, 'We meant no more than goodwill and conciliation!'﴾

(Qur'an 4: 61-62)

BELIEF IN ALLAH

Introduction: The Importance of this Principle

The first principle of *'aqeedah* is belief in Allah. This is the most important principle of belief and action, and it is the focal point of Islam and the essence of the Qur'an. We would not be exaggerating if we said that the whole of the Qur'an speaks about this belief, because the Qur'an either speaks directly about Allah (ﷻ), and His Essence, Names, Attributes and actions, as in *Aayaat al-Kursi* and *Soorah al-Ikhlaaṣ*.

Or it calls mankind to worship Him Alone, with no partner or associate, and to give up the worship of false gods - all of which has to do with telling about Allah, calling for the fulfilment of our duties toward Him and forbidding the direction of worship to anyone else.

Or it commands us to obey Him and forbids us to disobey Him, which are the obligations of faith.

Or it tells us about the people of faith and the honour that was bestowed upon them in this world, and how they are rewarded in the Hereafter. This is the reward of the people who believe in Allah.

Or it tells us about the *kaafireen* — disbelievers — and how Allah humiliates them in this world, and what He will do to them in the Hereafter, in the abode of punishment. This is the punishment for turning away from belief.

So the entire Qur'an speaks about belief in Allah. This explains why we find that Allah is mentioned in the Qur'an, by one or another of His Names and Attributes, 10,062 times; on every page of the Qur'an, He is mentioned approximately twenty times on average.

We can say that belief in Allah, in relation to all the other principles and minor matters of faith is like the root of a tree in relation to its trunk and branches. It is the basis of all other principles, the foundation of the religion. The more a person has faith in Allah, the more he is progressing in Islam.

Issues of Belief in Allah

The issues of this topic which the researcher must examine and discuss are as follows:

Firstly: He must examine the evidence that Allah (ﷻ) exists, and refute the specious arguments that have been raised in this respect.

Secondly: He must know about Allah (ﷻ), which is achieved in two ways in the Qur'an:

1) Understanding the wonders in creation which point to the greatness of Allah's power and the perfection of His creation.

2) Studying the *aayaat* (verses) of the Qur'an which speak directly of Allah, His essence, His Names, His attributes and His actions.

Thirdly: He must affirm that Allah alone is the only One to be worshipped, with no partner or associate, and reject anything else that is worshipped instead of Him.

Fourthly: He should look at the history of belief in Divinity and examine what has been said on this topic.

CHAPTER ONE
EVIDENCE OF THE EXISTENCE OF THE CREATOR

1 - THE FIRST PROOF: THE EVIDENCE OF THE *FIṬRAH* (HUMAN INSTINCT)

Sound Human Instinct Bears Witness to the Existence of Allah Without (Any Need for Further) Evidence

The Qur'an does not discuss at length the matter of proving the existence of Allah (ﷻ), because it states that sound human instinct, and minds that are not contaminated with the filth of *shirk*, affirm His existence (without any need for further evidence). Not only that, *Tawḥeed* or the affirmation of Divine Unity, is something which is natural and instinctive.

In the Qur'an it says:

﴿ فَأَقِمْ وَجْهَكَ لِلدِّينِ حَنِيفًا ۚ فِطْرَتَ ٱللَّهِ ٱلَّتِى فَطَرَ ٱلنَّاسَ عَلَيْهَا ۚ لَا تَبْدِيلَ لِخَلْقِ ٱللَّهِ ۚ ذَٰلِكَ ٱلدِّينُ ٱلْقَيِّمُ ... ﴿٣٠﴾ ﴾

﴿So set you [O' Muhammad] your face towards the religion [of pure Islamic Monotheism] Ḥaneef [worship none but Allah Alone]. Allah's *Fiṭrah* [i.e. Allah's Islamic Monotheism] with which He has created mankind. No change let there be in *Khalq-illaah* [i.e. the religion of Allah, Islamic Monotheism], that is the straight religion...﴾ *(Qur'an 30: 30)*

This *fiṭrah* is the thing which explains the phenomenon that has been noted by those who research the history of religions, that all nations whose history has been studied have adopted gods which they have turned to and venerated.[1]

It may be said at this point, "If turning towards Allah is something natural, then people would not have worshipped different gods at different times."

The answer is, that the *fiṭrah* (natural instinct) calls man to turn towards his Creator, but man is surrounded by many other influences which make him deviate towards the worship of other gods.

Parents, writers, teachers and others instil into children's minds ideas which change and contaminate this *fiṭrah*, placing a veil over the *fiṭrah* so that they are not able to turn towards the truth.

The Messenger (ﷺ) stated that what we have referred to here is true. Bukhari and Muslim narrated on the authority of Abu Hurayrah (رضي الله عنه) that the Messenger of Allah (ﷺ) said:

> "Every child is born in a state of *fiṭrah*, then his parents make him into a Jew or a Christian or a Magian.'"[2]

— He did not say that they make him Muslim, because Islam is in accordance with the *fiṭrah*.

It may be said: "If we were to leave a child with no influences to affect his *fiṭrah*, would he turn out to be a monotheist, knowing his Lord?" We say: "If the devils among men leave him alone, and do

---

[1] Even the communists nowadays who wanted to free themselves from the worship of gods - as they claimed - worship the founder of their Party, so you see them passing by his preserved body in Red Square on the anniversary of his death, bowing their heads in humility. They have made him a god; instead of worshipping the Creator of man they worship a dead man, may they perish!

(Comment added by the author in the new, revised edition): This is what I wrote fifteen years ago. A few years ago the guards of communism destroyed their own Party and cast aside their leaders and they threw out the body of their founder just as they threw out their beliefs and ideas.

[2] Bukhari, 3/245, hadith no. 1385; Muslim, 4/2047, hadith no. 2658.

not contaminate his *fiṭrah*", but the devils among the jinn (*shayaaṭeen*) will never leave him alone, as the *Shayṭaan* made a vow that he would misguide the children of Adam:

﴿ قَالَ فَبِعِزَّتِكَ لَأُغْوِيَنَّهُمْ أَجْمَعِينَ ﴿٨٢﴾ إِلَّا عِبَادَكَ مِنْهُمُ الْمُخْلَصِينَ ﴿٨٣﴾ ﴾

﴿[*Iblees* (Satan)] said: 'By Your Might, then I will surely, mislead them all, Except Your chosen slaves amongst them [i.e. faithful, obedient, true believers of Islamic Monotheism].'﴾ *(Qur'an 38: 82-83)*

The *Shayṭaan* has been given the power to reach people's hearts, as stated in the *ṣaḥeeḥ* hadith:

"The *Shayṭaan* flows in man like blood flows through his veins, and I fear that he may cast some evil - or he said, something - into both your hearts."[3]

The Qur'an describes the *Shayṭaan*, from whom we must seek refuge with Allah (ﷻ), as one who,

﴿ ... يُوَسْوِسُ فِي صُدُورِ النَّاسِ ﴿٥﴾ ﴾

﴿...Whispers into the hearts of mankind.﴾ *(Qur'an 114: 5)*

It is also true that every person has a hidden mate (*qareen*) from among the jinn who urges and encourages him to do evil. In the Qur'an it says:

﴿ ۞ قَالَ قَرِينُهُ رَبَّنَا مَا أَطْغَيْتُهُ وَلَٰكِن كَانَ فِي ضَلَٰلٍ بَعِيدٍ ﴿٢٧﴾ ﴾

﴿His companion [Satan-devil] will say: 'Our Lord! I did not push him to transgression, [in disbelief, oppression, and evil deeds], but he was himself in error far astray.'﴾ *(Qur'an 50: 27)*

---

[3] Muslim, 4/1712, hadith no. 2175.

No one can be safe from this unless he turns to Allah (ﷻ) for refuge.

﴿قُلْ أَعُوذُ بِرَبِّ ٱلنَّاسِ ﴿١﴾ مَلِكِ ٱلنَّاسِ ﴿٢﴾ إِلَٰهِ ٱلنَّاسِ ﴿٣﴾ مِن شَرِّ ٱلْوَسْوَاسِ ٱلْخَنَّاسِ ﴿٤﴾ ٱلَّذِى يُوَسْوِسُ فِى صُدُورِ ٱلنَّاسِ ﴿٥﴾ مِنَ ٱلْجِنَّةِ وَٱلنَّاسِ ﴿٦﴾﴾

> ﴿Say: 'I seek refuge with [Allah] the Lord of mankind, The King of mankind, The *Ilaah* [God] of mankind, From the evil of the whisperer [devil who whispers evil in the hearts of men] who withdraws [from his whispering in one's heart after one remembers Allah]. Who whispers into the hearts of mankind. Of jinn and men.'﴾ *(Qur'an 114: 1-6)*

The *shayaaṭeen* among the jinn play a major role in corrupting and contaminating human nature. It is reported in Muslim from 'Iyaaḍ ibn Ḥimaar that the Messenger of Allah (ﷺ) addressed one day, and one of the things he said in his *khuṭbah* (address) was:

> "My Lord has commanded me to teach you what you do not know of what He has taught me today: all the wealth that I have given to My slaves is *ḥalaal*, and I created all of My slaves as *ḥaneefs* [worshipping Allah Alone], then the *shayaaṭeen* came to them and led them astray from their religion. They forbade them things that I had permitted for them, and commanded them to associate others in worship with Me for which I had not sent down any authority."[4]

Calamities Purify the Essence of the *Fiṭrah*

It is often the case that the veils covering the *fiṭrah* and preventing it from seeing the truth will be removed when calamity strikes or

---

[4] Muslim, 4/2197, hadith no. 2865.

problems arise for which no help is forthcoming from any human being and there is no means of saving oneself. How many atheists have acknowledged their Lord and turned to Him when overwhelmed with calamity, and how many *mushrikeen* (idolaters and polytheists) have made their devotion solely for Allah alone when disaster strikes?

﴿ ... حَتَّىٰٓ إِذَا كُنتُمۡ فِي ٱلۡفُلۡكِ وَجَرَيۡنَ بِهِم بِرِيحٖ طَيِّبَةٖ وَفَرِحُواْ بِهَا جَآءَتۡهَا رِيحٌ عَاصِفٞ وَجَآءَهُمُ ٱلۡمَوۡجُ مِن كُلِّ مَكَانٖ وَظَنُّوٓاْ أَنَّهُمۡ أُحِيطَ بِهِمۡ دَعَوُاْ ٱللَّهَ مُخۡلِصِينَ لَهُ ٱلدِّينَ لَئِنۡ أَنجَيۡتَنَا مِنۡ هَٰذِهِۦ لَنَكُونَنَّ مِنَ ٱلشَّٰكِرِينَ ٢٢ ﴾

﴿...Till when you are in the ships, and they sail with them with a favourable wind, and they are glad therein, then comes a stormy wind and the waves come to them from all sides, and they think that they are encircled therein. Then they invoke Allah, making their Faith pure for Him Alone, [saying]: 'If You [Allah] deliver us from this, we shall truly, be of the grateful.'﴾ *(Qur'an 10: 22)*

We have heard how airplane passengers turned to their Lord when their plane developed problems and started to shake and swing about in the air, and the pilot - let alone the passengers - was not able to do anything about it. Their atheism vanished and they were screaming prayers, and their hearts turned to their Lord in all sincerity. There was no room for *shirk* (polytheism) and atheism in the face of such a terrifying ordeal.

The *Mushrikeen* (Polythiests — the Idolaters) to Whom the Messenger (ﷺ) was Sent Acknowledged the Existence of the Creator

The Arabs whom the Messenger (ﷺ) confronted acknowledged the existence of Allah and that He Alone is the Creator of the universe.

They also believed that He Alone was the Provider and that He alone could bring benefit or cause harm... but they worshiped others alongside Him, and they did not devote their worship to Him alone.

When the Qur'an calls the *mushrikeen* to worship Allah Alone and to make their religion for Him Alone, it asks them Who the Creator and Sovereign of the heavens and the earth is, for they knew that, and they never denied it:

﴿ وَلَئِن سَأَلْتَهُم مَّنْ خَلَقَ ٱلسَّمَٰوَٰتِ وَٱلْأَرْضَ لَيَقُولُنَّ ٱللَّهُ... ﴿٢٥﴾ ﴾

> ﴾And if you [O' Muhammad] ask them: 'Who has created the heavens and the earth,' they will certainly say: 'Allah'...﴿ *(Qur'an 31: 25)*

In *Soorah al-Mu'minoon* (the chapter: The Believers) it says:

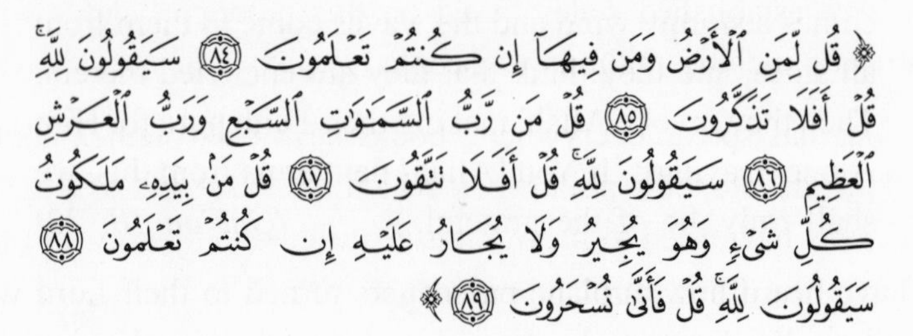
﴿ قُل لِّمَنِ ٱلْأَرْضُ وَمَن فِيهَآ إِن كُنتُمْ تَعْلَمُونَ ﴿٨٤﴾ سَيَقُولُونَ لِلَّهِ ۚ قُلْ أَفَلَا تَذَكَّرُونَ ﴿٨٥﴾ قُلْ مَن رَّبُّ ٱلسَّمَٰوَٰتِ ٱلسَّبْعِ وَرَبُّ ٱلْعَرْشِ ٱلْعَظِيمِ ﴿٨٦﴾ سَيَقُولُونَ لِلَّهِ ۚ قُلْ أَفَلَا تَتَّقُونَ ﴿٨٧﴾ قُلْ مَنۢ بِيَدِهِۦ مَلَكُوتُ كُلِّ شَىْءٍ وَهُوَ يُجِيرُ وَلَا يُجَارُ عَلَيْهِ إِن كُنتُمْ تَعْلَمُونَ ﴿٨٨﴾ سَيَقُولُونَ لِلَّهِ ۚ قُلْ فَأَنَّىٰ تُسْحَرُونَ ﴿٨٩﴾ ﴾

> ﴾Say: 'Whose is the earth and whosoever is therein? If you know!' They will say: 'It is Allah's!' Say: 'Will you not then remember?' Say: 'Who is [the] Lord of the seven heavens, and [the] Lord of the Great Throne?' They will say: 'Allah.' Say: 'Will you not then fear Allah [believe in His Oneness, obey Him, believe in the Resurrection and Recompense for every good or bad deed]?' Say: 'In Whose Hand is the sovereignty of everything [i.e. treasures of everything]? And He protects [all], while against Whom there is no protector [i.e. if Allah saves anyone, none can punish or harm him; and if Allah punishes or harms anyone, none can save

> him], if you know?' They will say: '[All that belongs] to Allah.' Say: 'How then are you deceived and turn away from the truth?'﴾ *(Qur'an 23: 84-89)*

It is well known that the Arabs used to venerate the Ka'bah and perform Ḥajj, and they had other acts of worship that they did.

The *Kufr* (Disbelief) of People Nowadays is Greater

We should not have had to pause too long to prove the existence of Allah, because sound human nature bears witness to His existence. We hardly know of anyone in the past who denied the existence of the Creator; those that did were so few as to be hardly worth mentioning.

But deviation has reached its lowest point nowadays. We see people who have established states based on this principle, states whose inhabitants include millions of people.

This idea has spread everywhere, books have been written about it and it has developed a philosophy which is the subject of study. Its proponents have tried to make it a scientific methodology and have tried to bring forth proof to support it.

Because of this, we have no choice but to produce our own proof concerning this matter.

2 - THE SECOND PROOF: THIS UNIVERSE MUST HAVE A CREATOR

The Qur'an offers the disbelievers and deniers proof which rational minds have no option but to affirm and which no sound mind can possibly reject. Allah (ﷻ), says:

﴿ أَمْ خُلِقُوا۟ مِنْ غَيْرِ شَىْءٍ أَمْ هُمُ ٱلْخَٰلِقُونَ ﴿٣٥﴾ أَمْ خَلَقُوا۟ ٱلسَّمَٰوَٰتِ وَٱلْأَرْضَ بَل لَّا يُوقِنُونَ ﴿٣٦﴾ ﴾

﴾Were they created by nothing? Or were they themselves the creators? Or did they create the heavens and the earth? Nay, but they have no firm Belief.﴿

(Qur'an 52: 35-36)

The Qur'an says to them: "You exist, and you cannot deny this"; the heavens and the earth exist, beyond any doubt. It is simply common sense, to the rational mind, that the things which exist must have a cause for their existence. The camel herder in the desert knows this. He says, "Camel dung indicates the presence of a camel and footsteps indicate that someone walked here. So the heavens with their stars and the earth with its mountains and valleys must indicate the existence of the All-Knowing, All-Aware." The great scientists who research into life and living beings also know this.

What is referred to in this *aayah* (verse) is known to the scientists as the law of cause and effect. This law states that a (possible) thing cannot happen by itself without another thing (causing it), because it does not possess in itself the power to exist by itself, and it cannot by itself cause something else to exist, for it cannot give to others that which it does not itself possess.

Let Us Give an Example to Explain This Law More Clearly

A few years ago, the sands in the Rub' al-Khaali desert (the Empty Quarter) were blown away by a windstorm to reveal the ruins of a city that had been covered by the sands. Scientists began to examine the contents of the city to try to determine the period in which it had been built. Nobody among the archaeologists or others even suggested that this city could have appeared as a result of the natural actions of the wind, rain, heat and cold, and not by the actions of man.

If anyone had suggested such a thing, people would have regarded him crazy and would have taken pity on him. So how about if someone had said that this city was formed by the air from nothing in the far distant past, then it settled on the earth? This suggestion is no less strange than the previous, in fact it is far stranger.

Why? Because nothing cannot create something, which is simply the matter of common sense, and a thing cannot create itself.

According to the way we know the city, there has to be someone who brought it into existence. What we see tells us something about the people who made it. The city must have been made by intelligent people who were skilled in construction and planning.

If we see a person going from the bottom of a building to the top, we see nothing strange in that, because a person has the ability to do that. But if we see that a rock which was in the courtyard of the building has moved to the top of the building, we will be certain that it did not move by itself. There has to have been someone who picked it up and moved it, because a rock does not have the ability to move or climb.

It is strange that people are certain that the city could not have come into existence without a creator, and that it could not have built itself, and they are certain that the rock must have had someone who would take it up to the top of the building, but there are those among them who insist that this universe came into being without a creator, even though the structure of the universe is far more complex.

﴿ لَخَلْقُ ٱلسَّمَٰوَٰتِ وَٱلْأَرْضِ أَكْبَرُ مِنْ خَلْقِ ٱلنَّاسِ... ﴿٥٧﴾ ﴾

﴾The creation of the heavens and the earth is indeed greater than the creation of mankind;...﴿ *(Qur'an 40: 57)*

But when these deniers are confronted with scientific logic that addresses their reason, they have to either accept it or stubbornly reject it.

This is the evidence with which the scholars of Islam are still confronting the deniers. One of the scholars was approached by some of these heretics who deny the Creator. He asked them: what would you say about a man who tells you, I have seen a ship laden with cargo, filled with goods, in the middle of the ocean, being buffeted by waves and winds, yet, despite all that, it is sailing smoothly and following a straight course, with no sailors controlling or steering it. Is this reasonable to believe?

They said, "This is irrational."

The scholar said: "*Subhaan Allah*! If it is not rationally possible for a ship to sail smoothly across the sea without any sailors or crew, then how is it possible for this world, with all its different forces and factors, with its vastness and huge variety, to exist without a Creator or Keeper?" They all wept and said, you have spoken the truth, and they repented.

This law, which is rationally acceptable, is what is referred to in the *aayah*:

﴿ أَمْ خُلِقُوا۟ مِنْ غَيْرِ شَىْءٍ أَمْ هُمُ ٱلْخَـٰلِقُونَ ﴿٣٥﴾ ﴾

﴿Were they created by nothing? Or were they themselves the creators?﴾ *(Qur'an 52: 35)*

This is evidence which forces rational minds to accept that there is a Creator Who is to be worshipped. The *aayah* is worded in such an eloquent and moving way that anyone who hears it will be moved deeply.

Bukhari narrated in his *Saheeh* that Jubayr ibn Mut'im said: "I heard the Messenger of Allah (ﷺ) reciting *Soorah at-Toor* in *Maghrib* (prayer). When he reached this passage —

﴿ أَمْ خُلِقُوا۟ مِنْ غَيْرِ شَىْءٍ أَمْ هُمُ ٱلْخَـٰلِقُونَ ﴿٣٥﴾ أَمْ خَلَقُوا۟ ٱلسَّمَـٰوَٰتِ وَٱلْأَرْضَ ۚ بَل لَّا يُوقِنُونَ ﴿٣٦﴾ أَمْ عِندَهُمْ خَزَآئِنُ رَبِّكَ أَمْ هُمُ ٱلْمُصَيْطِرُونَ ﴿٣٧﴾ ﴾

> ﴾'Were they created by nothing? Or were they themselves the creators? Or did they create the heavens and the earth? Nay, but they have no firm Belief. Or are with them the treasures of your Lord? Or are they the tyrants with the authority to do as they like?'﴿ *(Qur'an 52: 35-37)*

— my heart almost began to soar."[5]

Al-Bayhaqi said that the Abu Sulaymaan al-Khaṭṭaabi said: "The reason why he was so moved when he heard these *aayaat* was because he understood the *aayaat* so well and because what he learned from the strong evidence contained therein touched his sensitive nature, and with his intelligence he understood it..."

With regard to the meaning of the *aayah* (verse),

﴾Were they created by nothing?...﴿ *(Qur'an 52: 35),* Al-Khaṭṭaabi said: "Or were they brought into being without a creator? That could not happen, because the creation must inevitably be connected to the Creator. There has to have been a Creator. If they deny the Divine Creator, but they could not have come into being without a creator creating them, then did they create themselves? That is an even more fallacious argument, because if something does not exist, how can it be described as having power, and how could it create anything? How could it do anything? If these two arguments are refuted, then it is established that they have a Creator, so let them believe in Him.

Then Allah (ﷻ), says: ﴾Or did they create the heavens and the earth? Nay, but they have no firm Belief﴿ *(Qur'an 52: 36)*. This is something which they cannot lay any claim to. Thus they are defeated (in argument) and proof is established against them."

---

[5] Bukhari, 8/603, hadith no. 4854.

The point of what Al-Khaṭṭaabi said about that to which the *kuffaar* could not lay any claim is to put an end to this argument and dispute, because there could be some arrogant person who says "I created myself," just as one of his ilk who came before him claimed to have the power over life and death:

﴿ أَلَمْ تَرَ إِلَى ٱلَّذِى حَآجَّ إِبْرَٰهِـۧمَ فِى رَبِّهِۦٓ أَنْ ءَاتَىٰهُ ٱللَّهُ ٱلْمُلْكَ إِذْ قَالَ إِبْرَٰهِـۧمُ رَبِّىَ ٱلَّذِى يُحْىِۦ وَيُمِيتُ ... ﴿٢٥٨﴾ ﴾

> ﴿Have you not looked at him who disputed with Ibraheem [Abraham] about his Lord [Allah], because Allah had given him the kingdom? When Ibraheem said [to him]: 'My Lord [Allah] is He Who gives life and causes death.' He said, 'I give life and cause death.'...﴾
> *(Qur'an 2: 258)*

What was Ibraheem's response? He replied with another question which exposed the tyrant's incapability and proved him to be a liar:

﴿ ... قَالَ إِبْرَٰهِـۧمُ فَإِنَّ ٱللَّهَ يَأْتِى بِٱلشَّمْسِ مِنَ ٱلْمَشْرِقِ فَأْتِ بِهَا مِنَ ٱلْمَغْرِبِ ... ﴿٢٥٨﴾ ﴾

> ﴿...Ibraheem [Abraham] said, 'Verily, Allah brings the sun from the east; then bring it you from the west.'...﴾
> *(Qur'an 2: 258)*

The result of that was:

﴿ ... فَبُهِتَ ٱلَّذِى كَفَرَ ۗ وَٱللَّهُ لَا يَهْدِى ٱلْقَوْمَ ٱلظَّـٰلِمِينَ ﴿٢٥٨﴾ ﴾

> ﴿...So the disbeliever was utterly defeated. And Allah guides not the people, who are *Zaalimoon* [wrongdoers].﴾ *(Qur'an 2: 258)*

Let us suppose that someone said, "I created myself." Can he claim that he created the heavens and the earth? If nothing did not create the heavens and the earth, and if the heavens and the earth did not create themselves, and if these people cannot claim that they created all of that, then there must inevitably be a Creator Who created all of that, and this Creator is Allah, Glorified be He and Exalted.

The attitude of the empirical sciences towards this law

Human power and the nature of created beings is incapable of listing all the stages of cause and effect and tracing its sequence back, step by step, until it reaches the beginning of the universe. Hence the empirical sciences have no hope of finding out the origin of things. These sciences expressed refraining from such attempt. All that they have been able to do is to trace a few steps behind them, leaving everything beyond that to the realm of the unseen, concerning which scholars and ignorant people are on equal footing.

Reason has no choice but to admit

But this human despair of ever discovering the stages of creation in detail, with regard to both the past and the future, is counterbalanced by the general belief which every mind must acknowledge, voluntarily or otherwise, that no matter how long the list of cause and effect is, and whether it is considered to be finite or infinite, there should still be something else which carries in itself the cause of its existence and continued existence. This is the true beginning, before which there was nothing, otherwise all these created things would not have come into being (if they did not have an originator which exists independently).

Specious Arguments About the Origin of the Universe

We hear and read specious arguments which were put forward in the past, and those which are being proposed nowadays, which attempt to explain the existence of the universe. We shall quote some of these arguments and endeavour to explain where they went wrong.

1) The View that it Happened by Accident

Having examined the Qur'anic evidence which is addressed to the rational mind and which obliges it to acknowledge the existence of the Creator Who is to be worshipped, the notion that this universe came into being by accident without any creator is not only far from the truth, but also irrational. Whoever says this could be counted as one of those prattlers who have lost their minds, because they are stubbornly rejecting evidence which the rational mind has no choice but to accept and submit to.

There are yet others who said, "If six monkeys sat at typewriters and banged on the keys for billions of years, it is not unlikely that in the last pages they wrote we would find one of the sonnets of Shakespeare. This is the case with the universe that exists now. It came about as the result of random forces which played with matter for billions of years."

Waḥeed Uddeen Khan[6] said, after quoting this paragraph from Huxley:[7] "Any talk of this nature is utter nonsense. None of our branches of sciences — until the present day — know what type of accident could produce such a great reality with all its wonder and beauty."

He quotes another scientist who denounced this view by saying: "The idea that life happened as the result of an accident is like saying that you could get a dictionary as the result of an accidental explosion in a printing press."

---

[6] *Al-Islam Yataḥadda*, Pp. 66.

[7] Huxley is the atheist writer who wrote the famous book *Man Stands Alone*. Allah brought forth a scientist from his own nation, A. Christie Morrisson, the head of the New York Academy of Science and a former member of the Executive Committee of the US National Research Council, wrote the valuable book *Man Does Not Stand Alone* to refute Huxley. This book has been translated into Arabic under the title *Al-'Ilm yad'u ila'l-Eemaan* (Sciences call to Faith).

Waḥeeduddin Khan states, “Mathematics, which has given us the concept of probability, itself states that it is mathematically impossible for this universe to have come into existence by accident.”

Look at this example which Waḥeeduddin Khan quotes from the American scholar Christie Morrisson, which explains how it is impossible that the universe could have come into being by accident. He said: “If you take ten coins, and write on them the numbers from one to ten, then put them in your pocket and mix them well, then you try to take them out of your pocket in ascending numerical order (i.e., from one to ten), the chance of you taking out the coin on which is written the number one on the first attempt is one in ten. The chance of you taking out all ten coins in numerical order (1, 2, 3, 4...) is one in ten billion.”[8]

On this basis, how long would it take for this universe to assume its current shape if it had come about by accident? If we were to calculate that in the same manner, we would not be able to imagine or calculate the numbers, let alone comprehend them.

Everything in the universe tells us that it was brought into existence by an omniscient, wise Creator, but man is unjust (to himself) and ignorant.

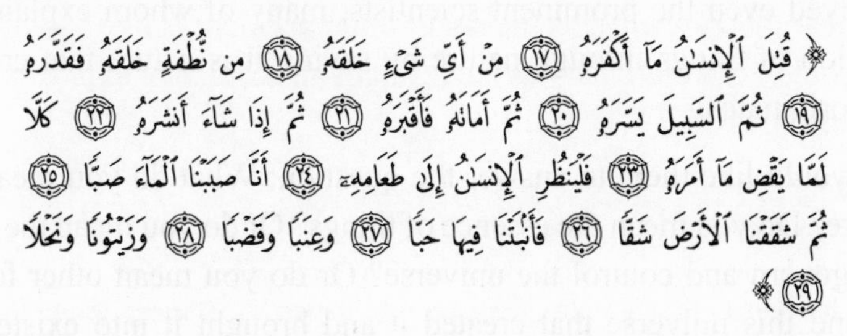

﴿Be cursed [the disbelieving] man! How ungrateful he

---

[8] *Al-'Ilm Yad'u ila'l-Eemaan*, Pp. 51.

is! From what thing did He create him? From *Nutfah* [male and female semen drops] He created him and then set him in due proportion. Then He makes the Path easy for him. Then He causes him to die and puts him in his grave. Then when it is His Will, He will resurrect him [again]. Nay, but [man] has not done what He commanded him. Then let man look at his food: We pour forth water in abundance. And We split the earth in clefts. And We cause therein the grain to grow. And grapes and clover plants [i.e. green fodder for the cattle]. And olives and date palms.﴾ *(Qur'an 80: 17-29)*

How could man have been created and formed by accident, when his food is created in such a well-planned manner that requires the co-operation of the heavens and the earth? Allah (ﷻ), indeed spoke the truth when He described man as:

﴿ ... إِنَّهُۥ كَانَ ظَلُومًا جَهُولًا ﴿٧٢﴾ ﴾

﴿...Verily he was unjust [to himself] and ignorant.﴾ *(Qur'an 33: 72).*[9]

2) The View that Nature is the Creator

This is a lie which has become widespread in our own time, and has deceived even the prominent scientists, many of whom explain the creation of things through nature by saying it is nature that creates and originates.

We would like them to answer the question: What do you mean by nature? Do you mean the essence of things? Or do you mean the laws that govern and control the universe? Or do you mean other forces beyond this universe that created it and brought it into existence?

---

[9] This matter will be discussed further when we look at the signs of Allah in the universe, *In sha Allah* (God willing).

If they say that by nature they mean the universe itself, then we do not need to bother refuting them, because the falseness of this view is obvious from what we have said above. This view repeats the idea referred to above, that a thing can bring itself into existence. In other words, they are saying that the universe created the universe, i.e., the heavens created the heavens, the earth created the earth, the universe created man and animals. We have already explained that human reason refuses to accept that a thing could create itself. To make matters clearer, we say that a thing cannot create something that is more developed than itself. Nature, such as the heavens, earth, stars, sun and moon, does not possess reason or the faculties of hearing and seeing, so how could it create man who hears, sees and knows? This cannot be.

If they say, all of that was created by accident, we say, we know for sure that there was no accident involved in the creation of the universe. We have already explained this above.

The theory of self-generation (a specious argument that has been proven to be false)

One of the things that helped to spread this new idolatry (the view that nature is the creator) was the scientists' observation of the appearance of maggots in the excrement of humans and animals, and the formation of bacteria which ate food and caused it to rot. They said, these are living beings which are generated by nature alone.

This idea lent weight to the new idolatry of "nature" in the eyes of those who were misguided far astray from the true religion of Allah. But the guidance of Allah soon exposed the falsehood of this theory at the hands of the famous French scientist Pasteur who proved that these maggots and bacteria referred to did not generate themselves from nature, but their origins lay in something even smaller that was invisible to the naked eye. He produced evidence which convinced other scientists that what he said was true. He sealed some food away from the open air, and killed the bacteria by boiling it; no new bacteria formed in the food and it did not turn rotten. This is the theory on which the food canning industry is based.[10]

Nature is the laws which govern the universe

Another group suggests that nature is the laws which govern the universe. This is the view of those who claim to have knowledge and who believe that nature is the creator. They say: this universe is running according to certain laws which regulate its affairs down to the last detail. The events that happen in this universe happen according to these laws. This is like a clock which runs accurately and precisely for a long time, running by itself with no controller.

In fact, these people are not answering the question that has been asked: Who created the universe? They tell us about the way in which the universe operates, and they tell us how these laws affect things, but we want to know who created the universe and who created the laws that govern it.

Waḥeeduddin Khan says, "Ancient man knew that rain came from the sky, but nowadays we know everything about how water evaporates from the sea until drops of water fall on the land. All of this is a description of what happens, but it is not in itself an explanation. Science does not tell us how these events became laws, or how the water is held between heaven and earth in these stunning and beautiful forms (clouds). It is from these phenomena that the scientists derived these laws.

When man claims that by discovering the laws of nature he has solved the mystery of the universe, he is only deceiving himself. When he makes this claim, he is putting a link from the middle of the

---

[10] Az-Zandaani, *Kitaab at-Tawḥeed*, 2/74.

chain at the end.

Nature does not explain anything (about the universe). It itself is in need of explanation. Read this debate that could take place between an intelligent man and a doctor who is prominent in his field:

Questioner: Why is blood red?

Doctor: Because there are red cells in the blood. The size of each cell is 1/700 of an inch.

Questioner: OK, but why are these cells red?

Doctor: Because in the blood there is a substance called haemoglobin, which becomes red when it is mixed with oxygen in the heart.

Questioner: That's fair enough, but where do these cells which carry haemoglobin come from ?

Doctor: They are manufactured in your liver.

Questioner: Wonderful! But how are all these things — the blood, cells, liver etc. — connected to one another so perfectly, and how do they each play their part with such precision?

Doctor: This is what we call the laws of nature.

Questioner: But what do you mean by the laws of nature?

Doctor: What we mean by the laws is the blind internal operation of natural and chemical forces.

Questioner: But why do these forces always produce the same result? How are things regulated so that birds fly in the air, fish live in water and man lives in this world with all his amazing potentials and capabilities?

Doctor: Don't ask me about that. My science only tells me about what happens, it does not answer the question about why it happens.

From these questions it becomes clear the extent to which modern science can explain the causes and effects behind this universe. The universe is like a machine which operates beneath a cover, and we know nothing about it except the fact that it is running. "But if we lift the lid, we will see how the many parts and cogs of this machine are connected to one another, how they turn one another; we will see all the movements of this machine. But does this mean that we know who created this machine, just by looking at its parts spinning? How can our seeing the machine running be proof that the machine came into existence by itself and is running by itself?"[11]

Nature is a force

There are those who say that nature is a force which created the universe, and that it is a living, hearing, seeing, wise and powerful force... We say to them, this is right, but your mistake is that you call this force "nature." This creative, innovative force has told us the name by which it deserves to be called, and that is "Allah." Allah has told us of His beautiful Names and sublime Attributes, so we must call Him by the names which He has called Himself, Exalted is He and All-High.

Those who came before them said something similar

Those who attribute creation to nature had Predecessors who said something very similar. These were the *Dahriyah* — the atheists — who attributed events to *Ad-Dahr* (time). They saw that children grow into adults, adults grow into old men and old men die as time goes by and night and day alternate, so they attributed life and death to time.

﴿ وَقَالُوا۟ مَا هِىَ إِلَّا حَيَاتُنَا ٱلدُّنْيَا نَمُوتُ وَنَحْيَا وَمَا يُهْلِكُنَآ إِلَّا ٱلدَّهْرُ ۚ وَمَا لَهُم بِذَٰلِكَ مِنْ عِلْمٍ ۖ إِنْ هُمْ إِلَّا يَظُنُّونَ ﴿٢٤﴾ ﴾

[11] Waḥeeduddin Khan, *Al-Islam yataḥaddaa* (Islam challenges), 29-31; he also quotes from other western scientists.

﴾And they say: 'There is nothing but our life of this world, we die and we live and nothing destroys us except *Ad-Dahr* [time].' And they have no knowledge of it, they only conjecture.﴿ *(Qur'an 45: 24)*

Those people attributed events to time, and these people attribute them to the nature of things; both are equally misguided.

3) Darwin's Theory [12]

The supporters of this theory tried to use it to explain the existence of living beings. This theory is widespread; many people try to spread it with good intentions, because they think that it is a scientific fact, whilst others try to spread it with bad intentions, because it suits their desire, which is to prove religion wrong in its description of how man was created. Those who seek to undermine religion find evidence in science to support their stance and deceive people.

What does this theory say?

This theory claims that the origin of all creatures was small organisms which developed from water, then their environment changed them until new characteristics emerged in this life-form, and these characteristics, over millions of years, led to the development of more advanced characteristics which changed that primitive creature into a superior life form. This development of characteristics caused by the environment and evolution continued until it arrived at the appearance of man.

The bases of this theory

a) This theory is based on what was noted during excavations carried out during Darwin's time. They discovered that the more ancient levels contained primitive life-forms, and the levels above them

[12] Zandaani, *Kitaab at-Tawḥeed*, 3/81.

contained progressively more developed life-forms. Darwin said: "These more highly-developed animals came about as a result of evolution from earlier, primitive life-forms."

b) It was also based on what was known at Darwin's time about the resemblance of the embryos of different animals at the early stages of development, which could give the impression that the origin of all animals is the same as their embryos appear to be the same, and that evolution happened on earth along the same lines as the development of embryos in the wombs of living beings.

c) It was also based on the existence of the vermiform appendix in human beings, which helps in digesting plant matter, but it no longer has any function in man. This gave the impression that it was something left over from monkeys that did not evolve, because it does have a function in monkeys.

Darwin's explanation of the process of evolution

a) Natural selection. Destructive factors kill off the weaker specimens and leave the stronger specimens. This is what they call the principle of "the survival of the fittest." So the strong specimens remain and pass on their strong characteristics to their offspring. These strong characteristics are combined as time goes by to form a new feature in the species. This is "evolution" which makes the specimen develop into a superior specimen. This ongoing development is evolution.

b) Sexual selection. This has to do with the preference of both males and females to mate with strong specimens, so that the characteristics of stronger specimens will be passed on and the characteristics of weaker specimens will be eliminated because of the reluctance of others to mate with them.

c) Every time a new characteristic emerges, it is passed on to the offspring.

Refutation of the bases on which this theory is founded

Archaeology is not a precise science, and no one can claim that he has carried out a complete survey of all the layers of the earth, including those beneath mountains and oceans, and that he did not find anything new that would challenge previously-held concepts.

Even if we suppose that the statements of this branch of science (i.e., archaeology) are proven to be true, the fact that there were at first primitive life-forms which were then superceded by more advanced creatures does not prove that the advanced life-forms developed from their primitive counterparts. All that this proves is the order of their existence, which may simply be a reflection of changes in the environment which supported different life-forms at different times. The archaeological view at the time of Darwin was that man has existed for 600,000 years; recent discoveries in the field of archaeology put the age of man at 10 million years.

Does this not prove that archaeology is a changeable science on which no definitive proof can be based? Tomorrow the archaeologists may discover something that is the opposite of what we expect!

Dr. Muṣṭafa Shaakir Saleem has commented on the book *Al-Insaan fi'l-Mar'aah* (Man in the Mirror) by Clyde Colquhoun, which talks about Neanderthal man, which the supporters of Darwin's theory say, was the first man to evolve from monkeys and gorillas... Dr. Muṣṭafa said: "Neanderthal man is described as having the following main natural features: a larger brain than that of modern man, and a large, broad skull... In addition to that, the chain of evolution which the archaeologists are trying to piece together is not complete; there is something known as 'the missing link'."

Dr. Sooriyaal said in his book *Taṣaddu' Madhhab Darwin* (The Collapse of Darwin's Theory):

a) The missing links in the chain of evolution are not only missing between man and the life-forms beneath him, but there are also missing links between the primitive single-celled life-forms and multi-celled life-forms, between unjointed and jointed, between invertebrates and fish and amphibians, between the latter and reptiles, between reptiles and human beings. I have mentioned them according to the order in which they appear in the geological periods.

b) Similarities between the embryos of different species: this is a serious mistake which some scientists made because microscopes had not yet been developed which would show the minute differences in the formation of the embryos of different species. In addition, there was a hoax perpetrated by the German scientist Ernst Haeckel who juxtaposed pictures of similar embryos. When some embryologists criticized him, he admitted that he had had to touch up approximately 8 per cent of the pictures and make them look similar because they were incomplete.

c) With regard to the human appendix being an evolutionary left-over from the monkey stage, this does not prove definitively that man evolved from monkeys. The reason for its presence may be that it is inherited from early man, who was dependent on plants, so it was created to help him digest that plant matter. Moreover, science may yet discover that it has a function which we currently do not know.

Science is advancing every day. If hermaphroditism is a characteristic of lower life forms, and having two genders is a characteristic of higher life-forms, and if having nipples is a sign of femininity, then why do we find that male elephants have nipples like man does, whilst the males of hoofed animals such as horses and donkeys do not? If Darwin claimed that man evolved from lower life forms, why is this trace of hermaphroditism left in man when it is not left in lower life-forms?

Refuting Darwin's explanation of how evolution works

a) Darwin says that there is a law that works in extermination and extinction of living beings so that only the fittest survive to pass on their characteristics to their offspring, until the strong characteristics combine to form a new species. There is indeed a law which works in the annihilation of all living beings, strong and weak alike, because Allah has decreed death for all living beings. But there is also a parallel law whereby there is co-operation between living beings and their environment, because when Allah created life, He also created the means to sustain life. So we see the sun, the oceans, the wind, rain, plants, gravity... all of these and other things co-operate to sustain human and animal life.

Focusing on the destructive factors and overlooking the factors of sustenance creates an imbalance in one's way of thinking. If there is a law of death or destruction, then there is also a law of life, and each of them has a role to play in life. If these natural forces such as wind, thunder, heat, water, storms, etc. are able to cause damage to people or to destroy their works, such as blinding them or destroying what they have built, it is impossible to believe that these blind, unintelligent natural forces are able to create an eye for one who does not have an eye, or to repair a structure that is in a state of disrepair.

It is reasonable to say that natural forces could be destructive or fatal, but it is unreasonable to say that these forces explain this perfect, wonderful creation in which everything has been shaped perfectly and formed in a systematic way such that its parts fit together with such amazing precision and work together in perfect harmony. It is impossible to attribute this perfection to blind natural forces.

Jamaaluddeen al-Afghaani said in his book *Al-Radd 'ala ad-Dahriyeen* — Refutation of the atheists — where he discusses this theory. After that, I ask them, how does each separate part of a living being know what the other parts are trying to achieve when each of them serves a different function? By what means does one part inform the others of what it intends to do? What parliament or senate or assembly of elders was held to create this perfectly-assembled being? How do these parts know — when they are still inside the bird's egg — that they should come out in the form of a bird which eats grains, so it has to have the necessary beak and craw?

Darwin's principle of the survival of the fittest has destroyed human life, because it has given justification for every oppressor, whether an individual or a government. When the oppressor engages in oppression, confiscation, war and plots, he does not think that he is doing anything wrong — rather, he is following a natural law, according to Darwin's claims, the law of the survival of the fittest. This claim led to the ugliest excesses of colonialism.

b) Natural selection, the tendency to mate with stronger individuals so as to eliminate weaker individuals, does not prove that evolution takes place within that species. What we understand from it is that stronger individuals of a given species survive whilst weaker specimens are eliminated.

It may be said that if evolution occurs in some individuals, this may lead to a lack of sexual attraction because sexual attraction will be reduced according to the difference of form between males and females. This is what was suggested by the famous scientist Duwayr Zansky in 1958, a century after Darwin. Among the things that he suggested was: "Differences in physical form reduce sexual attraction, so the tendency to reproduce is reduced between animals of different shapes; the more different they are, the less attraction there is between them. Therefore it is wrong to say that new characteristics will be passed on from an individual in its genes. For example, a blacksmith with strong muscles will not pass on his muscular strength to his offspring, just as a scientist with deep knowledge will not pass his knowledge on to his sons in his genes."

c) The suggestion that some characteristics emerge accidentally and are then passed on has been rejected by the modern science of genetics. Every characteristic that is not carried in the genes is an earned or acquired characteristic which cannot be passed on to the offspring.

Professor Nabeel George, one of the reliable scientists in this field, says: "For that reason, natural selection does not explain the theory of evolution. It only explains that the least fit will die, and that some characteristics will spread among the species. Those who speak of evolutionary leaps mean that an animal which did not have an eye suddenly had an eye because of the action of some rays.

Some specialists have proved that x-rays can cause changes in the number of genes, but this change occurs in something that is already present — it does not create something that does not exist. The number of a monkey's genes differs from the number of a human's genes. X-rays only affect the genes that are present; how could these rays, which do not possess any form of intelligence, create the intelligence in man which distinguishes him from monkeys and other animals?

These rays can affect the genes, but it is more akin to distortion than reforming, as happens in the case of atomic rays (radiation). This is in addition to the fact that science of genetics disproves Darwin's theory, as experience shows. The Jews, and the Muslims after them, have been circumcising their sons for centuries, but this has not led to any of their children being born circumcised. The more science advances, the more Darwin's theory is proven wrong.

This theory is not supported by reality

a) If this theory were true, we would see many animals and people coming into existence through evolution, not only through reproduction. Even if evolution needs a long time, this does not mean that we would not see monkeys changing into men, one group after another.

b) Even if we accept that natural circumstances and natural selection turned a monkey into a man, for example, we cannot accept that these circumstances would also dictate that there would be a woman to accompany this man, so that they could reproduce and there would be a balance between men and women.

c) The ability to adapt which we see in creatures such as the chameleon, which changes its colour according to where it is, is an ability which is inherent in the formation of that creature. It is born with that ability which exists in some and is barely present in others. All creatures have limits beyond which they cannot pass. The ability to adapt is the matter of inborn potential, not a developed characteristic that has been formed by the environment as the proponents of this theory say. Otherwise, the environment would have forced rocks, soil, and other inanimate objects to adapt.

d) Frogs are distinguished from man in their ability to live on the land and in water. Birds are distinguished from man by their ability to fly and move rapidly without the aid of a machine. A dog's nose is far more sensitive than that of a human — so is a dog's nose more advanced than a human's nose? Are frogs and birds more advanced than humans in some ways? Camels', horses' and donkeys' eyes see equally well by day and by night, whereas human eyes are unable to see in the dark. An eagle's vision is far more acute than that of a human. So are eagles and donkeys more advanced than man? If we take self-sufficiency as the basis of superiority, then plants are superior to man and all animals, because they manufacture their own food and food for others, with no need for nourishment from elsewhere.

If we take size as the basis of superiority, then camels and elephants and prehistoric animals (dinosaurs for example) would be superior to man.

The attitude of natural scientists towards this theory

a) Those who support this theory want to support the freedom of thought which the Church opposed and resisted. The natural scientists launched a war against the priests of the Church and their thought after the conflict between the two sides took a vicious turn.

b) Those who oppose it demand tangible evidence that natural selection has changed any species, especially mankind. Those who oppose it because they want natural proof are no less in number or in the fierceness of their resistance than the theologians in Europe who oppose it.

These are some of the views of the scientists who oppose this theory as quoted by Prof. Ibraaheem Ḥouraani: "The scientists have not proven the theory of Darwin; in fact they have disproved it and criticized it, even though they know that he researched it for twenty years." Among them are the scientists Nechel and Dallas, whose comments may be summed up as follows: "Evolution by natural selection cannot apply in the case of man; he can only have been created directly."

Another scientist, Farkho, said: "It is clear to us from real life that there is a big difference between humans and monkeys. We cannot say for sure that man is descended from monkeys or from any other animal, so we should not say any such thing."

Another scientist, Mivart, said, after examining the realities of life in detail: "The theory of Darwin is insupportable and is a childish opinion."

Von Biskoun said, after he and Farkho had conducted a comparative study of humans and monkeys: "The difference between the two is basic and a very great difference..."

Agassiz said in a paper which he delivered during a seminar on Victorian science that Darwin's theory was in fact wrong and false, his methods had nothing to do with science, and his theory was of no use at all.

Huxley, who was a skeptic and a friend of Darwin said that according to the evidence we have, it can never be proven that any kind of plants or animals evolved through either natural selection or artificial selection.

Tyndall, who was like Haeckel, said: "Undoubtedly those who believe in evolution are unaware of the fact that it is based on principles which are not proven (i.e., hypothetical principles). It is obvious to me that Darwin's theory needs to be altered."

Theory not fact

For all of these reasons, what Darwin said about evolution is called the theory of evolution. In the eyes of scientists, there is gulf of difference between a theory and a fact or law. According to their terminology, a theory is something which may be either true or false, whereas a fact or law is something which cannot be false in any way.

So why did it become so widespread?

The reason why this theory became so widespread is that it appeared at a time when Allah (ﷻ), willed that the falsehood of that distorted and altered religion (Christianity) should become apparent through the actions of some of its followers. The advance of science played a major role in exposing the falsehood of this religion, which led to the outbreak of a fierce battle in which thousands of scientists were killed. In this heated battle each side started to use all kinds of weapons against the other, and this theory spread as a weapon wielded by the scientists against their own religion, then against the religion of every land they colonized. They did this because they believed the theory to be true, and as an act of vengeance against the false religion which had stood in the way of scientific research. Then they used it as a means of destroying the religions of the colonized nations so that it would become easy for the colonialists to dominate those peoples.

Thus the colonialist education system, after destroying the people's religion, imposed the study of this theory in the curriculum, introducing it in scientific garb so that students would believe it to be true, thus instilling in students' minds the difference between this falsified science and religion, so that people would reject religion.

It is sufficient for the reader to know that because of this theory, many Muslims deviated from their religion. For this reason the colonialists were keen to teach this theory to Muslim children in their schools at the time when American law forbade teaching this theory in schools from 1935 CE.

But in Europe, after they had dealt the final blow to their deviated religion, they announced that Darwin's theory, which they had used in the battle to support science against religion, was not a scientific fact; it was no more than a theory, and the more science advanced, the more the falsehood of this theory became apparent.

The Qur'an and Darwin's theory

When the Qur'an speaks about the realities of past eternity, people must listen and pay heed to.

﴿ وَإِذَا قُرِئَ ٱلْقُرْءَانُ فَٱسْتَمِعُواْ لَهُۥ وَأَنصِتُواْ ... ﴿٢٠٤﴾ ﴾

﴿So, when the Qur'an is recited, listen to it, and be silent...﴾ *(Qur'an 7: 204)*

— because it comes from the All-Knowing, All-Aware, Who encompasses all things with His knowledge. What does man know? In comparison to the knowledge of Allah, he knows nothing.

﴿ ...وَٱللَّهُ يَعۡلَمُ وَأَنتُمۡ لَا تَعۡلَمُونَ ﴿٢١٦﴾ ﴾

﴾...Allah knows but you do not know.﴿ *(Qur'an 2: 216)*

How could He not know about His creatures' affairs when He is the one Who has created them?

﴿ أَلَا يَعۡلَمُ مَنۡ خَلَقَ وَهُوَ ٱللَّطِيفُ ٱلۡخَبِيرُ ﴿١٤﴾ ﴾

﴾Should not He Who has created know? And He is the Most Kind and Courteous [to His slaves], All-Aware [of everything].﴿ *(Qur'an 67: 14)*

How can people let themselves talk about their origins when they did not witness that act of creation?

﴿ ۞ مَّآ أَشۡهَدتُّهُمۡ خَلۡقَ ٱلسَّمَٰوَٰتِ وَٱلۡأَرۡضِ وَلَا خَلۡقَ أَنفُسِهِمۡ ... ﴿٥١﴾ ﴾

﴾I [Allah] made them [*Iblees* and his offspring] not to witness [nor took their help in] the creation of the heavens and the earth and not [even] their own creation...﴿ *(Qur'an 18: 51)*

Because they did not witness it, what they get right concerning this matter is very little, and the mistakes they make are many.

The opposite of this theory is the truth

What the All-Knowing All-Aware, the Creator of man, says is diametrically opposed to what these ignorant people said. Allah (ﷻ), tells us that He created man as a complete and independent creature. He told His angels that He was going to create him before He brought him into being.

﴿ وَإِذْ قَالَ رَبُّكَ لِلْمَلَـٰٓئِكَةِ إِنِّى جَاعِلٌ فِى ٱلْأَرْضِ خَلِيفَةً ... ﴿٣٠﴾ ﴾

﴾And [remember] when your Lord said to the angels: 'Verily, I am going to place [mankind] generations after generations on earth.'...﴿ *(Qur'an 2: 30)*[13]

Allah (ﷻ), has told us of the substance from which He created man. He created him from dust:

﴿ ... فَإِنَّا خَلَقْنَـٰكُم مِّن تُرَابٍ... ﴿٥﴾ ﴾

﴾...We have created you [i.e. Adam] from dust...﴿ *(Qur'an 22: 5)*

Abu Moosa al-Ash'ari said that he heard the Messenger of Allah (ﷺ) say:

> "Allah created Adam from a handful which He gathered from throughout the earth, so the sons of Adam vary as the earth varies; some are red, some are white, some are black, and some are of colours in between, some are easy-going, some are difficult, some are evil and some are good."[14]

Water is an element in the creation of man:

﴿ وَٱللَّهُ خَلَقَ كُلَّ دَآبَّةٍ مِّن مَّآءٍ... ﴿٤٥﴾ ﴾

﴾Allah has created every moving [living] creature from water...﴿ *(Qur'an 24: 45)*

Man is created from water and dust:

---

[13] ﴾So when your Lord told the angels: "I am placing an overlord on earth."﴿ - T.B. Irving. ﴾Behold, thy Lord said to the angels: "I will create a vicegerent on earth."﴿ - A. Yusuf 'Ali.

[14] Aḥmad, Tirmidhi and Abu Dawood (*Mishkaat al-Maṣaabeeḥ*, 1/36, hadith no. 100).

﴿ هُوَ ٱلَّذِى خَلَقَكُم مِّن طِينٍ... ﴿٢﴾ ﴾

﴿He it is Who has created you from clay...﴾ *(Qur'an 6: 2)*

This clay turned into sounding clay like the clay of pottery,

﴿ خَلَقَ ٱلْإِنسَٰنَ مِن صَلْصَٰلٍ كَٱلْفَخَّارِ ﴿١٤﴾ ﴾

﴿He created man [Adam] from sounding clay like the clay of pottery.﴾ *(Qur'an 55: 14)*

Allah (ﷻ), created him with His hands:

﴿ قَالَ يَٰٓإِبْلِيسُ مَا مَنَعَكَ أَن تَسْجُدَ لِمَا خَلَقْتُ بِيَدَىَّ... ﴿٧٥﴾ ﴾

﴿[Allah] said: "O' *Iblees* [Satan]! What prevents you from prostrating yourself to one whom I have created with Both My Hands...﴾ *(Qur'an 38: 75)*

Allah (ﷻ), has created him hollow from the beginning. According to the hadith narrated from Anas (رضي الله عنه), the Messenger of Allah (ﷺ) said:

> "When Allah formed Adam in Paradise, He left him for as long as He willed to leave him, and *Iblees* started walking around him, looking at him. When he saw that he was hollow, he knew that this was a creature which was not solid (strong)."[15]

Allah (ﷻ), blew into this clay of His Spirit, and life entered into it, so he started to hear, see, speak, think and be aware. Allah commanded the angels to prostrate to Adam when He breathed into him of His Spirit and life entered into him.

﴿ فَإِذَا سَوَّيْتُهُۥ وَنَفَخْتُ فِيهِ مِن رُّوحِى فَقَعُوا۟ لَهُۥ سَٰجِدِينَ ﴿٧٢﴾ ﴾

---

[15] Muslim, 4/2016, hadith no. 2611.

﴿So when I have fashioned him and breathed into him [his] soul created by Me, then you fall down prostrate to him.﴾ *(Qur'an 38: 72)*

Allah (ﷻ), tells us of the place where He caused him to dwell after He had created him:

﴿ وَقُلْنَا يَٰٓـَٔادَمُ ٱسْكُنْ أَنتَ وَزَوْجُكَ ٱلْجَنَّةَ... ﴿٣٥﴾ ﴾

﴿And We said: 'O' Adam! Dwell you and your wife in the Paradise...'﴾ *(Qur'an 2: 35)*

As soon as his creation was completed, he began to speak and he understood what was said to him:

﴿ وَعَلَّمَ ءَادَمَ ٱلْأَسْمَآءَ كُلَّهَا ثُمَّ عَرَضَهُمْ عَلَى ٱلْمَلَـٰٓئِكَةِ فَقَالَ أَنۢبِـُٔونِى بِأَسْمَآءِ هَـٰٓؤُلَآءِ إِن كُنتُمْ صَـٰدِقِينَ ﴿٣١﴾ قَالُوا۟ سُبْحَـٰنَكَ لَا عِلْمَ لَنَآ إِلَّا مَا عَلَّمْتَنَآ ۖ إِنَّكَ أَنتَ ٱلْعَلِيمُ ٱلْحَكِيمُ ﴿٣٢﴾ قَالَ يَـٰٓـَٔادَمُ أَنۢبِئْهُم بِأَسْمَآئِهِمْ ۖ ... ﴿٣٣﴾ ﴾

﴿And He taught Adam all the names [of everything], then He showed them to the angels and said, 'Tell Me the names of these if you are truthful.' They [angels] said: 'Glory is to You, we have no knowledge except what you have taught us. Verily, it is You, the All-Knower, the All-Wise.' He said: 'O' Adam! Inform them of their names,'...﴾ *(Qur'an 2: 31-33)*

Abu Hurayrah (رضي الله عنه) reported that the Messenger of Allah (ﷺ) said:

"When Allah created Adam and breathed His Spirit into him, he sneezed and said, *'Al-Ḥamdu lillah* (praise be to Allah),' praising Allah by His Leave. His Lord said to him, 'May Allah have mercy on you, O' Adam. Go to those angels' — to a group of them who were sitting — 'and say, *As-Salaamu 'alaykum.'* They said, "*Wa 'alayk as-salaam wa raḥmatullah.*"[16]

This first man was Adam, who is the father of all people. From Adam, Allah (ﷻ), created his wife Ḥawwaa' (Eve),

﴿ يَٰٓأَيُّهَا ٱلنَّاسُ ٱتَّقُوا۟ رَبَّكُمُ ٱلَّذِى خَلَقَكُم مِّن نَّفْسٍ وَٰحِدَةٍ وَخَلَقَ مِنْهَا زَوْجَهَا ... ﴿١﴾ ﴾

﴿O' mankind! Be dutiful to your Lord, Who created you from a single person [Adam], and from him [Adam] He created his wife [Ḥawwaa (Eve)],...﴾ *(Qur'an 4: 1)*

Man was not created imperfect and then completed as the proponents of the theory of evolution say. On the contrary, he was complete, then his form started to diminish. According to a hadith narrated by Bukhari and Muslim in their *ṣaḥeeḥs* from Abu Hurayrah, the Prophet (ﷺ) said:

"Allah created Adam and his height was sixty cubits."[17]

Hence the believers will enter Paradise physically perfect, in the form of Adam. The remainder of the hadith quoted above says: "Everyone who enters Paradise will do so in the form of Adam (عليه السلام), whose height was sixty cubits." Then he (the Prophet) (ﷺ) said:

"Man's form kept decreasing (in height) from that time until now."[18]

Allah (ﷻ), informs us that He transformed some misguided humans into monkeys and pigs, so the higher level of creation can be reduced

---

[16] Tirmidhi, *Mishkaat al-Maṣaabeeḥ*, 2/542, hadith no. 4662. The editor of *Al-Mishkaat* said: this is classed as *ṣaḥeeḥ* by Al-Ḥaakim and Adh-Dhahabi agreed with him. And it is as they said.

[17] Bukhari, 6/362, hadith no. 3326; Muslim, 4/2183, hadith no. 2841. This version is by Bukhari.

[18] Ibid. Here the version quoted is by Muslim.

to a lower level, but the idea of monkeys and pigs turning into humans is an idea that occurs only to those with the weakest powers of reasoning.

This is a brief look at what the Qur'an and *aḥaadeeth* say about the creation of man. We did not quote at length all of the texts of the Qur'an and Sunnah on this topic, but what we have said gives a clear picture and leaves no room for confusion and imagination. This is what Islam says about the noble origins of man, which he should feel proud of to belong to. The origins of man as described by the proponents of the theory of evolution, where a monkey evolved from a rat or a cockroach, is an origin which man would feel embarrassed to belong to.

This idea of early man taught to children by the scholars of history, as a savage who cannot speak and cannot do anything well, who learns from the animals, has cast many aspersions on the noble origin of man.

In conclusion

It is high time for us to wake up and return to our religion which brought the Book of our Lord, filled with goodness. It tells of what happened before you, what will happen after you, it judges between you. It is a serious matter, not a joke, and whoever follows guidance from any other source will be sent astray by Allah...

It is high time for us to keep away from the products of corrupt minds in such areas, i.e., matters concerning which Allah has spoken decisively and left no room for people's opinions.

We must put a stop to this intellectual defeat which has made us hasten to accept every new thing without pausing to think. We realize our mistake only when those who started it are destroyed.

to a lower level, but the idea of monkeys and pigs turning into humans is an idea that occurs only to those with the weakest powers of reasoning.

This is a brief look at what the Qur'an and Sunnah say about the creation of man. We did not quote at length all of the texts of the Qur'an and Sunnah on this topic, but what we have said gives a clear picture and leaves no room for confusion and imagination. This is what Islam says about the noble origins of man, which he should feel proud of to belong to. The origins of man as described by the proponents of the theory of evolution, where a monkey evolved from a rat or a cockroach, is an origin which man would feel embarrassed to belong to.

This idea of early man-human as described by the modern history as a savage who cannot speak and cannot do anything well, who learns from the animals, has cast many aspersions on the noble origin of man.

In conclusion

It is high time for us to wake up and return to our religion which contains the Book of our Lord (that) which tells us what happened before you, what will happen after you, it judges between you, it is a serious matter, not a joke, and whoever seeks guidance from any other source will be sent astray by Allah.

It is high time that we keep away from the pitfalls of contradictions and short-sightedness in matters concerning which Allah has spoken decisively and left no room for people's opinions.

We must put a stop to this intellectual defeat which has made us hasten to accept every new thing without pausing to think. We realize our mistake only when those who started it are destroyed.

CHAPTER TWO
DEFINITION OF ALLAH AND CONNECTING HEARTS TO HIM

INTRODUCTION

We would not have needed to discuss the previous issue at length were it not for the fact that so many doubts and specious arguments surround it that the researcher is obliged to examine their fallacy.

Now it is time for us to discuss in detail the second issue, which is the most important topic of this book, the issue which lies at the heart of the matter.

We have already stated that the Qur'an tackles this issue in two ways, to confirm this great reality:

a) It speaks of the perfection of Allah's creation and describes the wonders of the universe which indicate the greatness of the Creator.

b) It speaks directly of Allah, the Exalted, - His essence, names, attributes, blessings and creations. We shall endeavour - *In sha Allah* (God willing) - to discuss this in detail, and Allah (ﷻ), is the One Whose help we seek.

1 - EVIDENCE OF THE UNIVERSAL SIGNS WHICH POINT TO THE CREATOR AND INITIATOR

1) The Qur'anic Methodology in Using the Universal Signs as Evidence

i) Exploring the universe through the Qur'anic description

The Qur'an takes us on one journey after another through the horizons of the heavens and the different parts of the earth, pausing to consider the flowers of the meadows, taking us up to the stars in their orbits. In this way it opens our eyes and our hearts, showing us how the power and decree of Allah operate in His creation, uncovering for us the mysteries of creation, guiding us to the wisdom behind creation, and explaining the immense blessings which He has bestowed upon us and the universe around us.

This is a long discussion about it in the Book of Allah which is conveyed in long and short *soorahs* (chapters). It is a very interesting discussion which captivates the soul, is a pleasure to listen to. It stirs the emotions and senses.

I have studied much of what science and scientists have discovered about all aspects of life, explaining the mysteries of creation and how creation points to the Creator, but I have never found anything in all of that which is like the beautiful descriptions given in the Qur'an, with so much detail that stirs the emotions and guides the heart, reaching precise conclusions. How could it be otherwise, when the Qur'an has been sent down by the All-Wise, Most Praiseworthy?

Allah's Actions in the Universe

Come with me on a journey through the *aayaat* (verses) of the Qur'an, where we will explore this universe to see how the power of Allah operates in different areas: in a seed thrown into the soil, which splits and sends its roots down into the earth, so that from an inanimate seed comes forth life which is represented in its stem, leaves, fragrant flowers and fruits which nourish both men and beasts... in the dawn when it breaks... in the still of night... in the movements of the sun and the moon...

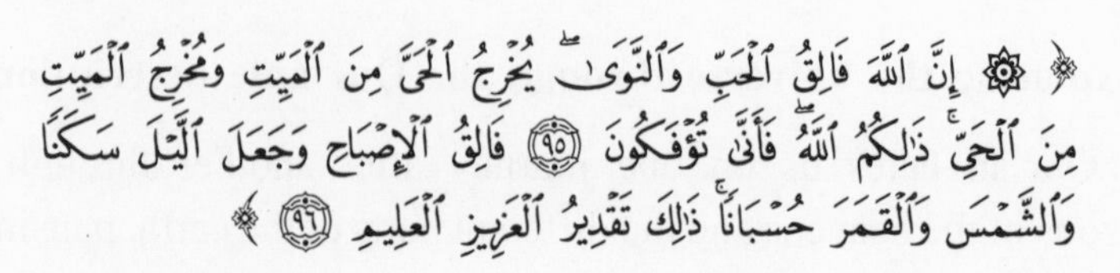

﴾Verily, it is Allah Who causes the seed grain and the fruit stone [like date stone] to split and sprout. He brings forth the living from the dead, and it is He Who brings forth the dead from the living. Such is Allah, then how are you deluded away from the truth? [He is the] Cleaver of the daybreak. He has appointed the night for resting, and the sun and the moon for reckoning. Such is the measuring of the All-Mighty, the All-Knowing.﴿

(Qur'an 6: 95-96)

Look how the clouds are formed by Allah:

﴿ أَلَمْ تَرَ أَنَّ ٱللَّهَ يُزْجِى سَحَابًا ثُمَّ يُؤَلِّفُ بَيْنَهُۥ ثُمَّ يَجْعَلُهُۥ رُكَامًا فَتَرَى ٱلْوَدْقَ
يَخْرُجُ مِنْ خِلَٰلِهِۦ وَيُنَزِّلُ مِنَ ٱلسَّمَآءِ مِن جِبَالٍ فِيهَا مِنۢ بَرَدٍ فَيُصِيبُ بِهِۦ مَن يَشَآءُ
وَيَصْرِفُهُۥ عَن مَّن يَشَآءُ يَكَادُ سَنَا بَرْقِهِۦ يَذْهَبُ بِٱلْأَبْصَٰرِ ﴿٤٣﴾ ﴾

﴾See you not that Allah drives the clouds gently, then joins them together, then makes them into a heap of layers, and you see the rain comes forth from between them; and He sends down from the sky hail [like] mountains, [or there are in the heaven mountains of hail from where He sends down hail], and strikes therewith whom He wills, and averts it from whom He wills. The vivid flash of its [clouds] lightning nearly blinds the sight.﴿ *(Qur'an 24: 43)*

Allah (سبحانه وتعالى), tells us how He deals with the shade or shadow:

﴿ أَلَمْ تَرَ إِلَىٰ رَبِّكَ كَيْفَ مَدَّ ٱلظِّلَّ وَلَوْ شَآءَ لَجَعَلَهُۥ سَاكِنًا ثُمَّ جَعَلْنَا
ٱلشَّمْسَ عَلَيْهِ دَلِيلًا ﴿٤٥﴾ ثُمَّ قَبَضْنَٰهُ إِلَيْنَا قَبْضًا يَسِيرًا ﴿٤٦﴾ ﴾

﴾Have you not seen how your Lord spread the shadow. If He willed, He could have made it still But We have made the sun its guide [i.e. after the sunrise, the shadow shrinks and vanishes at midnoon and then again appears in the afternoon with the decline of the sun, and had there been no sunlight, there would have been no shadow]. Then We withdraw it to Us - a gradual concealed withdrawal.﴿ *(Qur'an 25: 45-46)*

Look how He (ﷻ), deals with matters of life and living beings, and with the night and day:

﴾ قُلِ ٱللَّهُمَّ مَٰلِكَ ٱلْمُلْكِ تُؤْتِى ٱلْمُلْكَ مَن تَشَآءُ وَتَنزِعُ ٱلْمُلْكَ مِمَّن تَشَآءُ وَتُعِزُّ مَن تَشَآءُ وَتُذِلُّ مَن تَشَآءُ ۖ بِيَدِكَ ٱلْخَيْرُ ۖ إِنَّكَ عَلَىٰ كُلِّ شَىْءٍ قَدِيرٌ ﴿٢٦﴾ تُولِجُ ٱلَّيْلَ فِى ٱلنَّهَارِ وَتُولِجُ ٱلنَّهَارَ فِى ٱلَّيْلِ ۖ وَتُخْرِجُ ٱلْحَىَّ مِنَ ٱلْمَيِّتِ وَتُخْرِجُ ٱلْمَيِّتَ مِنَ ٱلْحَىِّ ۖ وَتَرْزُقُ مَن تَشَآءُ بِغَيْرِ حِسَابٍ ﴿٢٧﴾ ﴿

﴾Say [O' Muhammad]: "O' Allah! Possessor of the kingdom, You give the kingdom to whom You will, and You take the kingdom from whom You will, and You endue with honour whom You will, and You humiliate whom You will. In Your Hand is the good. Verily, You are Able to do all things. You make the night to enter into the day, and You make the day to enter into the night [i.e. increase and decrease in the hours of the night and the day during winter and summer], You bring the living out of the dead, and You bring the dead out of the living. And You give wealth and sustenance to whom You will, without limit [measure or account].﴿ *(Qur'an 3: 26-27)*

The Qur'an does not only tell us of the power of Allah and how it operates in the universe, how His knowledge encompasses all His creatures and how He is the disposer of all affairs - it also tells us the purpose for which He created the universe.

Allah (ﷻ), created this earth for the sake of man:

﴾ هُوَ ٱلَّذِى خَلَقَ لَكُم مَّا فِى ٱلْأَرْضِ جَمِيعًا... ﴿٢٩﴾ ﴿

﴿He it is Who created for you all that is on earth...﴾
(Qur'an 2: 29)

He created it for us in a manner that is suited to our nature and serves our interests. This is what the Qur'an calls subjugation (*taskheer*). He does not only tell us that by way of information; He explains to us the subjugation that Allah has created in the universe:

﴿ أَلَمۡ تَرَوۡاْ أَنَّ ٱللَّهَ سَخَّرَ لَكُم مَّا فِى ٱلسَّمَٰوَٰتِ وَمَا فِى ٱلۡأَرۡضِ ... ﴿٢٠﴾ ﴾

﴿See you not [O' men] that Allah has subjected for you whatsoever is in the heavens and whatsoever is in the earth,...﴾ *(Qur'an 31: 20)*

The stars were created for us to navigate by at night on land and sea:

﴿ وَهُوَ ٱلَّذِى جَعَلَ لَكُمُ ٱلنُّجُومَ لِتَهۡتَدُواْ بِهَا فِى ظُلُمَٰتِ ٱلۡبَرِّ وَٱلۡبَحۡرِۗ قَدۡ فَصَّلۡنَا ٱلۡأٓيَٰتِ لِقَوۡمٖ يَعۡلَمُونَ ﴿٩٧﴾ ﴾

﴿It is He Who has set the stars for you, so that you may guide your course with their help through the darkness of the land and the sea. We have [indeed] explained in detail Our *Aayaat* [proofs, evidences, verses, lessons, signs, revelations, etc.] for people who know.﴾
(Qur'an 6: 97)

The earth and the heavens, the coming down of rain from the sky, the ships that sail in the sea, the rivers which flow throughout the land, the sun and moon, the succession of night and day... all of these have been created for our benefit:

﴿ ٱللَّهُ ٱلَّذِى خَلَقَ ٱلسَّمَٰوَٰتِ وَٱلۡأَرۡضَ وَأَنزَلَ مِنَ ٱلسَّمَآءِ مَآءٗ فَأَخۡرَجَ بِهِۦ مِنَ ٱلثَّمَرَٰتِ رِزۡقٗا لَّكُمۡۖ وَسَخَّرَ لَكُمُ ٱلۡفُلۡكَ لِتَجۡرِىَ فِى ٱلۡبَحۡرِ بِأَمۡرِهِۦۖ وَسَخَّرَ لَكُمُ ٱلۡأَنۡهَٰرَ ﴿٣٢﴾ وَسَخَّرَ لَكُمُ ٱلشَّمۡسَ وَٱلۡقَمَرَ

دَآئِبَيْنِ وَسَخَّرَ لَكُمُ ٱلَّيْلَ وَٱلنَّهَارَ ﴿٣٣﴾ وَءَاتَىٰكُم مِّن كُلِّ مَا سَأَلْتُمُوهُ... ﴿٣٤﴾ ﴾

﴿Allah is He Who has created the heavens and the earth and sends down water [rain] from the sky, and thereby brought forth fruits as provision for you; and He has made the ships to be of service to you, that they may sail through the sea by His Command; and He has made rivers [also] to be of service to you. And He has made the sun and the moon, both constantly pursuing their courses, to be of service to you; and He has made the night and the day, to be of service to you. And He gave you of all that you asked for,...﴾ *(Qur'an 14: 32-34)*

ii) The blessings of Allah in the universe

The Qur'an tells us that Allah (ﷻ), has created this universe and subjugated it for us. He has made it compatible with our nature, and ordered it in such a way that suits the life of man. The Qur'an uses this explanation as a means to make man give thanks to his Lord, for man is inclined by nature to love the one who is kind to him:

﴿ هَلْ جَزَآءُ ٱلْإِحْسَٰنِ إِلَّا ٱلْإِحْسَٰنُ ﴿٦٠﴾ ﴾

﴿Is there any reward for good other than good?﴾ *(Qur'an 55: 60)*

Hence the Qur'an speaks in detail about the blessings which Allah (ﷻ), has bestowed upon His slaves in themselves:

﴿ قُلْ هُوَ ٱلَّذِىٓ أَنشَأَكُمْ وَجَعَلَ لَكُمُ ٱلسَّمْعَ وَٱلْأَبْصَٰرَ وَٱلْأَفْـِٔدَةَ ۖ قَلِيلًا مَّا تَشْكُرُونَ ﴿٢٣﴾ ﴾

﴿Say it is He Who has created you, and endowed you with hearing [ears] and seeing [eyes], and hearts. Little thanks you give.﴾ *(Qur'an 67: 23)*

- and in the universe around them:

﴿ ٱلَّذِى جَعَلَ لَكُمُ ٱلْأَرْضَ مَهْدًا وَجَعَلَ لَكُمْ فِيهَا سُبُلًا لَّعَلَّكُمْ
تَهْتَدُونَ ﴿١٠﴾ وَٱلَّذِى نَزَّلَ مِنَ ٱلسَّمَآءِ مَآءًۢ بِقَدَرٍ فَأَنشَرْنَا بِهِۦ بَلْدَةً
مَّيْتًا ۚ كَذَٰلِكَ تُخْرَجُونَ ﴿١١﴾ وَٱلَّذِى خَلَقَ ٱلْأَزْوَٰجَ كُلَّهَا وَجَعَلَ لَكُم مِّنَ
ٱلْفُلْكِ وَٱلْأَنْعَٰمِ مَا تَرْكَبُونَ ﴿١٢﴾ لِتَسْتَوُۥا۟ عَلَىٰ ظُهُورِهِۦ ثُمَّ تَذْكُرُوا۟ نِعْمَةَ
رَبِّكُمْ إِذَا ٱسْتَوَيْتُمْ عَلَيْهِ... ﴿١٣﴾ ﴾

﴾Who has made for you the earth like a bed, and has made for you roads therein, in order that you may find your way. And Who sends down water [rain] from the sky in due measure, then We revive a dead land therewith, and even so you will be brought forth [from the graves]. And Who has created all the pairs and has appointed for you ships and cattle on which you ride, In order that you may mount on their backs, and then may remember the Favour of your Lord when you mount thereon,...﴿ *(Qur'an 43: 10-13)*

He (سبحانه وتعالى), has created the sun and the moon for us in a manner that serves our interests and benefits us:

﴿ هُوَ ٱلَّذِى جَعَلَ ٱلشَّمْسَ ضِيَآءً وَٱلْقَمَرَ نُورًا وَقَدَّرَهُۥ مَنَازِلَ لِتَعْلَمُوا۟
عَدَدَ ٱلسِّنِينَ وَٱلْحِسَابَ ۚ... ﴿٥﴾ ﴾

﴾It is He Who made the sun a shining thing and the moon as a light and measured out for it stages that you might know the number of years and the reckoning...﴿

(Qur'an 10: 5)

The *an'aam* - camels, cattle and sheep - and horses, mules and donkeys, have all been created for us to use, and they have all been created in a manner that suits our nature:

﴿ وَٱلۡأَنۡعَٰمَ خَلَقَهَاۗ لَكُمۡ فِيهَا دِفۡءٞ وَمَنَٰفِعُ وَمِنۡهَا تَأۡكُلُونَ ۝٥ وَلَكُمۡ فِيهَا جَمَالٌ حِينَ تُرِيحُونَ وَحِينَ تَسۡرَحُونَ ۝٦ وَتَحۡمِلُ أَثۡقَالَكُمۡ إِلَىٰ بَلَدٖ لَّمۡ تَكُونُواْ بَٰلِغِيهِ إِلَّا بِشِقِّ ٱلۡأَنفُسِۚ إِنَّ رَبَّكُمۡ لَرَءُوفٞ رَّحِيمٞ ۝٧ وَٱلۡخَيۡلَ وَٱلۡبِغَالَ وَٱلۡحَمِيرَ لِتَرۡكَبُوهَا وَزِينَةٗۚ وَيَخۡلُقُ مَا لَا تَعۡلَمُونَ ۝٨ ﴾

﴾And the cattle, He has created them for you; in them there is warmth [warm clothing], and numerous benefits, and of them you eat. And wherein is beauty for you, when you bring them home in the evening, and as you lead them forth to pasture in the morning. And they carry your loads to a land that you could not reach except with great trouble to yourselves. Truly, your Lord is full of kindness, Most Merciful. And [He has created] horses, mules and donkeys, for you to ride and as an adornment. And He creates [other] things of which you have no knowledge.﴿ *(Qur'an 16: 5-8)*

The sea has also been created for us; in its creation and in the (ships) that sail on it are many things that benefit us:

﴿ وَهُوَ ٱلَّذِي سَخَّرَ ٱلۡبَحۡرَ لِتَأۡكُلُواْ مِنۡهُ لَحۡمٗا طَرِيّٗا وَتَسۡتَخۡرِجُواْ مِنۡهُ حِلۡيَةٗ تَلۡبَسُونَهَاۖ وَتَرَى ٱلۡفُلۡكَ مَوَاخِرَ فِيهِ وَلِتَبۡتَغُواْ مِن فَضۡلِهِۦ وَلَعَلَّكُمۡ تَشۡكُرُونَ ۝١٤ ﴾

﴾And He it is Who has subjected the sea [to you], that you eat thereof fresh tender meat [i.e. fish], and that you bring forth out of it ornaments to wear. And you see the ships ploughing through it, that you may seek [thus] of His Bounty [by transporting the goods from place to place] and that you may be grateful.﴿ *(Qur'an 16: 14)*

Allah (ﷻ), created bees to do their wonderful work, to produce for us this drink of varying colours, to provide nourishment and a healing for man:

﴿وَأَوۡحَىٰ رَبُّكَ إِلَى ٱلنَّحۡلِ أَنِ ٱتَّخِذِي مِنَ ٱلۡجِبَالِ بُيُوتٗا وَمِنَ ٱلشَّجَرِ وَمِمَّا يَعۡرِشُونَ ﴿٦٨﴾ ثُمَّ كُلِي مِن كُلِّ ٱلثَّمَرَٰتِ فَٱسۡلُكِي سُبُلَ رَبِّكِ ذُلُلٗاۚ يَخۡرُجُ مِنۢ بُطُونِهَا شَرَابٞ مُّخۡتَلِفٌ أَلۡوَٰنُهُۥ فِيهِ شِفَآءٞ لِّلنَّاسِۚ إِنَّ فِي ذَٰلِكَ لَأٓيَةٗ لِّقَوۡمٖ يَتَفَكَّرُونَ ﴿٦٩﴾﴾

﴾And your Lord inspired the bee, saying: 'Take you habitations in the mountains and in the trees and in what they erect. Then, eat of all fruits, and follow the ways of your Lord made easy [for you].' There comes forth from their bellies, a drink of varying colour wherein is healing for men. Verily, in this is indeed a sign for people who think.﴿ *(Qur'an 16: 68-69)*

The Qur'an urges us to seek and know Allah through His Universal Signs

The Qur'an urges the slaves of Allah to look at the signs of Allah in the universe — the earth, the heavens, everything in them and in between them — and to let that looking and pondering be the kind of reminder which benefits the believers.

I like the way in which some contemporary people called this method "the law of walking and looking," because the Qur'an frequently tells man to travel in the land and see and learn from that. This could be either in the literal, physical sense or it may mean thinking and pondering.

The command to do this is given in general terms:

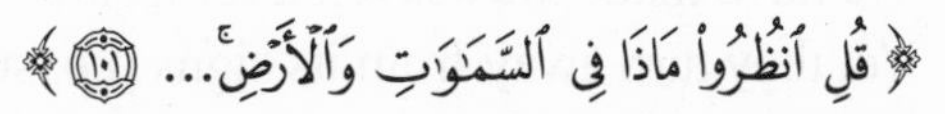

﴾Say: 'Behold all that is in the heavens and the earth,'...﴿
(Qur'an 10: 101)

— and in specific terms:

﴿ فَلْيَنظُرِ ٱلْإِنسَٰنُ مِمَّ خُلِقَ ۝٥ ﴾

﴾So let man see from what he is created!﴿ *(Qur'an 86: 5)*

﴿فَلْيَنظُرِ ٱلْإِنسَٰنُ إِلَىٰ طَعَامِهِۦٓ ۝٢٤﴾

﴾Then let man look at his food.﴿ *(Qur'an 80: 24)*

iii) How the Qur'an uses its *aayaat* (verses) to prove that the Creator is deserving of Lordship and Divinity and to prove the falseness of everything that is worshipped instead of Allah

The Qur'an takes the signs in the universe as material to debate with the *mushrikeen* (polytheists) and establish proof against them:

﴿ أَوَلَمْ يَرَ ٱلَّذِينَ كَفَرُوٓا۟ أَنَّ ٱلسَّمَٰوَٰتِ وَٱلْأَرْضَ كَانَتَا رَتْقًا فَفَتَقْنَٰهُمَا وَجَعَلْنَا مِنَ ٱلْمَآءِ كُلَّ شَىْءٍ حَىٍّ أَفَلَا يُؤْمِنُونَ ۝٣٠ وَجَعَلْنَا فِى ٱلْأَرْضِ رَوَٰسِىَ أَن تَمِيدَ بِهِمْ وَجَعَلْنَا فِيهَا فِجَاجًا سُبُلًا لَّعَلَّهُمْ يَهْتَدُونَ ۝٣١ وَجَعَلْنَا ٱلسَّمَآءَ سَقْفًا مَّحْفُوظًا وَهُمْ عَنْ ءَايَٰتِهَا مُعْرِضُونَ ۝٣٢ وَهُوَ ٱلَّذِى خَلَقَ ٱلَّيْلَ وَٱلنَّهَارَ وَٱلشَّمْسَ وَٱلْقَمَرَ كُلٌّ فِى فَلَكٍ يَسْبَحُونَ ۝٣٣ ﴾

﴾Have not those who disbelieve known that the heavens and the earth were joined together as one united piece, then We parted them? And We have made from water every living thing. Will they not then believe? And We have placed on the earth firm mountains, lest it should shake with them, and We placed therein broad highways for them to pass through, that they may be guided. And We have made the heaven a roof, safe and well-guarded. Yet they turn away from its signs [i.e. sun, moon, winds, clouds, etc.]. And He it is Who has created the night and the day, and the sun and the moon, each in an orbit floating.﴿ *(Qur'an 21: 30-33)*

He points out to them the corrupt nature of their belief in their gods who do not possess the attributes of Lordship (*Ruboobiyah*) and Divinity (*Uloohiyah*) which would qualify them to be deserving of worship and to be taken as gods instead of Allah (ﷻ):

﴿ قُلِ ٱلْحَمْدُ لِلَّهِ وَسَلَٰمٌ عَلَىٰ عِبَادِهِ ٱلَّذِينَ ٱصْطَفَىٰٓ ۗ ءَآللَّهُ خَيْرٌ أَمَّا يُشْرِكُونَ ﴿٥٩﴾ أَمَّنْ خَلَقَ ٱلسَّمَٰوَٰتِ وَٱلْأَرْضَ وَأَنزَلَ لَكُم مِّنَ ٱلسَّمَآءِ مَآءً فَأَنۢبَتْنَا بِهِۦ حَدَآئِقَ ذَاتَ بَهْجَةٍ مَّا كَانَ لَكُمْ أَن تُنۢبِتُوا۟ شَجَرَهَآ ۗ أَءِلَٰهٌ مَّعَ ٱللَّهِ ۚ بَلْ هُمْ قَوْمٌ يَعْدِلُونَ ﴿٦٠﴾ أَمَّن جَعَلَ ٱلْأَرْضَ قَرَارًا وَجَعَلَ خِلَٰلَهَآ أَنْهَٰرًا وَجَعَلَ لَهَا رَوَٰسِىَ وَجَعَلَ بَيْنَ ٱلْبَحْرَيْنِ حَاجِزًا ۗ أَءِلَٰهٌ مَّعَ ٱللَّهِ ۚ بَلْ أَكْثَرُهُمْ لَا يَعْلَمُونَ ﴿٦١﴾ أَمَّن يُجِيبُ ٱلْمُضْطَرَّ إِذَا دَعَاهُ وَيَكْشِفُ ٱلسُّوٓءَ وَيَجْعَلُكُمْ خُلَفَآءَ ٱلْأَرْضِ ۗ أَءِلَٰهٌ مَّعَ ٱللَّهِ ۚ قَلِيلًا مَّا تَذَكَّرُونَ ﴿٦٢﴾ أَمَّن يَهْدِيكُمْ فِى ظُلُمَٰتِ ٱلْبَرِّ وَٱلْبَحْرِ وَمَن يُرْسِلُ ٱلرِّيَٰحَ بُشْرًۢا بَيْنَ يَدَىْ رَحْمَتِهِۦٓ ۗ أَءِلَٰهٌ مَّعَ ٱللَّهِ ۚ تَعَٰلَى ٱللَّهُ عَمَّا يُشْرِكُونَ ﴿٦٣﴾ أَمَّن يَبْدَؤُا۟ ٱلْخَلْقَ ثُمَّ يُعِيدُهُۥ وَمَن يَرْزُقُكُم مِّنَ ٱلسَّمَآءِ وَٱلْأَرْضِ ۗ أَءِلَٰهٌ مَّعَ ٱللَّهِ ۚ قُلْ هَاتُوا۟ بُرْهَٰنَكُمْ إِن كُنتُمْ صَٰدِقِينَ ﴿٦٤﴾ ﴾

﴾Say [O' Muhammad]: 'Praise and thanks be to Allah, and peace be on His slaves whom He has chosen [for His Message]! Is Allah better, or [all] that you ascribe as partners [to Him]?' [Of course, Allah is Better]. Is not He [better than your gods] Who created the heavens and the earth, and sends down for you water [rain] from the sky, whereby We cause to grow wonderful gardens full of beauty and delight? It is not in your ability to cause the growth of their trees. Is there any *ilaah* [god] with Allah? Nay, but they are a people who ascribe equals [to Him]! Is not He [better than your gods] Who has made the earth as a fixed abode, and has placed rivers in its midst, and has placed firm mountains therein, and has set a barrier between the two seas [of salt and sweet water]? Is there any *ilaah* [god] with Allah? Nay, but most of them know not! Is not He [better than your gods] Who responds to the distressed one, when he calls on Him, and Who removes the evil, and makes you inheritors of the earth, generations after generations? Is there any *ilaah* [god] with Allah? Little is that you remember! Is not He [better than your gods] Who guides you in the darkness of the land and the sea, and Who sends the winds as heralds of glad tidings, going before His Mercy [rain]? Is there any *ilaah* [god] with Allah? High Exalted be Allah above all that they associate as partners [to Him]! Is not He [better than your so-called gods] Who originates creation, and shall thereafter repeat it, and Who provides for you from heaven and earth? Is there any *ilaah* [god] with Allah? Say: 'Bring forth your proofs, if you are truthful.'﴿

(Qur'an 27: 59-64)

These *aayaat* (verses) explain that their so-called gods are not fit to be worshipped, for Allah alone is the Creator of the heavens and the earth, Who sends down rain from the sky and brings forth the gardens which refresh the soul and are a delight to the eye. He is the One Who has made the earth as a fixed abode, and has placed rivers in its midst, and has placed firm mountains therein... He is the One Who is truly deserving of worship.

We must use this kind of evidence when confronting the disbelievers and atheists, for the Messengers have used this evidence before us to a great extent. Ibraaheem (Abraham) (ﷺ) (may peace be upon him), the close friend of *Ar-Raḥmaan* (Allah, the All-Merciful), debated with that heretic and established proof against him by using this kind of evidence, thus dazzling him and rendering him speechless:

﴿ أَلَمْ تَرَ إِلَى ٱلَّذِى حَآجَّ إِبْرَٰهِـۧمَ فِى رَبِّهِۦٓ أَنْ ءَاتَىٰهُ ٱللَّهُ ٱلْمُلْكَ إِذْ قَالَ
إِبْرَٰهِـۧمُ رَبِّىَ ٱلَّذِى يُحْىِۦ وَيُمِيتُ قَالَ أَنَا۠ أُحْىِۦ وَأُمِيتُ ۖ قَالَ إِبْرَٰهِـۧمُ
فَإِنَّ ٱللَّهَ يَأْتِى بِٱلشَّمْسِ مِنَ ٱلْمَشْرِقِ فَأْتِ بِهَا مِنَ ٱلْمَغْرِبِ فَبُهِتَ ٱلَّذِى
كَفَرَ ۗ وَٱللَّهُ لَا يَهْدِى ٱلْقَوْمَ ٱلظَّـٰلِمِينَ ﴿٢٥٨﴾ ﴾

﴿Have you not looked at him who disputed with Ibraaheem about his Allah, because Allah had given him the kingdom? When Ibraaheem said [to him]: 'My Allah is He Who gives life and causes death.' He said, 'I give life and cause death.' Ibraaheem said, 'Verily, Allah brings the sun from the east; then bring it you from the west.' So the disbeliever was utterly defeated. And Allah guides not the people, who are *Ẓaalimoon* [wrongdoers].﴾ *(Qur'an 2: 258)*

Moosa (Moses) (عليه السلام), the one who spoke with Allah, used the same argument when he confronted the tyrant of his age, Fir'awn (Pharaoh). He kept producing evidence after evidence until Pharaoh could no longer put up an argument, whereupon he resorted to the use of threats:

﴿ قَالَ فِرْعَوْنُ وَمَا رَبُّ ٱلْعَـٰلَمِينَ ﴿٢٣﴾ قَالَ رَبُّ ٱلسَّمَـٰوَٰتِ وَٱلْأَرْضِ وَمَا
بَيْنَهُمَآ ۖ إِن كُنتُم مُّوقِنِينَ ﴿٢٤﴾ قَالَ لِمَنْ حَوْلَهُۥٓ أَلَا تَسْتَمِعُونَ ﴿٢٥﴾ قَالَ رَبُّكُمْ
وَرَبُّ ءَابَآئِكُمُ ٱلْأَوَّلِينَ ﴿٢٦﴾ قَالَ إِنَّ رَسُولَكُمُ ٱلَّذِىٓ أُرْسِلَ إِلَيْكُمْ لَمَجْنُونٌ
﴿٢٧﴾ قَالَ رَبُّ ٱلْمَشْرِقِ وَٱلْمَغْرِبِ وَمَا بَيْنَهُمَآ ۖ إِن كُنتُمْ تَعْقِلُونَ ﴿٢٨﴾ قَالَ لَئِنِ
ٱتَّخَذْتَ إِلَـٰهًا غَيْرِى لَأَجْعَلَنَّكَ مِنَ ٱلْمَسْجُونِينَ ﴿٢٩﴾ ﴾

﴿Fir'awn [Pharaoh] said: 'And what is the Lord of the *'Aalameen* [mankind, jinn and all that exists]?' Moosa [Moses] said: 'The Lord of the heavens and the earth, and all that is between them, if you seek to be convinced with certainty.' Pharaoh said to those around: 'Do you not hear [what he says]?' Moosa said: 'Your Lord and

> the Lord of your ancient fathers!' [Pharaoh] said: 'Verily, your Messenger who has been sent to you is a madman!' [Moosa] said: 'Lord of the east and the west, and all that is between them, if you did but understand!' [Pharaoh] said: 'If you choose an *ilaah* [god] other than me, I will certainly put you among the prisoners.'﴾
>
> *(Qur'an 26: 23-29)*

This way of producing evidence is the way of all the Messengers. Look at *Soorah Ibraaheem* [*aayaat* (verses) 9, 10] and read what the disbelieving people, the people of Nooḥ (Noah) (عليه السلام) and 'Aad and Thamood, and those who came after them, said, and see how the Messengers replied by saying:

﴿ ... أَفِي ٱللَّهِ شَكٌّ فَاطِرِ ٱلسَّمَٰوَٰتِ وَٱلْأَرْضِ يَدْعُوكُمْ لِيَغْفِرَ لَكُم مِّن ذُنُوبِكُمْ ... ﴿١٠﴾ ﴾

> ﴾...Can there be a doubt about Allah, the Creator of the heavens and the earth? He calls you [to Monotheism and to be obedient to Allah] that He may forgive you of your sins...﴿ *(Qur'an 14: 10)*

They proved the veracity of their call by referring to the fact that Allah (سبحانه وتعالى), is the Creator of the heavens and the earth.

Kufr (disbelief) is reprehensible and strange in the face of such clear proof

Hence the Qur'an asks a question which indicates how strange it is that the disbelievers disbelieve when the proof and evidence are so clear:

﴿ كَيْفَ تَكْفُرُونَ بِٱللَّهِ وَكُنتُمْ أَمْوَٰتًا فَأَحْيَٰكُمْ ثُمَّ يُمِيتُكُمْ ثُمَّ يُحْيِيكُمْ ثُمَّ إِلَيْهِ تُرْجَعُونَ ﴿٢٨﴾ ﴾

> ﴾How can you disbelieve in Allah? Seeing that you were

dead and He gave you life. Then He will give you death, then again will bring you to life [on the Day of Resurrection] and then unto Him you will return.﴿

(Qur'an 2: 28)

In another *aayah* (verse), it asks:

﴾ يَٰٓأَيُّهَا ٱلْإِنسَٰنُ مَا غَرَّكَ بِرَبِّكَ ٱلْكَرِيمِ ﴿٦﴾ ٱلَّذِى خَلَقَكَ فَسَوَّىٰكَ فَعَدَلَكَ ﴿٧﴾ فِىٓ أَىِّ صُورَةٍ مَّا شَآءَ رَكَّبَكَ ﴿٨﴾ ﴿

﴾O' man! What has made you careless about your Lord, the Most Generous? Who created you, fashioned you perfectly, and gave you due proportion. In whatever form He willed, He put you together.﴿ *(Qur'an 82: 6-8)*

When man looks at himself and at the universe around him, he cannot but turn to his Creator and glorify Him. Hence it is strange that the disbelievers disbelieve and deny that.

﴾ مَّا لَكُمْ لَا تَرْجُونَ لِلَّهِ وَقَارًا ﴿١٣﴾ وَقَدْ خَلَقَكُمْ أَطْوَارًا ﴿١٤﴾ أَلَمْ تَرَوْا۟ كَيْفَ خَلَقَ ٱللَّهُ سَبْعَ سَمَٰوَٰتٍ طِبَاقًا ﴿١٥﴾ وَجَعَلَ ٱلْقَمَرَ فِيهِنَّ نُورًا وَجَعَلَ ٱلشَّمْسَ سِرَاجًا ﴿١٦﴾ وَٱللَّهُ أَنۢبَتَكُم مِّنَ ٱلْأَرْضِ نَبَاتًا ﴿١٧﴾ ثُمَّ يُعِيدُكُمْ فِيهَا وَيُخْرِجُكُمْ إِخْرَاجًا ﴿١٨﴾ ﴿

﴾What is the matter with you, that [you fear not Allah (His punishment), and] you hope not for reward [from Allah or you believe not in His Oneness]. While He has created you in [different] stages [i.e. first *Nutfah*, then *'Alaqah* and then *Mudghah*]. See you not how Allah has created the seven heavens one above another? And has made the moon a light therein, and made the sun a lamp? And Allah has brought you forth from the [dust of] earth? Afterwards He will return you into it [the earth], and bring you forth [again on the Day of Resurrection]?﴿

(Qur'an 71: 13-18)

iv) Those who benefit from the signs of the universe are those who have insight

The signs of Allah in the universe only become clear in all their inspiring reality to hearts which remember and worship Allah, because all veils have been removed from these hearts and they are open to the wonders of the universe. The Qur'an establishes this connection between human hearts and the rhythm of this immense and beautiful universe. This connection creates the insight that discovers the universe anew. This insight and discovery leave great impact on the human hearts and become so precious in the lives of the mankind. This connection is established by the Qur'an between understanding, learning and the man who learns and understands. Hence the Qur'an states that those who are guided by the signs of the universe are a certain type of people:

﴿ إِنَّ فِى خَلْقِ ٱلسَّمَٰوَٰتِ وَٱلْأَرْضِ وَٱخْتِلَٰفِ ٱلَّيْلِ وَٱلنَّهَارِ لَءَايَٰتٍ لِّأُو۟لِى ٱلْأَلْبَٰبِ ﴿١٩٠﴾ ٱلَّذِينَ يَذْكُرُونَ ٱللَّهَ قِيَٰمًا وَقُعُودًا وَعَلَىٰ جُنُوبِهِمْ وَيَتَفَكَّرُونَ فِى خَلْقِ ٱلسَّمَٰوَٰتِ وَٱلْأَرْضِ رَبَّنَا مَا خَلَقْتَ هَٰذَا بَٰطِلًا سُبْحَٰنَكَ فَقِنَا عَذَابَ ٱلنَّارِ ﴿١٩١﴾ ﴾

﴾Verily! In the creation of the heavens and the earth, and in the alternation of night and day, there are indeed signs for men of understanding. Those who remember Allah [always, and in prayers] standing, sitting, and lying down on their sides, and think deeply about the creation of the heavens and the earth, [saying]: 'Our Lord! You have not created [all] this without purpose, glory to You! [Exalted are You above all that they associate with You as partners]. Give us salvation from the torment of the Fire.'﴿ *(Qur'an 3: 190-191)*

These are the people who benefit from the signs of the universe, because they do not stop at the limit of the physical things that they can see; rather they look to the Hand that is running the universe and the Power that created it. They use their eyes, ears and minds in the best way in this matter, and they follow the guidance of the *aayaat* of the Qur'an, which help the ears, eyes and mind to understand the best that man can ever understand:

﴿وَمِنْ ءَايَٰتِهِۦٓ أَنْ خَلَقَ لَكُم مِّنْ أَنفُسِكُمْ أَزْوَٰجًا لِّتَسْكُنُوٓا۟ إِلَيْهَا وَجَعَلَ بَيْنَكُم مَّوَدَّةً وَرَحْمَةً ۚ إِنَّ فِى ذَٰلِكَ لَءَايَٰتٍ لِّقَوْمٍ يَتَفَكَّرُونَ ﴿٢١﴾ وَمِنْ ءَايَٰتِهِۦ خَلْقُ ٱلسَّمَٰوَٰتِ وَٱلْأَرْضِ وَٱخْتِلَٰفُ أَلْسِنَتِكُمْ وَأَلْوَٰنِكُمْ ۚ إِنَّ فِى ذَٰلِكَ لَءَايَٰتٍ لِّلْعَٰلِمِينَ ﴿٢٢﴾ وَمِنْ ءَايَٰتِهِۦ مَنَامُكُم بِٱلَّيْلِ وَٱلنَّهَارِ وَٱبْتِغَآؤُكُم مِّن فَضْلِهِۦٓ ۚ إِنَّ فِى ذَٰلِكَ لَءَايَٰتٍ لِّقَوْمٍ يَسْمَعُونَ ﴿٢٣﴾ وَمِنْ ءَايَٰتِهِۦ يُرِيكُمُ ٱلْبَرْقَ خَوْفًا وَطَمَعًا وَيُنَزِّلُ مِنَ ٱلسَّمَآءِ مَآءً فَيُحْىِۦ بِهِ ٱلْأَرْضَ بَعْدَ مَوْتِهَآ ۚ إِنَّ فِى ذَٰلِكَ لَءَايَٰتٍ لِّقَوْمٍ يَعْقِلُونَ ﴿٢٤﴾﴾

﴾And among His Signs is this, that He created for you wives from among yourselves, that you may find repose in them, and He has put between you affection and mercy. Verily, in that are indeed signs for a people who reflect. And among His Signs is the creation of the heavens and the earth, and the difference of your languages and colours. Verily, in that are indeed signs for men of sound knowledge. And among His Signs is your sleep by night and by day, and your seeking of His Bounty. Verily, in that are indeed signs for a people who listen. And among His Signs is that He shows you the lightning, for fear and for hope, and He sends down water [rain] from the sky, and therewith revives the earth after its death. Verily, in that are indeed signs for a people who understand.﴿ *(Qur'an 30: 21-24)*

So the signs become clear to those who ponder, listen and have understanding in the right direction and lead them to their objective.

The *kuffaar* (disbelievers), on the other hand, look at what happens, and their thoughts do not go beyond it, to the Creator. They do not understand the wisdom behind creation.

﴿ يَعْلَمُونَ ظَٰهِرًا مِّنَ ٱلْحَيَوٰةِ ٱلدُّنْيَا... ﴿٧﴾ ﴾

﴾They know only the outside appearance of the life of the world [i.e. the matters of their livelihood, like irrigating or sowing or reaping, etc.],...﴿ *(Qur'an 30: 7)*

The disbelievers do not benefit from the universal signs, because they do not look at them through the lens of the Qur'an:

﴿ قُلِ ٱنظُرُوا۟ مَاذَا فِى ٱلسَّمَٰوَٰتِ وَٱلْأَرْضِ ۚ وَمَا تُغْنِى ٱلْءَايَٰتُ وَٱلنُّذُرُ عَن قَوْمٍ لَّا يُؤْمِنُونَ ﴿١٠١﴾ ﴾

﴾Say: "Behold all that is in the heavens and the earth," but neither *Aayaat* nor warners benefit those who believe not.﴿ *(Qur'an 10: 101)*

The Qur'an denounces the disbelievers and the deniers for failing to look and learn:

﴿ أَوَلَمْ يَنظُرُوا۟ فِى مَلَكُوتِ ٱلسَّمَٰوَٰتِ وَٱلْأَرْضِ وَمَا خَلَقَ ٱللَّهُ مِن شَىْءٍ وَأَنْ عَسَىٰٓ أَن يَكُونَ قَدِ ٱقْتَرَبَ أَجَلُهُمْ ۖ فَبِأَىِّ حَدِيثٍۭ بَعْدَهُۥ يُؤْمِنُونَ ﴿١٨٥﴾ ﴾

﴾Do they not look in the dominion of the heavens and the earth and all things that Allah has created; and that it may be that the end of their lives is near. In what message after this will they then believe?﴿

(Qur'an 7: 185)

v) Modern sciences have severed the connection between mankind and the universe

Sayyid Quṭb (may Allah have mercy on him) said:

"The methodology of the so-called modern 'scientific' studies has severed the connection which Allah (ﷻ), established between mankind and the universe in which they live.

Mankind is part of this universe, and their life cannot be sound or healthy unless their hearts beat with the rhythm of the universe and are connected to the rhythm of this great universe. There has to be a connection between their hearts and everything they learn about one of the stars or planets, or about the characteristics of plants and animals, or the characteristics of the entire universe in general, and the living and inanimate worlds that it contains — if indeed there are inanimate worlds — or there is anything inanimate in this universe!

All 'scientific knowledge' must attune itself immediately to the rhythm of the human heart and to an amicable relationship with this universe, so as to strengthen the bonds between humans and inanimate objects and living beings. Every kind of knowledge, science and research that falls short of this vital, inspiring, moving objective in human life is imperfect knowledge, false information or fruitless research.

This universe is an open book of truth which can be read in every language and understood by all means. It can be understood by ordinary people living in tents and huts, and by city-dwellers living in apartments and palaces. Each person can understand it according to his own level and potential, and find in it some support for the truth when he searches it with the purpose of finding the truth. It is open at all times.

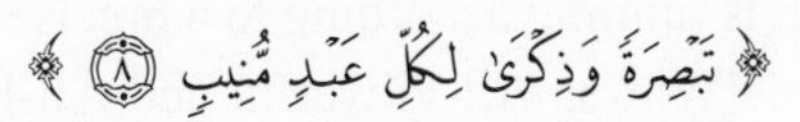

﴿An insight and a Reminder for every slave who turns to Allah in repentance [i.e. the one who believes in the Oneness of Allah and performs deeds of His obedience, and always begs His Pardon].﴾ *(Qur'an 50: 8)*

But modern science extinguishes this deep insight and cuts the ties between human hearts and this universe which speaks the truth, because it is the work of people who have no insight and are dominated by the myth of 'scientific method,' the method which cuts the ties between the universe and the creatures who live in it.

The methodology of faith does not detract from the results of the 'scientific methods' in understanding facts, but it adds the idea of connecting these facts to one another and referring them to the greater realities, and connecting the human heart to them, i.e., to the laws and realities of the universe, turning these laws and realities into moving rhythms that will stir people's emotions, not dry facts residing in their minds that disclose nothing of its beautiful mysteries. The methodology of faith is that which must take over in the field of study and research so that the facts that are discovered will have this strong connection..."[1]

vi) Evidence in creation of the attributes of the Creator

If we look at a machine which is beautifully crafted with great precision, strong and solidly constructed, doing its job in the best possible way, we will realize, with the minimum of mental effort, that its maker is alive and knowledgeable, and that he is possessed of power and will... and other attributes which the machine informs us of.

This universe tells us of many of the attributes of its Creator, such as:

His Power and Knowledge: This vast, immense, huge universe which is running according to a precise system must have been made by One Who is All-Powerful and All-Knowing. Allah (ﷻ), created the universe in this huge form and created this perfect system to tell us of His power and knowledge.

---

[1] *Fi Ẓilaal al-Qur'an, Tafseer Soorah Qaaf, aayah* (verse) 8.

﴿ ٱللَّهُ ٱلَّذِى خَلَقَ سَبْعَ سَمَٰوَٰتٍ وَمِنَ ٱلْأَرْضِ مِثْلَهُنَّ يَتَنَزَّلُ ٱلْأَمْرُ بَيْنَهُنَّ لِتَعْلَمُوٓا۟ أَنَّ ٱللَّهَ عَلَىٰ كُلِّ شَىْءٍ قَدِيرٌ وَأَنَّ ٱللَّهَ قَدْ أَحَاطَ بِكُلِّ شَىْءٍ عِلْمًۢا ﴿١٢﴾ ﴾

﴾It is Allah Who has created seven heavens and of the earth the like thereof [i.e. seven]. His Command descends between them [heavens and earth], that you may know that Allah has power over all things, and that Allah surrounds all things in [His] Knowledge.﴿

(Qur'an 65: 12)

The knowledge which controls this universe must be perfect and all-encompassing:

﴿ ... وَيَعْلَمُ مَا فِى ٱلْبَرِّ وَٱلْبَحْرِ ۚ وَمَا تَسْقُطُ مِن وَرَقَةٍ إِلَّا يَعْلَمُهَا وَلَا حَبَّةٍ فِى ظُلُمَٰتِ ٱلْأَرْضِ وَلَا رَطْبٍ وَلَا يَابِسٍ إِلَّا فِى كِتَٰبٍ مُّبِينٍ ﴿٥٩﴾ ﴾

﴾...And He knows whatever there is in the land and in the sea; not a leaf falls, but He knows it. There is not a grain in the darkness of the earth nor anything fresh or dry, but is written in a Clear Record.﴿ *(Qur'an 6: 59)*

He is Wise: Looking at this universe we find that it is well made with everything in its rightful place, created in the right proportions, in the most perfect and precise manner.

﴿ وَتَرَى ٱلْجِبَالَ تَحْسَبُهَا جَامِدَةً وَهِىَ تَمُرُّ مَرَّ ٱلسَّحَابِ ۚ صُنْعَ ٱللَّهِ ٱلَّذِىٓ أَتْقَنَ كُلَّ شَىْءٍ ... ﴿٨٨﴾ ﴾

﴾And you will see the mountains and think them solid, but they shall pass away as the passing away of the clouds. The Work of Allah, Who perfected all things,...﴿

(Qur'an 27: 88)

﴿ ٱلَّذِىٓ أَحْسَنَ كُلَّ شَىْءٍ خَلَقَهُۥ ۖ وَبَدَأَ خَلْقَ ٱلْإِنسَٰنِ مِن طِينٍ ﴿٧﴾ ﴾

﴾Who made everything He has created good and He

began the creation of man from clay.﴾ *(Qur'an 32: 7)*

The one who looks closely at the creation of Allah will not find anything but perfection and precision, and if he looks for any fault in creation he will not find it.

﴿ ٱلَّذِى خَلَقَ سَبْعَ سَمَٰوَٰتٍ طِبَاقًا ۖ مَّا تَرَىٰ فِى خَلْقِ ٱلرَّحْمَٰنِ مِن تَفَٰوُتٍ ۖ
فَٱرْجِعِ ٱلْبَصَرَ هَلْ تَرَىٰ مِن فُطُورٍ ﴿٣﴾ ثُمَّ ٱرْجِعِ ٱلْبَصَرَ كَرَّتَيْنِ يَنقَلِبْ إِلَيْكَ
ٱلْبَصَرُ خَاسِئًا وَهُوَ حَسِيرٌ ﴿٤﴾ ﴾

﴾Who has created the seven heavens one above another; you can see no fault in the creation of the Most Gracious. Then look again: 'Can you see any rifts?' Then look again and yet again, your sight will return to you in a state of humiliation and worn out.﴿ *(Qur'an 67: 3-4)*

Other attributes: What we have said about the universe indicating the attributes of the Creator is by way of example; we have not listed everything. These examples pave the way for further research and investigation, for in the universe there are many signs that point to the greatness, might and kindness of Allah. Listen to the Divine attributes which Allah (سُبْحَانَهُ وَتَعَالَىٰ), mentions at the end of each of these *aayaat* (verses):

﴿ أَلَمْ تَرَ أَنَّ ٱللَّهَ أَنزَلَ مِنَ ٱلسَّمَآءِ مَآءً فَتُصْبِحُ ٱلْأَرْضُ مُخْضَرَّةً ۗ
إِنَّ ٱللَّهَ لَطِيفٌ خَبِيرٌ ﴿٦٣﴾ لَّهُۥ مَا فِى ٱلسَّمَٰوَٰتِ وَمَا فِى ٱلْأَرْضِ ۗ
وَإِنَّ ٱللَّهَ لَهُوَ ٱلْغَنِىُّ ٱلْحَمِيدُ ﴿٦٤﴾ أَلَمْ تَرَ أَنَّ ٱللَّهَ سَخَّرَ لَكُم مَّا فِى
ٱلْأَرْضِ وَٱلْفُلْكَ تَجْرِى فِى ٱلْبَحْرِ بِأَمْرِهِۦ وَيُمْسِكُ ٱلسَّمَآءَ أَن تَقَعَ عَلَى
ٱلْأَرْضِ إِلَّا بِإِذْنِهِۦٓ ۗ إِنَّ ٱللَّهَ بِٱلنَّاسِ لَرَءُوفٌ رَّحِيمٌ ﴿٦٥﴾ ﴾

﴾See you not that Allah sends down water [rain] from the sky, and then the earth becomes green? Verily, Allah is the Most Kind and Courteous, Well-Acquainted with all things. To Him belongs all that is in the heavens and all that is on the earth. And verily, Allah He is Rich [Free of all needs], Worthy of all praise. See you not that Allah has subjected to you [mankind] all that is on the earth, and the ships that sail through the sea by His Command? He withholds the heaven from falling on the earth except by His Leave. Verily, Allah is, for mankind, full of kindness, Most Merciful.﴾ *(Qur'an 22: 63-65)*

vii) Allah is the only One Who is deserving of worship

Looking at and contemplating the signs of the universe leads us to worship Allah alone, for Allah alone is the Creator, the Controller, the Sustainer of the heavens and the earth, the Provider, the Giver of life and death. Hence He, and no one else, is deserving of worship.

﴿ يَٰٓأَيُّهَا ٱلنَّاسُ ٱعۡبُدُواْ رَبَّكُمُ ٱلَّذِي خَلَقَكُمۡ وَٱلَّذِينَ مِن قَبۡلِكُمۡ لَعَلَّكُمۡ
تَتَّقُونَ ٢١ ٱلَّذِي جَعَلَ لَكُمُ ٱلۡأَرۡضَ فِرَٰشٗا وَٱلسَّمَآءَ بِنَآءٗ وَأَنزَلَ مِنَ
ٱلسَّمَآءِ مَآءٗ فَأَخۡرَجَ بِهِۦ مِنَ ٱلثَّمَرَٰتِ رِزۡقٗا لَّكُمۡۖ فَلَا تَجۡعَلُواْ لِلَّهِ أَندَادٗا
وَأَنتُمۡ تَعۡلَمُونَ ٢٢ ﴾

﴿O' mankind! Worship your Lord [Allah], Who created you and those who were before you so that you may become *Al-Muttaqoon*. Who has made the earth a resting place for you, and the sky as a canopy, and sent down water [rain] from the sky and brought forth therewith fruits as a provision for you. Then do not set up rivals unto Allah [in worship] while you know [that He Alone has the right to be worshipped].﴾ *(Qur'an 2: 21-22)*

﴿ يَٰٓأَيُّهَا ٱلنَّاسُ ٱذۡكُرُواْ نِعۡمَتَ ٱللَّهِ عَلَيۡكُمۡۚ هَلۡ مِنۡ خَٰلِقٍ غَيۡرُ ٱللَّهِ يَرۡزُقُكُم مِّنَ
ٱلسَّمَآءِ وَٱلۡأَرۡضِۚ لَآ إِلَٰهَ إِلَّا هُوَۖ فَأَنَّىٰ تُؤۡفَكُونَ ٣ ﴾

﴿O' mankind! Remember the Grace of Allah upon you! Is there any creator other than Allah who provides for you from the sky [rain] and the earth? *Laa ilaaha illa Huwa* [none has the right to be worshipped but He]. How then are you turning away [from Him]?》

(Qur'an 35: 3)

In this manner - as we have stated above - the Qur'an proves the falsity of other so-called gods and that they do not deserve any kind of worship at all.

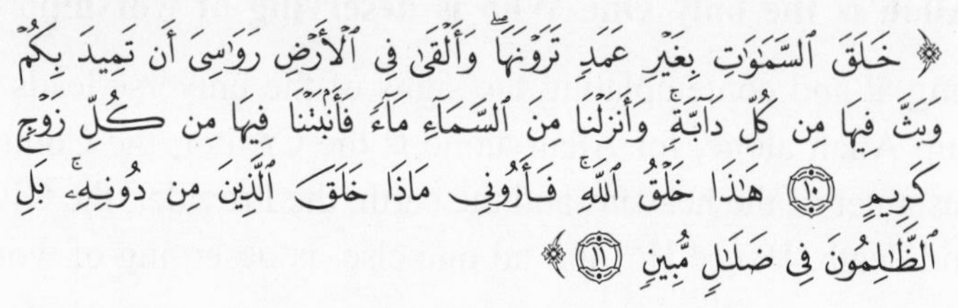

《He has created the heavens without any pillars that you see, and has set on the earth firm mountains lest it should shake with you. And He has scattered therein moving [living] creatures of all kinds. And We send down water [rain] from the sky, and We cause [plants] of every goodly kind to grow therein. This is the creation of Allah. So show Me that which those [whom you worship] besides Him have created. Nay, the *Ẓaalimoon* [polytheists, wrongdoers and those who do not believe in the Oneness of Allah] are in plain error.》

(Qur'an 31: 10-11)

Thus Allah (ﷻ), reminds His creation, through the universal signs and the way in which He controls all their affairs. In many *aayaat* of the Qur'an, He follows that by saying: 《Such is Allah your Lord》 *(Qur'an 39: 6)*, i.e., this is the God besides Whom none is deserving of worship.

Listen to these *aayaat* (verses) and then ponder the ending of each *aayah*:

﴿ خَلَقَ ٱلسَّمَٰوَٰتِ وَٱلْأَرْضَ بِٱلْحَقِّ ۖ يُكَوِّرُ ٱلَّيْلَ عَلَى ٱلنَّهَارِ وَيُكَوِّرُ ٱلنَّهَارَ عَلَى ٱلَّيْلِ ۖ وَسَخَّرَ ٱلشَّمْسَ وَٱلْقَمَرَ ۖ كُلٌّ يَجْرِى لِأَجَلٍ مُّسَمًّى ۗ أَلَا هُوَ ٱلْعَزِيزُ ٱلْغَفَّٰرُ ۝٥ خَلَقَكُم مِّن نَّفْسٍ وَٰحِدَةٍ ثُمَّ جَعَلَ مِنْهَا زَوْجَهَا وَأَنزَلَ لَكُم مِّنَ ٱلْأَنْعَٰمِ ثَمَٰنِيَةَ أَزْوَٰجٍ ۚ يَخْلُقُكُمْ فِى بُطُونِ أُمَّهَٰتِكُمْ خَلْقًا مِّنۢ بَعْدِ خَلْقٍ فِى ظُلُمَٰتٍ ثَلَٰثٍ ۚ ذَٰلِكُمُ ٱللَّهُ رَبُّكُمْ لَهُ ٱلْمُلْكُ ۖ لَآ إِلَٰهَ إِلَّا هُوَ ۖ فَأَنَّىٰ تُصْرَفُونَ ۝٦ ﴾

﴿He has created the heavens and the earth with truth. He makes the night to go in the day and makes the day to go in the night. And He has subjected the sun and the moon. Each running [on a fixed course] for an appointed term. Verily, He is the All-Mighty, the Oft-Forgiving. He created you [all] from a single person [Adam]; then made from him his wife [Ḥawwa' (Eve)]. And He has sent down for you of cattle eight pairs [of the sheep, two, male and female; of the goats, two, male and female; of the oxen, two, male and female; and of the camels, two, male and female]. He creates you in the wombs of your mothers, creation after creation in three veils of darkness. Such is Allah your Lord. His is the kingdom. *Laa ilaaha illa Huwa* [none has the right to be worshipped but He]. How then are you turned away?﴾

(Qur'an 39: 5-6)

2) Scholars Explain the Wonders that Allah has Made in His Creation

Scholars — past and present — have explained the wonders of Allah in His creation. They exhort themselves thereby as they exhort others. We will quote below some of the conclusions reached by scholars of the past and the present.

Reading these quotes, the reader should bear in mind the words of Moosa (Moses) to Fir'awn (Pharaoh):

﴿... رَبُّنَا ٱلَّذِىٓ أَعْطَىٰ كُلَّ شَىْءٍ خَلْقَهُۥ ثُمَّ هَدَىٰ ۝٥٠﴾

﴾..."Our Lord is He Who gave to each thing its form and nature, then guided it aright."﴿ *(Qur'an 20: 50).*

Allah (ﷻ), has given each thing that He has created which suits it, and has guided it to that which befits it... we will see examples of this giving and guiding below.

i) Bodies are formed of cells, which divide

a) What are the living bodies formed of, and how?

Explaining this matter a modern researcher, Dr. Yusuf 'Izz Uddeen says, "Most animals and plants are formed of a huge number of these tiny units which we call cells, just as a building is formed of stones laid next to one another."

b) Why are cells continually dividing?

Dr. Yusuf 'Izz Uddeen explains the secret behind the division of cells:

"The cells of our bodies and the bodies of other animals are always dividing. This division makes the body grow, or makes up for cells that have been lost or have died for various reasons. Each of these cells is basically formed from a wondrous substance called protoplasm.

The contents of each cell perform specific functions; among these contents are minute "bodies" which carry the genetic factors. These are called chromosomes.

The number of chromosomes in the cells of each species of animals and plants is fixed. The number of chromosomes in cats, for example, is different from the number in dogs or elephants or carrots or beans.

In each cell of the human body, the number of chromosomes is forty-six.

When a cell divides into two in our bodies, each cell must contain the same number of chromosomes, i.e., forty-six. If this number were distorted or changed, man would not be man. As we have mentioned, this division of cells happens continually, at all hours of the day, even when we are sleeping. Even now, we still do not know the real nature of the forces that control this amazing action of cell division. Science stops as describing the practical steps that have been observed through regular microscopes or electron microscopes which can magnify things far more than regular microscopes."

c) Why are reproductive cells different from other cells?

Dr. Yusuf says: "All the cells which are produced by cellular division in our bodies must contain forty-six chromosomes, apart from two types of cells, which are the reproductive cells, i.e., the male sperm and the female egg. When the tissue cells divide to produce these reproductive cells, they produce cells which do not contain forty-six chromosomes; instead, they contain half that number, so that each reproductive cell, whether male or female, contains twenty-three chromosomes."

Then he explains why this happens, and says:

"This happens for a great reason: the male cell (sperm) must join with the female cell (egg) to form the first cell in the body of the embryo, which we call the fertilized cell, where the twenty-three chromosomes in the male cell join the twenty-three chromosomes in the female cell, so that the number of chromosomes in the new cell is restored to the original number, forty-six chromosomes.

This fertilized cell which now contains forty-six chromosomes continues to divide, becoming two cells, then four, then eight, and so on, until the foetus is fully formed and emerges from its mother's womb. (The foetus) continues to grow by cell division until it becomes a fully-grown human being, with forty-six chromosomes in each of its cells, as in the cells of the bodies of its mother, father, grandparents and all other members of the human race."

"This halving of the number of chromosomes in the reproductive cells so that they can join together and restore the number to the original could never happen as the result of blind forces. It has to be the result of precise calculation on the part of a sublime power that knows what it is doing.

At the same time, this operation cannot be the result of trial and error. If only one mistake had happened at the beginning of creation, it would have dealt a final blow to the life form before the second generation had been created. This arrangement has to have been completed before the first foetus ever to appear was formed. Is this not sufficient evidence of the existence of a wise, capable and controlling higher power?"

d) Why do not brain cells divide?

The other type of cell that is unlike all the others is the brain cell which, unlike all other cells in the body, does not divide. Concerning the reason why it does not divide, Dr. Yusuf says:

"It could not have come about through trial and error that the only cells that do not divide are the nerve cells from which the brain and the rest of the nervous system are formed. If these cells were to divide like other cells, the results would be disastrous. In this case the brain cells would not be able to preserve a person's personality and all the features of his memory would disappear within a few hours.

The number of brain cells that are present in a person or animal does not increase even by one cell until the individual dies, whereas the red blood cells are cells which die and are replaced by new cells every hundred days or so. Red blood cells are manufactured in the bone marrow, then sent to join the flow of blood to take the place of cells that have died."

e) The reason why muscles in the body vary in strength.

On this topic Dr. Yusuf also says:

"The strongest muscles in the body of both humans and mammals are the muscles of the uterus in females, the muscles which push the foetus out of its mother's womb. If these muscles had not been so strong from the beginning of creation, the first newborn would never have emerged from its mother's womb.

The next strongest muscles after those of the uterus are the muscles of the jaw, and the muscles of the heart which must continue to work night and day to push the blood around the circulatory system for a period which may last for more than a hundred years. Similarly, the jaw muscles must remain able to bring the teeth together to chew tons of food over a lifetime."

ii) Resistance of living beings to destructive factors

Dr. Yusuf says:

"There is an important characteristic which is shared by all living beings from the most primitive to the most advanced. This characteristic is the resistance to destructive factors, because the Creator of all these beings wants them to survive.

The influenza virus changes shape from time to time, to make it harder to resist and destroy. Generation after generation of insects gains immunity to chemical insecticides, thus resisting destructive factors and extinction.

In the case of man, too, it has been noted that more babies are born during times of war, and that when women take birth control pills for an extended period, if they forget to take the pills for a few days, the result is often twins, to make up for the lack of offspring caused by the period of contraception. If a person loses one of his kidneys for some reason, the remaining kidney increases in size in order to do the work of two kidneys. It is as if the body realizes that something is missing and is trying to compensate for it.

Allah Alone is the One Who has provided these created beings with this wonderful ability to maintain the balance so that they are not exposed to the risk of extinction. He has also equipped many animals with the means of defending themselves. In this sense man is no different than scorpions, snakes, centipedes, etc.

This principle or law, to which all living beings are subject, could not have come about as the result of a blind accident. An accident cannot take the shape of a law that applies to all creatures."

iii) How Allah inspired the bee and the wonders of how Allah has created it

Ibn al-Qayyim[2] (may Allah have mercy on him) tells us about the wonders that Allah (ﷻ), has created in the universe. He tells us how Allah has guided the bee in the matters of its life: "The way in which the bee is guided is one of the most wondrous things. It has a leader and controller, the chief, which is bigger than all the other bees and more beautiful in colour and appearance.

The female bees give birth at the beginning of spring,[3] and most of the offspring are females. If a male is born they do not let him stay among them. Either they expel him or kill him, apart from a few, because the males do not do any work of value or earn a living.

---

[2] *Shifaa' al-'Aleel*, 101. What we quote here from Ibn al-Qayyim demonstrates that our righteous predecessors (*As-Salaf aṣ-Ṣaaliḥ*) used to ponder the creation of Allah. Although the observations of the Muslim scholars reached an advanced level, they are not free from errors, as bees do not have a king, but a queen.

[3] The only bee which lays eggs is the queen.

The bees are divided into groups, one of which stays with the king and never leaves him. Another group makes wax, which is made from the dregs of honey and is sweet like figs. The bees take great care of this, more than they do with the honey. They clean it and purify it from any contamination such as urine and the like. Another group builds the houses, another group brings water, carrying it on their backs. A third group sweeps the hive and cleans it of any dead bodies (of bees). If they see a slow, lazy bee, they kill it so that it cannot corrupt the other workers and infect them with its idleness and laziness.

The first thing to be built in the hive is the throne and house of the king. A raised house like a bed is built for him, and he sits there, with a group of bees like princes, servants and advisers around him, who never leave him. The bees make something like a trough in front of him, into which they pour the finest possible honey. They fill the trough with it, and this is the food of the king and his courtiers.

Then they start to build the houses in a straight line, like streets and shops. Their houses are regular six-sided shapes (hexagons), as if they have read the book of Euclid and know that this is the best shape for their houses, because what is needed when a house is built is a structure which is stable and spacious, and of all shapes, the hexagon takes on a round shape like a millstone when several of them are joined together. No holes or gaps are left, and the shapes support one another so that they form a single, solid layer, such that the point of a needle cannot be inserted between the houses.

Blessed be the One Who inspired the bee to build its houses in this solid, well-constructed manner which man cannot do. The bee knows that it needs to build its houses with two important qualities: the first is that the corners should not be so sharply-angled that this narrow space would be wasted, and the other is that the houses should be of such a shape that when they are joined together, no space is wasted.

The bee knows that the only shape which has these two qualities is the hexagon. Although triangles and squares could fill the space, their angles are too narrow. Other shapes may have wider angles, but they do not fill the space properly — they would leave gaps which would be a waste of space. The hexagon has these two qualities, so Allah guided the bee to build its houses in this shape, without any ruler or tools or example to follow. The most proficient of the sons of Adam would not be able to build a hexagonal house without the use of big tools.

Blessed be the One Who guided the bee to find its way to its "pasture" where it finds its food in an easy manner, without difficulty and without losing its way. It gathers the best of what it finds in the pasture, then comes back to its empty house and pours into it a drink of varying colour wherein is healing for men. Verily, in this is indeed a sign for people who think *(cf. Qur'an 16: 68-69).*

When it has finished building these houses, the bee goes out with an empty stomach, wandering in the plains and mountains, feeding on the nectar in the tops of flowers and tree leaves, and it comes back with a full stomach.

Allah (ﷻ), has created in its mouth a (kind of) heat which processes what it has collected and turns it into something sweet, then it brings it forth in the houses until they are full, then it seals them and covers the top with pure wax. When these houses are full, it goes to another place, if it finds a suitable site, and starts to build houses in it as it did with the first houses.

If it gets cold and the "pastures" are no longer available, and the bee cannot earn its living, it stays in its house and feeds on the stored honey. When it is earning its living, it goes out early and wanders in its pastures, and each group of bees does the work that it is designed to do. Then in the evening they go back to their houses.

The king only goes out of the hive on rare occasions when he wants to have fresh air. So he goes out, with his princes and servants, and goes around in the meadows and gardens for a while, then he goes back to his place.

One of the wonders of bees is that if someone offends the king, whether it is another bee, the owner of the hive or the person who is looking after the hive, he gets angry and leaves the hive and stays away from it. All the bees follow him, and the hive is left empty.

If their owner sees that and is afraid that the king may take all the bees away to another place, he plays a trick to bring the king back and make him happy. He tries to find out where he has taken the bees, which he can find out because all the bees are gathered around him. They never leave him, rather they gather around him until they look like a bunch of grapes. When the king goes out in anger, he settles in a high part of a tree, and the bees fly around him and join him, until they look like a ball. The owner of the bees takes a spear or a long stick, and puts a bunch of fragrant vegetation on his head, then he brings it near to where the king is. He has with him either a kind of tambourine or a reed, or some kind of musical instrument, which he starts to play, and he brings those (fragrant) plants near to him. He continues like that until the king is happy, and when he is happy and his anger has ceased, he jumps onto the plants, and his servants and all the other bees follow him, and their owner carries them back to the hive. Then he and his troops get down and go into the hive. Bees never feed on dead bodies, animals or food.

Another of the wonders of bees is that they kill corrupt and oppressive kings, and never obey them. The small, perfectly formed bees are the ones which make the honey, and they try to kill the long, useless bees and expel them from the hive. If they do that, the honey will be good. They try to kill the ones that they want to kill outside the hive, so as to protect the hive from (the contamination of) dead bodies.

There is a kind of bee that is of little use, with a large body. There is a war between these and the honey-makers. They try to get to them to kill them and destroy their houses, and get rid of them. The honey-makers are very alert and careful. If they are attacked in their houses, they try to push their attackers to the doors of their houses and make them fall into the honey, so that they will not be able to fly. So no one can escape them except the one who has a long life. When the war is over and everything has settled down, they go back to the ones that have been killed and throw them out of the hive.

Among the bees there are noble workers who are energetic and strive hard, and ignoble, lazy bees who are of little use and prefer not to do anything. The noble workers always try to expel these from the hive; they do not like to live with them lest the good bees follow in their footsteps and thus become corrupted.

The bee is one of the most refined and clean of animals, so it only defecates when flying. It dislikes rotten, putrid smells. The young, virgin bees strive harder than the older ones; they sting less and make better honey. When they do sting, it is less harmful than the sting of older bees.

Because the bee is one of the most useful and most blessed of insects, it was singled out to be inspired by its Lord unlike other animals, and the product of its stomach has been made a healing for sickness and a light which shines in the darkness. Hence the bee in relation to other animals is like those who are guided in relation to the rest of mankind. The bee has more enemies than other animals and its enemies are the least useful and least blessed of animals. This is the way of Allah with His creation, and He is the Almighty, Most Wise."[4]

---

[4] *Shifaa' al-'Aleel*, Pp. 101.

Contemporary scientists describe the world of the bee [5]

Science has advanced nowadays, telling us much about the wonders of creation and the mysteries of the universe. The scientists have confirmed for us that which we already knew about bees being divided into three groups: the queen bee, the male bees and the worker bees.

The queen bee is the mother of the whole hive; all the bees in the hive are her children. The queen bee lays between 1500 and 2000 eggs each day with the sun rise; the number may even reach 3500. This continues throughout the reproductive season, which starts in early spring and ends in late summer.

The huge number of eggs serves to make up for the continual shortfall which happens to bees. For the bee's lifespan is short, lasting 5-7 weeks. Hence the hive needs new generations in large numbers to support the hive and to make up for the continual shortfall, so that the hive will continue to provide the necessities of the bee's world and protect the bees from enemies and danger, otherwise the hive would cease to exist.

One of the wonders of the way in which Allah has created the bee is that the queen bee lays her eggs in houses built by the workers in different sizes. The largest houses are prepared for future queens, and the eggs which are laid in these houses will become queens. The eggs which the queen lays in the smaller houses, which are 1/4 of an inch across, will become male bees, and the eggs that are laid in the small houses which are 5 inches across will become worker bees. It remains for us to note that the queen bee deposits three or four sperms with the worker eggs so that the eggs will be fertilized and will become

---

[5] The information given here is adapted from the book *An-Naḥlah tusabbiḥ Allah*, by Muhammad Ḥasan Ḥomṣi.

worker bees, whilst she lays unfertilized eggs in the houses of male bees.

Another of the wonders of the way in which Allah has created the bee is that it does not mate except in the air when it is flying. There is a reason for this. The male bee cannot mate with the queen when she is sitting on the ground, because the male organ remains latent and invisible and can only emerge when it is soaring in the air, when air-sacs that exist in the male bee fill with air, exerting pressure on the male member, which then emerges.

One of the wonders of the way in which Allah has created the virgin queen bee is that she is able to call the male to mate with her, by making sounds which attract the male. She comes out of the hive and hovers around it, issuing these sounds, which are heard not only by the males in her hive, but in all the neighbouring hives. So groups of males come out and follow the queen, who keeps flying fast in the huge space; the strongest and fastest male is the one who gets to mate with her, but he loses his life in the process, because after mating he loses his male organ, which stays in the queen, and this results in his bleeding to death.

The reader may ask how the males hear the queen's call. The answer is that Allah has equipped all bees with sensory antennae, consisting of connected rings, twelve in males, and eleven in workers and queens consisting a number of holes.

The number of holes in the sensory antennae of the male is 2800, in the worker it is 2400 and in the queen it is 1600.

The sensory antennae of bees work like a radio antenna; they are used to detect the sound made by the queen, and other sounds. They are also used to smell, hear and feel.

If a bee — worker, male or queen — loses its antennae, it cannot fulfil its role, because most of its senses — hearing, smell and touch — are concentrated in the antennae, as stated above.

The formation of the male bee suits the role for which it has been created. It is large and strong, it eats a lot and it does not do anything. It does not gather nectar, or make it, or build, or guard the hive. Even its food is placed in its mouth by the workers. All that it is able to do is to fertilize the queen. Therefore after it has played its role, the worker bees stop feeding it. They rather, attack the male members and kill or expel them.

We should also note that the number of males is small in relation to the total number of bees; there are no more than two hundred males in a hive.

The worker bees form the largest number in the hive, and are the active element in it. They are the ones that perform various tasks and difficult missions.

They are the ones that collect nectar, gather pollen, make honey, prepare the queen's special food, build the honeycomb in which the honey is kept, raise the new generations of bees, guard the hive, keep it clean, maintain it and even ventilate and heat it.

The various tasks in the hive are distributed as specialized tasks, and these specialized tasks are connected to the age of the bee. At every stage in the bee's life there is a task which it does, and the longer a bee lives, the more tasks she does in turn. Thus when a bee has completed her lifespan, she will have done all the tasks required for the upkeep of the hive. We may note that the bee starts with easy tasks which do not require a great effort, and ends with the most difficult task, which is going about in the fields to gather nectar and pollen and water, then making and storing honey. We may also note that the tasks become progressively more difficult according to the characteristics that Allah (ﷻ), has bestowed upon the bee. Each task that the bee does is suited to the physical characteristics enabling her to play the new role and do the new task.

During the first two days of her life, the worker bee cleans the houses from which the newly-hatched bees have emerged. She cleans these houses and prepares them for the next generation. The queen will not lay eggs in these houses until she has inspected them and found them to be perfectly clean.

On the third and fourth days, she takes care of the young worker and male bees which are older than three days, bringing to them something which the scientists call "bee's bread," a mixture of honey and pollen, which she takes from what the bees have stored in the hexagonal cells (of the hive).

From the fifth day to the twelfth day, she works to feed the queen bee with the royal food which the latter eats all her life. This special food is also fed to the small worker and male bees during the first three days of their lives. The bees do this particular task at this age (5-12 days) because of the emergence at that time of special glands on both sides of the oesophagus, which enable the bee to manufacture the royal food.

After the twelfth day, the bee is able to fly, but she does not go far. All that she does is learn and practise. Her main task from day 12 to day 18 is to build the wax honeycomb which is prepared for storing honey, and raising the new generation of bees.

The reason why the bee performs this task at this stage in its life is because it grows four pairs of glands on the rings of its abdomen, and from this wax, by using its jaws, the bee at this age builds these houses which are so perfectly constructed with precise dimensions and geometrical shapes of the utmost beauty and order.

On the nineteenth and twentieth days, the bee cleans and guards the hive. After the twentieth day, she goes out to the fields and gathers nectar and pollen, and makes honey, and brings water to the hive. This final stage forms the largest part of the bee's life cycle.

Generations of bees come and go, and the bees progress through this sequence of tasks which ensures that all jobs are done continually, without allocating groups of bees to do one task all their life; each stage of life has its own specialty.

Glory be to the One, the Only, the Unique, the Self-Sufficient Master, Who has created these small beings, and taught them to do these tasks with such precision. This beauty and wonder point to the existence of the All-Knowing, All-Aware.

Among the wonders of the way in which Allah has formed the bee is that He has given it two stomachs, one of which it uses to collect all the raw materials derived from the nectar of flowers, or to carry water, and bring it to the hive, and the other it uses only for its own food, to digest it and be nourished by it.

Another of the wonders of the bee is that when it collects in its first stomach all the nectar that it gathers, it does not simply transport it; whilst it is bringing it to the hive, it performs the preliminary process required to turn it into honey, by producing the yeast that is required for this process.

The bee needs pollen for a variety of purposes in the hive. Its Creator has equipped it with special hollow pouches, called pollen sacs, for storing this pollen, on the outside of its hind legs. He (Allah) has given it something that looks like brushes on the inside ankle of its hind legs, which the bee uses to sweep up the pollen and collect it in the pollen sacs.

Another of the amazing features that the scientists have discovered in bees is the gland in the bee's back which the scientists call Nasanov's gland. This gland produces a special scent, and amazingly the bees of each hive have their own scent which distinguishes them from the bees of other hives. A bee can return to its own home from far away by following this unique scent which is distinct from the scent of other bees. The doorkeepers and guards of the hive recognize the bees which belong to their hive by the distinctive scent emitted by the bee.

What is amazing is that bees are able to agree upon a new scent if there is a reason for doing so. For example, when a group of bees set out to form a new hive, the members of the new hive agree upon by a new scent. By way of experiment, scientists mixed one group of bees with another, and found that after the bees had mixed, they agreed upon one new scent that distinguished them from others.

Another of the wonders of bees is that they build six-sided houses of pure wax which are completely airtight. But when they seal the doors of the houses which contain the larvae, they mix the wax with pollen, which allows air in through the grains of pollen, so the larvae stay alive. If their Lord did not inspire them to do this, the larvae would die and the bees would become extinct and vanish from the face of the earth.

Our Lord has told us about the things we have mentioned here, in eloquent *aayaat* (verses) which invite us to think about and ponder the wondrous way in which He (ﷻ), has guided the bee:

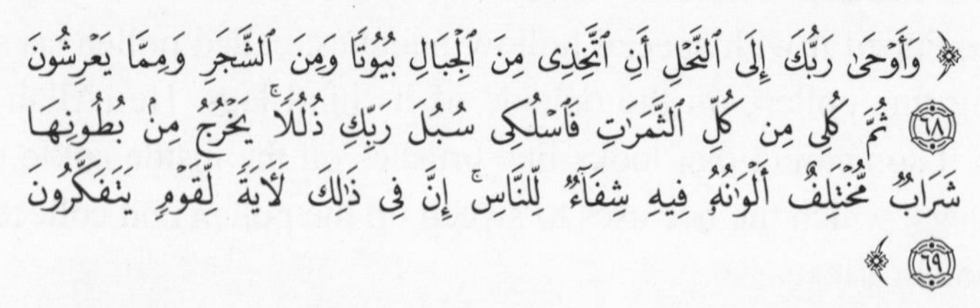

﴾And your Lord inspired the bee, saying: ‘Take you habitations in the mountains and in the trees and in what

> they erect. Then, eat of all fruits, and follow the ways of your Lord made easy [for you].' There comes forth from their bellies, a drink of varying colour wherein is healing for men. Verily, in this is indeed a sign for people who think.﴿ *(Qur'an 16: 68-69)*

The Muslims were guided to the great benefits that exist in honey, but those who have gone astray from the guidance of Allah have only recently discovered the benefits in it. Researchers have discovered amazing facts. They have found out that honey is both food and medicine. It is a high quality food that contains features that can hardly be found elsewhere, and it is a medicine which can be used to treat almost all diseases. Science is still discovering new benefits in honey every day.

How do bees tell one another where food is?

One of the things noted by contemporary scientists is the way in which bees tell one another where food is to be found. Dr. Yusuf 'Izz Uddeen says:

"If one of the worker bees discovers a field or a certain amount of vegetation which it thinks is a source of food, it goes back to the colony to tell the rest of the workers about the treasure that it has found. It does this by performing a ritual dance which it does by instinct, without knowing why it does so.

This strange dance has a certain significance, during which its body makes angles which refer to the angle of the sun. If the field that the bee has discovered is near to the colony, the dance in this case is different from the dance which it performs if the field is further away.

From these dances, the bees know that the field of clover or other flowering plants from which they gather their food, is a certain distance away, and that they have to travel at a certain angle in relation to the position of the sun in order to get there.

Then some of the workers will perform the same dance, from which the bee which discovered the field will be sure that the other bees have understood what she was trying to tell them. Then the other bees will fly off and head directly for the field, to gather more food. The bee which made the discovery conveys a number of pieces of information to the other bees in the colony by her dance. If we humans tried to match the bee's achievement in understanding these mysteries by drawing diagrams, it would take us no less than twenty minutes, if we had sufficient understanding of mathematics. But the bee understands that in an instant, and flies directly to the field in a straight line to get what it needs of food.

This is an amazing thing which we cannot explain unless we believe in the existence of Divine inspiration whereby the Creator of these small beings which are not able to think or reason, has enabled them to do what they need."

The bee sees a colour that we do not see

Dr. Yusuf also tells us that another of the bee's wonders is that it is able to see "a colour which we humans are unable to see or imagine. This colour is ultra-violet, which we see as black, so the bee is able to see ultra-violet rays." Then he explains to us the reason behind the bee's ability to see this colour:

"The reason for that is that these rays are the only ones which are able to penetrate clouds.

Bees may live in areas where there is cloud cover for much of the year, and it is essential for them to see the sun in order to know the way to the fields where their food is. This is the reason why bees are able to see this ultra-violet colour: this enables them to see the sun through the clouds, so they do not die of hunger when the sun is hidden behind the clouds. This is a wondrous fact which indicates that there is a Creator Who controls and decrees and know what He is doing, and that the ability to see this colour could not have been acquired by bees with the passage of time. It has to have been present from the very moment that Allah created bees, otherwise bees would have become extinct in those (cloudy) areas a long time ago."

iv) How Allah guides the ant and the wonders of its creation

Ibn al-Qayyim tells us of another of Allah's creatures, and explains to us how Allah (ﷻ), has guided it in the way in which it lives:

"The ant is one of the most guided of creatures, and the way in which it is guided is most wondrous. The tiny ant comes out of its home and looks for its food, even if it is far away. When it finds it, it carries it and drags it through winding paths, uphill and downhill, no matter how difficult the route, until it brings it back to its home, where it stores its food when possible.

When it has stored it, it goes to the things that can grow and splits them into two so that they will not grow. If they grow even after being split into two, it then splits them into four. If (the stored food) gets wet and the ant is afraid that it may go rotten, it waits for a sunny day, then it brings the food out and spreads it out by the entrance to its house, then it puts it back, and no ant eats the food that another has collected.

In order to know how Allah (ﷻ), has guided the ant, it is sufficient for us to know what Allah has said in the Qur'an about the ant which Sulaymaan (Solomon) (عليه السلام) (may peace be upon him) heard speaking to its companions and saying,

﴿... يَٰٓأَيُّهَا ٱلنَّمْلُ ٱدْخُلُوا۟ مَسَٰكِنَكُمْ لَا يَحْطِمَنَّكُمْ سُلَيْمَٰنُ وَجُنُودُهُۥ وَهُمْ لَا يَشْعُرُونَ ۝١٨﴾

﴾..."O' ants! Enter your dwellings, lest Sulaymaan and his hosts should crush you, while they perceive not."﴿

(Qur'an 27: 18)

The ant started by calling out in a manner that would be heard by those whom she was addressing, then she mentioned the ants in general terms because she was addressing them as a whole. Then she told them to enter their dwellings and protect themselves from the army, and told them why they should go in, which was because she was afraid that the army would step on them and that Sulaymaan and his army would crush them. Then she excused the Prophet of Allah and his army by noting that they would not realize that. This is amazing guidance.

Think about how Allah (ﷻ), speaks highly of the ant when He says:

﴿ وَحُشِرَ لِسُلَيْمَٰنَ جُنُودُهُۥ مِنَ ٱلْجِنِّ وَٱلْإِنسِ وَٱلطَّيْرِ فَهُمْ يُوزَعُونَ ﴿١٧﴾ ﴾

> ﴿And there were gathered before Sulaymaan [Solomon] his hosts of jinn and men, and birds, and they all were set in battle order [marching forward].﴾ *(Qur'an 27: 17)*

Then He (ﷻ) says:

﴿ حَتَّىٰٓ إِذَآ أَتَوْا۟ عَلَىٰ وَادِ ٱلنَّمْلِ ... ﴿١٨﴾ ﴾

> ﴿Till, when they came to the valley of the ants...﴾ *(Qur'an 27: 18)*

Allah tells us that they all passed through this valley, and that this valley was known for its ants, as *Wadi as-Sibaa'* (valley of the wild animals) (was known for its wildlife) etc. Then Allah tells us something which indicates how clever and precise this ant was, because she told the other ants to go into their homes. She and the other ants knew that each group of them had its own home which others would not enter. Then she said: ﴿...Lest Sulaymaan [Solomon] and his hosts should crush you...﴾ *(Qur'an 27: 18)*. So she both referred to him by name and acknowledged who he was; she knew that they were his troops and he was their leader. Then she said: ﴿...while they perceive not...﴾ *(Qur'an 27: 18)*. It is as if she both excused the army for not realizing the harm that they caused, whilst blaming the ants for not taking precautions and entering their homes. For this reason the Prophet of Allah smiled at what she said, because it was appropriate to smile in amazement at this point.

Az-Zuhri narrated from ‘Abdullah ibn ‘Abdullah ibn ‘Uyaynah from Ibn ‘Abbaas that the Messenger of Allah (ﷺ),

> “forbade the killing of ants, bees, hoopoes and hawks.”[6]

Muslim narrated from Abu Hurayrah (رضي الله عنه) that the Prophet (ﷺ) said:

> “One of the Prophets stopped beneath a tree, and an ant bit him. He ordered that his luggage should be taken away and that the ant’s village (nest) should be burned. Then Allah revealed to him: one ant bit you and you burned an entire community of ants who glorify (their Lord)! Was not one ant enough?”[7]

‘Awf ibn Abi Jameelah narrated that Qusaamah ibn Zuhayr said: Abu Moosa al-Ash‘ari narrated: ‘Everything has a leader, even ants have leaders.’

Among the wonders of the way in which ants are guided is that the ant knows that its Lord is above the heavens on His Throne. Imam Aḥmad narrated in *Kitaab az-Zuhd* from Abu Hurayrah, (رضي الله عنه) who attributed it to the Prophet (ﷺ):

> “One of the Prophets went out with the people to pray for rain, and they saw an ant raising its legs to heaven, praying lying on its back. He said: ‘Go back, for

---

[6] Attributed by Al-Majd ibn Taymiyah in *Al-Muntaqa*, Pp. 759, to Aḥmad, Abu Dawood and Ibn Maajah with the wording: “The Messenger of Allah forbade the killing of four (creatures): ants, bees, hoopoes and hawks.”

[7] Bukhari: 6/154, hadith no. 3019; 6/356, hadith no. 3318. Muslim: 4/1759, hadith no. 2241. The hadith is taken from the collection of reports narrated there.

> someone else has sufficed for you, or has ensured that you will be granted rain.'"

There are a number of isnads for this report, which is also narrated by Aṭ-Ṭaḥaawi in *At-Tahdheeb*, and by others.

In *Musnad al-Imam Aḥmad* it says that Sulaymaan ibn Dawood went out to pray for rain, and he saw an ant lying on its back, raising its legs towards the heavens and saying, "O' Allah, we are part of Your creation, and we cannot do without Your rain and Your provision. Either send us rain and provision or let us die. He (Sulaymaan) said: Go back, for you will be given rain by the *du'aa'* of someone else."

I was told about an ant which came out of its home and found part of a locust's body. It tried to carry it but was not able, so it went and brought others to help carry it. I (the person who told this story) picked it up, and the ant walked around in the place where it had been, and did not find it. The other ants went away and left the first ant. Then I put the locust down, and the ant tried to carry it and could not, so she went to bring the others back. I picked it up, and the ant walked around in the place where it had been, and did not find it, so the others went away. I did this several times, and the last time I did it, the ants made a circle around the first ant and tore it apart. I told this story to our *shaykh* and he said: Allah has created these ants in such a way that they hate lies and punish liars.

The ant is one of the most careful of creatures whose caution is proverbial. It is mentioned that when Sulaymaan (Solomon) saw how cautious the ant was and how careful it was to store food, he brought out an ant and asked it how much an ant eats each year? It said, three grains of wheat. So he ordered that the ant should be placed in a bottle, and be given three grains of wheat, and the bottle should be sealed and be left there for a year. When the year had passed, he commanded that the bottle should be opened, and he found one and a half grains of wheat left. He said, Did you not claim that you needed three grains of wheat per year?

The ant said, Yes, but when I saw that you were busy with the affairs of your own kind, I thought of how much of my life was left, and I realized that it was longer than the time that you had allocated for me, so I limited myself to eating half of the food, and I left half in order to ensure my survival. Sulaymaan was impressed by how cautious the ant was, which was part of the guidance given to it.

This caution makes the ant strive hard all summer, gathering food for the winter, because it knows that it will be difficult to find anything during the winter. Although the ant is small, it is very strong and is able to carry many more times more than its own body weight, and drag it to its home.

Ants do not have a leader who is in charge, as is the case with bees, but they do have scouts who look for food. If the scout finds something, it tells its companions, who all come out. Each ant works hard for the good of all, without stealing any grain to keep for itself.

Among the wonders of the ant is that if a man wants to prevent ants from falling into honey etc., if he digs a hole and surrounds it with water or fills a large vessel with water, and puts that thing (honey or whatever) in it, then an ant comes and cannot get to it, it will try to climb a wall and walk across the ceiling until it is above the thing, then it will drop down onto it. We ourselves have tried this.

A craftsman once heated a ring in the fire, then threw it on the floor to cool off. It so happened that some ants were trapped in the middle of the ring. The ants tried in all directions to get out, but the heat pushed them back. So they stayed in the middle of the ring, precisely in the centre, which was the furthest point from the circumference.[8]

---

[8] *Shifaa' al-'Aleel*, by Ibn al-Qayyim, Pp. 104.

The white ant (termite): its food and habitation

Professor Yusuf 'Izz Uddeen tells us about what science has discovered about the mysteries of this creature:

"Among the instincts that Allah, the Almighty, has given to such tiny creatures are amazing things which make every thinking person fall down in prostration to the Mighty Creator.

For example, let us look at a colony of the kind of insects that are known as 'white ants' (termites). These insects also live in colonies, and when the number of individuals in the colony is too much in proportion to the amount of food available, they know this instinctively, so they start to eat a large number of their eggs. This solves both the problem of overpopulation and the problem of food shortages, because eating the eggs provides some nourishment and at the same time reducing the numbers of offspring.

These insects do not know why they do this; it is divine inspiration which makes them do things which they cannot understand, but which are of benefit to them and help them to avoid extinction.

These insects themselves feed on wood, which they devour avidly. In some places which are infested with termites, a family may eat their food at the table, then the following morning they go to eat their breakfast, and they find that the legs of the table have collapsed in a single night.

In some areas of Australia which are infested with this destructive insect, tourists have been known to ask the name of a village which they can see in the distance from the train in which they are travelling; they are astounded when they are told that no people live in that village, and that these are the dwellings of white ants.

These dwellings may be several meters tall, and they are made from a strange substance which is a mixture of the termites' saliva and other things. It is stronger than reinforced concrete, and the walls cannot be penetrated by insects or by water. Inside these dwellings is a network of tunnels in which the white ants live.

These ants use a kind of code like Morse code to communicate from afar. One ant taps its head on the wall of the tunnel a certain number of times, and the other ants understand what it is trying to say from these coded taps. They do that without knowing what they are doing; they do it because of the divine inspiration which is called instinct.

The scientists were confused for a long time about how these insects could live by eating wood, because wood does not contain any digestible organic substances, but finally they discovered the secret. In the digestive tracts of this insect, they discovered tiny, primitive, one-celled animals which secrete a substance which turns wood into easily-digested material, and this nourishes the termite.

It is amazing indeed that there are no termites whose digestive tracts are free of these primitive creatures. If these creatures had not existed in the digestive tracts of termites from the very beginning they would not have been able to survive, and they would have become extinct in the first generation. Could this have happened by accident or is it something that has been planned and decreed [by Allah (ﷻ)]?"

Ants keep flocks and plow the soil

Among the wonders of the ant is that which has been mentioned by Dr. Yusuf 'Izz Uddeen, who says that ants have tamed hundreds of kinds of creatures which are inferior to themselves, whilst man has tamed only about twenty kinds of wild animals which he has subjugated for his own benefit. Ants know how to farm and care for their "flocks" by instinct.

The insects called aphids, which we see on the leaves of some plants, are tended by ants who gain some benefits from them. In early spring, the ants send out scouts to gather the eggs of these aphids. They bring the eggs to the colony and keep them in the same place where they keep their own eggs, and take care of them just as they take care of their own. When the eggs hatch, they feed the small aphids and take care of them. After a short while, the aphids start to excrete a substance which is sweet like honey, just as cows excrete milk. The ants "milk" the aphids for this substance, just as if they were cows.

Ants do not only care for these "flocks," they also engage in farming and plowing the soil. One of the scientists noticed a piece of land in a forest where a semi-wild kind of short-grain rice was growing. This plot of land measured five feet by three feet, and the rice was growing nearly six centimeters tall. It seemed to the observer that there should be someone taking care of this piece of land, for the soil around the roots was well-tilled and the weeds had been uprooted. Strangely enough, there were no other rice plants growing nearby. This rice had not planted itself there - someone was tending it.

It was noted that groups of ants were coming and going from this plot of land. The scientist lay on his stomach on the ground, and watched what they were doing. It was not long before he realized that these ants were the ones who were tending the rice in that piece of land. They had taken it upon themselves to "farm" that land, where they worked all the time. Some of them tilled and plowed the land, whilst others uprooted the weeds. If any shoots of other kinds of plants showed themselves, some of the ants would go to them and cut them, then carry them far away from the "farm."

The rice grew until it reached a height of sixty centimeters and the grains of rice had matured. When the "harvest season" began, a line of worker ants was seen to come non-stop to the stems of rice, which they climbed until they reached the grains. Then each worker ant would take a grain of rice and quickly bring it down to the ground, then take it to their underground stores.

What is amazing is that one group of ants would climb the stem, pick up the grains and throw them down, then other ants would take the grains to the stores.

This kind of ant lives a civil life in houses like ours, with chambers and stories, parts of which are below ground and others above ground. In these cities we find servants and slaves.

What is more amazing is that they have nurses who tend the sick night and day, and others who take away the dead bodies of ants which have died...

They do all this kind of work without thinking. It happens by instinct, which Allah (سُبْحَانَهُ وَتَعَالَىٰ), has instilled in their tiny bodies.

v) How Allah guides the hoopoe, and the wonders of its creation

Ibn al-Qayyim tells us, in his eloquent manner, of another of Allah's creatures which is mentioned in the Book of Allah, the hoopoe. Ibn al-Qayyim speaks of how Allah (سُبْحَانَهُ وَتَعَالَىٰ), guides and inspires it:

"The hoopoe is one of the most guided of animals, and the most able to see where water is located beneath the ground, which others cannot see. One of the ways in which it is guided is what Allah tells us in the Qur'an, where He tells us what the hoopoe said to the Prophet of Allah Sulaymaan (Solomon) (عَلَيْهِ السَّلَامُ), who had threatened him when he could not find him. When the hoopoe came, he immediately gave his excuse, before Sulaymaan could threaten him with the punishment. He addressed him in a manner that encouraged him to listen and accept what he said. He said:

﴿... فَقَالَ أَحَطتُ بِمَا لَمْ تُحِطْ بِهِۦ ... ﴿٢٢﴾﴾

﴾...'I have grasped [the knowledge of a thing] which you have not grasped...'﴿ *(Qur'an 27: 22)*,

— which implied: I have brought you (news of) something which I know very well, and it is important and serious. Hence he said:

﴿... وَجِئْتُكَ مِن سَبَإٍ بِنَبَإٍ يَقِينٍ ﴿٢٢﴾﴾

﴾...And I have come to you from Saba' [Sheba] with true news.﴿ *(Qur'an 27: 22).*

This was important news, which was worth knowing. Then he described it as true news, with no element of doubt. This was his preamble to his telling the Prophet of Allah the news, so that he would forget everything else and focus only on this news. It made him eager to hear it and find out what it was. This is an eloquent way of introducing something and making people listen.

Then he (hoopoe - *hud hud*) started to tell him the news in an affirmative manner, and said:

﴿إِنِّي وَجَدتُّ ٱمْرَأَةً تَمْلِكُهُمْ ... ﴿٢٣﴾﴾

﴾I found a woman ruling over them...﴿ *(Qur'an 27: 23).*

Then he described the status of that queen, and that she was one of the greatest monarchs because she had been given everything that is fit for rulers. Then he added further detail of her high status by describing the throne on which she sat, which was a mighty throne. Then he told him why he should go and deal with these people and attack them in their own land after calling them to Allah. He said:

﴿وَجَدتُّهَا وَقَوْمَهَا يَسْجُدُونَ لِلشَّمْسِ مِن دُونِ ٱللَّهِ ... ﴿٢٤﴾﴾

﴾I found her and her people worshipping the sun instead of Allah,...﴿ *(Qur'an 27: 24).*

The conjunction *wa* ("and") is omitted here; this sentence is made independent and is not connected to the previous sentence, in order to indicate that this is the main point and that what was said before was merely an introduction. Then he pointed out what had tempted and motivated them to do that, which was the way in which the *Shayṭaan* (Satan) had made their deeds fair-seeing to them and had barred them from the right way, prostrate to Allah Alone, for none is deserving of prostration except Him.

Then he mentioned that one of the things which Allah (ﷻ) does is to bring to light what is hidden in the heavens and the earth, i.e., things which are concealed such as rain, plants, minerals and other kinds of things that come down from the sky or come forth from the earth. When the hoopoe mentioned that Allah Alone does these things, he was also referring to the special talent which Allah (ﷻ) had bestowed upon him, which was the ability to detect water below the ground.

The author of *Al-Kashshaaf* said: The phrase 'bringing to light what is hidden' indicates that this is part of what the hoopoe said, because of his skill in knowing where water is hidden beneath the ground, which is due to the inspiration of the One Who brings to light what is hidden in the heavens and the earth, Glorified be He. The one who has insight and is guided by the light of Allah can hardly miss the fact that each person is influenced by his particular craft or branch of knowledge, which affects the way he speaks and thinks. No human does any kind of work, but Allah clothes him in the dress of that work (i.e., it shows in his features and characteristics)."

vi) How pigeons are guided, and the wonders of their creation

When Ibn al-Qayyim describes the wonders of the pigeon's creation and how Allah (ﷻ), inspires it, he speaks at length in the most fascinating manner, which indicates that pondering Allah's creation is a method which the scholars take upon themselves in order to fulfil Allah's command to His slaves.

Concerning this Ibn al-Qayyim said:

“The pigeon is one of the most amazingly guided animals. Ash-Shaafa‘i said: the wisest of birds is the pigeon, and the carrier pigeon is the one which brings messages and letters and may be worth more than a slave, for the service that it provides cannot be carried out by slaves, or by any other kinds of creature. It travels huge distances and brings news and other things which states and kingdoms need.

Those who care for and breed pigeons pay a great deal of attention to their bloodlines. They separate males and females during the mating season, taking the males to different females and vice versa, and fearing that their bloodlines may become corrupted. They are always afraid that the females may attract males of the common type of pigeon, thus corrupting the bloodline. Those who care for pigeons do not pay as much attention to the conduct of their own womenfolk or take as many precautions to protect them as they do for their pigeons.

Their carers have rules and methods to which they pay a great deal of attention, so that if a pigeon suddenly lands, there will be no mystery as to its pedigree and country of origin. They respect the person who has experience and knowledge in this field, and they treat him very generously indeed.

Only males are selected for carrying letters and messages, and they say that he longs more for his home because his mate is there, and he is physically stronger and has a better sense of direction. Others prefer females for this task, and say that if a male is kept away for too long, he will long for a mate, so he might see a female on his route and not be able to keep away from her, so he will forget about travelling and will want to stay with his new mate.

Pigeons can be trained, and they are regarded as a good omen and are used to people. They like people and people like them. When they get used to a place, they will stay there and remain loyal to their owner, even if he mistreats them. They will return there from long distances, and if they are prevented from doing so, they will remain loyal even if ten years have passed since they left their homeland, and as soon as the opportunity arises and they are able to do so, they will return.

When the male pigeon wants to mate, he approaches the female with the utmost gentleness. Once he realizes that the female may have conceived, he and his mate look for straw, grass and small twigs, with which they build a nest, by weaving together these materials. They give the nest a raised edge, so that the eggs will not roll out, and so it will provide a safe place for the young. Then they take turns sitting on the nest, to keep it warm and to replace its original smell with a new, pleasant smell which is derived from their own bodies and scents, so that when the eggs are laid they will be in a place that is similar to the womb, and there will be the right balance between heat and cold, softness and hardness.

Then when "labour" starts, the bird hastens to that place (the nest) and lays its eggs in it. If it is startled by thunder, it throws the egg out of the nest that it has prepared, just like when a woman miscarries out of fright.

When the eggs are laid, the pair keep on taking turns sitting on the nest, until the time for brooding is over and the chick starts to break out of the egg. The parents help it to emerge, then they blow air into its throat so that its crop will become bigger, because they know that the crop is too small for food until it has been widened in this manner.

But they also know that even after the crop has been widened, it is still too small for food, so they feed it with saliva mixed with food, which has a strong taste.

They also know that the crop cannot continually take in food, and that it needs to gain strength, so they pick up soft grains from ponds and feed them to the chick, then they move on to giving it stronger food.

They keep on feeding it with grains and water in stages, according to the chick's strength, and demands food from them, until they know that he is able to pick up food by itself. Then they gradually stop feeding it so that he gets used to picking up food. When they know that its lungs have developed and grown strong, they wean it so that it can fend for himself, and they hit it if it asks for food after that.

Then they no longer feel that amazing compassion, once they know that it is able to fend by itself.

Among the wonders of the way in which the pigeon is inspired is that when it is carrying a message, it follows remote routes, far from cities where people are to be found, so that no one will be able to detain it. It does not look for water among people, rather it seeks out water where people do not go.

Male and female pigeons share out their duties towards the chicks. Caring for and raising the chick is done by the female, and bringing food and feeding it to the chick are done by the male. The father is the head of the family who provides for them, and the mother is the one who gives birth and nurses the young.

Among the wonders of pigeons is that which was mentioned by Al-Jaaḥiẓ, who said: a man had a pair of pigeons whose wings had been clipped, and another pair which could fly. The pair which could fly had chicks. He said: I made a hole for them at the top of their coop so that they could go out and come in and feed their chicks. I was detained unexpectedly by some government officials, and I became very concerned about the birds whose wings were clipped. I was certain that they would have died, because they could not get out of the hole, and they had nothing to eat or drink. When I was let go, I did not care about anything except (these birds). I opened the door and found that the chicks had matured, and the pair with clipped wings were in the best of health. I was amazed. It was not long before the pair who could fly came back and came to the pair who could not fly; the latter were asking for food like chicks, and the former fed them.

Look at the way they are guided. The pair who could not fly saw how the chicks asked their parents for food when they became hungry and thirsty, so they did the same as the chicks did. The pair who could fly took pity on them and fed them as they fed their own chicks.

Another amazing thing about pigeons is that when they are flying and they see people from the air, they know which type of people they want to go to, and they know which is the opposite type. When pigeons first begin to fly, they are heedless and they will fly among vultures, eagles, falcons, crows and hawks, and they know which ones will pursue them and which will not. But if a pigeon sees an Indian falcon (*shaheen*), it is as if it has seen a lethal poison; it starts to panic like a sheep when it sees a wolf, or a donkey when it sees a lion.

More about the wonders of Allah's creation

Ibn al-Qayyim also tells us about other wonders of Allah's creation and how He inspires His creatures which the scholars of his time had noted, such as the following:

vii) A dog which nursed a child whose family had died

Al-Jaaḥiẓ said: When the plague had killed the members of a household, the people of that area were certain that no one was left alive among them, so they went and sealed the door of the house. But there was an infant boy left who was still suckling, and they overlooked him. After a while, some of the heirs went to that house and opened the door. When they entered the middle of the house, they were astounded to see a young boy playing with some pups belonging to the dog that had lived with the family. It was not long before they saw the dog that had belonged to the family. When the child saw her, he crawled over to her and she let him suckle from her.

When the child had gotten hungry and had seen the pups suckling, he had crawled over to them. The mother dog had taken pity on him and let him suckle, and when she had done that once, she continued to let him suckle, and he had kept asking for it.

viii) The whistling bird kills the viper

Ibn al-A'raabi said that a snake ate the eggs of a whistling bird, and the bird started screeching and flying at the snake's head, until the snake opened its mouth. Then the bird threw a fish spine into its mouth, and it stuck in the snake's throat until it died.

ix) The cunning of the fox

Among the amazing features of the fox is that when it gets infested with fleas, it takes a piece of wool in its mouth then goes to some shallow water, where it submerges itself gradually until the fleas jump onto that piece of wool. Then it lets the wool go and comes out of the water.

Another of its amazing features is that once a wolf ate the young of a fox, and the wolf also had young. There was an enclosed place like a pitfall nearby, so the fox went there and dug a tunnel to get out, then it went to the wolf and killed its young, then sat down and waited for him. When the wolf came back and realized that it was the fox that had done this, he started to chase him. The fox threw himself into that pitfall, then escaped through the tunnel. The wolf threw himself in after him, but he could not find him and he could not escape. Then the people who lived nearby came and killed him.

Once there was a man who had two chickens. The fox hid from him and snatched one, then ran away. Then he thought about how he could get the other chicken. He presented himself to the man from a distance, with something in his mouth that looked like a bird. By dropping it and running away, he made the man think it was his chicken. When the man rushed towards it, the fox doubled back and took the other chicken, then ran away.

Once a fox came to an island on which there were birds, and he tried hard to catch one of them, but he could not. Then he went and brought a bunch of grass which he threw into the water which was flowing towards the island, and the birds were afraid of it, but when they realized that it was only grass, they settled down again. The fox did this again, a second time, and a third and a fourth, until the birds got used to it. Then he brought a bigger bunch of grass and hid in it, and went over to where the birds were. The birds were sure that it was the same as the previous bunches of grass, so they did not fly away from it. Then the fox pounced on a bird and devoured it.

When the fox is starving, its body swells up, then it goes and throws itself down in the desert, as if it is dead. Birds come to see what it is, and it appears to be neither moving nor breathing. The birds are sure that it is dead, and when they start to peck at it, the fox pounces and kills them.

When a fox comes across a hedgehog, it flips it onto its back because of its spines, and it curls itself up into a ball. Then the fox urinates on the hedgehog's belly, which makes it uncurl, and the fox grabs it by the belly, separates the meat from the spiny skin and eats it.

x) The wonders of the wolf

Once a wolf attacked a man and wanted to kill him, but he saw that the man had a bow and arrows. He went and got the skull of a camel, and faced the man, holding it in his mouth. Every time the man shot an arrow at him, he deflected it with that skull, until the man was worn out. When the man realized that his arrows had run out, he called someone else to help him drive the wolf away.

xi) The wonders of monkeys

Bukhari mentioned in his *ṣaḥeeḥ* that 'Amr ibn Maymoon al-Awdi said: During the *Jaahiliyah* (Pre-Islamic period), I saw a male monkey and a female monkey committing zinaa. The other monkeys gathered together and stoned them to death. These monkeys upheld the limits of Allah when the sons of Adam were neglecting them.

xii) The wonders of cows

Cows are proverbially seen as being slow and stupid, but the Prophet (ﷺ) said:

> "Whilst a man was driving a cow, he rode on it, and she said, 'I was not created for this.'" The people said, "*Subḥaan Allah*! Can a cow speak?" He said: "I believe it and Abu Bakr and 'Umar believe it, and that is enough."

And he said: "Whilst a man was tending his sheep, the wolf attacked a ewe, and he saved her. The wolf said: 'You saved her from me, but who will save her on the day of the carnivores, the day when she will have no other shepherd but me?'" The people said, "*Subḥaan Allah*! Can a wolf talk?" The Messenger of Allah (ﷺ) said:

> "I believe it and Abu Bakr and 'Umar believe it, and that is enough."

xiii) The wonders of mice

Among the wonders of mice is that if a mouse drinks oil from the top of a vessel, then the level of the oil drops and it can no longer reach it, it goes and gets a mouthful of water. It then pours into the vessel, so that the level of oil will come up again and it can drink some more.

xiv) Some animals use medicine

Doctors claim that the idea of using enemas was taken from a kind of bird that has a long beak. If it is finding it difficult to defecate, it goes to salty water, takes some water in its beak, and gives itself an enema, then the droppings are passed quickly.

When weasels and hedgehogs eat snakes, they go and eat crabs, as a kind of medicine for that.

When the fox suffers a headache or a wound, it goes to a certain kind of dye and puts it on the wound like a kind of ointment. When the bear suffers a wound, it goes to a plant which is known to it, but is unknown to the herbalists, and treats itself with it, and it gets better.

xv) How people learn from animals

Many wise people learn things from "dumb" animals that are of use to them in their daily lives, their attitudes, their work and in war; they learn resolution and patience. Animals are more and more guided than many people.

Allah (ﷻ), says:

﴿أَمْ تَحْسَبُ أَنَّ أَكْثَرَهُمْ يَسْمَعُونَ أَوْ يَعْقِلُونَ إِنْ هُمْ إِلَّا كَالْأَنْعَامِ بَلْ هُمْ أَضَلُّ سَبِيلًا ﴿٤٤﴾﴾

﴿Or do you think that most of them hear or understand? They are only like cattle nay, they are even farther astray from the Path.﴾ *(Qur'an 25: 44)*

Abu Ja'far al-Baaqir said: Allah (ﷻ), did not only liken them to cattle. He said that they are more misguided than the animals. One of the ways in which female carnivores are guided is that when they give birth to their young, they keep picking them up for the first few days to protect them from ants, because when they are born they are like pieces of meat. The mother is afraid that the ants will harm the young, so she keeps picking them up and moving them from one place to another, until they become stronger.

Ibn al-A'raabi said: It was said to a *shaykh* of Quraysh: Who taught you all of this, for what you know is known only to people who have experience and who have engaged in trade? He said: Allah taught me what He taught the pigeon, which turns its eggs so that both sides will have an equal share of her warmth and care, lest the earth damage the egg if it is left on one side.

It was said to another: who taught you to persist and persevere in seeking what you want, even if at first you do not succeed, until you get it? He said: the One Who taught the dung beetle, when it climbs a wall and falls off, to keep on climbing again and again, until it manages to reach the top of the wall.

It was said to another: who taught you to set out early in the day to do your business, and never to miss a day? He said, the One Who taught the bird to set out hungry each morning seeking its food near and far, and never to get tired or to fear an attack in the air or on land.

It was said to another: who taught you to be so calm, quiet and reserved until you see what you want, then when you get the chance you pounce like a lion attacking its prey? He said: the One Who taught the cat to watch the mouse's hole and not to move a muscle, but to remain immobile as if dead, until the mouse comes out, whereupon it pounces like a lion.

It was said to another: who taught you to be so patient and forbearing? He said: the One Who taught the camel to be so patient even when carrying these heavy burdens, and to put up with the long marches, exhaustion and harshness and beatings of the camel-driver, with the heavy burden and everything on his back and the bitterness of hunger and thirst in his stomach. Even though he is so tired and utterly exhausted, this does not make him lose his patience.

It was said to another: who taught you to prefer others to yourself and to be so generous? He said; the One Who taught the rooster, when he finds a grain on the ground, not to eat it although he needs it, but instead to call the hens to come, until one comes and picks up the grain, and the rooster is happy with that. And when a lot of grain is put out for him, he scatters it here and there even if there are no hens around, because his nature is to prefer others over himself and to be generous, and he thinks it is miserly to keep food for himself.

It was said to another: who taught you to be so smart in seeking provision and earning a living? He said, the One Who taught the fox all these tricks which even wise men are unable to learn and to do. For the fox's tricks are too many to be counted.

Who taught the lion, when it is walking and is afraid that hunters may follow its tracks and come after it, to erase its tracks with its tail? Who taught him to come to his cub three days after it is born, to breathe into its nose? For when the lioness gives birth to it, it is like a dead puppy, and she keeps looking after it until its father comes and does that.

Who inspired the noblest of lions not to eat from any prey except its own? For if it passes by the prey of any other animal, it will not go near it even if it is starving.

Who taught the female elephant, when the time to give birth approaches, to go and give birth in the water? For the elephant is the only animal which gives birth standing up, because its joints are not like the joints of other animals and it is very tall, so it is afraid that if it gives birth on land, the infant will be harmed by the fall. So she goes to water which is not too deep, and gives birth there, so it will be like a soft bed.

Who taught the fly, when it falls into some liquid, to keep the wing on which the cure is out of the water?

Who taught the dog, when it sees the gazelles, to know which ones are sickly, and which one is the male? For it goes after males, even though it knows that they can run and jump faster and are stronger, and it leaves the females alone even though they are weaker. The dog knows that if the male runs for a while, its bladder will fill, for when any animal is scared, its bladder fills. When the male gazelle needs to urinate, it cannot do so when it is running so fast, so it slows down, and then the dog catches it. The females, on the other hand, are able to urinate whilst running because their urethras are wider and it is easier for them, so they keep on running.

Who taught it, when the ground is covered with snow, to look for a place where the snow is thinner and has melted a little, creating a slight depression in its surface? For it knows that there is a rabbit warren under this spot, so it digs it out and hunts the rabbits, because it knows that the heat of the rabbits' breath has melted the snow and made it thinner.

Who taught the wolf, when it sleeps, to sleep with one eye open? So it sleeps with one eye open, until that eye becomes drowsy, then it opens the sleeping eye.

Who taught the birds, if a chick falls from the nest, to call for help, so that other birds in the area gather around it and fly around it, until it is motivated by their actions and gains the strength to get up and fly with them?

A hunter said that one day he saw a bird on a wall, so he waved his hand as if throwing something, and the bird did not move. Then he bent down as if to pick up something from the ground, and it did not move. Then he touched the smallest pebble or date stone, and the bird flew away before he could pick it up.

Who taught a certain type of spider to stay close to the ground and remain immobile so that the fly will think that it is preoccupied, then it pounces upon it like a leopard?

Who taught the spider to make its web so fine and strong, then to make a thread at the top and hang from it, then when a mosquito gets caught in the web it drops down to it and comes to hunt it?

Who taught the gazelle only to enter its home backwards, so that it can face whatever it fears may harm it or its offspring?

Who taught the cat, when it sees a mouse on the roof, to raise its head towards it as if pointing to it with a stick, then move its head back and forth until the mouse is distracted and falls?

Who taught the jerboa to dig its house in the sides of the valley so that it will be above the flood level and will be safe from the hooves of cattle or water flowing through? It makes its tunnels deep, then it makes numerous doors in them. It makes a thin barrier between it and the surface of the earth, so that when it senses danger, it can open one of these doors easily and escape. Because it is very forgetful, it only builds its home near a rock which will serve as a guidepost pointing to its home if it loses its way.

Who taught the leopard when it gets fat to stay out of sight because it is too heavy to move, until it loses that fat, whereupon it emerges again?

Who taught the stag, when its antlers fall off, to stay out of sight because it has lost its weapon and it gains weight as a result? Then when its antlers have grown again, it comes out into the sun and wind and starts to move around a lot. This makes its muscles grow strong again, and it loses the fat that prevented it from running.

This is a vast topic. It suffices us to quote the words of Allah (ﷻ):

﴿ وَمَا مِن دَآبَّةٍ فِى ٱلْأَرْضِ وَلَا طَٰٓئِرٍ يَطِيرُ بِجَنَاحَيْهِ إِلَّآ أُمَمٌ أَمْثَالُكُم ۚ مَّا فَرَّطْنَا فِى ٱلْكِتَٰبِ مِن شَىْءٍ ۚ ثُمَّ إِلَىٰ رَبِّهِمْ يُحْشَرُونَ ﴿٣٨﴾ وَٱلَّذِينَ كَذَّبُوا۟

بِـَٔايَٰتِنَا صُمٌّ وَبُكْمٌ فِي ٱلظُّلُمَٰتِۗ مَن يَشَإِ ٱللَّهُ يُضْلِلْهُ وَمَن يَشَأْ يَجْعَلْهُ عَلَىٰ صِرَٰطٍ مُّسْتَقِيمٍ ﴿٣٩﴾

﴾There is not a moving [living] creature on earth, nor a bird that flies with its two wings, but are communities like you. We have neglected nothing in the Book, then unto their Lord they [all] shall be gathered. Those who reject Our *aayaat* [proofs, evidences, verses, lessons, signs, revelations, etc.] are deaf and dumb in the darkness. Allah sends astray whom He wills and He guides on the Straight Path whom He wills.﴿

(Qur'an 6: 38-39)

Ways in which humans are likened to animals

Ibn 'Abbaas says, according to a report narrated by 'Aṭaa': ﴾...but are communities like you...﴿ *(Qur'an 6: 38)*. [Allah] means: they recognize Me, affirm My Unity, glorify Me and praise Me. This is like the *aayah* (verse):

﴿ ... وَإِن مِّن شَيْءٍ إِلَّا يُسَبِّحُ بِحَمْدِهِۦ ... ﴿٤٤﴾ ﴾

﴾...And there is not a thing but glorifies His Praise...﴿

(Qur'an 17: 44)

﴿ أَلَمْ تَرَ أَنَّ ٱللَّهَ يُسَبِّحُ لَهُۥ مَن فِي ٱلسَّمَٰوَٰتِ وَٱلْأَرْضِ وَٱلطَّيْرُ صَٰٓفَّٰتٍۖ كُلٌّ قَدْ عَلِمَ صَلَاتَهُۥ وَتَسْبِيحَهُۥ ... ﴿٤١﴾ ﴾

﴾See you not [O' Muhammad] that Allah, He it is Whom glorify whosoever is in the heavens and the earth, and the birds with wings outspread [in their flight]? Of each one He [Allah] knows indeed his *ṣalaah* [prayer] and his glorification [or everyone knows his *ṣalaah* (prayer) and his glorification]...﴿ *(Qur'an 24: 41)*

This is also referred to in the following verses:

﴿ أَلَمْ تَرَ أَنَّ ٱللَّهَ يَسْجُدُ لَهُۥ مَن فِى ٱلسَّمَـٰوَٰتِ وَمَن فِى ٱلْأَرْضِ وَٱلشَّمْسُ وَٱلْقَمَرُ وَٱلنُّجُومُ وَٱلْجِبَالُ وَٱلشَّجَرُ وَٱلدَّوَآبُّ ... ﴿١٨﴾ ﴾

﴾See you not that whoever is in the heavens and whoever is on the earth, and the sun, and the moon, and the stars, and the mountains, and the trees, and *Ad-Dawaabb* [moving (living) creatures, beasts],...﴿ *(Qur'an 22: 18)*

﴿ وَلِلَّهِ يَسْجُدُ مَا فِى ٱلسَّمَـٰوَٰتِ وَمَا فِى ٱلْأَرْضِ مِن دَآبَّةٍ وَٱلْمَلَـٰٓئِكَةُ وَهُمْ لَا يَسْتَكْبِرُونَ ﴿٤٩﴾ ﴾

﴾And to Allah prostrate all that is in the heavens and all that is in the earth, of the moving [living] creatures and the angels, and they are not proud [i.e. they worship their Lord (Allah) with humility].﴿ *(Qur'an 16: 49)*

﴿ ... يَـٰجِبَالُ أَوِّبِى مَعَهُۥ وَٱلطَّيْرَ ... ﴿١٠﴾ ﴾

﴾..."O' you mountains. Glorify [Allah] with him! And you birds [also]!..."﴿ *(Qur'an 34: 10)*

﴿ وَأَوْحَىٰ رَبُّكَ إِلَى ٱلنَّحْلِ ... ﴿٦٨﴾ ﴾

﴾And your Lord inspired the bees,...﴿ *(Qur'an 16: 68)*

﴿ ... قَالَتْ نَمْلَةٌ يَـٰٓأَيُّهَا ٱلنَّمْلُ ... ﴿١٨﴾ ﴾

﴾...One of the ants said: 'O' ants!...'﴿ *(Qur'an 27: 18)*

﴿ ... عُلِّمْنَا مَنطِقَ ٱلطَّيْرِ ... ﴿١٦﴾ ﴾

﴾[Sulaymaan (Solomon) said:] '... We have been taught the language of birds,...'﴿ *(Qur'an 27: 16)*

Mujahid said, 'Communities like you' (means) species and categories which you know by their names. Az-Zajjaaj said, 'Communities like you' means, 'In that they will be resurrected.'

Ibn Qutaybah said: 'Communities like you' means, 'In that they search for food, seek provision and try to protect themselves from danger.'

Sufyaan ibn 'Uyaynah said: there is no human being on earth who does not resemble animals in some way. Some crush the heads of their victims like lions; some run like wolves; some bark like dogs; and some flaunt themselves like peacocks. Some people resemble pigs in that if you offer them good food they will not touch it, but if a man gets up from defecating, they will come and roll in it. Hence you find some people who, if they hear fifty words of wisdom they will not remember anything of that, but if a man does one thing wrong, that will stay in their memory.

Al-Khaṭṭaabi said: how well Sufyaan understood this *aayah* (verse) and reached this wise conclusion. That is if a statement could not be interpreted literally, it should be interpreted according to the subtle meaning to which it refers. Allah has told us of the similarities between men and every kind of bird and beast; this cannot be taken in the physical sense or in the sense of speech and knowledge, so it must be interpreted as a resemblance in terms of characteristics and attitude.

Allah (ﷻ), has made some animals smart and resourceful, and others relaxed and trusting. Some insects store a year's worth of food for themselves, and others rely on the fact that daily provision is guaranteed for them. Some do not know their offspring at all; some look after their own offspring but no others; some neglect their own offspring and care for the offspring of others; some never acknowledge their offspring once they become independent. Some creatures save whilst others have no means of earning. Some care for their offspring and never lose touch with them.

Some animals do not seek to produce offspring, whilst others devote all their time and effort to having children. Some recognize and appreciate kind treatment, whilst for others it does not mean a thing. Some prefer others to themselves, whilst others, if they gain enough to provide for an entire community of their species, will not let any other individual come near it.

Some animals like humans and feel at home with them, whilst others are very nervous of man. Some eat only good and pure things whilst others eat filth and yet others eat both.

Some animals will not harm unless severely provoked, whilst others will hurt without provocation. Some bear grudges and never forget if someone hurts them, whilst others do not remember at all. Some never get angry, whilst others get angry quickly and are not easily calmed. Some have very precise knowledge of things which most people know nothing about, and some do not know about anything at all. Some are able to detect and avoid things which are ugly or bad, and for others good and bad are the same. Some learn quickly, some learn slowly, and some never learn.

All of this points to the Creator and how wise and perfect He is in His creation. It shows how wonderful is the knowledge which He has instilled in His creation, how subtle the stratagems, how precise the management, how patient His creatures are in the pursuit of their goals. All of this makes us glorify Allah. It fills our hearts with knowledge of Allah and His wisdom and power. What every rational being knows is that He did not create all this in vain and He does not neglect His creation. In all that He creates He has the clearest wisdom and definitive proof, which indicates that He is the Lord and Sovereign of all things, that He alone is perfect, and that He is able to do all things and knows all things.

xvi) How the Creator guides living beings to multiply

Dr. Yusuf 'Izz Uddeen explains this topic as follows:

"Among the amazing things which all living beings have in common is the ability to multiply, to produce offspring which will ensure the continuation of the species and that it will not become extinct.

The act of reproducing is accomplished by different means in different creatures, but they all reach the intended goal. Bacteria (which are kinds of plants) multiply, as do all other kinds of plants and animals, according to their various levels. From a mathematical point of view, it is impossible that a series of accidental events could have led to the appearance of males and females in thousands of plants and animals to serve a specific purpose, which is the production of offspring to protect the species from extinction.

There are some plants and animals in which there is no distinction between males and females, but they still multiply and produce offspring. Tiny primitive animals such as the amoeba, which lives in water and whose body consists of a single cell, multiply in an amazing fashion. One amoeba divides into two parts, each of which turns into an amoeba. The creatures formed by this cell division divide into two in turn, and so on. This happens when the circumstances of life are suitable.

But if this creature feels any sense of danger, it creates a bubble around itself and divides into two, and into tens of new creatures inside that bubble, so as to make up for the time which it may otherwise have wasted inside the bubble waiting for circumstances to return to normal.

Multiplication by division occurs in numerous other primitive animals apart from the amoeba, such as the animal called a paramecium, which also lives in water and also multiplies by dividing into two in suitable circumstances, like the amoeba. But from time to time when it needs to renew its energy and vitality, it resorts to another kind of reproduction which is very complicated. It mobilizes its nucleus (and every cell has a nucleus, as is well known) to make every cell divide into four, instead of only two.

In animals which are superior to these primitive animals, if circumstances prevent females from mating with males in order to produce offspring, the animal becomes both male and female, i.e., it becomes a hermaphrodite, with both female and male reproductive organs side by side in its body. Thus it is able to produce offspring without having to wait for the opportunity for the two sexes to come together. This happens, for example, in the case of the liver-worm which lives in the ducts of the gall-bladder of some animals, where it is very difficult for them to move about in this constricted space to seek out the other sex. At the same time, if it so happens that two of these worms are able to fertilize one another, one will become like the female and the other will become like the male.

The notion that millions of accidents happened at the same time and served a specific, common goal in many different species and in many different ways is something that is inconceivable by scientific and mathematical standards. In this case we have no option but to accept the existence of an active, creative power behind all of this.

From the time of the first appearance of mammals on earth, the female was equipped to produce milk which would guarantee nourishment for the young as soon as they emerged from the mother's womb. If these mammary glands, which protrude from the mother's body, had not existed from the first moment that mammals appeared, the young would have had no chance to grow and survive. This is something that has been decreed and decided from the beginning, and is not subject to trial and error because there is no room for even the slightest mistake.

Can any rational person imagine that this provision of food for the newborn would happen as the result of blind chance? The milk of female mammals, in addition to providing nourishment, has also been found to contain materials which give the newborn immunity against diseases until it grows stronger and its body is able to protect itself. All efforts to manufacture the milk needed to nourish newborns have failed to produce milk that has the same characteristics as the milk that Allah has supplied to the female."

The importance of the sexual instinct

Dr. Yusuf also tells us about the sexual instinct and its importance and impact. He says:

"Among the things that puzzle scientists is the sexual instinct, which makes males attracted to females and vice versa.

The sexual instinct is the strongest of instincts, because it is the most important for ensuring the survival of the species and protecting it from extinction. The main purpose in life for some animals is to mate and perpetuate the species, and they die immediately after that.

The complete life cycle of the insect known as the may-fly is no more than a few days. During its entire life cycle it does not eat, because it is not equipped with a mouth at all. Its primary role during this short period of time is to mate and produce offspring. The mother dies as soon as she has fulfilled her role, and the father dies likewise."

xvii) How the Creator causes animals to make up for lost parts of their bodies

In his articles in *Al-Ahraam* newspaper, Dr. Yusuf discusses the characteristic which Allah (ﷻ), has bestowed upon His creatures, whereby they are able to make up for any part of their bodies that they lose:

"Among the other amazing features that we see in all animals and plants is the ability to make up for missing body parts. We find this ability, to one degree or another, in different living beings.

In many animals such as that which is called the hydra, we find an amazing feature which science can only describe, but it cannot explain. This animal lives in water and takes the form of a tube which is no more than a few millimeters in length. The tube is closed at the bottom and is open at the top. This opening serves as a mouth to take in food, and it is also used to expel waste matter. Around this mouth there are a number of hollow tentacles which are connected to the hollow tube inside its body.

If we cut this animal into two, an upper half and a lower half, we find that some cells in each half multiply to complete the part that is missing, and the result is two animals which look like the original. But it does not stop there. If we cut the animal into several pieces, each piece will grow and will make up the missing parts, and will become a perfectly formed animal.

The walls of the hydra's body are composed of two layers of cells, an outer layer and an inner layer which surrounds the hollow space inside its body. In each layer there are different types of cells, each of which performs a specific function. Most of the cells in the outer layer serve to protect the body, whilst the main function of the inner cells is to digest the food which the animal swallows through its mouth opening.

If we turn this animal inside-out, like a sock, so that the outer cells are on the inside surrounding its hollow centre, and the cells which were inside are now on the outside, what happens? The scientists who carried out this experiment discovered that the cells which are now on the outside migrate towards the inside, and the cells which are now on the inside migrate towards the outside, so that the animal will go back to the way it was. If this did not happen, the animal would die, because the cells which surround its hollow middle have to be digestive cells which can process the food in the animal's hollow middle. At the same time, the cells which are on the outside have to be protective cells which can defend the animal's body.

If an earthworm is cut in half, each half will grow, and will make up for the missing parts.

In other animals, such as the shrimp and others, if it loses one of its legs, it grows a new leg to replace the lost limb. If the wall gecko senses danger or a person or animal grabs it by the tail, it will detach that tail from its body and escape from the danger, and it grows a new tail.

If we humans cut ourselves when shaving or for any other reason, new cells form to replace the cells that are lost. If that did not happen, it would be impossible to perform surgery.

If we break a bone, new cells form and the break heals.

This could not have happened as the result of an accident. It has to be the result of a plan aimed at a specific goal, which is the preservation of the life of the individual. It is controlled by inner forces residing in the animal, the nature of which is not fully understood by science. It is a force which Allah has created in animals, but the animal knows nothing of it and does not know what it is doing."

xviii) All living beings have the function of breathing in common, although they achieve it in different ways

Dr. Yusuf also discusses this topic in his valuable articles, where he says:

"The function of breathing, which we find in all living creatures from the lowest to the highest, is an amazing process. In all cases it is simply the process of oxidization, i.e., the union of oxygen with nutrients in the cells of the body, which results in the release of energy which the organism needs and without which it would not be able to undertake any of its activities.

This oxidization takes place in different ways in different animals, but in all cases the result is the same: the release of energy. At the same time, water and carbon dioxide are formed as a result of this process. So the main stages of breathing are the intake of oxygen needed to oxidize the nutrients and the release of carbon dioxide and water as a result of this process.

In simple animals like the amoeba, where the body consists of a single cell, the process of breathing is completed in a very simple manner. The creature that looks like a piece of soft jelly, lives in water. There is a certain amount of diluted oxygen. This oxygen which is diluted in the water penetrates the amoeba's body, where it oxidizes the nutrients in its body, and the energy is released which it needs to move and grow and perform other necessary functions of life.

Carbon dioxide and water are formed as a result of this oxidization process, in addition to the release of energy.

The amoeba gets rid of the excess water in an amazing fashion. It collects the drops of water until they form a bubble filled with water. It then moves to the edge of the creature's body. Then it bursts, expelling the water from its body, then it starts to form a new bubble, and so on.

The carbon dioxide simply passes out from the amoeba's body into the surrounding water.

In insects, the function of breathing takes place through openings in the sides of the insect's body which lead to a network of fine tubes and get progressively smaller until they reach almost all its cells. Oxygen enters this system through the external holes, and reaches the cells of the body directly.

In man and a number of other animals, the oxygen reaches the tissues of the body through red blood cells which are carried by the blood and which contain a substance called haemoglobin.

One of the amazing features of this substance is that it binds readily with oxygen and carbon dioxide, and is also able to detach itself quickly from them. When these red blood cells reach the lungs, they pick up oxygen and travel through the arteries until they reach the small capillaries in the tissues of the body, where they release the oxygen. The oxygen passes through the thin walls of the capillaries into the tissues, where it is used to oxidize the nutrients. The carbon dioxide which results from this process of oxidization attaches itself to the haemoglobin and is carried back to the lungs, where it detaches itself and is expelled from the body by exhalation. Then more oxygen is picked up, and so on.

Breathing happens in different ways in different animals, but the result in all cases is the same, that is, bringing oxygen to the cells of the body and expelling carbon dioxide.

This offers definitive proof of two things:
First, the precise nature of this process has to be the action and decree of a Creator, because it could not have happened any other way. This result which all creatures have in common could not have come about by accident.

Second, the Creator is absolutely One, for the style of creation is based on one principle and leads to one unchanging result."

xix) Living beings get their food in different ways

On this topic, Dr. Yusuf tells us:

"All living beings, plants and animals, need nourishment. The way in which plants get their food is completely different from the way in which animals get theirs. Plants stay in one place and are not able to move around to look for their food as animals do so. Hence they manufacture their own food on the spot, by using solar energy.

Animals, on the other hand, find their food ready-made, whether it is plant material or from other animals. The food which animals eat has to be digested and absorbed by the body so that it can benefit from it. The process of digestion is very complicated, as it breaks down complex substances into simple substances which the body is then able to absorb and benefit from.

The food substances may be fats, proteins, starches, etc. Each type of food is digested by specific enzymes which affect it but do not affect other substances which may be present side by side with it. Enzymes which work on fats will not work on proteins, and enzymes which work on proteins will not work on fats.

Is it possible that all of this could have come about as the result of blind chance or accidents, or as the result of trial and error?

Any mind which is able to think must realize that this is impossible, just as this idea is rejected outright by the mathematical laws of probability.

The minute amoeba, which is formed of a single cell, takes in its food in a strange manner. It extends a pseudopodium which surrounds the piece of food which is to be found in the water surrounding it. The food may be either tiny animal organisms or single-celled plants which are smaller than the amoeba. In this case the food will be moving if it is a tiny animal organism, and stationary if it is a single-celled plant, such as some water mosses.

It is indeed remarkable that a simple creature such as the amoeba, which has no brain or nervous system, is able to distinguish between food that is stationary and food that is moving. If the food is a moving animal, the amoeba approaches it with caution from a distance so that it will not run away. If the food is stationary and is not moving, the amoeba approaches it without caution, touching it as it surrounds it, because in this case the food is not able to escape. How does a simple creature like the amoeba, which we can barely see without the aid of a microscope, and which has no brain, nerves, eyes or other sensory organs, know this?

Once the food has been surrounded by the pseudopodium, it is now inside the amoeba's body, encased in a drop of water. Then the amoeba's body begins to secrete an acidic digestive enzyme which kills the prey which it has caught, if it is still alive. Then it secretes an alkaline enzyme. There is a reason for this, the most important enzyme, which is the one which digests proteins, can only work in an alkaline environment."

xx) How blood circulates in the bodies of all living beings

Dr. Yusuf tells us about the circulation of the blood:

"Blood circulation takes place in different ways in different parts of the animals' bodies, just as the formation of the heart varies in different kinds of animals, but the result is the same, blood circulation in parts of the body.

If we look at how the heart and circulatory system is formed in man and in a number of other animals, we will see that the heart — this beautifully designed organ — is formed of interconnected chambers whose openings are equipped with valves. The job of these valves is to allow blood to pass through in one direction, and to prevent it going back in the opposite direction.

We find similar valves in the large veins for the same reason.

The network of blood vessels, with its arteries, veins and capillaries, is designed in an amazing manner. The arteries branch out, getting smaller and smaller, until they become capillaries with thin walls.

The reason why the capillaries have such thin walls is to allow the gaseous exchange of oxygen from the haemoglobin carried in the red blood cells to the tissues of the body. At the same time, carbon dioxide passes from the tissues into the capillaries, where it attaches itself to the red blood cells. Then the capillaries join back together to form veins which lead back to the lungs, where the red blood cells get rid of the carbon dioxide and pick up more oxygen, and so on.

The heart beats rhythmically for a lifetime, whereby some of its chambers expand whilst others contract, to push the pure, oxygen-bearing blood through the arteries, whilst the blood that has passed through the body returns carrying carbon dioxide, to send it to the lungs where it picks up more oxygen and gets rid of the carbon dioxide.

There circulate in the bodies of man and some other animals fluids which have specific functions, such as blood and lymph. The lymph acts as a mediator between the blood and the tissues. Blood has many functions, such as delivering nutrients to all parts of the body. If blood does not exist in the bodies of some animals, such as the liver-worm, the bodies of these animals are designed in such a way that nutrients are delivered by some other means.

In our bodies and in the bodies of a number of other animals, blood is composed of a liquid in which there float huge numbers of cells which have different forms and functions. These are called red blood cells and white blood cells.

The red blood cells, as mentioned above, play a role in the function of breathing. The white blood cells appear in a variety of forms and perform different functions. Some of them serve to swallow and destroy any germs that enter the human's or animal's body; they swallow them in a manner similar to that of the amoeba swallowing its food. We breathe in from the air millions of germs day and night, but we do not get sick every day, because these amazing cells which float in our blood and which are able to move from the bloodstream into the tissues in cases of emergency, swallow these germs and kill them. So we do not fall ill unless the body's resistance is weakened for some reason, or if there are more germs than usual."

xxi) The way in which the senses are formed in living beings

Dr. Yusuf explains to us that "most animals have sensory organs such as sight, smell, touch and hearing. The basic format of the eye is similar in all mammals and other creatures. Its formation is very complex and amazing. The eye has a lens through which light passes and an opening through which light enters the lens. This opening through which light enters the eye automatically becomes wider in low light and smaller in bright light. The reason for that is clear. When the light is low, the eye needs more light in order to see objects clearly, and when the light is bright, it needs less light.

The eye sees things in low light, but man has not yet been able to invent a camera that can take pictures in such low light.

The bee is able to see ultra-violet rays, and the owl is able to see infra-red rays, which we are not able to see. These are heat rays which enable the owl to see a mouse in deep darkness, by seeing these heat rays which are emitted by the mouse's warm body.

The rays of light which enter the eye fall on the retina at the back of the eye. The retina is formed of nine different layers, which all together are no thicker than a piece of paper. The layer which is at the back of the eye is formed of millions of rods and cones arranged in a certain order which allows them to distinguish colours. The optic nerve transmits these sensations to a specific area of the brain which translates these sensations into a clear image of what the eye sees.

This amazing formation of the lens, rods and cones, and nerves can only have happened at one time. If they were not all created at the same time, sight would have been impossible. How can it be that all these factors complement one another at the same time?

The science of mathematics tells us that it is impossible for all these things to have happened at one time by chance. A television camera is a primitive imitation of the process of vision which is accomplished by the eye. All the things that the human mind has invented are primitive imitations of what exists in nature. If a simple camera needed so much thought and reasoning to be invented, does it make any sense to say that the eye of a human or any other animal could have been formed by chance?

It is truly amazing that for every animal which needs to be able to see, Allah (ﷻ), has created eyes with which it can see. Although those eyes may differ greatly from our own in the way they are formed, they still meet the same goal, which is to see. So we find in the earthworm, for example, cells in its skin which are sensitive to light and darkness. This is all that is needed by creatures such as this worm, which lives in tunnels beneath the ground.

Insects have eyes which are formed differently from the eyes of humans, monkeys, cows, turtles and fish, but despite these differences the insects still see whatever they look at with these eyes. The fact that these different means all reach the same goal is not something that could have come about by chance; it has to be the result of a plan aimed at reaching a specific goal.

Allah (ﷻ), has blessed every creature with senses and understanding according to its needs. The housefly, for example, needs eyes to see food, and it feels every movement aimed at attacking it. Hence the Creator equipped it with a pair of compound eyes, as He gave to most insects. Each of these compound eyes is composed of hundreds of units which resemble one another and are packed close together.

Each one of these units sees part of the object that is being viewed, and these partial images combine to give the fly a complete picture. Its Creator has also given it another kind of eye, called the simple eye. There are three of these simple eyes on the top of the fly's head; their function is to spot any movement. It is these eyes which make catching the fly almost impossible."

xxii) How the bones and joints are designed

The bones of our bodies and those of a number of other animals can be moved at the joints. Certain muscles contract whilst others simultaneously expand in harmony, and the hand, leg, finger or other part of the body moves in the way in which the person or animal wants it to move. The joints are formed in such a way that they are able to slide, so the creature does not feel any friction.

The vertebrae of the spinal column are joined in a way that is designed to take pressure and avoid friction. The vertebrae are connected to one another, and it is an amazing design. The spinal column encloses the spinal cord to protect it just as the skull protects the brain inside it, and nerves extend from the spinal cord through holes in the vertebrae. All these design features have to have happened at the same time, because if even one aspect of this design was lacking, the animal would not be able to move. Does it make sense to suggest that all of these features could have happened at the same time as the result of an accident?

xxiii) The reason why blood clots

It is well-known that if we are wounded, the blood which comes out of the veins at the site of the wound quickly clots. There is a reason behind this. The congealed blood seals the wounded blood vessels, thus stemming the flow of blood. If this clotting did not happen, the individual would bleed to death.

What it indicates is that a deliberate plan on the part of the Creator to protect living beings is the fact that we find it happening in different ways in different creatures. The result in all cases is the same. In most insects, if the insect such as a cockroach, for example, is wounded, a number of cells gather and form a seal over the wound so that no blood can come out. In some insects we find that the blood clots just as our blood does.

The fact that the same goal is reached by different means, as we have stated above, offers definitive proof of the existence of a Creator Who controls and designs things in different ways in order to reach a specific goal for which He keeps the living being alive.

xxiv) The sensory antennae of mosquitoes

It cannot be accidental that the sensory antennae of the male mosquito have longer hairs than those on the antennae of the female. In the past, it was believed that these longer hairs served as an adornment, to make the male attractive to the female. But it then became apparent that these hairs of the antennae of the male mosquito are able to pick up special sounds made by the female from a great distance. These sounds made by the female travel by waves which, to a large extent, resemble the waves of a broadcast.

The male waves his antennae in different directions just as we move the antenna of a television in order to get a clearer picture. In certain positions the antennae pick up the female's sound clearly, and from the angle of his antennae, he knows instinctively where the female is who is making the sound. So he flies towards her, taking the shortest route, in order to mate with her.

Thus we note that the Creator has given the mosquito this amazing ability to detect the female's sound from dozens of meters away, despite the fact that there are many other sounds crowding the airwaves. If this did not happen, the male mosquito would not be able to find the female easily, and mosquitoes would not be able to survive generation after generation.

This is like a broadcast receptor in the mosquito's antennae which it used millions of years before man was able to discover the secrets of wireless communication. Is it possible that such a thing could have happened as the result of blind chance?

xxv) Creatures which flash in the darkness

The females of some species of insects flash in the darkness, with a frequency which is distinguishable to the males of the same species and which they do not confuse with the flashes of other species which are emitted on a different frequency. When the male sees these flashes, which are barely discernible to our eyes, he flies to the female and mating takes place, thus ensuring the continued survival of the species.

Mathematics proves that a system of this kind could never be formed by the blind and unreasonable forces of "nature." It is a system devised by a Creator Who knows what He is doing and Who orders things in the most amazing fashion in order to achieve a certain goal.

xxvi) The digestive process in animals

We know that it is essential to cut food into small pieces to make it easy to digest. The teeth have different structures and are arranged differently in different animals in order to perform the same function, which is cutting up food.

In man, the teeth are arranged in an amazing fashion. We see that man has incisors, canines and molars, arranged in such a fashion that each kind of tooth performs a specific function. Animals do not have any kind of teeth that they do not need. Animals which feed on liquids are equipped with special means of sucking up their liquid food and conveying it to the digestive tract. When animals, which have teeth, chew, the secretions of their salivary glands mix with the food to initiate the digestive process.

In the stomach and intestines — as we have mentioned above — the animal produces enzymes, each of which work on a certain kind of food and have no effect on others.

xvii) Formation of the embryo

The development of the embryo in any kind of animal is something amazing. Science is only able to describe the stages in this process; it is incapable of explaining its nature and the forces which push it towards a specific goal, namely the formation of the embryo of a given animal.

This process begins with the joining of the male cell (sperm) to the female cell (egg), to form the fertilized cell. The fertilized cell then begins to divide by means of an amazing force which resides in it, so the cell becomes two cells, then four cells, then eight cells, and so on... until the number of cells reaches a specific limit, and it becomes like a hollow ball, the wall of which consists of a single layer of cells. Then half of the ball goes inside the other half, making two layers of cells in the wall.

In most animals — including man — a third layer of cells forms between these two layers. The cells continue to divide, and each of these three layers develops into specific organs.

The outer layer develops into the skin and nervous system, and some other parts. The middle layer develops into muscles and bones. The inner layer develops into part of the digestive tract. The cells continue to divide until the foetus is fully formed inside its mother's womb, in mammals, or inside the egg, if it is an egg-laying animal. When the foetus is fully formed, the uterus of the mother expels it, in the case of mammals, or it breaks the egg and emerges, in the case of animals which lay eggs.

xviii) The formation of the ear

No reasonable person could imagine that the formation of the ear in man and in a number of other animals could have come about by accident. The ear has a drum which picks up sound waves and vibrates. These vibrations are carried to three tiny bones which are arranged in an amazing fashion. The pressure on both sides of the eardrum should always be equal; for that reason there is a tube behind the ear which connects to the nasal cavity. The internal part of the ear is connected to a bone which is shaped like a shell. Its function is to analyze noises and distinguish between tones; it also controls the sense of balance. If it were not for this, we would not be able to take even one step without tripping and falling.

The sounds then travel via the nerves to the auditory centre of the brain, so that the person or animal may understand the sounds he hears and distinguish them from one another. Could all of this have happened at the same time by chance? The mathematical laws of probability rule that out completely.

xxix) Filariae worms

Amazing things happen to living beings, things that cannot be counted. They point to the existence of a higher power which controls all things and enable living beings to survive. These are things which could not happen by chance, such as the lifecycle of the worm which causes the disease known as elephantiasis. These worms are called filariae worms.

In their adult stage, these worms sink into the human lymph vessels and lymph glands. They block the lymph glands, causing limbs to swell, especially the calves, one or both of them, where a person's calf may become as big as that of an elephant. These worms mate whilst they are inside the human lymph glands, thus producing small worms which move from the lymph vessels to the blood vessels. If these worms stay in human blood vessels, they cannot complete their lifecycle. They have to move to the body of certain types of mosquitoes in order to complete their life cycle. Then they become able to infect man. So when the mosquito sucks the blood of an infected person, it also takes in some of these small worms, which then grow inside the mosquito's body until they are fully grown. Then they are able to infect a man when the mosquito injects them into his bloodstream whilst feeding on his blood.

The scientists tried to obtain samples of these worms from the blood of people who were infected with this disease, but all their attempts met with failure, until something very strange happened.

One night, one of the scientists was staying up late at night in the laboratory. He took a blood sample from an infected person and examined it under the microscope, and was amazed to see huge numbers of these worms in the sample that he had taken. During the day he had taken a sample from the same patient and had not seen any trace of the worms. He was very curious to know the reason why the worms were present in the blood sample taken at night, when they were not present in a blood sample taken from the same person during the day.

It became clear that these tiny worms escape to the internal blood vessels during the day, and come back to the blood vessels which are closer to the surface of the skin at night. The reason for this is that the mosquitoes which feed on human blood in these places only come out at night. Hence the worms move to the blood vessels which are closer to the surface of the skin at that time, so that the mosquitoes can suck them up with the blood, and they can complete their life-cycle inside the mosquito's body. Of course, these worms do not know or understand anything about the mosquitoes in whose bodies they complete their life-cycle. They do this by instinct, i.e., there is a higher power which causes them to behave in this manner so that they can survive.

It is amazing that in places where the kinds of mosquitoes that suck blood are active in the day and not at night, we find that these worms do the opposite: they stay in the inner blood vessels at night and come to the blood vessels that are near the skin during the day, so that the mosquitoes in this case too are able to suck them up with the blood. Could this have happened by chance?

xxx) The magnetism of the earth

If we turn aside from the creation of living beings and their mind-boggling wonders, and look at this vast universe, we will find many amazing things. The first of these wonders is the magnetism that exists in the sphere of the earth. This is what keeps us attached to the earth and prevents us from being thrown off into space whilst the earth rotates.

This magnetism is different from the magnetism that exists in a bar magnet. We know that a bar magnet is able to attract some things, but not others such as meat, paper, glass, stones, sand, water, etc. But the magnetism of the earth attracts and holds everything, our bodies, glass, sand, water, stones and paper. If the earth did not hold these things, nothing would be left on its surface.

xxxi) The size, dimensions and orbit of heavenly bodies

Fred Hoyle, professor of astronomy at London University, says in his book *The Nature of the Universe* that there are some heavenly bodies whose size is so astoundingly vast that it almost defies imagination, and that in relation to one of these bodies the earth would look like a grain of sand.

The great American scholar Christie Morrison, the former head of the Academy of Science in New York, says: "The position of the heavenly bodies did not happen merely by chance. They are placed in a calculated manner in space. If the moon, for example, was closer to the earth by a quarter of the distance that separates us from it, the ebb and flow of the tides would become so strong that all dry land would be flooded at high tide, and as a result all creatures that live on the dry land would be drowned. If the axis of the earth was not at an angle of 23°, this would result in permanent night at the poles. Evaporation from the oceans would lead to the formation of huge icecaps, the pressure of which would cause the earth to bulge. There would be less rain, to an extent which would make life on earth impossible. The speed of the earth's revolution would approach 1000 mph. Even if we were to imagine it spinning at a speed of only 100 mph, this would make both night and day longer, with the result that all plants and animals would burn during the day from the intense heat, and freeze at night because of the intense cold."

In the voluminous book by Dr. Judd, Professor of philosophy at London University, there is a discussion of the different ways in which the universe and life could have come into being, discussed from a scientific and philosophical point of view. The summary of this detailed discussion is that the universe can only have come into being as the result of an amazing process of creation. Allah (سبحانه وتعالى), indeed spoke the truth when He said:

﴿سَنُرِيهِمْ ءَايَٰتِنَا فِى ٱلْءَافَاقِ وَفِىٓ أَنفُسِهِمْ حَتَّىٰ يَتَبَيَّنَ لَهُمْ أَنَّهُ ٱلْحَقُّ ... ﴿٥٣﴾﴾

﴾We will show them Our Signs in the universe, and in their own selves, until it becomes manifest to them that this [the Qur'an] is the truth...﴿ *(Qur'an 41: 53)*

2 - KNOWING ALLAH THROUGH THE TEXTS OF THE QUR'AN AND SUNNAH

The Divine Names and Attributes

We have already stated above that the second way in which we may know Allah (ﷻ), is through the texts of the Qur'an and *aḥaadeeth* which speak directly about Allah, describing His attributes, names and actions.

This is a safe way which will give guaranteed results, because finding out about Allah through His words and the words of His Messenger leaves no room for doubt or confusion.

We have endeavoured to quote the texts themselves in most cases, because this is the best way to make the matter clear, and is better than quoting what people say. I have also sought not to distort the texts by misinterpreting them, as many previous writers have done in an attempt to make the verses agree with their human opinions and analogies. People must change their opinions and analogies to fit the texts and not the other way round.

1) The Extent to Which the Human Mind can Comprehend the Attributes of Allah

The attributes of Allah which are mentioned in the Qur'an and spoken of in the Sunnah may be divided into two types:

a) Those which the human mind can never know and comprehend by itself, i.e., contrary to the texts, such as proving a Hand and a Face of Allah.

b) Those which the human mind can deduce, such as His attributes of Power and Wisdom.

We will not be able to discuss all the attributes of Allah here, but we will mention some of them in order to explain what we mean and to give a clear picture, *In sha Allah.*

2) Summary of the Attributes Which are Mentioned in the Texts

i) Allah has an essence (*dhaat*)

Allah, the All-Glorified, has an essence characterized by perfection and is far above any faults or shortcomings. Anyone who reads what the Qur'an says about Allah will know for sure that He has a self:

﴿ ٱللَّهُ لَآ إِلَٰهَ إِلَّا هُوَ ٱلْحَىُّ ٱلْقَيُّومُ ۚ لَا تَأْخُذُهُۥ سِنَةٌ وَلَا نَوْمٌ ... ﴿٢٥٥﴾ ﴾

﴿Allah! *Laa ilaaha illa Huwa* [none has the right to be worshipped but He], *Al-Ḥayyul-Qayyoom* [the Ever Living, the One Who sustains and protects all that exists]. Neither slumber nor sleep overtakes Him...﴾ *(Qur'an 2: 255)*

﴿ قُلْ هُوَ ٱللَّهُ أَحَدٌ ﴿١﴾ ٱللَّهُ ٱلصَّمَدُ ﴿٢﴾ لَمْ يَلِدْ وَلَمْ يُولَدْ ﴿٣﴾ وَلَمْ يَكُن لَّهُۥ كُفُوًا أَحَدٌۢ ﴿٤﴾ ﴾

﴿Say [O' Muhammad]: 'He is Allah, [the] One. *Allah-uṣ-Ṣamad* [Allah — the Self-Sufficient Master, Whom all creatures need, (He neither eats nor drinks)]. He begets not, nor was He begotten. And there is none co-equal or comparable unto Him.'﴾ *(Qur'an 112: 1-4)*

When the disbelievers wanted to kill Khubayb, he composed the following couplet:[9]

"I do not care when I am killed as a Muslim.
It does not matter to me how I die,
That is for the sake (lit. essence) of Allah, the Divine,
And if He wills, may He bless my scattered body."

The essence of Allah is not like the essence of created beings, just as His attributes are unlike the attributes of any created beings. Allah is

[9] *Ṣaḥeeḥ al-Bukhari bi Sharḥihi Fatḥ al-Baari*, 13/381.

the Perfection after Whom there is no perfection, whereas every created being must be imperfect in one way or another, the least of which is that they are all in need of another.

Allah (سبحانه وتعالى) says, pointing out that there is no resemblance between Him and His creation:

﴿... لَيْسَ كَمِثْلِهِۦ شَىْءٌۖ وَهُوَ ٱلسَّمِيعُ ٱلْبَصِيرُ ﴿١١﴾﴾

﴾...There is nothing like Him; and He is the All-Hearer, the All-Seer.﴿ *(Qur'an 42: 11)*

ii) His "Self"

Allah has a "Self" in a manner that befits His Perfection and Majesty, a "Self" which is nothing like the selves of His creation. Allah has told us of this in His Book. He (سبحانه وتعالى), says:

﴿وَإِذَا جَآءَكَ ٱلَّذِينَ يُؤْمِنُونَ بِـَٔايَـٰتِنَا فَقُلْ سَلَـٰمٌ عَلَيْكُمْۖ كَتَبَ رَبُّكُمْ عَلَىٰ نَفْسِهِ ٱلرَّحْمَةَۖ أَنَّهُۥ مَنْ عَمِلَ مِنكُمْ سُوٓءًۢا بِجَهَـٰلَةٍ ثُمَّ تَابَ مِنۢ بَعْدِهِۦ وَأَصْلَحَ فَأَنَّهُۥ غَفُورٌ رَّحِيمٌ ﴿٥٤﴾﴾

﴾When those who believe in Our *Aayaat* [proofs, evidences, verses, lessons, signs, revelations, etc.] come to you, say: "*Salaamun 'Alaykum*" [peace be on you]; your Lord has written [prescribed] Mercy for Himself, so that if any of you does evil in ignorance, and thereafter repents and does righteous good deeds [by obeying Allah], then surely, He is Oft-Forgiving, Most Merciful.﴿ *(Qur'an 6: 54)*

Allah (سبحانه وتعالى), tells us that He has a Self, and that He has written or prescribed for Himself mercy. Allah states this in another *aayah*:

﴿قُل لِّمَن مَّا فِى ٱلسَّمَـٰوَٰتِ وَٱلْأَرْضِۖ قُل لِّلَّهِۚ كَتَبَ عَلَىٰ نَفْسِهِ ٱلرَّحْمَةَۚ لَيَجْمَعَنَّكُمْ إِلَىٰ يَوْمِ ٱلْقِيَـٰمَةِ لَا رَيْبَ فِيهِ ... ﴿١٢﴾﴾

﴾Say [O' Muhammad]: 'To whom belongs all that is in the heavens and the earth?' Say: 'To Allah. He has prescribed Mercy for Himself. Indeed He will gather you together on the Day of Resurrection, about which there is no doubt...'﴿ *(Qur'an 6: 12)*

The Messenger (ﷺ) has explained something about this writing or prescription. According to the hadith narrated by Abu Hurayrah (رضي الله عنه), the Messenger of Allah (ﷺ) said:

"When Allah decreed His creation, He wrote a book which is with Him above the Throne: My Mercy precedes My wrath." According to another report: "...prevails over My wrath."[10]

It is the way of all the Messengers to affirm that Allah has a Self. 'Eesa (Jesus) Peace be upon him, said to the Lord of Might:

﴿... تَعۡلَمُ مَا فِي نَفۡسِي وَلَآ أَعۡلَمُ مَا فِي نَفۡسِكَۚ إِنَّكَ أَنتَ عَلَّٰمُ ٱلۡغُيُوبِ ١١٦﴾

﴾...You know what is in my inner-self though I do not know what is in Yours; truly, You, only You, are the All-Knower of all that is hidden [and unseen].﴿ *(Qur'an 5: 116)*

And Allah said to His Messenger Moosa (Moses) (عليه السلام):

﴿... ثُمَّ جِئۡتَ عَلَىٰ قَدَرٖ يَٰمُوسَىٰ ٤٠ وَٱصۡطَنَعۡتُكَ لِنَفۡسِي ٤١﴾

﴾...'Then you came here according to the fixed term which I ordained [for you], O' Moosa [Moses]! And I have chosen you, for Myself.'﴿ *(Qur'an 20: 40-41)*

Allah has warned us against Himself, as He (سبحانه وتعالى), says:

---

[10] *Mishkaat al-Maṣaabeeḥ*, 1/726, hadith no. 2364.

﴿ ... وَيُحَذِّرُكُمُ ٱللَّهُ نَفْسَهُۥ وَٱللَّهُ رَءُوفٌۢ بِٱلْعِبَادِ ﴿٣٠﴾ ﴾

﴾...And Allah warns you against Himself [His punishment] and Allah is full of kindness to [His] slaves.﴿ *(Qur'an 3: 30)*

Allah reminds His slaves about the slaves who remember Him in their hearts. Bukhari and Muslim narrated in their *ṣaḥeeḥs* from Abu Hurayrah (ﷺ) that the Messenger (ﷺ) said:

> "Allah says: I am as My slave thinks I am. I am with him when he remembers Me. If he remembers Me to himself, I remember him to Myself. If he remembers Me in an assembly, I remember him in an assembly better than it."[11]

Remembering Allah pleases the self of our Lord (ﷻ). According to a hadith narrated by Ibn 'Abbaas from Juwayriyah (the wife of Prophet), the Prophet (ﷺ) left her apartment one morning after he had prayed *ṣubḥ* (*Fajr* - Dawn), and she was in her prayer-place in her house. At mid-morning he came back, and she was still sitting there. He said, "Are you still as you were when I left you?" She said, "Yes." The Prophet said:

> "After I left you, I said only four words three times, but if they were weighed against what you have said since this morning, they would outweigh it. They are *Subḥaan Allahi wa bi ḥamdihi, 'adada khalqihi wa ridaa nafsihi wazinata 'arshihi wa midaada kalimaatihi* (Glory and praise be to Allah, as many as His creation are, as much as pleases Him, as much as His Throne weighs and as many as His words are)."[12]

---

[11] *Mishkaat al-Maṣaabeeḥ*, 1/693, hadith no. 2264.

[12] Muslim, 4/2090, hadith no. 2726.

iii) The Face of our Lord, the Exalted

Allah (ﷻ), has a Face which is unlike the faces of His creation. We affirm that and believe in it, because Allah has told us of that in His Book and His Messenger has stated that in his *aḥaadeeth*. Allah (ﷻ), says:

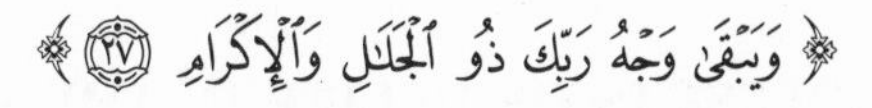

﴿And the Face of your Lord full of Majesty and Honour will remain forever.﴾ *(Qur'an 55: 27)*

Ibn Jareer said in his *Tafseer* of this *aayah*: full of Majesty and Honour describes the Face, hence it appears in the nominative form (*dhu*, i.e. it is in grammatical agreement with the word *wajh*, meaning Face).[13]

Some earlier writers denied that Allah has a Face, claiming that the phrase translated as "full of Majesty and Honour" refers to the word Lord. So in their view, the phrase translated as "full of Majesty and Honour" refers to the Lord, not to His Face.

This view was refuted by Ibn Khuzaymah, who said: This is the claim of one who is ignorant of the Arabic language, because Allah (ﷻ), says: ﴿And the Face of your Lord full of Majesty and Honour will remain forever.﴾ *(Qur'an 55: 27)*

The word *wajh* appears in the nominative form here (i.e. it is the subject), whilst the word Lord appears in a genitive (possessive) form in conjunction with the word *wajh*. If the phrase translated as "full of Majesty and Honour" referred to the word Lord here, it would appear as *Dhi'l-Jalaaali wa'l-Ikraam* (genitive) instead of *Dhu'l-Jalaali wa'l-Ikraam* (nominative).[14]

---

[13] *Tafseer aṭ-Ṭabari*. See his *Tafseer* of *Soorat ar-Raḥmaan* 55: 27.

[14] *At-Tawḥeed* by Ibn Khuzaymah, Pp. 21.

Another of the texts which affirm that Allah has a Face is the *aayah* (verse):

﴿ ... كُلُّ شَىْءٍ هَالِكٌ إِلَّا وَجْهَهُۥ... ﴿٨٨﴾ ﴾

﴾...Everything will perish save His Face...﴿
(Qur'an 28: 88)

THE EFFECTS OF BELIEF IN THE FACE OF ALLAH

a) Seeking the Face of Allah through righteous deeds

Once we know what Allah has said, we must seek the Face of our Lord through our (righteous) deeds, as Allah has told us in His Book. Any deed which is not done for the purpose of seeking His Face is false: ﴾...Everything will perish save His Face...﴿ *(Qur'an 28: 88)*

Among these deeds is spending money for the purpose of seeking His Face:

﴿ ... وَمَآ ءَاتَيْتُم مِّن زَكَوٰةٍ تُرِيدُونَ وَجْهَ ٱللَّهِ فَأُو۟لَٰٓئِكَ هُمُ ٱلْمُضْعِفُونَ ﴿٣٩﴾ ﴾

﴾...But that which you give in Zakah [*Ṣadaqah* - charity, etc.] seeking Allah's Countenance [Face], then those they shall have manifold increase.﴿ *(Qur'an 30: 39)*

He (ﷻ), has described His believing slaves as seeking His Face through their deeds, and nothing but His Face:

﴿ إِنَّمَا نُطْعِمُكُمْ لِوَجْهِ ٱللَّهِ لَا نُرِيدُ مِنكُمْ جَزَآءً وَلَا شُكُورًا ﴿٩﴾ ﴾

﴾[Saying]: 'We feed you seeking Allah's Countenance only. We wish for no reward, nor thanks from you.'﴿
(Qur'an 76: 9)

﴿ وَمَا لِأَحَدٍ عِندَهُۥ مِن نِّعْمَةٍ تُجْزَىٰٓ ﴿١٩﴾ إِلَّا ٱبْتِغَآءَ وَجْهِ رَبِّهِ ٱلْأَعْلَىٰ ﴿٢٠﴾ ﴾

﴿And who has [in mind] no favour from anyone to be paid back, Except to seek the Countenance [Face] of his Lord, the Most High.﴾ *(Qur'an 92: 19-20)*

﴿ وَٱصْبِرْ نَفْسَكَ مَعَ ٱلَّذِينَ يَدْعُونَ رَبَّهُم بِٱلْغَدَوٰةِ وَٱلْعَشِيِّ يُرِيدُونَ وَجْهَهُۥ... ﴿٢٨﴾ ﴾

﴿And keep yourself [O' Muhammad] patiently with those who call on their Lord [i.e. your companions who remember their Lord with glorification, praising in prayers, and other righteous deeds] morning and afternoon, seeking His Face;...﴾ *(Qur'an 18: 28)*

In *Aṣ-Ṣaḥeeḥayn* (Bukhari and Muslim) it is reported from 'Utbaan ibn Maalik that the Messenger of Allah (ﷺ) said:

"Allah has forbidden to the Fire those who say *Laa ilaaha illa-Allah*, seeking thereby the Face of Allah."[15]

b) Seeking refuge by the Face of Allah, the Exalted

This is what the Messenger (ﷺ) did. Jaabir ibn 'Abdullah narrated that when this *aayah* (verse) was revealed —

﴿ قُلْ هُوَ ٱلْقَادِرُ عَلَىٰٓ أَن يَبْعَثَ عَلَيْكُمْ عَذَابًا مِّن فَوْقِكُمْ... ﴿٦٥﴾ ﴾

﴿Say: 'He has power to send torment on you from above...'﴾ *(Qur'an 6: 65)*

— the Prophet (ﷺ) said: "I seek refuge by Your Face." Allah (سبحانه وتعالى), said:

﴿ ... أَوْ مِن تَحْتِ أَرْجُلِكُمْ ... ﴿٦٥﴾ ﴾

﴿...or from under your feet,...﴾ *(Qur'an 6: 65).*

---

[15] *Ṣaḥeeḥ al-Bukhari bi Sharḥihi Fatḥ al-Baari*, 1/519, hadith no. 425; Muslim, 1/455.

The Prophet (ﷺ) said: "I seek refuge by Your Face." Allah (سبحانه وتعالى), said:

﴿... أَوْ يَلْبِسَكُمْ شِيَعًا وَيُذِيقَ بَعْضَكُم بَأْسَ بَعْضٍ ... ﴿٦٥﴾﴾

﴾...Or to cover you with confusion in party strife, and make you to taste the violence of one another...﴿ *(Qur'an 6: 65).*

The Prophet (ﷺ) said: "That is easier."[16]

It is reported from 'Ali ibn Abi Ṭaalib (رضي الله عنه) that the Messenger of Allah (ﷺ) used to say, when he lay down:

> "*Allahumma inni a'oodhu bi wajhik al-kareem, wa bi kalimaatik at-taammaat min sharri kulli daabbah anta aakhidh bi naaṣitayatihaa* (O' Allah! I seek refuge by Your Noble Face and by Your perfect Words, from the evil of every beast whose forelock You have hold of)."

— This is narrated by Abu Dawood.[17]

c) Responding to the one who asks of you for the sake (lit. by the Face) of Allah

It is reported that Ibn 'Abbaas (رضي الله عنه) stated: the Messenger of Allah (ﷺ) said:

> "Whoever seeks refuge with Allah, protect him, and whoever asks of you for the sake (lit. by the Face) of Allah, give to him."[18]

---

[16] Bukhari, 13/388, hadith no. 7406.

[17] *Jaami' al-Uṣool*, 4/271, hadith no. 2263. Its isnad is *ḥasan*, as is mentioned by the editor of *Jaami' al-Uṣool.*

[18] Abu Dawood, 3/961, hadith no. 4260. Al-Albaani said: it is *ḥasan ṣaḥeeḥ*. See also *Al-Asma' wa'ṣ-Ṣifaat* by Al-Bayhaqi, 1/306.

d) Hoping to see the Face of Allah

It is reported from 'Ammaar ibn Yaasir that the Messenger (ﷺ) used to say in his supplication *(du'aa'):*

"*Allahumma bi 'ilmik al-ghaybi wa qudratika 'ala'l-khalq, aḥyini ma 'alimta al-ḥayaata khayran li wa tawaffani idha 'alimta al-wafaat khayran li. Allahumma wa as'aluka khashiyataka fi'l-ghaybi wa'sh-shahaadah, wa as'aluka kalimat al-ḥaqq wa'l-'adla fi'l-ghaḍab wa'r-riḍaa, wa as'aluka al-qaṣad fi'l-faqari wa'l-ghinaa. Wa as'aluka na'eeman laa yabeed, wa as'aluka qurrat 'aynin laa tanqaṭi', wa as'aluka ar-riḍaa ba'da al-qaḍaa', wa as'aluka burd al-'eeish ba'da al-mawt, wa as'aluka ladhdhatan-naẓr ila wajhika, wa as'aluka ash-shawqa ila liqaa'ika fi ghayru ḍaaraa'a muḍirrah, wa laa fitnata muḍillah. Allahumma zayyinnaa bi zeenat il-eemaan wa'j'alna hudaata muhtadeen* (O' Allah! By Your knowledge of the Unseen and Your Power over Your creation, keep me alive so long as you know that living is good for me, and cause me to die when You know that death is good for me. I ask You to make me fear You in secret and in public. I ask You to make me speak the truth and be fair when angry and when content. I ask You to make me to be economical in poverty and in richness. I ask You for a life of ease that never ends. I ask You for joy that never ceases. I ask You for contentment after You have issued Your decree. I ask You for tranquillity after death. I ask You for the joy of looking upon Your Face. I ask You to make me long to meet You without undergoing painful sickness or misguiding *fitnah*. O' Allah! adorn us with the beauty of faith and make us guides to others who are also guided.)."[19]

The Prophet (ﷺ) explained the "even more" mentioned in the *aayah*:

[19] Ibn Khuzaymah in *At-Tawḥeed*, Pp. 12; Nasaai, 1/280, hadith no. 1237, 1238. Its isnad is *ṣaḥeeḥ* (sound).

﴾For those who have done good is the best reward and even more [i.e. having the honour of glancing at the Countenance of Allah].﴿ *(Qur'an 10: 26)*

— as meaning looking at the face of our Lord (ﷻ). Similar statement is also narrated from Abu Bakr and Ḥudhayfah. Then he (the narrator) said: The reports to this effect from the *Ṣaḥaabah* and *Taabi'een* (may Allah be pleased with them) are many.[20]

Muslim narrated from Ṣuhayb that the Prophet (ﷺ) said:

"When the people of Paradise enter Paradise, Allah will say, 'Do you want anything more from Me?' They will say, 'Have You not made our faces white [honoured us]; have You not admitted us to Paradise; have You not saved us from the Fire?' Then the veil will be lifted, and they will never be given anything more beloved to them than looking upon the face of their Lord, the Exalted." Then he recited the *aayah*: ﴾For those who have done good is the best reward and even more [i.e. having the honour of glancing at the Countenance of Allah].﴿ *(Qur'an 10: 26)*[21]

Bukhari and Muslim narrated that the Messenger of Allah (ﷺ) said:

"Two gardens of silver, their vessels and all that is in them, and two gardens of gold, their vessels and all that is in them. And all that will stand between the people and their seeing the Lord will be the veil of pride over His Face in the Paradise of *'Aden*."[22]

---

[20] *Al-Asmaa' wa'ṣ-Ṣifaat* by Al-Bayhaqi, Pp. 308.

[21] Muslim, 1/163, hadith no. 180.

[22] Bukhari, 13/423, hadith no. 7444. Also narrated in 8/623, hadith no. 4878, with similar wording by Muslim, 1/163, hadith no. 180. Ibn Khuzaymah with the wording, "There will be nothing between the people and their seeing the Face of =

The veil of His Face

It is narrated that Abu Moosa reported: the Messenger of Allah (ﷺ) said:

> "Allah, the All-Powerful and All-High, does not sleep and it is not befitting that He should sleep. He lowers the scale and raises it. The deeds of the night are raised up to Him before the day, and the deeds of the day before the night. His veil is Light (according to the report of Abu Bakr: fire); if it were to be uncovered, the splendour of His Countenance would consume His creation as far as His Sight reaches."[23]

The narrator's uncertainty as to whether the word was *noor* (light) or *naar* (fire) does not matter, because it is like the pure fire through which Allah addressed Moosa (Moses), which may be called *noor* or *naar*. Allah called the fire in a lamp light, unlike the dark fire such as the fire of Hell, which cannot be called light.

This veil prevents His slaves from comprehending Allah, just as the clouds and ceilings prevent them from seeing the sun and moon. When the clouds move, the sun and moon appear. This does not mean that they prevent Allah from seeing, for no Muslim would say this. Nothing whatsoever is hidden from Allah, in the heavens or on earth, but His Light conceal Him from His creation, as it says in the hadith: "if it were to be uncovered, the splendour of His Countenance would consume His creation as far as His Sight reaches." His Sight reaches all of His creation, but the splendour is concealed by the veil of light or fire.

= their Lord (*Rabb*)." The commentator of *Kitaab at-Tawḥeed* noted that this hadith is narrated by Al-Bayhaqi in *Al-Asmaa' wa'ṣ-Ṣifaat*, Pp. 222.

[23] Muslim, 1/161, hadith no. 179.

iv) Allah has two Hands

Allah ﷻ, has two Hands, in a manner that is befitting to His Majesty and perfection. They do not resemble the hands of His creatures in any way. Allah (ﷻ) says:

﴿... بَلْ يَدَاهُ مَبْسُوطَتَانِ ... ﴿٦٤﴾﴾

﴿...Nay, both His Hands are widely outstretched...﴾ *(Qur'an 5: 64)*

And Allah said, rebuking *Iblees* when he refused to prostrate to Adam:

﴿قَالَ يَٰٓإِبۡلِيسُ مَا مَنَعَكَ أَن تَسۡجُدَ لِمَا خَلَقۡتُ بِيَدَيَّۖ... ﴿٧٥﴾﴾

﴿[Allah] said: 'O' *Iblees* [Satan]! What prevents you from prostrating yourself to one whom I have created with Both My Hands...'﴾ *(Qur'an 38: 75)*

Glorifying Allah by mentioning His Hands

A number of *aḥaadeeth* have been narrated in which the Lord - the Exalted and All-Glory - is glorified by mention of His Hands and stating that goodness is in them. The Lord will call the people of Paradise, saying to them: "O' people of Paradise!" They will say, "At Your service, O' Lord, all goodness in is Your Hands."[24]

Our Lord will call Adam on the Day of Resurrection, and Adam will say in response: "At Your service, O' Lord! All goodness is in Your Hands."[25]

Whenever the Prophet (ﷺ) stood to pray at night, his *du'aa'* (supplication) would include the words: "At Your service, O' Lord, all goodness is in Your hands."[26]

---

[24] Bukhari, 13/487, hadith no. 7518.

[25] Ibid, 11/388, hadith no. 6530; 6/382, hadith no. 3348; Muslim, 1/201, no. 201.

[26] Muslim, 1/534, hadith no. 771.

In his *Talbiyah*, Ibn 'Umar used to say: "At Your service, O' Lord, all goodness is in Your hands."[27]

Allah spreads His Hands

Allah (ﷻ), is Generous and spreads His hands to give and bestow.

﴿... بَلْ يَدَاهُ مَبْسُوطَتَانِ يُنفِقُ كَيْفَ يَشَآءُ وَلَيَزِيدَنَّ كَثِيرًا مِّنْهُم... ﴿٦٤﴾﴾

﴿...Nay, both His Hands are widely outstretched. He spends [of His Bounty] as He wills...﴾*(Qur'an 5: 64)*

And He spreads His Hands by night and by day to accept the repentance of His slaves. Abu Moosa al-Ash'ari narrated that the Messenger of Allah (ﷺ) said:

> "Allah spreads His Hands by night to accept the repentance of those who sinned by day, and He spreads His Hands by day to accept the repentance of those who sinned by night. (This will continue) until the sun rises from the west."[28]

Things which the All-Merciful has created with His Hands

Allah is not incapable of anything. When He wills something, He creates it with the word *Kun* ("Be!"), and it is as He wills. But He has created some things with His Hands, as a sign of honour and high status, and the care that Allah bestows upon them. The things that Allah has created with His Hand and that are mentioned in His Books or narrated in the Sunnah of His Messenger are the following:

a) Adam — Concerning this, Allah (ﷻ), said to *Iblees* (Satan):

﴿... يَٰٓإِبْلِيسُ مَا مَنَعَكَ أَن تَسْجُدَ لِمَا خَلَقْتُ بِيَدَيَّ ... ﴿٧٥﴾﴾

---

[27] Muslim, 2/841, hadith no. 1184.

[28] Ibid, 4/2113, hadith no. 5572.

> ﴿...O' *Iblees* [Satan]! What prevents you from prostrating yourself to one whom I have created with Both My Hands...﴾ *(Qur'an 38: 75)*

In a lengthy hadith about intercession, it says:

> "They will come to Adam and will say, 'You are Adam, the father of mankind. Allah created You with His Hands and caused you to dwell in His Paradise.'" (Agreed upon).[29]

According to the hadith which describes the debate between Adam and Moosa (Moses) (ﷺ), Moosa said to Adam:

> "You are the one whom Allah created with His Hands and breathed into you of His Spirit."[30]

Allah (ﷻ), tells us that He created Adam with his Hands, and the Messenger (ﷺ) tells us that the people will ask Adam to intercede for them, and they will mention the greatest of the blessings that Allah bestowed upon him, that is, Allah created him with His Hands. Moosa (Moses) also mentioned the blessing which Allah bestowed upon Adam, that He created Him with His Hands. The mention of this unique characteristic indicates the way in which Adam is distinguished above others. Otherwise, if Hand here referred to Power, how would Adam be better than anyone else, so that he might be praised in this manner?

b) Allah (ﷻ) wrote the *Tawraat* (Torah) with His Hand:

It is narrated in some reports of the hadith about the dispute between Adam and Moosa, that Adam said to Moosa:

---

[29] *Mishkaat al-Maṣaabeeḥ* (derived from Bukhari and Muslim), 3/69, hadith no. 5572.

[30] Muslim, 4/2043, hadith no. 2652.

> "You are Moosa (Moses) whom Allah chose to speak to, and He wrote for you the *Tawraat* with His Hand."[31]

According to a report narrated in Bukhari and Muslim:

> "Allah chose you to speak to, and He wrote for you with His Hand."[32]

c) Allah (ﷻ) wrote something which is placed with Him:

It is narrated from Abu Hurayrah (رضي الله عنه) that the Prophet (ﷺ) said:

> "When Allah finished His Creation, He wrote in a book, 'My Mercy prevails over — or precedes — My Wrath.' And it is with Him above the Throne." According to another report: "Allah wrote in a book before He created the universe: 'Verily My Mercy precedes my Wrath' — and it is written with Him above the Throne."[33]

It is also narrated by Ibn Maajah from Abu Hurayrah, with the wording:

> "Your Lord wrote for Himself by His Hand before He created the universe: My Mercy precedes My Wrath."[34]

It is also reported in *Kitaab as-Sunnah* by Abu 'Aaṣim that the Most Merciful wrote down something with His Hand, it says:

> "When Allah finished creating the universe, He wrote with His Hand in a Book with Him: My Mercy prevails over — or he said: precedes — My Wrath. And it is with Him above the Throne." Or words to that effect.[35]

---

[31] Abu Dawood, 3/891, hadith no. 3934; Ibn Maajah, 1/20, hadith no. 65.

[32] Bukhari, 11, hadith no. 6614; Muslim, 4/2042, hadith no. 2652.

[33] Bukhari: 13/522, hadith no. 7554. Muslim: 4/2107, hadith no, 2751.

[34] Ibn Maajah,1/37, hadith no. 156.

[35] *Kitaab as-Sunnah*, by Ibn Abi 'Aaṣim, 1/270, hadith no. 608.

d) Allah (ﷻ) planted the Paradise of *'Aden* with His Hands:

It is narrated in Muslim that the Messenger of Allah (ﷺ) said:

> "Moosa (Moses) asked: 'Who among the people of Paradise will be the lowest in status?' He said: 'It will be a man who will be brought after the people of Paradise have entered Paradise.' It will be said to him: 'Enter Paradise.' He will say, 'O' Lord, the people have settled in their places and taken what is theirs.' It will be said to him: 'Would you not be happy to have the equivalent of a king's possessions in the world?' He will say, 'I would be happy with that, O' Lord.' It will be said to him, 'You will have that, and the same again, and again and again.' The fifth time, he will say: 'I am happy with that O' Lord.' It will be said to him, 'And ten times that, and you will have whatever your heart desires and whatever delights you.' He will say, 'I am happy with that, O' Lord.' He said, 'O' Lord, and who will be the highest of them in status?' He said: 'Those whom I will; I have planted the place of their honour with My hand, and sealed it. No eye has seen, no ear has heard, nor has it entered the heart of man.' He said: And this is confirmed in the Book of Allah, where it says:
>
> ﴿فَلَا تَعْلَمُ نَفْسٌ مَّآ أُخْفِيَ لَهُم مِّن قُرَّةِ أَعْيُنٍ جَزَآءًۢ بِمَا كَانُوا۟ يَعْمَلُونَ ﴿١٧﴾﴾
>
> ﴾No person knows what is kept hidden for them of joy as a reward for what they used to do.﴿ *(Qur'an 32: 17)*."[36]

From this hadith we see that He planted the Garden with His own Hand.

---

[36] Muslim, 1/176, hadith no. 189.

The greatness of the Hands of the Lord (ﷻ)
It says in the Qur'an:

﴿ وَمَا قَدَرُوا۟ ٱللَّهَ حَقَّ قَدْرِهِۦ وَٱلْأَرْضُ جَمِيعًا قَبْضَتُهُۥ يَوْمَ ٱلْقِيَٰمَةِ وَٱلسَّمَٰوَٰتُ مَطْوِيَّٰتٌۢ بِيَمِينِهِۦ ... ﴿٦٧﴾ ﴾

﴿They made not a just estimate of Allah such as is due to Him. And on the Day of Resurrection the whole of the earth will be grasped by His Hand and the heavens will be rolled up in His Right Hand...﴾ *(Qur'an 39: 67)*

In *ṣaḥeeḥayn* it is narrated from Abu Hurayrah (رضي الله عنه) that the Prophet (ﷺ) said:

"Allah will grasp the earth on the Day of Resurrection, and will roll up the heavens in His Right Hand, then He will say: 'I am the King, where are the kings of the earth?'"[37]

Muslim narrated from 'Abdullah ibn 'Umar that the Prophet (ﷺ) said:

"Allah will roll up the heavens on the Day of Resurrection, then He will hold them in His Right Hand, and will say, 'I am the King, where are the tyrants? Where are the arrogant?' Then He will roll up the earth in His left Hand, and will say, 'I am the King. Where are the tyrants? Where are the arrogant?'"

According to another version he said: I saw the Messenger of Allah (ﷺ) on the *minbar*, saying:

"The Compeller — *Al-Jabbar* — the Almighty, will take His heavens and His earth in His Hands, and will say, 'I am Allah (and He will close His Fingers and then open

[37] Bukhari, 8/551, hadith no. 4812; Muslim, 4/2148, hadith no. 2787.

> them and say) I am the Sovereign.'"

And I looked at the minbar and saw it shaking from the bottom, and I thought it would collapse under the Messenger of Allah.[38]

Both of His Hands are Right Hands

It is narrated in a report in Muslim,

> "Then He will roll up the earth in His left Hand."

Al-Bayhaqi considered this report as weak in terms of the isnad, and said: The mention of the left hand in this report is narrated only by 'Umar ibn Ḥamzah from Saalim. This hadith is also narrated by Naafi' and 'Ubaydullah ibn Muqsim from Ibn 'Umar, but they did not mention the left hand.[39] He also classified it as *ḍa'eef* on the basis of the *matn* (text), and said: "How can that be *ṣaḥeeḥ* (sound) when it has been proven that the Prophet (ﷺ) described both of His Hands as right?[40]

It is narrated that 'Abdullah ibn 'Amr stated: the Messenger of Allah (ﷺ) said:

> "The just will be with Allah on thrones of light at the right hand of the Most Merciful, — the Almighty and All-Glory — and both His Hands are right, those who were just in their judgements and in the way they treated their families and those under their authority."[41]

v) The Fingers of the Most Merciful

Allah has Fingers which in no way resemble the fingers of any of His creation. They befit His Perfection and Majesty, the All-Glory and

---

[38] Muslim, 4/2148, hadith no. 2788.

[39] *Al-Asmaa' wa'ṣ-Ṣifaat* by Al-Bayhaqi, 1/324.

[40] Ibid.

[41] Muslim, 3/1458, hadith no. 1827.

Exalted. In the Bukhari and Muslim, it is narrated from 'Abdullah ibn Mas'ood that a Jew came to the Prophet (ﷺ) and said, "O' Muhammad, Allah holds the heavens on one Finger, the earth on one Finger, the mountains on one Finger, the trees on one Finger and all creatures on one Finger, and He says, 'I am the Sovereign.'" The Messenger of Allah (ﷺ) smiled so broadly that his eyeteeth could be seen, then he recited:

﴿وَمَا قَدَرُوا۟ ٱللَّهَ حَقَّ قَدْرِهِۦ ... ﴿٦٧﴾﴾

> ﴿They made not a just estimate of Allah such as is due to Him...﴾ *(Qur'an 39: 67)*

According to another version: The Messenger of Allah (ﷺ) smiled in amazement and confirmation.[42]

It is narrated that 'Abdullah ibn 'Amr ibn al-'Aaṣ (may Allah be pleased with them both) heard the Prophet (ﷺ) say:

> "The hearts of the sons of Adam are all as one heart between two of the fingers of the Most Merciful, and He directs them as He wishes." Then he said: "O' Allah, Director of the hearts, direct our hearts towards obedience to You."[43]

vi) What has been mentioned concerning His Foot

Al-Bayhaqi used this as a title in his book *Al-Asmaa' wa'ṣ-Ṣifaat* (348), where he mentioned a number of *aḥaadeeth*:

a) A hadith is narrated by Bukhari and Muslim from Anas ibn Maalik (رضي الله عنه) that the Prophet (ﷺ) said:

> "Hell will keep saying, 'Are there any more?' until the

---

[42] Bukhari, 13,393, hadith no. 7414; Muslim, 4/2147, hadith no. 2786.

[43] Muslim, 4/2045, hadith no. 2655.

Lord of Glory will put His Foot on it, then it will say, 'Enough, enough, by Your Glory!' Then it will shrink into itself." According to some reports: "And there will still be extra space in Paradise until Allah creates people for it and causes them to dwell in the extra space of Paradise."[44]

b) It is narrated from Abu Hurayrah (رضي الله عنه) that the Messenger of Allah (ﷺ) said:

> "Paradise and Hell engaged in a debate. Hell said: 'I was created to take the arrogant and the tyrannical.' Paradise said, 'Why is it that no one will enter me except the weak and lowly among mankind?' Allah said to Paradise: 'You are My Mercy, by which I will show mercy to whomsoever I will among My slaves.' And He said to Hell: 'You are My Punishment by which I will punish whomsoever I will among My slaves. Each of you will have its fill.' The Fire will not be filled until Allah puts His Foot, and it says, 'Enough, enough, enough!' Then it will be filled and will shrink into itself. And Allah does not treat any of His creation unjustly. As for Paradise, Allah will create people for it [to fill it]."[45]

c) It is narrated that Ibn 'Abbaas (رضي الله عنه) said concerning the *Kursiy*,

﴿ ... وَسِعَ كُرْسِيُّهُ ٱلسَّمَٰوَٰتِ وَٱلْأَرْضَ ... ﴿٢٥٥﴾ ﴾

﴾...His *Kursiy* extends over the heavens and the earth,...﴿
(Qur'an 2: 255)

---

[44] Bukhari, 8/594, hadith no. 4848, 4849; Muslim, 4/2187, 2188, hadith no. 2848. This version is narrated by Muslim.

[45] Bukhari, 8/595, hadith no. 4850; Muslim, 4/2186, hadith no. 2846. This version is narrated by Muslim.

- it is the place for the feet (i.e., a footstool).[46]

vii) Allah, the Exalted, has a Shin

It is obligatory for us to believe in this and not to deny it, because He - the Exalted - has told us of it.

Allah (ﷻ) says:

﴿ يَوْمَ يُكْشَفُ عَن سَاقٍ وَيُدْعَوْنَ إِلَى ٱلسُّجُودِ فَلَا يَسْتَطِيعُونَ ﴿٤٢﴾ ﴾

> ﴾[Remember] the Day when the *Shin* shall be laid bare [i.e. the Day of Resurrection] and they shall be called to prostrate themselves [to Allah], but they [hypocrites] shall not be able to do so.﴿ *(Qur'an 68: 42)*

There are reports in Bukhari and Muslim which explain this *aayah* (verse) and make it clear. It is narrated that Abu Sa'eed al-Khudri said: I heard the Messenger of Allah (ﷺ) say:

> "Our Lord will lay bare His *Shin*, and every believing man and believing woman will prostrate to Him. There will be left those who used to prostrate in the world in order to show off and gain a good reputation. Such a one will try to prostrate, but his backbone will become a single (solid) piece (and he will not be able to prostrate)."[47]

We must note here that affirming that Allah has a *Shin* is like affirming that He has a Hand, hearing, sight and any other attributes.

---

[46] See *Mukhtaṣar al-'Aluw* by Dhahabi, Pp. 102. The editor *Shaykh* Naaṣiruddeen al-Albaani said: this is *ṣaḥeeḥ mawqoof*, and attributed it to Ibn Khuzaymah in *At-Tawḥeed*, 71-72; to Daarimi in *Ar-Radd 'ala'l-Mareesi*, 71, 73-74; and Ibn Abi Shaybah in *Al-'Arsh*, 2/114.

[47] Bukhari, 8/664, hadith no. 4419; Muslim, 1/167, hadith no. 183. This version is narrated by Bukhari.

What has been narrated from Ibn 'Abbaas, who interpreted laying bare the *Shin* as referring to the seriousness of the matter, contradicts what is proven from Ibn Mas'ood, that our Lord will lay bare His *Shin*.[48]

How well Ash-Shawkaani spoke when he said: Allah has given us sufficient interpretation of this *aayah* (verse) in the ṣaḥeeḥ (sound) reports narrated from the Messenger of Allah. This does not imply thinking in physical or anthropomorphic terms, for there is nothing like unto Him.[49]

Ibn Jareer aṭ-Ṭabari and Ibn Katheer narrated the *tafseer* of Ibn 'Abbaas, just as they also narrated the hadith which explain the text of the Qur'an. They did not interpret the hadith in any way different than its apparent meaning, which indicates that they did not see any contradiction between the hadith and the view of Ibn 'Abbaas. The matter will indeed be serious on the Day of Resurrection, and this does not contradict the idea that Allah will lay bare His *Shin*.

viii) His rising over the Throne

The Throne is the greatest thing in all of creation, and Allah (ﷻ), refers in seven places in His Book to His rising over the Throne, by saying,

﴿ ٱلرَّحْمَٰنُ عَلَى ٱلْعَرْشِ ٱسْتَوَىٰ ۝٥ ﴾

﴾The Most Gracious [Allah] rose over [*Istawaa*] the [Mighty] Throne [in a manner that suits His Majesty].﴿ *(Qur'an 20: 5)*

The evidence that the Throne is one of the things created by Allah (ﷻ), the Almighty:

---

[48] *Fatḥ al-Qadeer* by Ash-Shawkaani, 5/319.
[49] Ibid, 5/320.

﴿ ... وَيَحۡمِلُ عَرۡشَ رَبِّكَ فَوۡقَهُمۡ يَوۡمَئِذٖ ثَمَٰنِيَةٞ ﴿١٧﴾ ﴾

﴿...And eight angels will, that Day, bear the Throne of your Lord above them.﴾ *(Qur'an 69: 17)*

- i.e., on the Day of Resurrection.

﴿ ٱلَّذِينَ يَحۡمِلُونَ ٱلۡعَرۡشَ وَمَنۡ حَوۡلَهُۥ يُسَبِّحُونَ بِحَمۡدِ رَبِّهِمۡ وَيُؤۡمِنُونَ بِهِۦ وَيَسۡتَغۡفِرُونَ لِلَّذِينَ ءَامَنُواْ ... ﴿٧﴾ ﴾

﴿Those [angels] who bear the Throne [of Allah] and those around it glorify the praises of their Lord, and believe in Him, and ask forgiveness for those who believe...﴾ *(Qur'an 40: 7)*

Allah (ﷻ), tells us that the Throne has bearers, and that they seek forgiveness for the believers. This negates the view of those who say that the Throne refers to Allah's Sovereignty or Dominion (*Al-Mulk*).

According to a hadith narrated by Bukhari, "When you ask Allah, ask Him for *Al-Firdaws*, for it is the middle of Paradise and is the highest part of Paradise. Above it is the Throne of the Most Merciful, and from it spring forth the rivers of Paradise."[50]

Bukhari narrated from Abu Hurayrah that the Messenger of Allah (ﷺ) said:

> "Do not prefer me over Moosa (Moses), for the people will fall unconscious on the Day of Resurrection; I will be the first to regain consciousness, and Moosa will be there, holding on to the side of the Throne. I do not know whether Moosa will be one of those who fell unconscious and then woke up before me, or whether he was one of those whom Allah exempted

[50] Bukhari, 13/404, hadith no. 7423.

(from falling unconscious)."[51]

According to a report narrated by Abu Sa'eed al-Khudri:

"Moosa (Moses) will be there, holding on to one of the pillars of the Throne."[52]

How can the Throne not be one of the things created by Allah (ﷻ), when it is the roof of *Al-Firdaws*. How can Moosa (Moses) hold onto one of the pillars of the Throne if it is not something that has been created?

The Messenger (ﷺ) said:

"When Allah completed His creation, He wrote down with Himself above His Throne: My mercy precedes My wrath."[53]

The great size of the Throne

Allah has described His Throne as being Great (*'Aẓeem*):

﴿... وَرَبُّ الْعَرْشِ الْعَظِيمِ ﴿٨٦﴾﴾

﴿...And Lord of the Great Throne.﴾ *(Qur'an 23: 86)*

The Messenger (ﷺ) described the Throne as being great in two ways:

a) By telling us of the great size of the angels who carry the Throne. In Sunan Abi Dawood it is narrated with a *ṣaḥeeḥ* (sound) isnad that the Messenger (ﷺ) said:

"I have been granted permission to speak about one of the angels of Allah, one of the bearers of the Throne. The

---

[51] Bukhari, 11/367, hadith no. 6517, 6518; the hadith is also narrated by Muslim, 4/1834, hadith no. 2373.

[52] Ibid, 13/405, hadith no. 7427.

[53] Ibid, hadith no. 7422.

> space between his earlobes and his shoulders is the distance of seven hundred years' travelling."[54]

b) The Messenger described the size of the Throne by contrasting its size with the size of the heavens and the *kursiy*. He (ﷺ) said:

> "The seven heavens in comparison to the *kursiy* are like no more than a ring thrown out into an empty field, and the superiority of the Throne in relation to the *kursiy* is like the superiority of that field in relation to that ring."[55]

Allah praises Himself by mentioning His rising over the Throne and by declaring that He is the Lord of the Throne

The Lord praises Himself by stating that He has risen over His Throne:

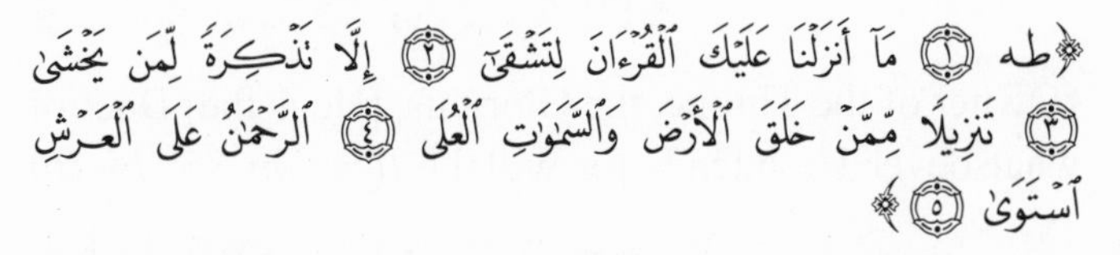

> ﴿*Ta-Ha*.[These letters are one of the miracles of the Qur'an, and none but Allah (Alone) knows their meanings.] We have not sent down the Qur'an unto you [O' Muhammad] to cause you distress, But only as a Reminder to those who fear [Allah]. A Revelation from Him [Allah] Who has created the earth and high heavens. The Most Gracious [Allah] rose over [*Istawaa*] the [Mighty] Throne [in a manner that suits His Majesty].﴾ *(Qur'an 20: 1-5)*

---

[54] Abu Dawood, 3/895, hadith no. 3953.

[55] Narrated by Muhammad ibn Abi Shaybah in *Kitaab al-'Arsh*, by Al-Bayhaqi in *Al-Asmaa' wa's-Ṣifaat*, by Ibn Jareer and by others. It is *ṣaḥeeḥ* (sound) when all its isnads are taken together. See *Shaykh* Al-Albaani's comments on its isnad in *Silsilat al-Aḥaadeeth aṣ-Ṣaḥeeḥah*, hadith no. 109.

﴿ هُوَ ٱلَّذِى خَلَقَ ٱلسَّمَٰوَٰتِ وَٱلْأَرْضَ فِى سِتَّةِ أَيَّامٍ ثُمَّ ٱسْتَوَىٰ عَلَى ٱلْعَرْشِ يَعْلَمُ مَا يَلِجُ فِى ٱلْأَرْضِ وَمَا يَخْرُجُ مِنْهَا وَمَا يَنزِلُ مِنَ ٱلسَّمَآءِ وَمَا يَعْرُجُ فِيهَا وَهُوَ مَعَكُمْ أَيْنَ مَا كُنتُمْ وَٱللَّهُ بِمَا تَعْمَلُونَ بَصِيرٌ ﴿٤﴾ ﴾

﴾He it is Who created the heavens and the earth in six Days and then rose over [*Istawa*] the Throne [in a manner that suits His Majesty]. He knows what goes into the earth and what comes forth from it, and what descends from the heaven and what ascends thereto. And He is with you [by His Knowledge] wheresoever you may be. And Allah is the All-Seer of what you do.﴿ *(Qur'an 57: 4)*

And Allah (ﷻ), praises Himself on more than one occasion as being the Master of the Throne:

﴿ ذُو ٱلْعَرْشِ ٱلْمَجِيدُ ﴿١٥﴾ فَعَّالٌ لِّمَا يُرِيدُ ﴿١٦﴾ ﴾

﴾Owner of the Throne, the Glorious, [He is the] Doer of whatsoever He intends [or wills].﴿ *(Qur'an 85: 15-16)*

﴿ ... إِذًا لَّٱبْتَغَوْا۟ إِلَىٰ ذِى ٱلْعَرْشِ سَبِيلًا ﴿٤٢﴾ ﴾

﴾...Then they would certainly have sought out a way to the Lord of the Throne.﴿ *(Qur'an 17: 42)*

And Allah (ﷻ), praises Himself as being the Lord of the Throne:

﴿ ... عَلَيْهِ تَوَكَّلْتُ وَهُوَ رَبُّ ٱلْعَرْشِ ٱلْعَظِيمِ ﴿١٢٩﴾ ﴾

﴾...In Him I put my trust and He is the Lord of the Mighty Throne.﴿ *(Qur'an 9: 129)*

﴿ ... فَسُبْحَٰنَ ٱللَّهِ رَبِّ ٱلْعَرْشِ عَمَّا يَصِفُونَ ﴿٢٢﴾ ﴾

﴾...Glorified is Allah, the Lord of the Throne, [High is He] above all that [evil] they associate with Him!﴿ *(Qur'an 21: 22)*

﴿قُلْ مَن رَّبُّ ٱلسَّمَٰوَٰتِ ٱلسَّبْعِ وَرَبُّ ٱلْعَرْشِ ٱلْعَظِيمِ ﴿٨٦﴾﴾

﴾Say: 'Who is [the] Lord of the seven heavens, and [the] Lord of the Great Throne?'﴿ *(Qur'an 23: 86)*

'Abdullah ibn Rawaḥah praised his Lord in couplets as follows:

"I bear witness that the promise of Allah is true,
And that the Fire is the abode of the *kaafireen* (disbelievers).
And that the Throne is floating above the water,
And above the Throne is the Lord of the Worlds.
And it is borne by noble angels,
Angels of the Lord."

This couplet was transmitted by Ibn 'Abdul-Barr in *Al-Isti'aab*, where he says: We have narrated it through *ṣaḥeeḥ* isnads.

The meaning of His rising over the Throne (*istiwaa*)

We do not know how Allah (سبحانه وتعالى), rose over the Throne, because we do not know how He is, but we know the meaning of *istawaa* in the Arabic language. When the Arabs follow the word *istawaa* with the preposition *'ala*, they mean four things: settling, going over, rising above and ascending, as was affirmed by Ibn al-Qayyim.[56]

Abu'l-Ḥasan al-Ash'ari narrated that the *Mu'tazilah* interpreted the phrase ﴾rose over [*Istawaa*] the Throne﴿ *(Qur'an 57: 4)* as meaning that He possessed or took control of it.[57] Whoever interprets this phrase in this manner should note that his predecessors in this regard are the *Mu'tazilah*, and what bad predecessors they are.

The *Ahl as-Sunnah* and scholars of hadith affirm that Allah rose over the Throne. They do not deny it, but they do not discuss how it happened, as Abu'l-Ḥasan al-Ash'ari (may Allah have mercy on

---

[56] *Sharḥ al-Waaṣittiyah* by Al-Harraas, Pp. 80.

[57] *Maqaalaat al-Islamiyeen*, Pp. 157, 211.

him) narrated from them.[58]

Scholars of the Arabic language have narrated to us that the scholars whose *fiṭrah* has not been contaminated with alien philosophy refuse to interpret *istawaa* as meaning *istawla* (possess, take control).

Dawood ibn 'Ali al-Iṣbahaani said: I was with Ibn al-A'rabi, and a man came to him and asked, What is the meaning of the *aayah*,

﴿ ٱلرَّحْمَٰنُ عَلَى ٱلْعَرْشِ ٱسْتَوَىٰ ۝٥ ﴾

> ﴿The Most Gracious [Allah] rose over [*Istawaa*] the [Mighty] Throne [in a manner that suits His Majesty].﴾ *(Qur'an 20: 5)*

Ibn al-A'rabi said: He is on His Throne as He has told us. He said, O' Abu 'Abdullah, does it not mean *istawla* (possess, take control)? Ibn al-A'rabi said: How can you know that? The Arabs do not say *istawla* unless there are two people competing for a throne, then whichever of them prevails, they describe as *istawla*.[59]

This method, which is acknowledging the meaning of *istiwaa* whilst not seeking to know how, is the method of the righteous *salaf*. When Imam Maalik was asked about the *aayah*, ﴿The Most Gracious [Allah] rose over [*Istawaa*] the [Mighty] Throne [in a manner that suits His Majesty]'﴾ *(Qur'an 20: 5)* and was asked how He rose over it, he paused and broke out in a sweat. Then he raised his head and said: The Most Gracious rose over the Throne, as He described Himself. We do not ask how, because one cannot ask how with regard to Allah. You are guilty of *bid'ah* (innovation), throw him out.[60]

---

[58] *Maqaalaat al-Islamiyeen*, Pp. 211, 290.

[59] *Lisaan al-'Arab*, 2/249.

[60] Al-Bayhaqi, and classed as *ṣaḥeeḥ* by Adh-Dhahabi. See *Mukhtaṣar al-'Uluw li'l-'Aliy al-Ghaffaar*, by Adh-Dhahabi, Pp. 141, hadith no. 131.

According to a report, Maalik said: How is incomprehensible, *istiwaa* is not unknown, belief in it is obligatory, and asking about it is *bid'ah*.[61]

The phrase 'not unknown' means it is known; what is known is its meaning, because the word has a meaning in Arabic which the Arabs understand, and which scholars can explain and interpret. Hence many of those who narrated the above view from Imam Maalik narrated the meaning from him, and they mentioned that he replied to the man as follows: "*Istiwaa* is known, how is unknown, believing in it is obligatory and asking about it is *bid'ah*."[62] In fact there is no difference between saying that *istiwaa* is known and saying that it is not unknown - the meaning is the same.

Qurṭubi (may Allah have mercy on him) said: "The first generation — may Allah be pleased with them — did not deny direction (with regard to Allah), and they did not say anything to that effect. They affirmed direction in accordance with what Allah had said in His Book and what His Messenger had told them.

No one denies that He rose over His throne in a real sense. This applies only to the Throne because it is the greatest thing in His creation. But we do not know how He rose over it, because we cannot know the true nature of this.

Maalik said: the *istiwaa* is known — i.e., in the linguistic sense — but how it happened is unknown, and asking about it is *bid'ah*, as Umm Salmah (may Allah be pleased with her) said. And this is sufficient.[63]

ix) Where is Allah?

Allah (ﷻ), has told us that He is in the heavens, above His Throne:

---

[61] See *Mukhtaṣar al-'Aluw*, Pp. 141, hadith no. 132.

[62] *Tafseer al-Qurṭubi*, 2/219.

[63] Ibid.

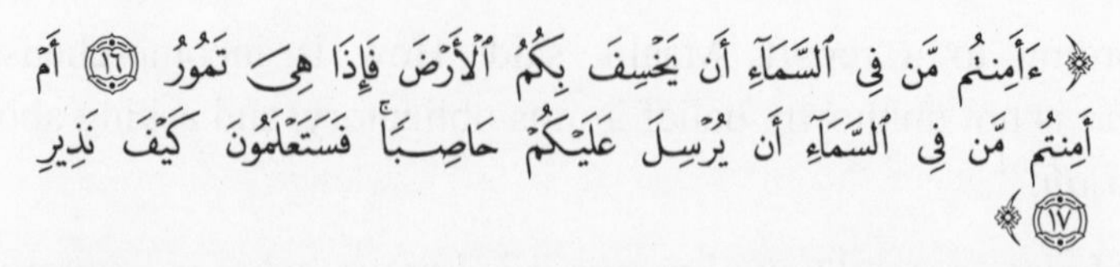

﴾Do you feel secure that He, Who is over the heaven [Allah], will not cause the earth to sink with you, and then it should quake? Or do you feel secure that He, Who is over the heaven [Allah], will not send against you a violent whirlwind? Then you shall know how [terrible] has been My Warning.﴿ *(Qur'an 67: 16-17)*

The Messenger (ﷺ) told us that His Lord is in the heavens. It is narrated from Abu Sa'eed al-Khudri that the Messenger of Allah (ﷺ) said:

> "Do you not trust me when I am the trustee of the One Who is in heaven, and the Revelation comes to me from heaven morning and evening?"[64]

And he testified that the slave girl was a believer when she told him that Allah was in heaven. It is narrated that Mu'aawiyah ibn al-Ḥakam al-Sulami beat a slave girl of his for being careless in minding his sheep. Then he regretted it, and came to the Messenger of Allah (ﷺ) to express his regret and ask for his permission to set her free. The Messenger (ﷺ) called for the girl and asked her,

> "Where is Allah?" She said, "In heaven." He asked, "Who am I?" She said, "You are the Messenger of Allah." He said, "Set her free, for she is a believer."[65]

---

[64] Bukhari, 8/66, hadith no. 4351; Muslim, 2/742, hadith no. 1064 1/382, hadith no. 537. Also narrated by Abu Dawood, 1/175, hadith no. 823; 3/632, hadith no. 2809.

[65] Muslim, 1/382, hadith no. 537; Abu Dawood, 1/175, hadith no. 823; 3/632, hadith no. 2809.

The Messenger (ﷺ) taught the sick person to pray for himself or for his brother with this *du'aa'* (supplication) in which it is stated that Allah (سبحانه وتعالى), is in the heaven:

"*Rabbana Allah alladhi fi's-samaa'i, taqaddasa ismuka, amruka fi's-samaa'i wa'l-arḍ, kama raḥmatuka fi's-samaa' faj'al raḥmataka fi'l-arḍ, ighfir lanaa ḥawbanaa wa khaṭaayaana, anta Rabb aṭ-Ṭayyibeen, anzil raḥmatan min raḥmatika wa shifaa'an min shifaa'ika 'ala haadha'l-waj'i fa yabra'* (O' our Lord Allah, Who are in heaven, sanctified be Your Name. Your Command prevails in the heavens and on earth. As Your Mercy is in heaven, make Your Mercy on earth. Forgive us our mistakes and sins. You are the Lord of the good. Send down Mercy from Your Mercy and healing from Your healing upon this pain, and heal it)."[66]

According to a hadith narrated by 'Abdullah ibn 'Amr, the Messenger of Allah (ﷺ) said:

> "The merciful will be shown mercy by the Most Merciful. Have mercy on those who are on earth, so that the One Who is in the heaven will have mercy on you."[67]

The meaning of His being in heaven

The phrase "Allah is in the heaven" does not mean that He is contained by its physical dimensions — Glorified and Exalted be He far above that. What is meant by heaven is highness and being above. Allah (سبحانه وتعالى), has described Himself as being the Most High:

﴿سَبِّحِ ٱسْمَ رَبِّكَ ٱلْأَعْلَى ۝١﴾

﴾Glorify the Name of your Lord, the Most High.﴿

(Qur'an 87: 1)

---

[66] Abu Dawood, 4/16, hadith no. 3892

[67] Tirmidhi, 2/180, hadith no. 1569. Tirmidhi said: a *ṣaḥeeḥ ḥasan* hadith.

And as the Most High, the Most Great:

﴿... وَسِعَ كُرْسِيُّهُ ٱلسَّمَٰوَٰتِ وَٱلْأَرْضَ ۖ وَلَا يَـُٔودُهُۥ حِفْظُهُمَا ۚ وَهُوَ ٱلْعَلِىُّ ٱلْعَظِيمُ ﴿٢٥٥﴾﴾

﴿...His *Kursiy* extends over the heavens and the earth, and He feels no fatigue in guarding and preserving them. And He is the Most High, the Most Great.﴾ *(Qur'an 2: 255)*

The All-High, tells us that He is above His slaves:

﴿يَخَافُونَ رَبَّهُم مِّن فَوْقِهِمْ وَيَفْعَلُونَ مَا يُؤْمَرُونَ ۩ ﴿٥٠﴾﴾

﴿They fear their Lord above them, and they do what they are commanded.﴾ *(Qur'an 16: 50)*

﴿وَهُوَ ٱلْقَاهِرُ فَوْقَ عِبَادِهِۦ ... ﴿١٨﴾﴾

﴿And He is the Irresistible [Supreme], above His slaves,...﴾ *(Qur'an 6: 18)*

When the Messenger (ﷺ) praised his Lord in his *du'aa'*, he said:

"And You are, and there is none above You."[68]

Zaynab used to boast to the other wives of the Messenger (ﷺ):

"Your families arranged your marriages, but my marriage was arranged by Allah from above the seven heavens."[69]

The Muslim cannot understand his *'aqeedah* (creed) properly if, when he thinks that Allah is in the heavens, he thinks that the heavens contain Him and that He is limited by the physical dimensions of the

---

[68] Muslim, 4/2084, hadith no. 2713.
[69] Tirmidhi, 3/92, hadith no. 2566.

heavens. Glorified be He far above such a thing. How can that be, when the heavens are nothing in relation to Him?

﴿ ... وَٱلسَّمَٰوَٰتُ مَطْوِيَّٰتُۢ بِيَمِينِهِۦ ... ﴿٦٧﴾ ﴾

﴿...And the heavens will be rolled up in His Right Hand...﴾ *(Qur'an 39: 67)*

﴿ يَوْمَ نَطْوِى ٱلسَّمَآءَ كَطَىِّ ٱلسِّجِلِّ لِلْكُتُبِ ... ﴿١٠٤﴾ ﴾

﴿And [remember] the Day when We shall roll up the heaven like a scroll rolled up for books...﴾ *(Qur'an 21: 104)*

Extensive evidence

The evidence in the Qur'an and Sunnah which shows that Allah (ﷻ), is in the heavens, above His slaves, is very clear and in abundance. To quote it all would take too long. But we can arrange it in the following categories:

1) Evidence which states clearly that He is in the heaven. We have mentioned this above.
2) Evidence which states that He rose above the Throne. We have quoted this above.
3) Evidence which proves that He is High, and that He is above His slaves. We have mentioned some of this above.
4) Texts which indicate that some of the things He has created are with Him.

﴿ إِنَّ ٱلَّذِينَ عِندَ رَبِّكَ لَا يَسْتَكْبِرُونَ عَنْ عِبَادَتِهِۦ ... ﴿٢٠٦﴾ ﴾

﴿Surely, those [angels] who are with your Lord are never too proud to perform acts of worship to Him,...﴾ *(Qur'an 7: 206)*

And Allah (ﷻ) says concerning the *shuhadaa'* (martyrs):

﴿... بَلۡ أَحۡيَآءٌ عِندَ رَبِّهِمۡ يُرۡزَقُونَ ﴿١٦٩﴾﴾

﴾...Nay, they are alive, with their Lord, and they have provision.﴿ *(Qur'an 3: 169)*

And there are many other similar texts.

5) Texts which state that some things are raised or ascend to Him, such as the *aayaat* (verses) which clearly state that 'Eesa ibn Maryam (Jesus) (Peace be upon him) was raised up to Him:

﴿بَل رَّفَعَهُ ٱللَّهُ إِلَيۡهِۚ... ﴿١٥٨﴾﴾

﴾But Allah raised him ['Eesa (Jesus)] up [with his body and soul] unto Himself...﴿ *(Qur'an 4: 158)*

And texts which state that good deeds ascend to Him:

﴿... إِلَيۡهِ يَصۡعَدُ ٱلۡكَلِمُ ٱلطَّيِّبُ وَٱلۡعَمَلُ ٱلصَّٰلِحُ يَرۡفَعُهُۥۚ... ﴿١٠﴾﴾

﴾...To Him ascend [all] the goodly words, and the righteous deeds exalt it...﴿ *(Qur'an 35: 10)*

And texts which state that the souls of the believers ascend to Him:

﴿إِنَّ ٱلَّذِينَ كَذَّبُواْ بِـَٔايَٰتِنَا وَٱسۡتَكۡبَرُواْ عَنۡهَا لَا تُفَتَّحُ لَهُمۡ أَبۡوَٰبُ ٱلسَّمَآءِ... ﴿٤٠﴾﴾

﴾Verily, those who belie Our *Aayaat* [proofs, evidences, verses, lessons, signs, revelations, etc.] and treat them with arrogance, for them the gates of heaven will not be opened...﴿ *(Qur'an 7: 40)*

The texts indicate that the gates of heaven will be opened for the believers, and numerous *aḥaadeeth* explain this.

Another example is that the angels ascend to Him:

﴿تَعۡرُجُ ٱلۡمَلَٰٓئِكَةُ وَٱلرُّوحُ إِلَيۡهِ ... ﴿٤﴾﴾

﴾The angels and the *Rooḥ* [Jibreel (Gabriel)] ascend to Him...﴿ *(Qur'an 70: 4)*

6) And Allah (ﷻ), tells us that the angels descend:

﴿ يُنَزِّلُ ٱلْمَلَٰٓئِكَةَ بِٱلرُّوحِ مِنْ أَمْرِهِۦ... ﴿٢﴾ ﴾

﴾He sends down the angels with the *Rooḥ* [Revelation] of His Command...﴿ *(Qur'an 16: 2)*

And He tells us that He sent down His Books:

﴿ وَهَٰذَا كِتَٰبٌ أَنزَلْنَٰهُ مُبَارَكٌ ... ﴿٩٢﴾ ﴾

﴾And this [the Qur'an] is a blessed Book which We have sent down...﴿ *(Qur'an 6: 92)*

7) And there is the raising of one's hands and eyes to Him. There are many *aḥaadeeth* in which it is stated that the Messenger (ﷺ) raised his hands when making *du'aa'*, and everyone who is stricken with distress raises his hands when calling upon Allah, the Almighty.

Similarly, the gaze is also lifted, as is narrated in the reports of the *du'aa'* (supplication) after *wuḍoo'* (ablution).

8) Another example is the way in which the Prophet (ﷺ) pointed upwards with his finger, as in the hadith describing his Farewell Pilgrimage, when they said,

> "We bear witness that you have conveyed the message and fulfilled (your mission) and advised us sincerely." Then he pointed with his forefinger towards the heavens and then towards the people, and said: "O' Allah, bear witness! O' Allah, bear witness!"[70]

[70] Abu Dawood, 1/358, hadith no. 1905. A very similar hadith is narrated in Bukhari and Muslim, but I could not find any mention there of the Messenger raising his forefinger towards the heavens and then towards the people. (Author)

If you want to learn more about the evidence and the views of the *salaf* (pious predecessors) of this ummah, then refer to what the scholars have compiled on this topic in their books.

His being All-High does not contradict His being close

Allah (ﷻ), is close and answers the call of the one who calls upon Him. He knows their secret ideas and their secret counsels. He is closer to the one who calls upon Him than the neck of his riding-beast. He knows what hearts whisper to themselves, and He is closer to (His slaves) than their jugular veins. He knows the secret and that which is yet more hidden. He knows what sinks into the earth and what emerges therefrom, what comes down from the heavens and what ascends thereto. He is with His creation by His knowledge and power. Nothing whatsoever of them is hidden from Him. And nothing is hidden from your Lord (so much as) the weight of an atom (or small ant) on the earth or in the heaven. Not what is less than that or what is greater than that. He is close although He is Most High, and He is Most High although He is close. He is the First (nothing is before Him) and the Last (nothing is after Him), the Most High (nothing is above Him) and the Most Near (nothing is nearer than Him) *(cf. Qur'an 57:3).*

x) The laugh of our Lord, the Exalted

Allah laughs at when He wills and as He wills. We believe in that and affirm it, but we do not know how it happens, nor are we required to know that.

Several *ṣaḥeeḥ* (sound and authentic) reports have been narrated concerning that:

1) It is narrated from Abu Hurayrah (رضي الله عنه) that the Messenger of Allah (ﷺ) said:

> "Allah laughs at two men, one of whom killed the other

> but they will both enter Paradise. One fought for the sake of Allah and was killed, then Allah accepted the repentance of the killer, then he died as a *shaheed* (martyr)."[71]

2) It is narrated from Abu Hurayrah that a man came to the Prophet (ﷺ) and said: "O' Messenger of Allah, I am tired and hungry." He sent word to his wives, and they did not find anything (to offer him). The Messenger of Allah (ﷺ) said:

> "Will any man host him tonight, Allah will bless him?" A man from among the *Anṣaar* stood up and said, "I will do it, O' Messenger of Allah." He went to his family and told his wife, "The guest of the Messenger of Allah - do not withhold anything from him." She said, "By Allah, I do not have anything except food for the children." He said: "When the children want their supper, get them to sleep, then come and extinguish the lamp, and we will leave our own stomachs empty tonight." So she did that. The next day he came to the Messenger of Allah, who said: "The All-Glory and Exalted liked and appreciated — or he said, He laughed at — the action of So-and-so and So-and-so (this couple)."

Then Allah (ﷻ), revealed the words:

﴿... وَيُؤْثِرُونَ عَلَىٰٓ أَنفُسِهِمْ وَلَوْ كَانَ بِهِمْ خَصَاصَةٌ ... ﴿٩﴾﴾

> ﴿...And give them [emigrants] preference over themselves even though they were in need of that...﴾ *(Qur'an 59: 9)*[72]

---

[71] Bukhari, 6/39, hadith no. 2826; Muslim, 3/1504, hadith no. 1890. This version is narrated by Bukhari.

[72] Bukhari, 8/631, hadith no. 4889; Muslim, 3/1625, hadith no. 2054. This version is narrated by Bukhari.

3) There is a lengthy *marfoo'* hadith in Bukhari narrated from Abu Hurayrah (ﷺ), it says:

> "Then Allah (ﷻ), will finish judging among His slaves, and there will be left a man with his face in the direction of Hell. He will be the last of the people of Hell to enter Paradise. He will say, 'O' Lord, turn my face away from the Fire, for its smell is disturbing me and its heat is burning me.' So he will keep praying to Allah as long as He wills that he should pray.
> Then Allah will say, 'If I give you that, will you ask Me for anything else?' He will say, 'No, by Your Glory, I will not ask for anything else,' and he will give whatever promises he wants to his Lord. Then Allah will turn his face away from the Fire. When he turns towards Paradise and sees it, he will remain silent for as long as Allah wills that he should remain silent, then he will say: 'O' Lord, bring me to the gate of Paradise.' Allah will say to him, 'Did you not give me your solemn promise that you would not ask Me for anything else ever again? Woe to you, O' son of Adam, how treacherous you are!' Then he will say, 'O' Lord,' and he will pray to Allah until He says: 'Perhaps if I give you that, you will not ask for anything else.' He will say, 'No, by Your Glory, I will not ask for anything else.' He will give whatever promises he wants. So he will be brought close to the gate of Paradise, and when he stands at the gate of Paradise, it will become apparent to him what is in Paradise, the joys and delights that exist therein. Then he will remain silent for as long as Allah wills that he should remain silent, then he will say: 'O' Lord, admit me to Paradise.' Allah will say to him, 'Did you not give me your solemn promise that you would not ask Me for

> anything else ever again? Woe to you, O' son of Adam, how treacherous you are!' Then he will say, 'O' Lord, I do not want to be the most miserable of Your creation.' And he will keep on praying until Allah will laugh at him, and when Allah laughs at him, He will say, 'Enter Paradise.'"[73]

According to a report narrated by Muslim from the hadith of 'Abdullah ibn Mas'ood, Allah will say to that man:

> "Will it not please you if I were to give you the world and another the like thereof? He will say, 'O' Lord, are You mocking me when You are the Lord of the Worlds?' The Messenger of Allah laughed, and they said, 'Why are you laughing, O' Messenger of Allah?' He said, 'Because the Lord of the Worlds will laugh when (that man) says, 'Are You mocking] me when You are the Lord of the Worlds?' and He will say, 'I am not mocking you, but I am able to do whatsoever I will.'"[74]

xi), xii) Descending and Coming of the Exalted

It is narrated from Abu Hurayrah that the Messenger of Allah (ﷺ) said:

> "Our Lord — the All-Glorious, All-High — comes down every night to the nearest heaven, when one-third of the night remains. He says: 'Whoever calls upon Me, I will answer him, and whoever asks of Me, I will give him, and whoever seeks forgiveness of Me, I will forgive him.'"[75]

---

[73] Bukhari, 13/420, hadith no. 7437.

[74] Muslim, 1/175, hadith no.187.

[75] Bukhari, 3/29, hadith no. 1145; Muslim, 1/521, hadith no. 758. This version is narrated by Bukhari.

The Qur'an states that Allah (ﷻ), will come on the Day of Resurrection to pass judgement:

﴿ هَلْ يَنظُرُونَ إِلَّآ أَن يَأْتِيَهُمُ ٱللَّهُ فِى ظُلَلٍ مِّنَ ٱلْغَمَامِ وَٱلْمَلَٰٓئِكَةُ وَقُضِىَ ٱلْأَمْرُ ۚ وَإِلَى ٱللَّهِ تُرْجَعُ ٱلْأُمُورُ ﴿٢١٠﴾ ﴾

﴾Do they then wait for anything other than that Allah should come to them in the shadows of the clouds and the angels? [Then] the case would be already judged. And to Allah return all matters [for decision].﴿

(Qur'an 2: 210)

﴿ كَلَّآ إِذَا دُكَّتِ ٱلْأَرْضُ دَكًّا دَكًّا ﴿٢١﴾ وَجَآءَ رَبُّكَ وَٱلْمَلَكُ صَفًّا صَفًّا ﴿٢٢﴾ ﴾

﴾Nay! When the earth is ground to powder. And your Lord comes with the angels in rows.﴿

(Qur'an 89: 21-22)

It is narrated from Ibn Mas'ood (رضي الله عنه) that the Messenger of Allah (ﷺ) said:

"Allah will gather together the first and the last for an appointed time, forty years, when they will be looking up at the heavens, waiting for judgement to be passed, and Allah will come in the shadows of clouds from the Throne to the *Kursiy.*"[76]

xiii) The speech of Allah

Allah (ﷻ), speaks when He wills and in the manner He wills. His speech does not resemble the speech of any of His creatures. Allah

---

[76] By Ibn Mandah. Adh-Dhahabi said: its isnad is *ḥasan*. A group of scholars who had memorized *aḥaadeeth* and were well-versed in the criticism thereof classed it as *ṣaḥeeḥ* (sound), such as Al-Ḥaakim, Al-Mundhiri and Al-Haythami.

spoke to some of His creation, and they spoke with Him, such as the Prophet of Allah, Moosa (Moses) (عليه السلام):

﴿... وَكَلَّمَ ٱللَّهُ مُوسَىٰ تَكۡلِيمٗا ١٦٤﴾

﴿...And to Moosa [Moses] Allah spoke directly.﴾
(Qur'an 4: 164)

﴿وَلَمَّا جَآءَ مُوسَىٰ لِمِيقَٰتِنَا وَكَلَّمَهُۥ رَبُّهُۥ... ١٤٣﴾

﴿And when Moosa [Moses] came at the time and place appointed by Us, and his Lord [Allah] spoke to him;...﴾
(Qur'an 7: 143)

Allah (سبحانه وتعالى), mentioned for us the talks between Him and Moosa (Moses) (عليه السلام):

﴿... قَالَ رَبِّ أَرِنِيٓ أَنظُرۡ إِلَيۡكَۚ قَالَ لَن تَرَىٰنِي وَلَٰكِنِ ٱنظُرۡ إِلَى ٱلۡجَبَلِ فَإِنِ ٱسۡتَقَرَّ مَكَانَهُۥ فَسَوۡفَ تَرَىٰنِيۚ فَلَمَّا تَجَلَّىٰ رَبُّهُۥ لِلۡجَبَلِ جَعَلَهُۥ دَكّٗا وَخَرَّ مُوسَىٰ صَعِقٗاۚ فَلَمَّآ أَفَاقَ قَالَ سُبۡحَٰنَكَ تُبۡتُ إِلَيۡكَ وَأَنَا۠ أَوَّلُ ٱلۡمُؤۡمِنِينَ ١٤٣ قَالَ يَٰمُوسَىٰٓ إِنِّي ٱصۡطَفَيۡتُكَ عَلَى ٱلنَّاسِ بِرِسَٰلَٰتِي وَبِكَلَٰمِي فَخُذۡ مَآ ءَاتَيۡتُكَ وَكُن مِّنَ ٱلشَّٰكِرِينَ ١٤٤﴾

﴿...He said: 'O' my Lord! Show me [Yourself], that I may look upon You.' Allah said: 'You cannot see Me, but look upon the mountain; if it stands still in its place then you shall see Me.' So when his Lord appeared to the mountain, He made it collapse to dust, and Moosa [Moses] fell down unconscious. Then when he recovered his senses he said: 'Glory be to You, I turn to You in repentance and I am the first of the believers.' [Allah] said: 'O' Moosa I have chosen you above men by My Messages, and by My speaking [to you]. So hold that which I have given you and be of the grateful.'﴾ *(Qur'an 7: 143-144)*

Allah (ﷻ), spoke to Adam and Ḥawwa' (Eve):

﴿ ... وَنَادَىٰهُمَا رَبُّهُمَآ أَلَمْ أَنْهَكُمَا عَن تِلْكُمَا ٱلشَّجَرَةِ وَأَقُل لَّكُمَآ إِنَّ ٱلشَّيْطَٰنَ لَكُمَا عَدُوٌّ مُّبِينٌ ﴿٢٢﴾ ﴾

﴿...And their Lord called out to them [saying]: 'Did I not forbid you that tree and tell you: Verily, *Shayṭaan* [Satan] is an open enemy unto you?'﴾ *(Qur'an 7: 22)*

Allah speaks to Jibreel (Gabriel) (ﷺ): It is narrated that Abu Hurayrah (ﷺ) said; the Messenger of Allah (ﷺ) said:

"When Allah, the All-Glorious, All-High, loves a slave, He calls out Jibreel (Gabriel): 'Verily Allah loves So and so, so love him.' Then Jibreel loves him, and calls out to the people of heaven: 'Verily Allah loves So and so, so love him.' Then the people of heaven love him, and Allah causes him to find acceptance among the people of the earth."[77]

The angels hear their Lord when He speaks. It is narrated from Abu Hurayrah that the Prophet (ﷺ) said:

"When Allah decrees a matter in the heaven, the angels beat their wings in submission to His decree, (with a sound like) a chain striking a rock. When fear is banished from their hearts, they say, 'What is it that your Lord has said?' They say, 'The truth, and He is the Most High, the Great.'"[78]

This hadith is narrated by Bukhari to explain the *aayah*:

[77] Bukhari, 13/461, hadith no. 7485; Muslim, 4/2030, hadith no. 2637. This version is narrated by Bukhari.

[78] Bukhari, 13/453, hadith no. 7481.

﴿ وَلَا تَنفَعُ ٱلشَّفَٰعَةُ عِندَهُۥٓ إِلَّا لِمَنْ أَذِنَ لَهُۥ ۚ حَتَّىٰٓ إِذَا فُزِّعَ عَن قُلُوبِهِمْ قَالُوا۟ مَاذَا قَالَ رَبُّكُمْ ۖ قَالُوا۟ ٱلْحَقَّ ۖ وَهُوَ ٱلْعَلِىُّ ٱلْكَبِيرُ ﴿٢٣﴾ ﴾

﴾Intercession with Him profits not except for him whom He permits. So much so that when fear is banished from their [angels'] hearts, they [angels] say: 'What is it that your Lord has said?' They say: 'The truth. And He is the Most High, the Most Great.'﴿ *(Qur'an 34: 23)*

Bukhari devoted a chapter to this *aayah*, then he said: But he did not say what your Lord created. He has transmitted all the reports narrated by Masrooq from Ibn Mas'ood that ends with him (Masrooq) — *mu'allaq mawqoof*, under this chapter. It says: "When Allah speaks with the *Waḥy* (Revelation/inspiration), the people of the heavens hear something, and when fear is banished from their hearts and the sound has ceased, they know that it is the truth, and they call out, What did your Lord say?

Yet there is another *mu'allaq* hadith transmitted by Jaabir from 'Abdullah ibn Unays, who said: I heard the Messenger of Allah (ﷺ) say:

> "Allah will gather His slaves and will call them with a voice which will be heard from afar as clearly as it will be heard from up close: 'I am the Sovereign, I am the Judge.'"[79]

Bukhari in his book, *Khalq af'aal al-'Ibaad* (creation of the deeds of Allah's slaves), commenting on this hadith said: This proves that the voice of Allah does not resemble the voices of His creation, because the voice of Allah can be heard from afar as clearly as it can be heard from nearby, and the angels swoon from His voice.[80]

---

[79] Bukhari, 13/452.

[80] *Khalq Af'aal al-'Ibaad*, Pp. 149.

Allah (ﷻ), speaks with a voice that does not resemble any of the voices of His creation at all, as stated in the hadith narrated by Bukhari from Abu Sa'eed al-Khudri, who stated: The Messenger of Allah (ﷺ) said:

> "Allah will say, 'O' Adam!' and he will say, 'At Your service.' Then a voice will call out: 'Allah commands you to send forth from your progeny those who are to be sent to Hell.'"[81]

On the Day of Resurrection, He (ﷻ), will speak to His angels:

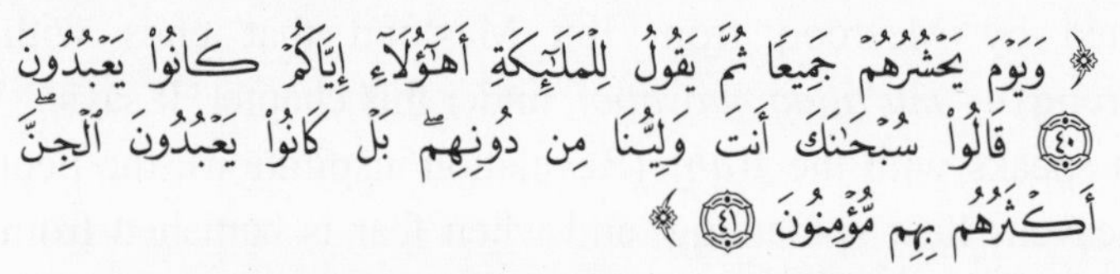

> ﴿And [remember] the Day when He will gather them all together, then He will say to the angels: 'Was it you that these people used to worship?' They [the angels] will say: 'Glorified be You! You are our *Wali* [Lord] instead of them. Nay, but they used to worship the jinn; most of them were believers in them.'﴾ *(Qur'an 34: 40-41)*

And He (ﷻ), will address the disbelievers and the deniers (of the truth), rebuking them:

﴿ وَيَوْمَ نَحْشُرُ مِن كُلِّ أُمَّةٍ فَوْجًا مِّمَّن يُكَذِّبُ بِـَٔايَٰتِنَا فَهُمْ يُوزَعُونَ ﴿٨٣﴾ حَتَّىٰٓ إِذَا جَآءُو قَالَ أَكَذَّبْتُم بِـَٔايَٰتِى وَلَمْ تُحِيطُوا۟ بِهَا عِلْمًا أَمَّاذَا كُنتُمْ تَعْمَلُونَ ﴿٨٤﴾ ﴾

> ﴿And [remember] the Day when We shall gather out of every nation a troop of those who denied Our *Aayaat*

---

[81] Bukhari, 13/453, hadith no. 7483. See also 8/441, hadith no. 4741. Muslim, 1/201, hadith no. 222. This version is narrated by Bukhari.

[proofs, evidences, verses, lessons, signs, revelations, etc.], and [then] they [all] shall be driven [to the place of reckoning], till, when they come [before their Lord at the place of reckoning], He will say: 'Did you deny My *Aayaat* [proofs, evidences, verses, lessons, signs, revelations, etc.] whereas you comprehended them not by knowledge [of their truth or falsehood], or what [else] was it that you used to do?'﴿ *(Qur'an 27: 83-84)*

And He (ﷻ), will greet the people of Paradise with *salaam*:

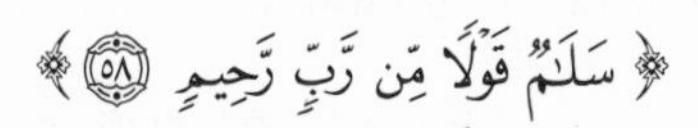

﴾[It will be said to them]: *Salaam* [peace be on you] - a Word from the Lord [Allah], Most Merciful.﴿ *(Qur'an 36: 58)*

Allah (ﷻ), will speak to them. It is narrated from Abu Sa'eed al-Khudri that the Prophet (ﷺ) said:

"Allah will say to the people of Paradise: 'O' people of Paradise!' They will say, 'At Your service, all good is in Your hand.' He will say, 'Are you content?' They will say, 'How could we not be content, O' Lord, when You have given us what You have not given to anyone else among Your creation?' He will say, 'Shall I not give you something even better than that?' They will say, 'O' Lord, what can be better than that?' He will say, 'I grant you My pleasure and I will never be angry with you again after that.'"[82]

Allah's speech is not limited or restricted

Allah (ﷻ), says:

[82] Bukhari, 13/487, hadith no. 7518; Muslim, 4/2176, hadith no. 2829. This version is narrated by Bukhari.

﴿ قُل لَّوْ كَانَ ٱلْبَحْرُ مِدَادًا لِّكَلِمَٰتِ رَبِّى لَنَفِدَ ٱلْبَحْرُ قَبْلَ أَن تَنفَدَ كَلِمَٰتُ رَبِّى وَلَوْ جِئْنَا بِمِثْلِهِۦ مَدَدًا ﴿١٠٩﴾ ﴾

﴿Say [O' Muhammad to mankind]: 'If the sea were ink for [writing] the Words of my Lord, surely, the sea would be exhausted before the Words of my Lord would be finished, even if We brought [another sea] like it for its aid.'﴾ *(Qur'an 18: 109)*

The Qur'an is truly the Word of Allah

The Qu'ran is undoubtedly the Word of Allah. Allah (ﷻ), says:

﴿ وَإِنْ أَحَدٌ مِّنَ ٱلْمُشْرِكِينَ ٱسْتَجَارَكَ فَأَجِرْهُ حَتَّىٰ يَسْمَعَ كَلَٰمَ ٱللَّهِ ... ﴿٦﴾ ﴾

﴿And if anyone of the *Mushrikoon* [polytheists, idolaters, pagans, disbelievers in the Oneness of Allah] seeks your protection then grant him protection so that he may hear the Word of Allah [the Qur'an] ...﴾ *(Qur'an 9: 6)*

﴿ سَيَقُولُ ٱلْمُخَلَّفُونَ إِذَا ٱنطَلَقْتُمْ إِلَىٰ مَغَانِمَ لِتَأْخُذُوهَا ذَرُونَا نَتَّبِعْكُمْ ۖ يُرِيدُونَ أَن يُبَدِّلُوا۟ كَلَٰمَ ٱللَّهِ ۚ قُل لَّن تَتَّبِعُونَا كَذَٰلِكُمْ قَالَ ٱللَّهُ مِن قَبْلُ ... ﴿١٥﴾ ﴾

﴿Those who lagged behind will say, when you set forth to take the spoils, 'Allow us to follow you.' They want to change Allah's Words. Say: 'You shall not follow us; thus Allah has said beforehand.'...﴾ *(Qur'an 48: 15)*

﴿ وَلَوْ أَنَّمَا فِى ٱلْأَرْضِ مِن شَجَرَةٍ أَقْلَٰمٌ وَٱلْبَحْرُ يَمُدُّهُۥ مِنۢ بَعْدِهِۦ سَبْعَةُ أَبْحُرٍ مَّا نَفِدَتْ كَلِمَٰتُ ٱللَّهِ ... ﴿٢٧﴾ ﴾

﴿And if all the trees on the earth were pens and the sea [were ink wherewith to write], with seven seas behind it

> to add to its [supply], yet the Words of Allah would not be exhausted...﴿ *(Qur'an 31: 27)*

Ibn Katheer said in his *Tafseer* of this *aayah* (verse):[83]

Here Allah (ﷻ), refers to His Might, Pride, Majesty, Beautiful Names, Sublime Attributes and Perfect Words which none can encompass, and whose nature and essence none can know, as the Master of mankind [i.e., the Prophet (ﷺ)] said:

> "I cannot praise You sufficiently; You are as You have praised Yourself."[84]

Allah (ﷻ), says: ﴾And if all the trees on the earth were pens...﴿ *(Qur'an 31: 27)* meaning, even if all the trees on earth were made into pens, and the seas were made into ink, and seven times as many seas were provided along with that, to write down the words of Allah indicating His Might, Attributes and Majesty, the pens would break and the sea would run dry, even if more seas were brought.

Al-Ḥasan al-Baṣri said: If the trees of the earth were made into pens, and the sea was made into ink, and Allah (ﷻ), were to say, My Decree is such and such, My Decree is such and such..., the sea would run dry and the pens would break. Allah indeed spoke the truth when He said:

﴿ ... وَمَآ أُوتِيتُم مِّنَ ٱلْعِلْمِ إِلَّا قَلِيلًا ﴿٨٥﴾ ﴾

> ﴾...And of knowledge, you [mankind] have been given only a little.﴿ *(Qur'an 17: 85)*

[83] *Tafseer ibn Katheer*, 5/394.

[84] Muslim, 1/353, hadith no. 486.

xiv) The love of Allah

It is stated in the Qur'an and Sunnah that Allah (ﷻ), loves certain deeds, certain words and some of His creation who have certain characteristics which He has stated that He loves.

He has told us that so that we may strive to attain these characteristics that He loves and do the deeds that He loves, and utter the words that He loves. Thus He will love us.

Allah (ﷻ), loves the pious:

﴿... إِنَّ ٱللَّهَ يُحِبُّ ٱلْمُتَّقِينَ ﴿٤﴾﴾

﴾...Surely, Allah loves *Al-Muttaqeen* [the pious].﴿
(Qur'an 9: 4)

He (ﷻ), loves those who do good:

﴿... وَٱللَّهُ يُحِبُّ ٱلْمُحْسِنِينَ ﴿١٣٤﴾﴾

﴾...Verily, Allah loves *Al-Muḥsineen* [the good-doers].﴿
(Qur'an 3: 134)

He (ﷻ) loves those who repent to Him and purify themselves:

﴿... ٱللَّهَ يُحِبُّ ٱلتَّوَّٰبِينَ وَيُحِبُّ ٱلْمُتَطَهِّرِينَ ﴿٢٢٢﴾﴾

﴾...Truly, Allah loves those who turn unto Him in repentance and loves those who purify themselves.﴿
(Qur'an 2: 222)

He (ﷻ) loves those who are patient:

﴿... وَٱللَّهُ يُحِبُّ ٱلصَّٰبِرِينَ ﴿١٤٦﴾﴾

﴾...And Allah loves *Aṣ-Ṣaabireen* [the patient].﴿
(Qur'an 3: 146)

He (ﷻ) loves those who are just:

﴿ ... إِنَّ ٱللَّهَ يُحِبُّ ٱلْمُقْسِطِينَ ﴿٤٢﴾ ﴾

﴾...Verily, Allah loves those who act justly.﴿
(Qur'an 5: 42)

He (ﷻ) loves those who put their trust in Him:

﴿ ... إِنَّ ٱللَّهَ يُحِبُّ ٱلْمُتَوَكِّلِينَ ﴿١٥٩﴾ ﴾

﴾...Certainly, Allah loves those who put their trust [in Him].﴿ *(Qur'an 3: 159)*

He (ﷻ) loves those who fight for His sake in ranks:

﴿ إِنَّ ٱللَّهَ يُحِبُّ ٱلَّذِينَ يُقَٰتِلُونَ فِي سَبِيلِهِۦ صَفًّا كَأَنَّهُم بُنْيَٰنٌ مَّرْصُوصٌ ﴿٤﴾ ﴾

﴾Verily, Allah loves those who fight in His Cause in rows [ranks] as if they were a solid structure.﴿
(Qur'an 61: 4)

Ṣaḥeeḥayn (Bukhari and Muslim) narrated from Abu Hurayrah (رضي الله عنه) that the Messenger of Allah (ﷺ) said:

"Two words which are light on the tongue but they are heavy in the Balance and are beloved to the Most Merciful: *Subḥaan Allahi wa bi ḥamdihi, Subḥaan Allah il-'Aẓeem* (Glory and praise be to Allah, glory be to Allah the Almighty)."[85]

It is narrated that Sumrah ibn Jundub said: The Messenger of Allah (ﷺ) said:

"The most beloved of speech to Allah is four (phrases):

[85] Bukhari, 11/206, hadith no. 1406; Muslim, 4/2072, hadith no. 2694.

> *Subḥaan Allahi wa'l-ḥamdu Lillaahi wa laa ilaaha illa-Allahu wa Allahu Akbar* (Glory be to Allah, praise be to Allah, there is no god except Allah, and Allah is Most Great). And it does not matter which of them you start with."[86]

The Prophet (ﷺ) said to Ashajj 'Abd al-Qays:

> "You have two characteristics which Allah loves: patience and deliberation."[87]

It is narrated from 'Ubaadah ibn aṣ-Ṣaamit that the Prophet (ﷺ) said:

> "Whoever loves to meet Allah, Allah loves to meet him; whoever hates to meet Allah, Allah hates to meet him."[88]

All the actions, attitudes and words that Allah loves are those which were brought by the Messenger (ﷺ) or which were part of his character. Hence Allah stated in a comprehensive *aayah* (verse) that the way to earn His love is to follow the Messenger (ﷺ):

﴿ قُلْ إِن كُنتُمْ تُحِبُّونَ ٱللَّهَ فَٱتَّبِعُونِي يُحْبِبْكُمُ ٱللَّهُ ... ﴿٣١﴾ ﴾

> ﴾Say [O' Muhammad to mankind]: "If you [really] love Allah, then follow me [i.e. accept Islamic Monotheism, follow the Qur'an and the Sunnah], Allah will love you...﴿ *(Qur'an 3: 31)*

xv), xvi) Allah's hatred and anger

There are actions which Allah does not love; in fact He hates them and is angry with them. His hatred and anger are real in a manner that

---

[86] Muslim, 3/1685, hadith no. 2137.

[87] Ibid, 1/48, hadith no. 17.

[88] Ibid, 4/2065, hadith no. 2684.

befits His noble nature. Among these actions is *fasaad* (corruption or mischief):

﴿... وَٱللَّهُ لَا يُحِبُّ ٱلْفَسَادَ ﴿٢٠٥﴾﴾

﴾...And Allah likes not mischief.﴿ *(Qur'an 2: 205)*

﴿... وَٱللَّهُ لَا يُحِبُّ ٱلْمُفْسِدِينَ ﴿٦٤﴾﴾

﴾...And Allah does not like the *Mufsideen* [mischief-makers].﴿ *(Qur'an 5: 64)*

It is also stated in the texts that Allah does not like the *kaafiroon* (disbelievers), *ẓaalimoon* (wrongdoers or oppressors), extravagants, aggressors, betrayers and those who exult in their riches. He does not like such as are proud and boastful *(cf. Qur'an 4: 36)*, the disbelievers and sinners *(cf. Qur'an 2: 276)*, or those who betray their trusts and indulge in crime *(cf. Qur'an 4: 107)*. In the Qur'an it says:

﴿... وَلَٰكِن كَرِهَ ٱللَّهُ ٱنۢبِعَاثَهُمْ فَثَبَّطَهُمْ ... ﴿٤٦﴾﴾

﴾...But Allah was averse to their being sent forth, so He made them lag behind...﴿ *(Qur'an 9: 46)*

We have mentioned above the hadith in which Allah (ﷻ), says:

"Whoever hates to meet Allah, Allah hates to meet him."[89]

It is narrated from 'Aa'ishah (may Allah be pleased with her) that: the Prophet (ﷺ) said:

"The most hated of men to Allah is the tough and argumentative type."[90]

[89] Muslim, 4/2065, hadith no. 2684.

[90] Bukhari, 13/180, hadith no. 7188; Muslim, 4/2054, hadith no. 2668.

It is narrated from Al-Baraa' ibn 'Aazib that he heard the Messenger of Allah (ﷺ) say concerning the *Anṣaar*:

> "Whoever loves them, Allah will love him, and whoever hates them, Allah will hate him."[91]

xvii) Seeing Allah

No one can see Allah (سبحانه وتعالى), in this world. Moosa (Moses) (عليه السلام) hoped to see Allah, but his Lord told him that he would not and could not see Him in this world; even the strong and solid mountain could not bear that:

﴿ وَلَمَّا جَآءَ مُوسَىٰ لِمِيقَٰتِنَا وَكَلَّمَهُۥ رَبُّهُۥ قَالَ رَبِّ أَرِنِىٓ أَنظُرْ إِلَيْكَ ۚ قَالَ لَن تَرَىٰنِى وَلَٰكِنِ ٱنظُرْ إِلَى ٱلْجَبَلِ فَإِنِ ٱسْتَقَرَّ مَكَانَهُۥ فَسَوْفَ تَرَىٰنِى ۚ فَلَمَّا تَجَلَّىٰ رَبُّهُۥ لِلْجَبَلِ جَعَلَهُۥ دَكًّا وَخَرَّ مُوسَىٰ صَعِقًا... ﴿١٤٣﴾ ﴾

> ﴾And when Moosa [Moses] came at the time and place appointed by Us, and his Lord [Allah] spoke to him; he said: 'O' my Lord! Show me [Yourself], that I may look upon You.' Allah said: 'You cannot see Me, but look upon the mountain; if it stands still in its place then you shall see Me.' So when his Lord appeared to the mountain, He made it collapse to dust, and Moosa fell down unconscious...﴿ *(Qur'an 7: 143)*

The scholars differed as to whether the Messenger (ﷺ) saw his Lord when he was taken up into the heavens (the *Mi'raaj*). The correct view is that he did not see his Lord during the *Mi'raaj*. It is narrated in a *ṣaḥeeḥ* (sound) report that 'Aa'ishah said:

> "Whoever claims that Muhammad (ﷺ) saw his Lord has invented a great lie against Allah."[92]

---

[91] Bukhari, 7/113, hadith no. 3783; Muslim, 1/85, hadith no. 75.

[92] Muslim, 1/159, hadith no. 177.

This is the case in this world. But in the Hereafter it will be different. People will be created anew. Do you not see that the sun will be brought close to people's heads on the Day of Resurrection, until there is no more than one mile between it and them, yet they will not melt! Do you not see that after people are resurrected and brought forth from their graves, they will not be susceptible to death any more! When the disbelievers (*kuffaar*) enter the Fire, every time their skins are roasted through, Allah, the All-Powerful, will change them for other skins so that they can (continue to) taste the torment, but they will not die.

On the Day of Resurrection, the believers will be able to see their Lord. The greatest delight that they will be given in Paradise will be looking upon the face of the Mighty and Generous Lord, Exalted be He.

This great blessing will be denied to the disbelievers:

﴿ كَلَّآ إِنَّهُمْ عَن رَّبِّهِمْ يَوْمَئِذٍ لَّمَحْجُوبُونَ ﴿١٥﴾ ﴾

> ﴿Nay! Surely, they [evil doers] will be veiled from seeing their Lord that Day.﴾ *(Qur'an 83: 15)*

But those whom Allah (ﷻ), has chosen and made their faces beautiful, they will not be veiled or deprived:

﴿ وُجُوهٌ يَوْمَئِذٍ نَّاضِرَةٌ ﴿٢٢﴾ إِلَىٰ رَبِّهَا نَاظِرَةٌ ﴿٢٣﴾ ﴾

> ﴿Some faces that Day shall be *Naaḍirah* [shining and radiant]. Looking at their Lord [Allah].﴾
> *(Qur'an 75: 22-23)*

There are the *Abraar* (righteous):

﴿ إِنَّ ٱلْأَبْرَارَ لَفِى نَعِيمٍ ﴿٢٢﴾ عَلَى ٱلْأَرَآئِكِ يَنظُرُونَ ﴿٢٣﴾ ﴾

> ﴿Verily, *Al-Abraar* [the pious believers of Islamic

Monotheism] will be in Delight [Paradise]. On thrones, looking [at all things].﴿ *(Qur'an 83: 22-23)*

This looking at His Noble Face is the *ziyaadah* ("even more," additional) which is promised to the believers:

﴿ لِّلَّذِينَ أَحْسَنُوا۟ ٱلْحُسْنَىٰ وَزِيَادَةٌ ... ﴿٢٦﴾ ﴾

﴾For those who have done good is the best reward and even more [i.e. having the honour of glancing at the Countenance of Allah]...﴿ *(Qur'an 10: 26)*

And it is the *mazeed* (more) referred to in the *aayah* (verse):

﴿ لَهُم مَّا يَشَآءُونَ فِيهَا وَلَدَيْنَا مَزِيدٌ ﴿٣٥﴾ ﴾

﴾There they will have all that they desire and We have more [for them, i.e. a glance at the All-Mighty, All-Majestic].﴿ *(Qur'an 50: 35)*

There are *mutawaatir aḥaadeeth* which clearly state this. It is reported from Abu Hurayrah that some people said to the Messenger of Allah (ﷺ): "O' Messenger of Allah, will we see our Lord on the Day of Resurrection?" The Messenger of Allah (ﷺ) said:

"Do you doubt that you can see the moon on the night when it is full?" They said, "No, O' Messenger of Allah." He said, "Do you doubt that you can see the sun when there are no clouds in the way?" They said, "No, O' Messenger of Allah." He said: "Verily you will see Him likewise."[93]

Bukhari has narrated that Jareer ibn 'Abdullah said: "We were sitting with the Prophet when he looked at the full moon and said:

---

[93] Bukhari, 13/419, hadith no. 7437; Muslim, 1/163, hadith no. 183. This version is narrated by Muslim.

> "You will see your Lord just as you are seeing this moon, do not doubt this. And if you can avoid missing a prayer before the sun rises and before the sun sets, then do that (i.e., strive not to miss *Fajr* and *'Aṣr* prayers)."[94]

In *Ṣaḥeeḥ* Muslim it is narrated from Ṣuhayb that the Prophet (ﷺ) said:

> "When the people of Paradise enter Paradise, Allah will say, 'Do you want anything else from Me?' They will say, 'Have You not made our faces white? Have You not granted us admittance to Paradise and saved us from Hell?' Then the veil will be lifted and they will never be given anything more beloved to them than looking at their Lord, the All-glory." Then he recited this *aayah* (verse):
>
> ﴿ لِّلَّذِينَ أَحْسَنُوا الْحُسْنَىٰ وَزِيَادَةٌ ... ﴾
>
> ﴾For those who have done good is the best reward and even more [i.e. having the honour of glancing at the Countenance of Allah]...﴿ *(Qur'an 10: 26)* [95]

Ṣaḥeeḥayn (Bukhari and Muslim) narrated from Abu Moosa that the Prophet (ﷺ) said:

> "Two gardens of silver, their vessels and everything in them, and two gardens of gold, their vessels and everything in them. And there will be nothing between the people and seeing their Lord except the veil of pride over His face in the Paradise of *'Aden*."[96]

---

[94] Bukhari, 13/419, hadith no. 7434.

[95] Muslim, 1/163, hadith no. 181.

[96] Bukhari, 13/423, hadith no. 7444; Muslim, 1/163, hadith no. 180.

xviii) The Knowledge of Allah

We know that Allah (ﷻ), bears the attribute of knowledge, and that He has called Himself by a number of Names which reflect this attribute, such as *Al-'Aleem* (All-Knowing):

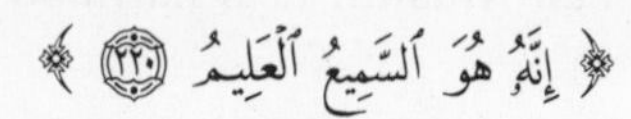

﴾Verily, He, only He, is the All-Hearer, the All-Knower.﴿ *(Qur'an 26: 220)*

Another of these Names is *Al-Khabeer* (the All-Aware), which means that He knows what will be before it happens; *Al-Ḥakeem* (the Wise), which means that He knows the details of things; *Ash-Shaheed* (the Witness), which means that He knows what is unseen and what is seen, i.e., that nothing is unknown to Him; *Al-Ḥaafiẓ* (the Protector), meaning that He does not forget what He knows; *Al-Muḥṣiy* (the Reckoner), which means that the fact that He knows so much does not distract Him from knowing the tiniest details, such as the light of the day and how strong the wind is, and when the leaves fall. He knows the numbers and the movements of each leaf.

His Knowledge encompasses generalities and minor details

Philosophers claim that Allah knows things in general terms, but He does not know minor details — but this is a lie. The Knowledge of Allah is comprehensive and all-encompassing, and nothing whatsoever is hidden from Him on earth or in the heavens. He knows every movement on land and sea, and there is no leaf that falls from a tree or a seed that is planted in the ground, or a small plant that cleaves the earth, or dries out or dies, but the Knowledge of Allah encompasses it.

﴿ ... وَيَعْلَمُ مَا فِي ٱلْبَرِّ وَٱلْبَحْرِ ۚ وَمَا تَسْقُطُ مِن وَرَقَةٍ إِلَّا يَعْلَمُهَا وَلَا حَبَّةٍ فِي ظُلُمَٰتِ ٱلْأَرْضِ وَلَا رَطْبٍ وَلَا يَابِسٍ إِلَّا فِي كِتَٰبٍ مُّبِينٍ ﴿٥٩﴾ ﴾

﴿...And He knows whatever there is in the land and in the sea; not a leaf falls, but He knows it. There is not a grain in the darkness of the earth nor anything fresh or dry, but is written in a Clear Record.﴾ *(Qur'an 6: 59)*

Nothing of these innumerable animals is hidden from Allah:

﴿ ۞ وَمَا مِن دَآبَّةٍ فِي ٱلْأَرْضِ إِلَّا عَلَى ٱللَّهِ رِزْقُهَا وَيَعْلَمُ مُسْتَقَرَّهَا وَمُسْتَوْدَعَهَا ۚ كُلٌّ فِي كِتَٰبٍ مُّبِينٍ ﴿٦﴾ ﴾

﴿And no moving [living] creature is there on earth but its provision is due from Allah. And He knows its dwelling place and its deposit [in the uterus or grave]. All is in a Clear Book [*Al-Lawḥ al-Maḥfooẓ* — the Book of Decrees with Allah].﴾ *(Qur'an 11: 6)*

There is nothing that goes down into the earth, or ascends from the earth to the heavens, but Allah encompasses it with His knowledge:

﴿ يَعْلَمُ مَا يَلِجُ فِي ٱلْأَرْضِ وَمَا يَخْرُجُ مِنْهَا وَمَا يَنزِلُ مِنَ ٱلسَّمَآءِ وَمَا يَعْرُجُ فِيهَا ۚ وَهُوَ ٱلرَّحِيمُ ٱلْغَفُورُ ﴿٢﴾ ﴾

﴿He knows that which goes into the earth and that which comes forth from it, and that which descends from the heaven and that which ascends to it. And He is the Most Merciful, the Oft-Forgiving.﴾ *(Qur'an 34: 2)*

Nothing of man is hidden from Allah (ﷻ), whatsoever. Allah's knowledge of man is comprehensive, encompassing his apparent and visible actions, but He also knows what is hidden in the depths of his soul:

﴿ قُلْ إِن تُخْفُوا۟ مَا فِي صُدُورِكُمْ أَوْ تُبْدُوهُ يَعْلَمْهُ ٱللَّهُ... ﴿٢٩﴾ ﴾

﴿Say [O' Muhammad]: 'Whether you hide what is in your breasts or reveal it, Allah knows it...'﴾

(Qur'an 3: 29)

﴿ وَهُوَ ٱللَّهُ فِي ٱلسَّمَٰوَٰتِ وَفِي ٱلْأَرْضِ يَعْلَمُ سِرَّكُمْ وَجَهْرَكُمْ... ﴿٣﴾ ﴾

﴾And He is Allah [to be worshipped Alone] in the heavens and on the earth; He knows what you conceal and what you reveal...﴿ *(Qur'an 6: 3)*

This is knowledge which encompasses all the minor details of man's life:

﴿ وَمَا تَكُونُ فِي شَأْنٍ وَمَا تَتْلُوا۟ مِنْهُ مِن قُرْءَانٍ وَلَا تَعْمَلُونَ مِنْ عَمَلٍ إِلَّا كُنَّا عَلَيْكُمْ شُهُودًا إِذْ تُفِيضُونَ فِيهِ ... ﴿٦١﴾ ﴾

﴾Neither you [O' Muhammad] do any deed nor recite any portion of the Qur'an, nor you [O' mankind] do any deed [good or evil], but We are Witness thereof, when you are doing it...﴿ *(Qur'an 10: 61)*

Look at the Knowledge, from which nothing is hidden, not even the smallest grain:

﴿ يَٰبُنَيَّ إِنَّهَآ إِن تَكُ مِثْقَالَ حَبَّةٍ مِّنْ خَرْدَلٍ فَتَكُن فِي صَخْرَةٍ أَوْ فِي ٱلسَّمَٰوَٰتِ أَوْ فِي ٱلْأَرْضِ يَأْتِ بِهَا ٱللَّهُ إِنَّ ٱللَّهَ لَطِيفٌ خَبِيرٌ ﴿١٦﴾ ﴾

﴾O' my son! If it be [anything] equal to the weight of a grain of mustard seed, and though it be in a rock, or in the heavens or in the earth, Allah will bring it forth. Verily, Allah is Subtle [in bringing out that grain], Well-Aware [of its place].﴿ *(Qur'an 31: 16)*

In the knowledge of Allah, secret and open, small and great, unseen and seen, are all the same:

﴿ ٱللَّهُ يَعْلَمُ مَا تَحْمِلُ كُلُّ أُنثَىٰ وَمَا تَغِيضُ ٱلْأَرْحَامُ وَمَا تَزْدَادُ وَكُلُّ شَيْءٍ عِندَهُۥ بِمِقْدَارٍ ﴿٨﴾ عَٰلِمُ ٱلْغَيْبِ وَٱلشَّهَٰدَةِ ٱلْكَبِيرُ

ٱلْمُتَعَالِ ﴿٩﴾ سَوَآءٌ مِّنكُم مَّنْ أَسَرَّ ٱلْقَوْلَ وَمَن جَهَرَ بِهِۦ وَمَنْ هُوَ مُسْتَخْفٍۭ بِٱلَّيْلِ وَسَارِبٌۢ بِٱلنَّهَارِ ﴿١٠﴾ ﴾

﴿Allah knows what every female bears, and by how much the wombs fall short [of their time or number] or exceed. Everything with Him is in [due] proportion. All-Knower of the unseen and the seen, the Most Great, the Most High. It is the same [to Him] whether any of you conceals his speech or declares it openly, whether he be hid by night or goes forth freely by day.﴾

(Qur'an 13: 8-10)

Allah (ﷻ), indeed spoke the truth when He said:

﴿ ... وَمَا يَعْزُبُ عَن رَّبِّكَ مِن مِّثْقَالِ ذَرَّةٍ فِى ٱلْأَرْضِ وَلَا فِى ٱلسَّمَآءِ وَلَآ أَصْغَرَ مِن ذَٰلِكَ وَلَآ أَكْبَرَ إِلَّا فِى كِتَٰبٍ مُّبِينٍ ﴿٦١﴾ ﴾

﴿...And nothing is hidden from your Lord [so much as] the weight of an atom [or small ant] on the earth or in the heaven. Not what is less than that or what is greater than that but is [written] in a Clear Record.﴾ *(Qur'an 10: 61)*

xix), xx) His Life, Sustainment and Eternity

Allah (ﷻ), is Alive and His Life is eternal:

﴿ هُوَ ٱلْحَىُّ لَآ إِلَٰهَ إِلَّا هُوَ ... ﴿٦٥﴾ ﴾

﴿He is the Ever Living, *Laa ilaaha illa Huwa* [none has the right to be worshipped but He];...﴾ *(Qur'an 40: 65)*

His life is different from the lives of His creation, all of whom die and cease to exist; nothing will remain except Allah (ﷻ):

﴿ كُلُّ مَنْ عَلَيْهَا فَانٍ ﴿٢٦﴾ وَيَبْقَىٰ وَجْهُ رَبِّكَ ذُو ٱلْجَلَٰلِ وَٱلْإِكْرَامِ ﴿٢٧﴾ ﴾

﴿Whatsoever is on it [the earth] will perish. And the Face

> of your Lord full of Majesty and Honour will remain forever.﴾ *(Qur'an 55: 26-27)*

Bukhari has narrated from Ibn 'Abbaas that the Prophet (ﷺ) used to say:

> "'*A'oodhu bi 'izzatika alladhi laa ilaaha illa anta, alladhi laa yamoot wa'l-jinn wa'l-ins yamootoon* (I seek refuge in Your Glory, there is no god except You, Who never dies, whilst the jinn and mankind will die)."[97]

Whoever is like this is the One Who deserves to have trust placed in Him:

﴿ وَتَوَكَّلْ عَلَى ٱلْحَيِّ ٱلَّذِى لَا يَمُوتُ... ﴿٥٨﴾ ﴾

> ﴾And put your trust [O' Muhammad] in the Ever Living One Who dies not,...﴿ *(Qur'an 25: 58)*

He is *Al-Qayyoom*, the Self-Sustaining who sustains all that exists. All created beings are in need of Him, and they have no other maintainer except Him:

﴿ وَمِنْ ءَايَٰتِهِۦٓ أَن تَقُومَ ٱلسَّمَآءُ وَٱلْأَرْضُ بِأَمْرِهِۦ ... ﴿٢٥﴾ ﴾

> ﴾And among His Signs is that the heaven and the earth stand by His Command...﴿ *(Qur'an 30: 25)*

Allah, the Exalted, mentions these two Names together

The All-Exalted, mentions these two names together in more than one *aayah* of His Book:

﴿ ٱللَّهُ لَآ إِلَٰهَ إِلَّا هُوَ ٱلْحَىُّ ٱلْقَيُّومُ ﴿٢﴾ ﴾

> ﴾Allah! *Laa ilaaha illa Huwa* [none has the right to be worshipped but He], *Al-Ḥayy al-Qayyoom* [the Ever

[97] Bukhari, 13/368, hadith no. 7383.

Living, the One Who sustains and protects all that exists].﴾ *(Qur'an 3: 2)*

The perfection of His Life and Sustainment

One of the aspects of the perfection of His Life and Sustainment is that He (سُبْحَانَهُ وَتَعَالَى), does not sleep:

﴿ ٱللَّهُ لَآ إِلَٰهَ إِلَّا هُوَ ٱلْحَىُّ ٱلْقَيُّومُ ۚ لَا تَأْخُذُهُۥ سِنَةٌ وَلَا نَوْمٌ ۚ... ﴿٢٥٥﴾ ﴾

﴾Allah! *Laa ilaaha illa Huwa* [none has the right to be worshipped but He], *Al-Ḥayy al-Qayyoom* [the Ever Living, the One Who sustains and protects all that exists]. Neither slumber nor sleep overtakes Him...﴿ *(Qur'an 2: 255)*

"Slumber" refers to the beginning of sleep. Slumber and sleep are shortcomings, and the Creator is far above having these shortcomings. Muslim has narrated that Abu Moosa said: The Messenger of Allah (ﷺ) stood up among us and told us five things. He said:

> "Allah, the All-Glory and All-Exalted, does not sleep, and it is not befitting that He should sleep; He lowers and raises the scale; the deeds of the night ascend to Him before the deeds of the day, and the deeds of the day before the deeds of the night."[98]

Glorifying Allah by mentioning His Life and Sustainment

Allah praises Himself by describing Himself as being Alive, the Self-Sustaining Who sustains all that exists, as can be seen in the texts quoted above. The Messenger (ﷺ) used to praise his Lord by mentioning these attributes. It is narrated that Ibn 'Abbaas (رَضِيَ ٱللَّهُ عَنْهُ) said: When the Prophet (ﷺ) used to get up at night to pray *tahajjud*, he

---

[98] Muslim, 1/162, hadith no. 179.

would say: "*Allahumma laka'l-ḥamd, anta qayyim as-samawaati wa'l-arḍ wa man fihinna, wa laka'l-ḥamd, lakas-samaawaatu wa'l-arḍ wa man fihinna, wa laka'l-ḥamd, anta noor as-samawaati wa'l-arḍ, laka'l-ḥamd, anta malik as-samaawaati wa'l-arḍ* (O' Allah, to You be praise, You are the Sustainer of the heavens and the earth and all that are in them. To You be praise, to You belong the heavens and the earth and all that are in them. To You be praise, You are the Light of the heavens and the earth. To You be praise, You are the Sovereign of the heavens and the earth)..."[99]

xxi), xxii) His hearing and sight

These two attributes of Allah are confirmed by the text of the Qur'an:

﴿... لَيْسَ كَمِثْلِهِۦ شَىْءٌ ۖ وَهُوَ ٱلسَّمِيعُ ٱلْبَصِيرُ ﴿١١﴾﴾

﴾...There is nothing like Him, and He is the All-Hearer, the All-Seer.﴿ *(Qur'an 42: 11)*

﴿ذَٰلِكَ بِأَنَّ ٱللَّهَ يُولِجُ ٱلَّيْلَ فِى ٱلنَّهَارِ وَيُولِجُ ٱلنَّهَارَ فِى ٱلَّيْلِ وَأَنَّ ٱللَّهَ سَمِيعٌۢ بَصِيرٌ ﴿٦١﴾﴾

﴾That is because Allah merges the night into the day, and He merges the day into the night. And verily, Allah is All-Hearer, All-Seer.﴿ *(Qur'an 22: 61)*

And Allah (ﷻ), said to Moosa (Moses) and Haaroon (Aaron) (may peace be upon them):

﴿قَالَ لَا تَخَافَآ ۖ إِنَّنِى مَعَكُمَآ أَسْمَعُ وَأَرَىٰ ﴿٤٦﴾﴾

﴾Fear not, verily, I am with you both, hearing and seeing.﴿ *(Qur'an 20: 46)*

---

[99] Bukhari, 3/3, hadith no. 1120; Muslim, 1/532, hadith no. 799. This version is narrated by Bukhari.

The Greatness of Allah's hearing and sight

Allah (ﷻ), says:

﴿ قُلِ ٱللَّهُ أَعْلَمُ بِمَا لَبِثُوا۟ ۖ لَهُۥ غَيْبُ ٱلسَّمَٰوَٰتِ وَٱلْأَرْضِ ۖ أَبْصِرْ بِهِۦ وَأَسْمِعْ ... ﴿٢٦﴾ ﴾

﴾Say: Allah knows best how long they stayed. With Him is [the knowledge of] the Unseen of the heavens and the earth. How clearly He sees, and hears [everything]!...﴿ *(Qur'an 18: 26)*

Ibn Jareer said: The meaning here is very emphatic, praising Allah. It is as if it is saying, How well He sees and hears. The interpretation is: how well Allah sees all that exists, and how well He hears all that is to be heard; nothing whatsoever of that is hidden from Him.[100]

Allah (ﷻ), hears and sees the righteous, and rewards them:

﴿ ٱلَّذِى يَرَىٰكَ حِينَ تَقُومُ ﴿٢١٨﴾ وَتَقَلُّبَكَ فِى ٱلسَّٰجِدِينَ ﴿٢١٩﴾ إِنَّهُۥ هُوَ ٱلسَّمِيعُ ٱلْعَلِيمُ ﴿٢٢٠﴾ ﴾

﴾Who sees you [O' Muhammad] when you stand up [alone at night for *Tahajjud* prayers]. And your movements among those who fall prostrate [to Allah in the five compulsory congregational prayers]. Verily, He, only He, is the All-Hearer, the All-Knower.﴿ *(Qur'an 26: 218-220)*

Allah (ﷻ), sees the evildoers and punishes them:

﴿ لَّقَدْ سَمِعَ ٱللَّهُ قَوْلَ ٱلَّذِينَ قَالُوٓا۟ إِنَّ ٱللَّهَ فَقِيرٌ وَنَحْنُ أَغْنِيَآءُ ۘ سَنَكْتُبُ مَا قَالُوا۟ وَقَتْلَهُمُ ٱلْأَنۢبِيَآءَ بِغَيْرِ حَقٍّ وَنَقُولُ ذُوقُوا۟ عَذَابَ ٱلْحَرِيقِ ﴿١٨١﴾ ﴾

[100] *Tafseer ibn Jareer*, 15/232.

﴾Indeed, Allah has heard the statement of those [Jews] who say: 'Truly, Allah is poor and we are rich!' We shall record what they have said and their killing of the Prophets unjustly, and We shall say: 'Taste you the torment of the burning [Fire].'﴿ *(Qur'an 3: 181)*

'Aa'ishah (may Allah be pleased with her) said, explaining the vastness of Allah's hearing:

"Praise be to Allah Whose hearing encompasses all sounds."[101]

When the woman who disputed (*Al-Mujaadilah* — Khawlah bint Tha'labah) came to speak to the Prophet (ﷺ) in a corner of his house, I could not hear her, but Allah revealed the words:

﴿ قَدْ سَمِعَ ٱللَّهُ قَوْلَ ٱلَّتِى تُجَـٰدِلُكَ فِى زَوْجِهَا وَتَشْتَكِىٓ إِلَى ٱللَّهِ وَٱللَّهُ يَسْمَعُ تَحَاوُرَكُمَآ إِنَّ ٱللَّهَ سَمِيعٌۢ بَصِيرٌ ۝١ ﴾

﴾Indeed Allah has heard the statement of her [Khawlah bint Tha'labah] that disputes with you [O' Muhammad] concerning her husband [Aus ibn Aṣ-Ṣaamit], and complains to Allah. And Allah hears the argument between you both. Verily, Allah is All-Hearer, All-Seer.﴿ *(Qur'an 58: 1)*[102]

Bukhari narrated that Abu Moosa al-Ash'ari (رضي الله عنه) said: We were with the Prophet (ﷺ) on a journey, and whenever we climbed up we would shout *Allahu Akbar* (Allah is All-Great). He said:

---

[101] Bukhari, 13/372. Ibn Hajar said in *Fatḥ al-Baari* (13/373): Aḥmad, Nasaai and Ibn Maajah narrated this, with the same wording.

[102] This conversations is narrated by Aḥmad, Nasaai and Ibn Maajah, as stated by Al-Ḥaafiẓ in *Fatḥ al-Baari*, 13/374.

"Take it easy! You are not calling the One Who is deaf or absent; you are calling the One Who is All-Hearing, All-Seeing and Who is near."[103]

The *mushrikeen's* ignorance of how far the hearing of Allah extends

Bukhari narrated that 'Abdullah (رضي الله عنه) said: Two Thaqafis and a Qurayshi (or two Qurayshis and a Thaqafi) gathered by the House (the Ka'bah). They had fat bellies and little understanding in their hearts. One of them said: Do you think that Allah can hear what we say? The other said, He can hear if we raise our voices, but not if we lower them. The other said: If He can hear us when we raise our voices, then He can hear us when we lower them.

Then Allah (سبحانه وتعالى), revealed the words:

﴿وَمَا كُنتُمْ تَسْتَتِرُونَ أَن يَشْهَدَ عَلَيْكُمْ سَمْعُكُمْ وَلَآ أَبْصَٰرُكُمْ وَلَا جُلُودُكُمْ وَلَٰكِن ظَنَنتُمْ أَنَّ ٱللَّهَ لَا يَعْلَمُ كَثِيرًا مِّمَّا تَعْمَلُونَ ﴿٢٢﴾﴾

﴾And you have not been hiding yourselves [in the world], lest your ears and your eyes and your skins should testify against you; but you thought that Allah knew not much of what you were doing.﴿

(Qur'an 41: 22)[104]

3 - THE BEAUTIFUL NAMES OF ALLAH [105]

All the Names of Allah are beautiful:

---

[103] Bukhari, 13/372, hadith no. 7386.

[104] Ibid, 8/562, hadith no. 4817.

[105] I have written a separate book on the Names and Attributes of Allah, entitled *Asmaa' Allah wa Ṣifaatuhu fi Mu'taqad Ahl as-Sunnah wa'l-Jamaa'ah*; for more details on this topic, refer to this book.

﴿ وَلِلَّهِ ٱلْأَسْمَآءُ ٱلْحُسْنَىٰ فَٱدْعُوهُ بِهَا ... ﴿١٨٠﴾ ﴾

﴾And [all] the Most Beautiful Names belong to Allah, so call on Him by them...﴿ *(Qur'an 7: 180)*

Among these names are those that He has mentioned in *Soorah al-Ḥashr*:

﴿ هُوَ ٱللَّهُ ٱلَّذِى لَآ إِلَٰهَ إِلَّا هُوَ عَٰلِمُ ٱلْغَيْبِ وَٱلشَّهَٰدَةِ هُوَ ٱلرَّحْمَٰنُ ٱلرَّحِيمُ ﴿٢٢﴾ هُوَ ٱللَّهُ ٱلَّذِى لَآ إِلَٰهَ إِلَّا هُوَ ٱلْمَلِكُ ٱلْقُدُّوسُ ٱلسَّلَٰمُ ٱلْمُؤْمِنُ ٱلْمُهَيْمِنُ ٱلْعَزِيزُ ٱلْجَبَّارُ ٱلْمُتَكَبِّرُ سُبْحَٰنَ ٱللَّهِ عَمَّا يُشْرِكُونَ ﴿٢٣﴾ هُوَ ٱللَّهُ ٱلْخَٰلِقُ ٱلْبَارِئُ ٱلْمُصَوِّرُ لَهُ ٱلْأَسْمَآءُ ٱلْحُسْنَىٰ ... ﴿٢٤﴾ ﴾

﴾He is Allah, beside Whom *Laa ilaaha illa Huwa* [none has the right to be worshipped but He] the All-Knower of the unseen and the seen. He is the Most Gracious, the Most Merciful. He is Allah, beside Whom *Laa ilaaha illa Huwa* [none has the right to be worshipped but He], the King, the Holy, the One Free from all defects, the Giver of security, the Watcher over His creatures, the All-Mighty, the Compeller, the Supreme. Glory be to Allah! [High is He] above all that they associate as partners with Him. He is Allah, the Creator, the Inventor of all things, the Bestower of forms. To Him belong the Best Names...﴿ *(Qur'an 59: 22-24)*

1) The Number of His Names

Bukhari and Muslim narrated from Abu Hurayrah (رضي الله عنه) that the Prophet (ﷺ) said:

"Allah has ninety-nine Names, one hundred less one. Whoever counts them will enter Paradise. Allah is *Witr* (odd-numbered) and loves *Al-Witr* (that which is odd-numbered)."[106]

This hadith indicates that Allah has a limited number of Names, and states that they are ninety-nine.

But this conflicts with the report narrated by Ibn Mas'ood, according to which the Prophet (ﷺ) said:

> "No slave is ever afflicted with distress or grief, and says: '*Allahumma inni 'abduka ibnu 'abdika, ibnu amatika, naaṣiyati bi yadika, maaḍin fiyya ḥukmika, 'adlun fiyya qaḍaa'uka, as'aluka bi kulli ismin huwa laka, sammayta bihi nafsaka aw 'allamtahu aḥadan min khalqika, aw anzaltahu fi kitaabika, aw asta'tharta bihi fi 'ilm al-ghaybi 'indaka, an taj'al al-Qur'aana rabee' qalbi wa noora ṣadri, wa jalaa'a ḥuzni, wa dhihaaba hammi*
>
> (O' Allah, I am Your slave, son of Your slave, son of Your female slave. My forelock is in Your Hand, Your command over me is forever executed and Your decree over me is just. I ask You by every Name belonging to You which You have named Yourself with, or taught to any of Your creation, or revealed in Your Book, or You have preserved in the knowledge of the unseen with You, to make the Qur'an the life of my heart and the light of my breast, a departure for my sorrow and a release for my anxiety)' — but Allah will take away his distress and grief, and replace them with joy."[107]

And it is narrated that the Messenger praised his Lord as follows:

---

[106] Bukhari, 11/214, hadith no. 6410. Muslim, 4/2062, hadith no. 2677. This version is narrated by Muslim.

[107] Aḥmad, 1/391; Ibn Ḥajar in *Fatḥ al-Baari* attributed it to Aḥmad and Ibn Ḥibaan. *Fatḥ al-Baari*, 11/220.

"I cannot praise You sufficiently; You are as You have praised Yourself."[108]

The confusion that stems from this hadith is that it indicates that among the Names of Allah are Names which He has not revealed in His Book, but which He has told only to certain ones among His creation, or He has kept them to Himself and has not told them to any of His creation. The hadith of Abu Hurayrah, on the other hand, indicates that the Names of Allah number ninety-nine, all of which have been revealed and are known, as indicated by the phrase man *aḥṣaahaa* (whoever counts them) — this counting is impossible unless they are revealed and known. This implies that the Names which Allah has kept to Himself or revealed only to certain ones among His creation are other than these ninety-nine.

The truth which should be noted is that the number of Names which Allah has taught us in His Book, or His Messenger has mentioned, is ninety-nine and no more, because the Messenger (ﷺ) stated this number, and because he said "whoever counts them." Any additional names are something which we do not know, because they are part of the concealed Knowledge of Allah or have been revealed exclusively to certain ones among His creation. Otherwise it does not make sense to limit the number of the names of Allah to ninety-nine.

2) Defining the Names of Allah

The Messenger (ﷺ) told us that the Names of Allah which have been revealed and that we can know and count are ninety-nine names.

There is no *ṣaḥeeḥ* hadith which lists these Names in such a way as to leave no room for debate concerning them. These names have been narrated here and there in the Book of Allah and in the Sunnah of the Messenger (ﷺ). An *aayah* (verse) may mention one or two names, or

[108] Muslim, 1/353, hadith no. 486.

more, or an *aayah* may end with one or more Names, or list a group of these Names.

The scholars endeavoured to compile the Names of Allah from the Book of Allah and the Sunnah of His Messenger (ﷺ) and they endeavoured to interpret and explain them.

Qurṭubi wrote a book called *Ma'aani Asmaa' Allah il-Ḥusnaa* (The Meanings of the Most Beautiful Names of Allah). The Names were also listed by Ibn Jareer aṭ-Ṭabari, Abu Bakr ibn al-'Arabi, Ibn Ḥajar al-'Asqallaani and others. The scholars agreed on a large number of the names in the list, and disagreed over a few, which some regarded as being among the Names of Allah whilst others did not.[109]

The reason for these differences is that some scholars thought that everything that the Qur'an said about Allah could be counted as one of His Names and could be used on its own as a Name of Allah. Abu Bakr ibn al-'Arabi counted among His Names *Raabi' thalaathah* (the Fourth of three) and *Saadis khamsah* (the Sixth of five), on the basis of the *aayah*:

﴿أَلَمْ تَرَ أَنَّ ٱللَّهَ يَعْلَمُ مَا فِى ٱلسَّمَٰوَٰتِ وَمَا فِى ٱلْأَرْضِ ۖ مَا يَكُونُ مِن نَّجْوَىٰ ثَلَٰثَةٍ إِلَّا هُوَ رَابِعُهُمْ وَلَا خَمْسَةٍ إِلَّا هُوَ سَادِسُهُمْ... ﴿٧﴾﴾

﴾Have you not seen that Allah knows whatsoever is in the heavens and whatsoever is on the earth? There is no *Najwaa* [secret counsel] of three but He is their fourth [with His Knowledge, while He Himself is over the Throne, over the seventh heaven], - nor of five but He is their sixth [with His Knowledge],...﴿ *(Qur'an 58: 7)*

He also counted *Al-Faa'il* (the Doer) and *Az-Zaari'* (the Grower) as Names of Allah, on the basis of the *aayaat* (verses):

---

[109] *Talkheeṣ al-Ḥabeer*, 4/172.

﴿ يَوْمَ نَطْوِى ٱلسَّمَآءَ كَطَىِّ ٱلسِّجِلِّ لِلْكُتُبِ ۚ كَمَا بَدَأْنَآ أَوَّلَ خَلْقٍ نُّعِيدُهُۥ ۚ وَعْدًا عَلَيْنَآ ۚ إِنَّا كُنَّا فَٰعِلِينَ ﴿١٠٤﴾ ﴾

﴾And [remember] the Day when We shall roll up the heaven like a scroll rolled up for books. As We began the first creation, We shall repeat it. [It is] a promise binding upon Us. Truly, We shall do it.﴿ *(Qur'an 21: 104)* and:

﴿ أَفَرَءَيْتُم مَّا تَحْرُثُونَ ﴿٦٣﴾ ءَأَنتُمْ تَزْرَعُونَهُۥٓ أَمْ نَحْنُ ٱلزَّٰرِعُونَ ﴿٦٤﴾ ﴾

﴾Then tell Me about the seed that you sow in the ground. Is it you that make it grow, or are We the Grower?﴿ *(Qur'an 56: 63-64)*

The truth is that these are not Names of Allah, in the sense that Allah cannot be called or addressed as *Raabi' thalaathah* (the Fourth of three), *Saadis khamsah* (the Sixth of five), *Al-Faa'il* (the Doer) or *Az-Zaari'* (the Grower).[110]

There are actions mentioned in the Qur'an which Allah (ﷻ), attributes to Himself by way of showing that He punishes, is just and treats like with like, which in their context imply praise of Him and point to His perfection. But it is not permissible to derive Names of Allah from them, or to use them in any context other than the *aayaat* in which they are mentioned, such as:

﴿ إِنَّ ٱلْمُنَٰفِقِينَ يُخَٰدِعُونَ ٱللَّهَ وَهُوَ خَٰدِعُهُمْ ... ﴿١٤٢﴾ ﴾

﴾Verily, the hypocrites seek to deceive Allah, but it is He Who deceives them...﴿ *(Qur'an 4: 142)*

﴿ وَمَكَرُوا۟ وَمَكَرَ ٱللَّهُ ... ﴿٥٤﴾ ﴾

﴾And they [disbelievers] plotted [to kill 'Eesa (Jesus)],

---

110 *Ma'aarij al-Qubool*, 1/77.

and Allah planned too...﴿ *(Qur'an 3: 54)*

﴿ ... نَسُوا۟ ٱللَّهَ فَنَسِيَهُمْ ... ﴿٦٧﴾ ﴾

﴾...They have forgotten Allah, so He has forgotten them...﴿ *(Qur'an 9: 67)*

﴿ وَإِذَا لَقُوا۟ ٱلَّذِينَ ءَامَنُوا۟ قَالُوٓا۟ ءَامَنَّا وَإِذَا خَلَوْا۟ إِلَىٰ شَيَٰطِينِهِمْ قَالُوٓا۟ إِنَّا مَعَكُمْ إِنَّمَا نَحْنُ مُسْتَهْزِءُونَ ﴿١٤﴾ ٱللَّهُ يَسْتَهْزِئُ بِهِمْ... ﴿١٥﴾ ﴾

﴾And when they meet those who believe, they say: 'We believe,' but when they are alone with their *Shayaaṭeen* [devils - polytheists, hypocrites], they say: 'Truly, we are with you; verily, we were but mocking.' Allah mocks at them...﴿ *(Qur'an 2: 14-15)*

Allah cannot be called deceiver, plotter, forgetful, mocker, or other things above which He is exalted. It cannot be said that Allah mocks, deceives, plots or forgets in absolute terms, out of the context of these *aayaat*. Those who counted these as being among His Most Beautiful Names made a serious mistake, because deceit or plotting may imply praise or blame; it is not permissible to use them in reference to Allah except in a context where there is no room whatsoever for them to imply blame, as in the context of these *aayaat*.[111]

For the same reason, there is no mention among His names of Him being *Al-Mutakallim* (speaker), *Al-Mureed* (the One Who wills), *Al-Faa'il* (the Doer), *Aṣ-Ṣaani'* (the Maker), because these words may also imply both praise or blame. If it were permissible to derive names from the actions of Allah, such as the Deceiver, the Plotter, because these actions are mentioned in the Qur'an, then it would be permissible to make the Caller, the Comer, the Goer, the Forgetter, the Divider, the Angry, the Wrathful, the Curser, Names of Allah

---

[111] *Ma'aarij al-Qubool*, 1/76.

too... and other actions which the Qur'an attributes to Allah (ﷻ).

Allah (ﷻ), did not describe Himself as plotting and deceiving except to explain how He punishes those who do such things without justification. Punishing in kind is counted as something good if it is done by a created being, so how about when the Creator does it?

Among the Names of Allah are some which are not to be attributed to Him except in conjunction with their opposites, because if such a name is used on its own, it may imply imperfection. Examples of this include *Al-Maani'* (the Withholder), *Aḍ-Ḍaarr* (the Causer of Harm), *Al-Qaabiḍ* (the Seizer), *Al-Mudhill* (the Dishonourer), *Al-Khaafiḍ* (the Abaser). These names cannot be applied singly to Allah; they must be accompanied by their opposites, so that one says: *Al-Mu'ṭi al-Maani'* (the Giver the Withholder), *Aḍ-Ḍaarr an-Naafi'* (the Causer of Harm the Bringer of Benefit), *Al-Qaabiḍ al-Baasiṭ* (the Seizer the Bestower), *Al-Mu'izz al-Mudhill* (the Honourer the Dishonourer) *Al-Khaafiḍ ar-Raafi'* (the Abaser the Exalter).

Another example is *Al-Muntaqim* (the Avenger). The idea of vengeance only appears in the Qur'an in conjunction with the word *dhu* (owner of):

﴿... وَٱللَّهُ عَزِيزٌ ذُو ٱنتِقَامٍ ۝٩٥﴾

﴾...And Allah is All-Mighty, All-Able of Retribution [*Dhu Intiqaam*, lit. Owner of vengeance].﴿

(Qur'an 5: 95)

Or in the context of dealing with sinners:

﴿... إِنَّا مِنَ ٱلْمُجْرِمِينَ مُنتَقِمُونَ ۝٢٢﴾

﴾...Verily, We shall exact retribution from the *Mujrimoon* [criminals, disbelievers, polytheists, sinners].﴿

(Qur'an 32: 22)

3) The Greatest Name

The Messenger (ﷺ) has told us in more than one hadith that Allah (ﷻ), has one greatest Name which is distinguished from His other Names. Among these *aḥaadeeth* are the following:

a) It is narrated from Buraydah al-Aslami that the Messenger of Allah (ﷺ) heard a man saying: "O' Allah, I ask of You by the fact that You are Allah, there is no god except You, the One, the Self-Sufficient Master, who begets not, nor was He begotten, and there is none co-equal or comparable unto Him." He (the Prophet) (ﷺ) said:

> "He has called upon Allah by His Greatest Name, which if He is asked by it, He gives, and if He is called upon by it, He responds." — Tirmidhi and Abu Dawood[112]

b) It is narrated that Anas (رضي الله عنه) said: I was sitting with the Prophet (ﷺ) in the mosque, and a man was praying. He said,

> "O' Allah, I ask You by the fact that all praise is due to You, there is no god except You, *Al-Ḥannaan* (the Compassionate) *Al-Mannaan* (the Gracious), the Originator of the heavens and the earth, O' Owner of Majesty and Honour, O' Ever-Living, Self-Sustaining One, I ask of You." The Prophet said: "He has called upon Allah by His greatest Name, which if He is called upon by it, He responds, and if He is asked by it, He gives." — Tirmidhi, Abu Dawood, Ibn Maajah and Daarimi.[113]

c) Ibn Maajah narrated from Abu Umaamah that the Messenger of Allah (ﷺ) said:

---

[112] *Mishkaat al-Maṣaabeeḥ*, 1/703, hadith no. 2289; the editor of *Al-Mishkaat* judged its isnad to be *ṣaḥeeḥ* (sound).

[113] Ibid, 1/704, no. 2290; the editor of *Al-Mishkaat* judged its isnad to be *ṣaḥeeḥ*.

"The greatest Name of Allah is in three *soorahs* of the Qur'an, in *Al-Baqarah, Aal 'Imraan* and *Ṭa-Ha*." Ibn Maajah, Aṭ-Ṭaḥaawi in *Mushkil al-Aathaar*, and Ibn Mu'een in *At-Taareekh wa'l-'Ilal*, and others.[114]

d) The *aayaat* in *Al-Baqarah* (The Cow) and *Aal 'Imraan* in which the greatest Name of Allah has been mentioned have been described in a report. Tirmidhi, Abu Dawood, Ibn Maajah and Daarimi narrated from Asmaa' bint Yazeed (may Allah be pleased with her) that the Prophet (ﷺ) said: The greatest Name of Allah is in these two *aayaat* :

﴿ وَإِلَٰهُكُمْ إِلَٰهٌ وَاحِدٌ لَّا إِلَٰهَ إِلَّا هُوَ الرَّحْمَٰنُ الرَّحِيمُ ﴿١٦٣﴾ ﴾

﴿And your *Ilaah* [God] is One *Ilaah* [God - Allah], *Laa ilaaha illa Huwa* [there is none who has the right to be worshipped but He], the Most Gracious, the Most Merciful.﴾ *(Qur'an 2: 163),*

And in the beginning of *Aal 'Imraan*:

﴿ الم ﴿١﴾ اللَّهُ لَا إِلَٰهَ إِلَّا هُوَ الْحَيُّ الْقَيُّومُ ﴿٢﴾ ﴾

﴿*Alif-Laam-Meem*. [These letters are one of the miracles of the Qur'aan, and none but Allah (Alone) knows their meanings.] Allah! *Laa ilaaha illa Huwa* [none has the right to be worshipped but He], *Al-Ḥayyul-Qayyoom* [the Ever Living, the One Who sustains and protects all that exists].﴾ *(Qur'an 3: 1-2)*[115]

By comparing these texts in which the greatest Name of Allah is mentioned, it becomes clear that this name is "Allah," because this is the only name which is found in all of these texts in which the

---

[114] See its isnad in *Silsilat al-Aḥaadeeth aṣ-Ṣaḥeeḥah* by *Shaykh* Naaṣiruddeen al-Albaani, 2/382, hadith no. 746.

[115] *Mishkaat al-Maṣaabeeḥ*, 1/704, hadith no. 2291.

Messenger (ﷺ) said the greatest Name is mentioned.

What makes it most likely that "Allah" is the greatest Name is the fact that it is repeated in the Qur'an 2697 times, (two thousand six hundred and ninety seven times, according to the counting in *Al-Mu'jam al-Mufahras*) and the word *Allahumma* is repeated five times, at the time when another name which belongs exclusively to Allah, namely *Ar-Raḥmaan*, is repeated only 57 times. This idea (that "Allah" is the greatest Name) is also supported by the fact that it includes so many great meanings.

4) The Obligation of Believing in His Names

There is consensus among the righteous predecessors (*salaf*) that it is obligatory to believe in all the Most Beautiful Names of Allah and the Attributes to which they point, and the (Divine) actions which stem from those Attributes. For example, the Name *Al-Qadeer* (the Able) implies that we must believe that He is Able to do all things, and that His Ability is perfect, and that from His Ability stem all things that exist.

5) How the Muslim Counts the Names of Allah

The *aḥaadeeth* encourage us to count the Names of Allah. The one who counts them is promised admittance to Paradise.

The scholars differed as to what the phrase *man aḥṣaahaa* (whoever counts them) means.

Al-Khaṭṭaabi said: it may mean several things:

a) That a person recites them until he says all of them, and does not limit himself to only a few of them. So he calls upon Allah by all of them, and praises Him by all of them, and so he earns the promised reward.

This is the view which was favoured by Bukhari, who interpreted *iḥṣaa'* as meaning memorization, because of the existence of another report in which the words "whoever memorizes them" are narrated.

b) That *iḥṣaa'* means being able, i.e., to fulfil his duty towards these Names and act in accordance with their implications, which means that he should ponder their meanings and adhere to the ensuing obligations. So if he says "*Ar-Razzaaq* (the All-Provider)," he should have the certainty that his provision will come to him, and so on.

c) That it means understanding all their meanings.

And it is said that *iḥṣaa'* means acting according to their meanings, so that if a person says "*Al-Ḥakeem* (the All-Wise), He submits to all His commands and decrees, and believes that they are all in accordance with His Wisdom.

Ibn Baṭṭaal said: the way of acting in accordance with them is as follows:

(i) What it is appropriate to follow, such as *Ar-Raḥeem* (the Most Merciful) and *Al-Kareem* (the Most Generous), so that a person trains himself to develop these attributes in himself with regard to what he does.

(ii) Attributes which belong exclusively to Allah, such as *Al-Jabbaar* (the Compeller) and *Al-'Aẓeem* (the Most Great). The slave is obliged to affirm these attributes and submit to them, but not to try to develop these attributes in himself.

(iii) Attributes which imply a promise, where all the slave should do is hope for and desire that promise.

(iv) Attributes which imply a warning, where all the slave should do is fear it and hope to avoid it.

It seems that the meaning of *iḥṣaa'* (counting) is memorization and performing any acts of worship that this may require, just as there is no benefit in simply memorizing Qur'an if one does not act upon it. It is one of the features of those who have gone beyond the pale of Islam that they read the Qur'an but it does not go any further than their throats.[116]

6) List of the Names of Allah

It may be that Ibn Ḥajar al-'Asqallaani came closest to the truth when he listed ninety-nine Names taken from the Qur'an, thus complying with the number mentioned in the hadith of Abu Hurayrah (رضي الله عنه). We will quote them as he listed them:

S. No.	Name of Allah	Meaning
1	*Allah*	God
2	*Ar-Rabb*	The Lord, Sustainer, Cherisher
3	*Al-Ilaah*	The God
4	*Al-Waaḥid*	The One
5	*Ar-Raḥmaan*	The Most Beneficent
6	*Ar-Raḥeem*	The Most Merciful
7	*Al-Malik*	The King, Sovereign
8	*Al-Quddoos*	The Holy
9	*As-Salaam*	The One Free from all defects, the Author of Safety
10	*Al-Mu'min*	The Giver of Security
11	*Al-Muhaymin*	The Watcher over His Creatures, the Protector
12	*Al-'Azeez*	The All-Mighty

[116] It became clear to us, after studying this topic in our book *Asmaa' Allah wa Ṣifaatuhu fi Mu'taqada Ahl as-Sunnah*, that the correct view is that *iḥṣaa* means memorizing.

13	*Al-Jabbaar*	The Compeller
14	*Al-Mutakabbir*	The Supreme, the Majestic
15	*Al-Khaaliq*	The Creator
16	*Al-Baari'*	The Inventor of all things, the Maker
17	*Al-Muṣawwir*	The Bestower of forms, the Fashioner
18	*Al-Awwal*	The First
19	*Al-Aakhir*	The Last
20	*Aẓ-Ẓaahir*	The Most High, the Manifest
21	*Al-Baaṭin*	The Most Near, the Hidden
22	*Al-Ḥayy*	The Ever-Living
23	*Al-Qayyoom*	The Self-Suffcient, the One Who sustains and protects all
24	*Al-'Aliyy*	The Most High, the Sublime
25	*Al-'Aẓeem*	The Most Great
26	*At-Tawwaab*	The Acceptor of Repentance
27	*Al-Ḥaleem*	The Ever-Forbearing
28	*Al-Waasi'*	The All-Sufficient for His creatures' needs
29	*Al-Ḥaakim*	The All-Wise
30	*Ash-Shaakir*	The All-Appreciative
31	*Al-'Aleem*	The All-Knowing
32	*Al-Ghanee*	The Rich, Free from all wants and needs; Self-Sufficient
33	*Al-Kareem*	The Bountiful, The Generous
34	*Al-'Afuw*	The Oft-Pardoning
35	*Al-Qadeer*	The All-Powerful
36	*Al-Laṭeef*	The Most Subtle and Courteous
37	*Al-Khabeer*	The All-Aware
38	*As-Samee'*	The All-Hearing

39	*Al-Baṣeer*	The All-Seer
40	*Al-Mawlaa*	The Lord, Protector and Supporter, Patron
41	*An-Naṣeer*	The Helper
42	*Al-Qareeb*	The Near (to all, by His Knowledge)
43	*Al-Mujeeb*	The Responsive
44	*Ar-Raqeeb*	The All-Watcher
45	*Al-Ḥaseeb*	The All-Sufficient in taking account; the Recknoer
46	*Al-Qawee*	The Most Strong
47	*Ash-Shaheed*	The Witness
48	*Al-Ḥameed*	The One Who is Worthy of All Praise
49	*Al-Majeed*	The All-Glorious
50	*Al-Muḥeeṭ*	The Encompasser
51	*Al-Ḥafeeẓ*	The Guardian
52	*Al-Ḥaqq*	The Truth
53	*Al-Mubeen*	The Manifest
54	*Al-Ghaffaar*	The Oft-Forgiving
55	*Al-Qahhar*	The Irresistible, the Dominant
56	*Al-Khallaaq*	The Creator
57	*Al-Fattaḥ*	The Judge, the Reliever, the Opener
58	*Al-Wadood*	The Most Loving
59	*Al-Ghafoor*	The Oft-Forgiving
60	*Ar-Ra'oof*	The Full of Kindness
61	*Ash-Shakoor*	The Most Ready to Appreciate
62	*Al-Kabeer*	The Most Great
63	*Al-Mut'aal*	The Most High
64	*Al-Muqeet*	The Ever All-Able, All-Witness

65	*Al-Musta'aan*	The One Whose Help is to be sought
66	*Al-Wahhaab*	The Bestower
67	*Al-Ḥafi*	The Ever Most Gracious
68	*Al-Waarith*	The Inheritor
69	*Al-Wali*	The Protector of Guardian
70	*Al-Qaa'im*	The One Who Takes Charge (Guards, Maintains, Provides)
71	*Al-Qaadir*	The Able
72	*Al-Ghaalib*	The One Who has Full Power and Control, the Predominant
73	*Al-Qaahir*	The Irresistible
74	*Al-Ḥaafiẓ*	The Protector
75	*Al-Barr*	The Most Subtle, Kind, Courteous and Generous; The Source of All Goodness
76	*Al-Aḥad*	The One
77	*Aṣ-Ṣamad*	The Self-Sufficient Master, the Eternal
78	*Al-Maleek*	The King, the Owner, the Proprietor
79	*Al-Muqtadir*	The Omnipotent, All-Able to carry out what He wills
80	*Al-Wakeel*	The Disposer of Affairs
81	*Al-Haadi*	The Guide
82	*Al-Kafeel*	The Surety
83	*Al-Kaafi*	The Sufficient
84	*Al-Akram*	The Most Generous
85	*Al-A'alaa*	The Most High
86	*Ar-Razzaaq*	The All-Provider
87	*Dhu'l-Quwwat il-Mateen*	Owner of Power, the Most Strong
88	*Ghaafir adh-Dhanb*	The Forgiver of sin

89	*Qaabil at-Tawb*	The Acceptor of repentance
90	*Shadeed al-'Iqaab*	The Severe in Punishment
91	*Dhu'ṭ-Ṭawl*	The Bestower (of favours)
92	*Rafee' ad-Darajaat*	The Owner of High Ranks
93	*Saree' al-Ḥisaab*	The Swift in Reckoning
94	*Faaṭir as-Samawaati wa'l-Arḍ*	The Originator of the heavens and the earth
95	*Badee' as-Samawaati wa'l-Arḍ*	The Creator of the heavens and the earth
96	*Noor as-Samawaati wa'l-Arḍ*	The Light of the heavens and the earth
97	*Maalik al-Mulk*	The Possessor of the Kingdom
98, 99	*Dhul-Jalaali wa'l Ikraam*	Owner of Majesty and Honour

7) Special Effects of the Most Beautiful Names of Allah

Shaykh Ḥasan al-Banna mentioned in his book *Al-'Aqaa'id*[117] (the Creed) that some people say that each Name of Allah has special effects and secret meanings, which they have described in detail or in brief. Some people have gone to extremes and overstepped the mark by claiming that each Name has a spiritual servant who will serve anyone who persists in repeating that Name.

He said that some people claim that the greatest Name of Allah is a secret which is granted to some individuals, by means of which they overcome tremendous obstacles and perform extraordinary feats; this is something which is given only to them and not to other people.

[117] *Majmoo' ar-Rasaa'il*, 444-447; *Shaykh* Al-Banna (may Allah have mercy on him) mentioned this by way of denunciation.

These people to whom *Shaykh* Al-Banna referred to spoke without knowledge, and spoke of things concerning which there is no clear text in the Book of our Lord or the Sunnah of His Messenger (ﷺ). So there is no value in this and no proof for it, and at the same time we should remember that the Messenger (ﷺ) said:

> "Every action that is not a part of our directives and commands (i.e., Islam) is rejected."

These words and claims opened the door to myths and fables, and wasted a lot of time and energy in mistaken pursuits, which lead to a great deal of misguidance.

The virtue of which the Messenger (ﷺ) spoke in relation to the greatest name of Allah is that if He is called upon by it, He will respond, and if He is asked by it, He will give.

8) The Benefit of Knowing These Names

The real benefits which are to be gained from knowing the Names and Attributes of Allah can be summarized under the following points:

a) Getting to know Allah (سبحانه وتعالى), for the Names and Attributes of Allah are the greatest means for us to get to know our Lord. Without them, belief in Allah will remain an ambiguous idea which does not bear good fruits. We have spoken in detail about His Attributes and Names above, praise and blessings be to Allah.

b) Praising Him by His Names and Attributes. Praising Allah by His Names and Attributes is the greatest way of praising Him. This is one of the greatest kinds of *dhikr* (remembrance) that He has commanded us to say, as in the *aayah* (verse):

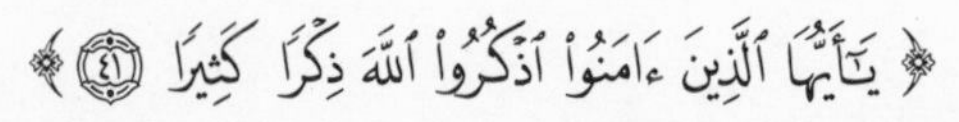

> ﴿O' you who believe! Remember Allah with much remembrance.﴾ *(Qur'an 33: 41)*

c) Calling upon Him by His Names and Attributes, as He (ﷻ), says:

﴿ وَلِلَّهِ ٱلْأَسْمَآءُ ٱلْحُسْنَىٰ فَٱدْعُوهُ بِهَا ... ﴿١٨٠﴾ ﴾

﴾And [all] the Most Beautiful Names belong to Allah, so call on Him by them...﴿ *(Qur'an 7: 180).*

The Messenger (ﷺ) told us on more than one occasion that one of the *ṣaḥaabah* called upon Allah (ﷻ), by His greatest Name, which if He is called upon by it, He will respond.

d) Increasing faith; the more a person learns about Allah and His Attributes, the more his faith increases.

e) Feeling strong and steadfast, because the person is putting his trust in the Most Strong, the All-Able, the One Who has full power and control.

f) Making one's heart feel attached to Allah. For the person who knows that his provision (*rizq*) comes from Allah will ask Him for provision; and the one who knows that Allah is the Compeller will fear Him; and the one who knows that Allah is All-Knowing will remember that He is watching... and so on.

g) The great reward which we will attain through this knowledge. Learning these Names and Attributes is the noblest thing that anyone can study, and learning and teaching them is one of the greatest works that anyone can undertake.

Examples of how the Messenger (ﷺ), blessings and peace be upon him, glorified and praised his Lord and called upon Him

I would like to quote some of the words — in addition to those mentioned above — with which the Prophet (ﷺ) glorified and praised Allah by His Names and Attributes, and called upon Him.

a) It is narrated from Abu Hurayrah that Abu Bakr aṣ-Ṣiddeeq (may Allah be pleased with them) said to the Messenger of Allah (ﷺ):

"Teach me something that I can say in the morning and in the evening." He (ﷺ) said:

> "Say: *Allahumma 'Aalim al-ghaybi wa'sh-shahaadah, Faaṭir as-samawaati wa'l-arḍ, Rabba kulli shay'in wa maleekahu, ashhadu an laa ilaaha illa anta, 'Aoodhu bika min sharri nafsi wa min sharr ish-shayṭaan wa sharakihi*
> (O' Allah, Knower of the unseen and the seen, Creator of the heavens and the earth, Lord and Sovereign of all things, I bear witness that there is no god except You. I seek refuge in You from the evil of my own self and from the evil and snares of the *Shayṭaan*)."

— This is narrated by Tirmidhi, Abu Dawood and Ad-Daarimi.[118]

b) Abu Sa'eed al-Khudri narrated that when the Messenger of Allah (ﷺ) would raise his head from *rukoo'*, he would say:

> "*Rabbanaa laka'l-ḥamd, mil' us-samawaati wa'l-arḍ, wa mil'u ma shi'ta min shay'in ba'd, ahl ath-thanaa'i wa'l-majd, aḥaqqu ma qaala al-'abd, wa kullunaa laka 'abd, Allahumma laa maani'a lima a'ṭayta wa laa mu'ṭiya limaa mana'ta, wa laa yanfa'u dhaa'l-jaddi minka al-jadd*
> (Our Lord, to You be praise, filling the heavens and the earth, filling whatever else You wish, Lord of Praise and Majesty. The truest thing a slave has said - and we are all slaves to You - is, O' Allah, none can withhold what You grant, and none can grant what You withhold, nor can the possessions of an owner benefit him in front of You)."[119]

---

[118] *Mishkaat al-Maṣaabeeḥ*, 1/734, hadith no. 2390.
[119] Muslim, 1/347, hadith no. 477.

c) It is narrated that Thawbaan (ﷺ) said: when the Messenger of Allah (ﷺ) would complete his *ṣalaah*, he would pray for forgiveness (say *astaghfirullah*) three times, and then say:

> "*Allahumma antas-salaam wa minkas-salaam, tabaarakta ya dhaa'l-jalaali wa'l-ikraam* [O' Allah, You are *As-Salaam* (The One Free from all defects), and from You comes peace, blessed are You O' Owner of Majesty and Honour]."[120]

d) Ibn 'Abbaas (ﷺ) narrated that the Messenger of Allah (ﷺ) used to say at times of distress:

> "*Laa ilaaha illa Allah al-'Aẓeem al-Ḥaleem, laa ilaaha illa Allah Rabb ul-'Arsh il-'Aẓeem, Laa ilaaha illa Allah Rabb us-samawaati wa Rabb ul-arḍ, Rabb ul-'Arsh il-kareem* (There is no god except Allah, the Most Great, the Ever Forbearing, there is no god except Allah, the Lord of the Mighty Throne, there is no god except Allah, the Lord of the heavens and the Lord of the earth, Lord of the Noble Throne)."[121]

e) It is narrated from Sumrah ibn Jundub that the Messenger of Allah (ﷺ) said:

> "The most beloved of speech to Allah are four phrases: *Subḥaan Allah, wa'l-ḥamdu Lillaah, wa laa ilaaha illa-Allah, w' Allahu Akbar* (Glory be to Allah, praise be to Allah, there is no god except Allah, and Allah is Most Great). And it does not matter with which of them you start."

According to another report:

---

[120] Muslim, 1/414, hadith no. 592.

[121] Bukhari, 11/145; Muslim, 4/2093, hadith no. 2730.

> "The best of speech is: *Subḥaan Allah, wa'l-ḥamdu Lillaah, wa laa ilaaha illa Allah, w' Allahu Akbar.*"[122]

f) It is narrated from Abu Hurayrah (رضي الله عنه) that the Messenger of Allah (ﷺ) said:

> "Two words which are light on the tongue but will weigh heavily in the Balance, and are beloved to the Most Merciful: *Subḥaan Allahi wa bi ḥamdihi, Subḥaan Allah il-'Aẓeem* (Glory and Praise be to Allah, Glory be to Allah the Most Great)."[123]

4 - THE METHODOLOGY IN THE LIGHT OF WHICH THE ATTRIBUTES OF ALLAH ARE TO BE UNDERSTOOD [124]

Shaykh Muhammad al-Ameen ash-Shanqeeṭi (may Allah have mercy on him) stated that the Holy Qur'an indicates that the issue of the Divine Attributes is focused on three principles. Whoever follows all of them has reached the correct view, and attained the belief which the Prophet (ﷺ) and his Companions and the righteous *Salaf* adhered to. Whoever misses out one of these three principles is misguided.

He stated that each of these three principles is indicated in the Qur'an:

The first principle: Declaring that Allah is far above any of His Attributes resembling any of the attributes of His creatures. This principle is indicated by the *aayaat* (verses):

﴿ ... لَيْسَ كَمِثْلِهِۦ شَىْءٌ ... ﴿١١﴾ ﴾

---

[122] Muslim. See *Mishkaat al-Maṣaabeeḥ*, 1/706, hadith no. 2294.

[123] Muslim, 4/2072, hadith no. 2694.

[124] See *Manhaj wa Diraasaat li Aayaat al-Asmaa' wa'ṣ-Ṣifaat*, by *Shaykh* Muhammad al-Ameen ash-Shanqeeṭi (may Allah have mercy on him).

﴿...There is nothing like Him...﴾ *(Qur'an 42: 11)*

﴿ وَلَمْ يَكُن لَّهُۥ كُفُوًا أَحَدٌۢ ﴿٤﴾ ﴾

﴿And there is none co-equal or comparable unto Him.﴾ *(Qur'an 112: 4)*

﴿ فَلَا تَضْرِبُوا۟ لِلَّهِ ٱلْأَمْثَالَ ... ﴿٧٤﴾ ﴾

﴿So put not forward similitudes for Allah [as there is nothing similar to Him, nor He resembles anything]...﴾ *(Qur'an 16: 74)*

The second principle: Believing in Allah as He has described Himself, because Allah cannot be described by anyone who knows Allah better than Allah:

﴿ ... قُلْ ءَأَنتُمْ أَعْلَمُ أَمِ ٱللَّهُ ... ﴿١٤٠﴾ ﴾

﴿...Say, 'Do you know better or does Allah?...'﴾ *(Qur'an 2: 140)*

And (this principle includes) believing in what the Messenger (ﷺ) has said describing Allah, because no one knows Allah, after Allah Himself, better than the Messenger of Allah (ﷺ) of whom Allah said:

﴿ وَمَا يَنطِقُ عَنِ ٱلْهَوَىٰٓ ﴿٣﴾ إِنْ هُوَ إِلَّا وَحْىٌ يُوحَىٰ ﴿٤﴾ ﴾

﴿Nor does he speak of [his own] desire. It is only a Revelation revealed.﴾ *(Qur'an 53: 3-4)*

The misguidance of those who follow only one of these two principles and not the other

The *Shaykh* (may Allah have mercy on him) condemned those who followed only one of these principles. He counted those who deny an Attribute which Allah has affirmed for Himself as people who are obstinate before the Lord of the heavens and the earth, and he regarded the actions of those who deny an Attribute which Allah has affirmed for Himself as an audacious attitude towards Allah.

He regarded this as being the ultimate misguidance, because the person who denies this, looks at the attributes of perfection and majesty which Allah has affirmed for Himself, then, this poor ignorant fool, comes before the Compeller of heaven and earth and says, what You have attributed to Yourself does not befit You, for it implies imperfection; I will interpret it (in a way that differs from its apparent meaning) and deny it, and replace it with something else from my own ideas, without any basis in the Qur'an or Sunnah.

Similarly misguided is the person who affirms the attributes of Allah, but he likens the attributes of the Creator to the attributes of His creatures.

The one who is successful and saved, who is following the straight path, is the one who believes in both of these principles, and does not distinguish between them. He believes in the attributes that Allah has affirmed for Himself, and at the same time he declares Him to be above resembling His creatures in any of His Attributes. Thus he is a believer who believes Allah to be above resembling His creation, and is free from any indulgence in either *tashbeeh* (anthropomorphism) or *ta'ṭeel* (denying all attributes of Allah).

These principles are indicated by a verse in the Book of Allah

These two principles are indicated by a verse in the Book of Allah, which is:

﴿ ... لَيْسَ كَمِثْلِهِۦ شَىْءٌ ۖ وَهُوَ ٱلسَّمِيعُ ٱلْبَصِيرُ ﴿١١﴾ ﴾

﴾...There is nothing like Him, and He is the All-Hearer, the All-Seer.﴿ *(Qur'an 42: 11).*

In this *aayah*, Allah affirms that He has the Attributes of hearing and seeing, whilst at the same time denying that there is anything like

Him. This clearly indicates that it is not permissible for people to deny that Allah can hear and see by claiming that only created beings possess hearing and sight and that affirming that Allah can hear and see will lead one to liken Allah to His creatures.

The meaning which the *aayah* points to is that Allah has the attributes of hearing and seeing, but His hearing and seeing in no way resemble the hearing and seeing of His creatures. His hearing and seeing befit His Majesty and Perfection, and the hearing and seeing of His creatures are suited to their situations. So there is no comparison between the attributes of Allah and the attributes of His creatures.

The third principle: the one on which the issue of the divine Attributes centres — as Ash-Shanqeeṭi says — is that there is no hope of understanding the true nature of how these attributes are, because understanding their true nature is impossible. Allah (ﷻ) has stated this clearly in *Soorah Ṭa-Ha* where He says:

﴿ يَعْلَمُ مَا بَيْنَ أَيْدِيهِمْ وَمَا خَلْفَهُمْ وَلَا يُحِيطُونَ بِهِۦ عِلْمًا ﴿١١٠﴾ ﴾

﴿He [Allah] knows what happens to them [His creatures] in this world, and what will happen to them [in the Hereafter] but they will never compass anything of His Knowledge.﴾ *(Qur'an 20: 110)*

This means that it is impossible for the human mind to encompass the attributes of the Lord of the heavens and the earth.

What the *Shaykh* said about the impossibility of ever knowing the true nature of Allah or His Attributes is sound logic, because the human mind, no matter how intelligent it is and how great its powers of understanding, is totally incapable of knowing the true nature of things.

Man is incapable of knowing the true nature of the soul that resides in his body; he is incapable of knowing the true nature of light which is the most apparent of things; he is incapable of understanding the true nature of matter, or of the atoms of which matter is composed, so how can he hope to understand the true nature of the Divine Essence and Attributes?

Those Who Deviate from the Correct Methodology and the Reasons for Their Deviation

Deviation from the correct methodology regarding the Names and Attributes of Allah comes about as a result of the undermining of one of the three principles mentioned above. We can divide the deviation of people, past and present, concerning the Names and Attributes of Allah, into three categories:

1) The deviation of the *mushrikeen*

The deviation of the *mushrikeen* was mentioned by Ibn 'Abbaas, Ibn Jurayj and Mujaahid. The *mushrikeen* misinterpreted the Names of Allah and changed them from their true meaning. They used them to name their idols, and distorted them by adding and taking away. So they derived "*al-Laat*" from "Allah", "*al-'Uzza*" from "*al-'Azeez*" and "*Manaat*" from "*al-Mannaan*".

Another aspect of their heresy is that they denied some of the names of Allah, such as *Ar-Raḥmaan*:

﴿ ... وَهُمْ يَكْفُرُونَ بِالرَّحْمَٰنِ ... ﴿٣٠﴾ ﴾

﴾...While they disbelieve in the Most Gracious [Allah]...﴿ *(Qur'an 13: 30)*

﴿ وَإِذَا قِيلَ لَهُمُ اسْجُدُوا لِلرَّحْمَٰنِ قَالُوا وَمَا الرَّحْمَٰنُ... ﴿٦٠﴾ ﴾

﴾And when it is said to them: 'Prostrate yourselves to the Most Gracious [Allah]!' They say: 'And what is the Most Gracious?'...﴿ *(Qur'an 25: 60)*

This also includes those who described Allah as being imperfect, such as the evil ones among the Jews who said:

﴿ ... إِنَّ ٱللَّهَ فَقِيرٌ وَنَحْنُ أَغْنِيَآءُ ... ﴿١٨١﴾ ﴾

﴿...'Truly, Allah is poor and we are rich!'...﴾
(Qur'an 3: 181)

﴿ ... يَدُ ٱللَّهِ مَغْلُولَةٌ ۚ غُلَّتْ أَيْدِيهِمْ وَلُعِنُوا۟ بِمَا قَالُوا۟ ... ﴿٦٤﴾ ﴾

﴿...Allah's Hand is tied up [i.e. He does not give and spend of His Bounty].' Be their hands tied up and be they accursed for what they uttered...﴾ *(Qur'an 5: 64)*

2) The deviation of *tashbeeh* (anthropomorphism)

These people attribute to Allah that which He attributed to Himself, but they do not declare Allah to be above any resemblance to His creatures. They focus only on the end of the *aayah*,

﴿ ... لَيْسَ كَمِثْلِهِۦ شَىْءٌ ۖ وَهُوَ ٱلسَّمِيعُ ٱلْبَصِيرُ ﴿١١﴾ ﴾

﴿...There is nothing like Him, and He is the All-Hearer, the All-Seer.﴾ *(Qur'an 42: 11)*

— and they overlook the beginning. If they had paid attention to the beginning, they would realize that there is nothing that is like unto Allah, and they would not have dared to say what they said, which is so utterly shocking and which makes the heart tremble, which is their suggestion that Allah has a hand, sight and hearing which is like our hands, hearing and sight — exalted be Allah far above what they say.

They made their object of worship like the idols. Hence the scholars of the *salaf* said: "The anthropomorphist worships an idol." They have uttered *kufr* by these words which take them beyond the pale of Islam. Among these people were Dawood al-Jawaaribi and Hishaam ibn al-Ḥakam ar-Raafiḍi. These two groups were opposites in their heresy: the former *mushrikeen* raised the creation to the level of the Creator and made them equal to Him, whilst the anthropomorphists brought the Creator down to the level of His physical creation, and likened Him to them. Exalted and sanctified be Allah above their lies and misguidance.

3) The deviance of the deniers, who fall into three categories

a) A group who denied the Names and the meanings to which they refer; they described Allah is terms of absolute negation (what He is not). These are the *Jahamiyah*. The fact of the matter is that their deviation is disbelief in Allah, just like the deviation of the *mushrikeen*.

b) A group who affirmed the names of Allah as words, without accepting the attributes of perfection that they imply. They said, *Raḥmaan* (Most Beneficent), *Raḥeem* (Most Merciful), without *Raḥmah* (Mercy) *Ḥakeem* (All-Wise) without wisdom, *Qadeer* (All-Powerful) without power, *Samee'* (All-Hearing) without hearing, etc. These are the *Mu'tazilah*.

c) A third group who affirmed seven of the *Ṣifaat al-Ma'aani* (characteristics), namely: life, knowledge, power, will, hearing, seeing and speech, but they denied all the other attributes. These are the *Ash'aris.*[125]

In the case of those who disbelieved in the names and Attributes of Allah, those who likened His Attributes to the attributes of His creatures and those who denied His Names and Attributes, their misguidance is quite clear, because they are opposing Allah and His Messenger, disbelieving in the Qur'an and Sunnah. Their position is

---

[125] Abu'l-Ḥasan al-Ash'ari (may Allah have mercy on him) did not subscribe to this view; we will discuss his belief concerning the attributes of the Creator below.

quite clear and does not require further explanation.

The ones whose faulty belief needs to be exposed are the *Ahl al-Kalaam* (Islamic philosophers / scholastics) who claim that they are declaring Allah to be above any resemblance to His creatures, so they deny attributes of Allah which have been narrated in the Qur'an and Sunnah, on the basis that this may lead to *tashbeeḥ* (anthropomorphism or thinking of Allah as being like His creation). So they resort to interpreting these attributes in a manner that takes them far away from their true meaning.[126]

5 - CATEGORIES OF ATTRIBUTES ACCORDING TO THE SCHOLARS OF *KALAAM*

Shaykh Muhammad al-Ameen ash-Shanqeeṭi (may Allah have mercy on him) explained the methodology of the scholars of *kalaam* with regard to their classification of the attributes of Allah. He described what they affirmed and what they denied, and where they fell into error and confusion. Then he discussed the Qur'anic evidence for ascribing these attributes to Allah and mentioned that it is not permissible to deny them in the case of Allah on the grounds that some of His creatures also have these attributes, because the Attributes of Allah befit His Majesty and the attributes of His creatures are suited to their inability.

---

[126] Some contemporary figures such as *Shaykh* Ḥasan al-Banna and *Shaykh* Ḥasan Ayyoob tried to be lenient towards those who made this mistake, who are known as the *khalaf* (successors), and they tried to reconcile between the views of the *salaf* (pious predecessors) and the *khalaf*. But the fact of the matter which must be understood is that the view of the *khalaf* who claim that the apparent meaning of the attributes of Allah is not what is meant, is far removed from the correct view. There is no meeting point between this and the view of the *salaf*. The fact that some of the *khalaf* had good intention is no excuse, because good intentions do not make falsehood true.

The *Shaykh* explained that the scholars of *kalaam* who indulged in this matter produced what they called rational evidence which they put together as rational analogies, and they divided the attributes of Allah into six categories, as follows:

a) *Ṣifah Nafsiyah* (attributes referring to "emotions" e.g., love, hate, etc.)
b) *Ṣifah Ma'na* (attributes which are part of the essence of Allah)
c) *Ṣifah Ma'nawiyah* (adjectival forms of the attributes which are part of the essence of Allah)
d) *Ṣifah Fay'liyah* (attributes describing actions)
e) *Ṣifah Salbiyah* (negative attributes)
f) *Ṣifah Jaami'ah* (encompassing attributes)

With regard to attributes other than these, they regarded them as relative attributes with no real, independent existence. Thus they caused a great deal of confusion.

Judging the Methodology of *Kalaam* Against the Qur'an and Sunnah

Shaykh Ash-Shanqeeṭi (may Allah have mercy on him) explained what the Qur'an says describing the Creator with these attributes, and describing His creatures with these attributes. The Qur'an states that the attributes of the Creator of the heavens and the earth are true, and that the attributes of created beings are true, and that there is no comparison between the attributes of the Creator and the attributes of His created beings. The attributes of the Creator befit His Divine Nature, and the attributes of His created beings are appropriate to their imperfect state and their need of Him. The difference between the attribute of the Divine and the attribute of the created beings is like the difference between the Divine essence and the essence of the created being.

Ṣifaat al-Ma'aani According to the Scholars of *Kalaam*

The *Shaykh* explained that according to the scholars of *kalaam* the *Ṣifaat al-Ma'aani* number no more than seven, and they deny all other attributes apart from these seven.

According to the scholars of *kalaam*, the *ṣifaat al-ma'aani* are defined as being those which are part of the essence of Allah.

The seven attributes which they affirm are power, will, knowledge, life, hearing, seeing and speech. The *Mu'tazilah* deny these seven attributes but affirm their implications, so they say: He is Able in and of Himself, All-Hearing in and of Himself, All-Knowing in and of Himself, Ever-Living in and of Himself. But they do not affirm that Allah has power, knowledge, life, hearing or seeing, because they are seeking to avoid implying that the Eternal is many, which all rational people know is a misguided and contradictory view. For if there were no knowledge in the essence of Allah, it would be impossible to say that He is All-Knowing without knowledge; this is clearly self-contradictory.

Then the *Shaykh* quoted the evidence for the *ṣifaat al-ma'aani*, and mentioned the differences between the attributes of the Creator and the attributes of the created being:

a) They described Allah as being powerful and affirmed that He has power. Allah (ﷻ) says in His Book:

﴿... إِنَّ ٱللَّهَ عَلَىٰ كُلِّ شَيْءٍ قَدِيرٌ ﴿٢٠﴾﴾

﴿...Certainly, Allah has power over all things.﴾
(Qur'an 2: 20).

We are certain that He has power in a manner that befits His Perfection and Majesty.

Some of His created beings are also described as having power. Allah (ﷻ) says:

﴿ إِلَّا ٱلَّذِينَ تَابُوا۟ مِن قَبْلِ أَن تَقْدِرُوا۟ عَلَيْهِمْ ... ﴿٣٤﴾ ﴾

﴾Except for those who [having fled away and then] came back [as Muslims] with repentance before they fall into your power...﴿ *(Qur'an 5: 34).*

— Here power is attributed to some created beings.

We know that everything in the Qur'an is true, that Allah has real power which befits His Perfection and Majesty and that some created beings have real power that is suited to their imperfect, transient state and their need for Allah. The difference between the attribute of the Divine and the attribute of the created beings is like the difference between the Divine essence and the essence of the created being, which is an immense difference.

b), c) Allah (ﷻ) described Himself as hearing and seeing in more than one *aayah* of His Book. He says:

﴿ ... إِنَّ ٱللَّهَ سَمِيعٌۢ بَصِيرٌ ﴿١﴾ ﴾

﴾...Verily, Allah is All-Hearer, All-Seer.﴿ *(Qur'an 58: 1)*

﴿ ... لَيْسَ كَمِثْلِهِۦ شَىْءٌ ۖ وَهُوَ ٱلسَّمِيعُ ٱلْبَصِيرُ ﴿١١﴾ ﴾

﴾...There is nothing like Him, and He is the All-Hearer, the All-Seer.﴿ *(Qur'an 42:11)*

Allah also described some of His created beings as being able to hear and see. He (ﷻ) says:

﴿ إِنَّا خَلَقْنَا ٱلْإِنسَٰنَ مِن نُّطْفَةٍ أَمْشَاجٍ نَّبْتَلِيهِ فَجَعَلْنَٰهُ سَمِيعًۢا بَصِيرًا ﴿٢﴾ ﴾

﴾Verily, We have created man from *Nutfah* [drops] of mixed semen [sexual discharge of man and woman], in order to try him, so We made him hearer and seer.﴿
(Qur'an 76: 2)

﴿ أَسْمِعْ بِهِمْ وَأَبْصِرْ يَوْمَ يَأْتُونَنَا ... ﴿٣٨﴾ ﴾

﴾How clearly will they [polytheists and disbelievers in the Oneness of Allah] see and hear, the Day when they will appear before Us!...﴿ *(Qur'an 19: 38)*

We do not doubt that what is in the Qur'an is true. Allah (ﷻ) can hear and see in a true sense, in a manner that befits His Majesty and Perfection, and created beings can hear and see in a real manner that suits their needful, transient and imperfect state. The difference between the attribute of the Divine and the attribute of the created beings is like the difference between the Divine essence and the essence of the created being.

d) Allah described Himself as being alive. He (ﷻ) says:

﴿ ٱللَّهُ لَآ إِلَٰهَ إِلَّا هُوَ ٱلْحَىُّ ٱلْقَيُّومُ... ﴿٢٥٥﴾ ﴾

﴾Allah! *Laa ilaaha illa Huwa* [none has the right to be worshipped but He], *Al-Ḥayyul-Qayyum* [the Ever Living, the One Who sustains and protects all that exists]...﴿ *(Qur'an 2: 255)*

﴿ هُوَ ٱلْحَىُّ لَآ إِلَٰهَ إِلَّا هُوَ ... ﴿٦٥﴾ ﴾

﴾He is the Ever Living, *Laa ilaaha illa Huwa* [none has the right to be worshipped but He]...﴿ *(Qur'an 40: 65)*

﴿ وَتَوَكَّلْ عَلَى ٱلْحَىِّ ٱلَّذِى لَا يَمُوتُ ... ﴿٥٨﴾ ﴾

﴾And put your trust [O' Muhammad] in the Ever Living One Who dies not...﴿ *(Qur'an 25: 58)*

He (ﷻ) has also described some of His created beings as being alive:

﴿... وَجَعَلْنَا مِنَ ٱلْمَآءِ كُلَّ شَىْءٍ حَىٍّ... ﴿٣٠﴾﴾

﴾...And We have made from water every living thing...﴿ *(Qur'an 21: 30)*

﴿وَسَلَٰمٌ عَلَيْهِ يَوْمَ وُلِدَ وَيَوْمَ يَمُوتُ وَيَوْمَ يُبْعَثُ حَيًّا ﴿١٥﴾﴾

﴾And *Salaam* [peace] be on him the day he was born, and the day he dies, and the day he will be raised up to life [again]!﴿ *(Qur'an 19: 15)*

﴿يُخْرِجُ ٱلْحَىَّ مِنَ ٱلْمَيِّتِ وَيُخْرِجُ ٱلْمَيِّتَ مِنَ ٱلْحَىِّ ... ﴿١٩﴾﴾

﴾He brings out the living from the dead, and brings out the dead from the living...﴿ *(Qur'an 30: 19)*

We are certain that Allah has the attribute of life in a real sense and in a manner that befits His Perfection and Majesty, just as created beings are also alive in a manner that suits their state of imperfection, transient nature and need (for Allah). The difference between the attribute of the Divine and the attribute of the created beings is like the difference between the Divine essence and the essence of the created being; there is an immense difference between the Creator and His creation.

e) Allah (ﷻ) has described Himself as having a will:

﴿فَعَّالٌ لِّمَا يُرِيدُ ﴿١٦﴾﴾

﴾He does what He intends [or wills].﴿ *(Qur'an 85: 16)*

﴿إِنَّمَآ أَمْرُهُۥٓ إِذَآ أَرَادَ شَيْـًٔا أَن يَقُولَ لَهُۥ كُن فَيَكُونُ ﴿٨٢﴾﴾

﴾Verily, His Command, when He intends [wills] a thing, is only that He says to it, 'Be!' and it is!﴿ *(Qur'an 36: 82)*

And He (ﷻ) described some of His creatures as having a will:

﴿ ...تُرِيدُونَ عَرَضَ ٱلدُّنْيَا... ﴿٦٧﴾ ﴾

﴾...You desire the good of this world...﴿ *(Qur'an 8: 67)*

﴿ ... إِن يُرِيدُونَ إِلَّا فِرَارًا ﴿١٣﴾ ﴾

﴾...They but wished to flee﴿ *(Qur'an 33: 13)*

﴿ يُرِيدُونَ لِيُطْفِئُوا۟ نُورَ ٱللَّهِ ... ﴿٨﴾ ﴾

﴾They intend to put out the Light of Allah [i.e. the religion of Islam]...﴿ *(Qur'an 61: 8)*

Undoubtedly Allah (ﷻ) has a will in a real sense, in a manner that befits His Perfection, and His created beings have wills which suit their state of imperfection, transient nature and need (for Allah). The difference between the attribute of the Divine and the attribute of the created beings is like that between the Divine essence and the essence of the created being.

f) Allah described Himself as having knowledge. He (ﷻ) says:

﴿ ... وَٱللَّهُ بِكُلِّ شَىْءٍ عَلِيمٌ ﴿٣٥﴾ ﴾

﴾...And Allah is All-Knower of everything.﴿ *(Qur'an 24: 35)*

﴿ لَّٰكِنِ ٱللَّهُ يَشْهَدُ بِمَآ أَنزَلَ إِلَيْكَ أَنزَلَهُۥ بِعِلْمِهِۦ ... ﴿١٦٦﴾ ﴾

﴾But Allah bears witness to that which He has sent down [the Qur'an] unto you [O' Muhammad]; He has sent it down with His Knowledge...﴿ *(Qur'an 4: 166)*

﴿ فَلَنَقُصَّنَّ عَلَيْهِم بِعِلْمٍ وَمَا كُنَّا غَآئِبِينَ ﴿٧﴾ ﴾

﴾Then surely, We shall narrate unto them [their whole

story] with knowledge, and indeed We have not been absent.﴿ *(Qur'an 7: 7)*

And He (ﷻ) has described some of His created beings as having knowledge:

﴿ ... وَبَشَّرُوهُ بِغُلَٰمٍ عَلِيمٍ ۝٢٨ ﴾

﴾...And they gave him glad tidings of a son having knowledge.﴿ *(Qur'an 51: 28)*

﴿ ... وَإِنَّهُۥ لَذُو عِلْمٍ لِّمَا عَلَّمْنَٰهُ ... ۝٦٨ ﴾

﴾...And verily, he was endowed with knowledge because We had taught him...﴿ *(Qur'an 12: 68)*

No doubt the Creator has real knowledge in a manner that befits His Perfection and Majesty, knowledge that encompasses all things, and His created beings have knowledge in a manner that suits their state of transience, imperfection and need (for Allah). The difference between the knowledge of the Creator and the knowledge of His created beings is like that between the essence of the Creator and the essence of His created beings.

g) Allah (ﷻ) has described Himself as speaking. He says:

﴿ ... وَكَلَّمَ ٱللَّهُ مُوسَىٰ تَكْلِيمًا ۝١٦٤ ﴾

﴾...And to Moosa Allah spoke directly.﴿ *(Qur'an 4: 164)*

﴿ ... فَأَجِرْهُ حَتَّىٰ يَسْمَعَ كَلَٰمَ ٱللَّهِ ... ۝٦ ﴾

﴾...Then grant him protection so that he may hear the Word of Allah [the Qur'an]...﴿ *(Qur'an 9: 6)*

And He (ﷻ) has described some of His created beings as speaking:

﴿ ... فَلَمَّا كَلَّمَهُۥ قَالَ إِنَّكَ ٱلْيَوْمَ لَدَيْنَا مَكِينٌ أَمِينٌ ۝٥٤ ﴾

﴿...Then, when he spoke to him, he said: 'Verily, this day, you are with us high in rank and fully trusted.'﴾ *(Qur'an 12: 54)*

﴿ ... وَتُكَلِّمُنَآ أَيۡدِيهِمۡ ... ﴿٦٥﴾ ﴾

﴿...And their hands will speak to Us...﴾ *(Qur'an 36: 65)*

Undoubtedly the Creator speaks in a real manner that befits His Perfection and Majesty, and His creatures speak in a manner that suits their transient state, imperfect nature and need (for Allah). The difference between the speech of the Creator and the speech of His created beings is like that between the essence of the Creator and the essence of His created beings.

The Discussion on the Negative Attributes According to the Scholars of *Kalaam*

Shaykh Ash-Shanqeeṭi (may Allah have mercy on him) explained the way in which the scholars of *kalaam* defined the negative attributes. He said: these are attributes which indicate an absolute absence, i.e., they indicate that Allah does not have attributes which are not befitting to Allah, without indicating something that does exist in His essence.

Those who say this list five negative attributes, with no sixth. According to them, these attributes are: eternity (no beginning), everlastingness (no end), difference from His created beings (no resemblance), oneness (no plurality), and absolute independence (no reliance on another), which they call self-sufficiency, by which they mean that He is not subject to any limitations of space and location.

i), ii) Eternity and Everlastingness

The *Shaykh* (may Allah have mercy on him) pointed out that eternity and everlastingness, which the scholars of *kalaam* attributed to Allah and claimed that He ascribed to Himself, are what is referred to in the *aayah*:

﴿ هُوَ ٱلْأَوَّلُ وَٱلْءَاخِرُ ... ﴿٣﴾ ﴾

﴾He is the First [nothing is before Him] and the Last [nothing is after Him]...﴿ *(Qur'an 57: 3)*

According to them, eternity (*al-qidam*, lit. ancientness) is intended to deny that there was any previous non-existence; in their view this is more specific than the word *al-azl* (eternity), because *al-azl* refers to something which has no beginning, whether it is something that exists, such as the essence and attributes of Allah, or does not exist. In their view, *al-qidam* refers to something which has no beginning, but which must also be something that does exist, such as the essence of Allah which is characterized by Perfection and Majesty.

The *Shaykh* (may Allah have mercy on him) explained that Allah described His created beings in terms of *al-qidam*:

﴿ قَالُواْ تَٱللَّهِ إِنَّكَ لَفِى ضَلَٰلِكَ ٱلْقَدِيمِ ﴿٩٥﴾ ﴾

﴾They said: 'By Allah! Certainly, you are in your old error [*ḍalaalika al-qadeem*]'﴿ *(Qur'an 12: 95)*

﴿ ... كَٱلْعُرْجُونِ ٱلْقَدِيمِ ﴿٣٩﴾ ﴾

﴾...Like the old [*qadeem*] dried curved date stalk.﴿ *(Qur'an 36: 39)*

﴿ أَنتُمْ وَءَابَآؤُكُمُ ٱلْأَقْدَمُونَ ﴿٧٦﴾ ﴾

﴾You and your ancient fathers.﴿ *(Qur'an 26: 76)*

And He (ﷻ) has described some of His created beings in terms of *al-baqaa'* (everlastingness):

﴿ وَجَعَلْنَا ذُرِّيَّتَهُۥ هُمُ ٱلْبَاقِينَ ﴿٧٧﴾ ﴾

﴿And, his progeny, them We made the survivors [*al-baaqeen*].﴾ *(Qur'an 37: 77)*

﴿ مَا عِندَكُمْ يَنفَدُ وَمَا عِندَ ٱللَّهِ بَاقٍ... ﴿٩٦﴾ ﴾

﴿Whatever is with you, will be exhausted, and whatever is with Allah [of good deeds] will remain [*baaqin*]...﴾ *(Qur'an 16: 96)*

Undoubtedly, the nature of the everlastingness that is attributed to Allah (ﷻ) is different from the nature of that which is attributed to His created beings.

The attribution of eternity (*al-qidam*) and everlastingness (*al-baqaa'*) to Allah has not been narrated in the Qur'an or Sunnah

The *Shaykh* (may Allah have mercy on him) pointed out that Allah has not described Himself in the Qur'an as being eternal in terms of *al-qidam*. Some of the *Salaf* regarded it as makrooh to describe Him in such terms, because it could imply prior non-existence, as in the phrases:

﴿...Like the old [*qadeem*] dried curved date stalk.﴾ *(Qur'an 36: 39)*
﴿They said: 'By Allah! Certainly, you are in your old error [*ḍalaalika al-qadeem*].'﴾ *(Qur'an 12: 95)*
﴿You and your ancient fathers [*al-aqdamoon*].﴾ *(Qur'an 26: 76)*

Some of them claimed that this usage [*al-qidam*] is narrated in a hadith, and some scholars say that this indicates that Allah may be described in this manner, whilst others say that this has not been proven.

With regard to the description of Allah as being First and Last, as in the *aayah*, ﴿He is the First [*Al-Awwal*] [nothing is before Him] and the Last [*Al-Aakhir*] [nothing is after Him].﴾ *(Qur'an 57: 3)*

- Allah has also described some of His created beings in terms of their being first and last:

﴿ أَلَمْ نُهْلِكِ ٱلْأَوَّلِينَ ﴿١٦﴾ ثُمَّ نُتْبِعُهُمُ ٱلْآخِرِينَ ﴿١٧﴾ ﴾

﴾Did We not destroy the ancients [*al-awwaleen* lit. the first ones]? So shall We make later generations [*al-aakhireen*] to follow them.﴿ *(Qur'an 77: 16-17)*

Undoubtedly, the manner of being First and Last which Allah attributes to Himself is befitting to His Majesty and Perfection, just as the manner in which His created beings may be first or last is suited to their transient state, imperfect nature and need (for Allah).

iii), iv) Oneness and Self-sufficiency

Allah (ﷻ) has described Himself as being One:

﴿ وَإِلَٰهُكُمْ إِلَٰهٌ وَٰحِدٌ ... ﴿١٦٣﴾ ﴾

﴾And your *Ilaah* [God] is One *Ilaah* [God - Allah]...﴿ *(Qur'an 2: 163)*

And He (ﷻ) has also described some of His created beings in similar terms:

﴿ ... يُسْقَىٰ بِمَآءٍ وَٰحِدٍ ... ﴿٤﴾ ﴾

﴾...Watered with the same water [lit. with one water]...﴿ *(Qur'an 13: 4)*

Allah (ﷻ) has described Himself as being Rich or Self-sufficient:

﴿ ... إِن تَكْفُرُوٓا۟ أَنتُمْ وَمَن فِى ٱلْأَرْضِ جَمِيعًا فَإِنَّ ٱللَّهَ لَغَنِىٌّ حَمِيدٌ ﴿٨﴾ ﴾

﴾...If you disbelieve, you and all on earth together, then verily, Allah is Rich [Free of all needs], Owner of all praise.﴿ *(Qur'an 14: 8)*

﴿ ... فَكَفَرُوا۟ وَتَوَلَّوا۟ ۚ وَّٱسْتَغْنَى ٱللَّهُ ۚ وَٱللَّهُ غَنِىٌّ حَمِيدٌ ﴿٦﴾ ﴾

﴿...So they disbelieved and turned away [from the truth]. But Allah was not in need [of them]. And Allah is Rich [Free of all needs], Worthy of all praise.﴾ *(Qur'an 64: 6)*.

And He (ﷻ) has described some of His created beings in similar terms:

﴿ ... وَمَن كَانَ غَنِيًّا فَلْيَسْتَعْفِفْ ۖ ... ﴿٦﴾ ﴾

﴿...And whoever [amongst guardians] is rich, he should take no wages...﴾ *(Qur'an 4: 6)*

﴿ ... إِن يَكُونُوا۟ فُقَرَآءَ يُغْنِهِمُ ٱللَّهُ مِن فَضْلِهِۦ ۗ ... ﴿٣٢﴾ ﴾

﴿...If they be poor, Allah will enrich them out of His Bounty...﴾ *(Qur'an 24: 32)*

These are the negative attributes which were mentioned in the Qur'an, which are used to describe both the Creator and His created beings. Undoubtedly the nature of these attributes when applied to the Creator befit His Perfection and Majesty, and when they are used to describe His created beings, their nature suits their imperfect state, transience and need (for Allah).

Conclusion concerning the *Ṣifaat al-Ma'nawiyah*

Then the Shaykh discusses what the scholars of *kalaam* called the seven *ṣifaat al-ma'nawiyah*, which refer to Allah being Able, Willing, All-Knowing, Ever-Living, All-Hearing, All-Seeing, and Speaking. He explains that the essence of these attributes has to do with the way these attributes apply to Allah.

Scholars of *kalaam* (scholastics) who counted them did so on the basis of there being an intermediate state between being absent and being present.

The *Shaykh* did not accept this concept. He said: "In fact this is a myth and is imaginary. No sound mind would accept something that comes in between a thing and its opposite. Everything that does not exist is simply non-existent or absent, and everything that is not absent exists. There is no in between at all, as is well known to all rational people."

Ṣifaat al-Af'aal (attributes describing some of Allah's actions)

Then the *Shaykh* discusses the *ṣifaat al-af'aal*, and says: these *ṣifaat al-af'aal* are mentioned frequently in the Qur'an, where they are attributed to both the Creator and His created beings. Undoubtedly the essence of these attributes as ascribed to the Creator is different from their essence as ascribed to His created beings, just as the essence of the Creator differs from the essence of His created beings.

These attributes include the following:

i) _Rizq_ (provision): Allah (ﷻ) has described Himself as granting provision to His creation. He says:

﴿ مَآ أُرِيدُ مِنْهُم مِّن رِّزْقٍ وَمَآ أُرِيدُ أَن يُطْعِمُونِ ﴿٥٧﴾ إِنَّ ٱللَّهَ هُوَ ٱلرَّزَّاقُ ذُو ٱلْقُوَّةِ ٱلْمَتِينُ ﴿٥٨﴾ ﴾

﴿I seek not any provision from them [i.e. provision for themselves or for My creatures] nor do I ask that they should feed Me [i.e. feed themselves or My creatures]. Verily, Allah is the All-Provider, Owner of Power, the Most Strong.﴾ *(Qur'an 51: 57-58)*

﴿ ...وَمَآ أَنفَقْتُم مِّن شَىْءٍ فَهُوَ يُخْلِفُهُۥ وَهُوَ خَيْرُ ٱلرَّٰزِقِينَ ﴿٣٩﴾ ﴾

﴿...And whatsoever you spend of anything [in Allah's Cause], He will replace it. And He is the Best of providers.﴾ *(Qur'an 34: 39)*

﴿ ... قُلْ مَا عِندَ ٱللَّهِ خَيْرٌ مِّنَ ٱللَّهْوِ وَمِنَ ٱلتِّجَٰرَةِ ۚ وَٱللَّهُ خَيْرُ ٱلرَّٰزِقِينَ ﴿١١﴾ ﴾

﴾...Say: 'That which Allah has is better than any amusement or merchandise! And Allah is the Best of providers.'﴿ *(Qur'an 62: 11)*

And Allah (ﷻ) has described some of His created beings in terms of *rizq*:

﴿ وَإِذَا حَضَرَ ٱلْقِسْمَةَ أُو۟لُوا۟ ٱلْقُرْبَىٰ وَٱلْيَتَٰمَىٰ وَٱلْمَسَٰكِينُ فَٱرْزُقُوهُم مِّنْهُ ... ﴿٨﴾ ﴾

﴾And when the relatives and the orphans and *Al-Masaakeen* [the poor] are present at the time of division, give them [*arzuqoohum* - lit. grant them provision] out of the property...﴿ *(Qur'an 4: 8)*

﴿ وَلَا تُؤْتُوا۟ ٱلسُّفَهَآءَ أَمْوَٰلَكُمُ ٱلَّتِى جَعَلَ ٱللَّهُ لَكُمْ قِيَٰمًا وَٱرْزُقُوهُمْ فِيهَا وَٱكْسُوهُمْ... ﴿٥﴾ ﴾

﴾And give not unto the foolish your property which Allah has made a means of support for you, but feed and clothe them [*arzuqoohum*] therewith...﴿ *(Qur'an 4: 5)*

﴿ ... وَعَلَى ٱلْمَوْلُودِ لَهُۥ رِزْقُهُنَّ ... ﴿٢٣٣﴾ ﴾

﴾...but the father of the child shall bear the cost of the mother's food [*rizquhunna*]...﴿ *(Qur'an 2: 233)*

Undoubtedly, the actions when ascribed to Allah are different from when they are ascribed to His created beings, just as the essence of Allah is different from the essence of His created beings.

ii) *'Amal* (action, doing): Allah (ﷻ) describes Himself as doing. He said:

﴿ أَوَلَمْ يَرَوْا۟ أَنَّا خَلَقْنَا لَهُم مِّمَّا عَمِلَتْ أَيْدِينَآ أَنْعَـٰمًا فَهُمْ لَهَا مَـٰلِكُونَ ﴿٧١﴾ ﴾

﴾Do they not see that We have created for them of what Our Hands have created [lit. done, made], the cattle, so that they are their owners.﴿ *(Qur'an 36: 71)*

And Allah (ﷻ) has described His creatures as doing, as He says:

﴿ ... إِنَّمَا تُجْزَوْنَ مَا كُنتُمْ تَعْمَلُونَ ﴿١٦﴾ ﴾

﴾...You are only being requited for what you used to do.﴿ *(Qur'an 52: 16)*

Undoubtedly this action as attributed to the created being is different from this action as attributed to the Creator, just as the essence of the Creator differs from the essence of the created being.

iii) *Ta'leem* (teaching): Allah (ﷻ) describes Himself as teaching His creation:

﴿ ٱلرَّحْمَـٰنُ ﴿١﴾ عَلَّمَ ٱلْقُرْءَانَ ﴿٢﴾ خَلَقَ ٱلْإِنسَـٰنَ ﴿٣﴾ عَلَّمَهُ ٱلْبَيَانَ ﴿٤﴾ ﴾

﴾The Most Gracious [Allah]! He has taught [you mankind] the Qur'an [by His Mercy]. He created man. He taught him eloquent speech.﴿ *(Qur'an 55: 1-4)*

﴿ ٱقْرَأْ وَرَبُّكَ ٱلْأَكْرَمُ ﴿٣﴾ ٱلَّذِى عَلَّمَ بِٱلْقَلَمِ ﴿٤﴾ عَلَّمَ ٱلْإِنسَـٰنَ مَا لَمْ يَعْلَمْ ﴿٥﴾ ﴾

﴾Read! And your Lord is the Most Generous. Who has taught [the writing] by the pen. He has taught man that which he knew not.﴿ *(Qur'an 96: 3-5)*

﴿ ... وَعَلَّمَكَ مَا لَمْ تَكُن تَعْلَمُ ۚ وَكَانَ فَضْلُ ٱللَّهِ عَلَيْكَ عَظِيمًا ﴿١١٣﴾ ﴾

﴿...And taught you that which you knew not. And Ever Great is the Grace of Allah unto you [O' Muhammad].﴾
(Qur'an 4: 113)

Allah (ﷻ) also describes some of His creation as having this attribute. He says:

﴿ هُوَ ٱلَّذِى بَعَثَ فِى ٱلْأُمِّيِّـۧنَ رَسُولًا مِّنْهُمْ يَتْلُوا۟ عَلَيْهِمْ ءَايَـٰتِهِۦ وَيُزَكِّيهِمْ وَيُعَلِّمُهُمُ ٱلْكِتَـٰبَ وَٱلْحِكْمَةَ ... ﴿٢﴾ ﴾

﴿He it is Who sent among the unlettered ones a Messenger [Muhammad] from among themselves, reciting to them His Verses, purifying them [from the filth of disbelief and polytheism], and teaching them the Book [this Qur'an, Islamic laws and Islamic jurisprudence] and *Al-Ḥikmah* [As-Sunnah: legal ways, orders, acts of worship of Prophet Muhammad].﴾
(Qur'an 62: 2)

Both examples of teaching are mentioned together in the *aayah*:

﴿ ... تُعَلِّمُونَهُنَّ مِمَّا عَلَّمَكُمُ ٱللَّهُ ... ﴿٤﴾ ﴾

﴿...Training and teaching them [to catch) in the manner as directed to you by Allah...﴾ *(Qur'an 5:4)*

iv) *Inbaa'* (telling, informing): Allah (ﷻ) describes Himself as telling or informing, and describes His created beings as also telling or informing. Both are mentioned together in the *aayah*:

﴿ وَإِذْ أَسَرَّ ٱلنَّبِىُّ إِلَىٰ بَعْضِ أَزْوَٰجِهِۦ حَدِيثًا فَلَمَّا نَبَّأَتْ بِهِۦ وَأَظْهَرَهُ ٱللَّهُ عَلَيْهِ عَرَّفَ بَعْضَهُۥ وَأَعْرَضَ عَنۢ بَعْضٍ ۖ فَلَمَّا نَبَّأَهَا بِهِۦ قَالَتْ مَنْ أَنۢبَأَكَ هَـٰذَا ۖ قَالَ نَبَّأَنِىَ ٱلْعَلِيمُ ٱلْخَبِيرُ ﴿٣﴾ ﴾

﴿And [remember] when the Prophet disclosed a matter in confidence to one of his wives [Ḥafsah], then she told it [to another i.e. 'Aa'ishah]. And Allah made it known to him; he informed part thereof and left a part. Then when he told her [Ḥafṣah] thereof, she said: 'Who told you this?' He said: 'The All-Knower, the All-Aware [Allah] has told me.'》 *(Qur'an 66: 3)*

Undoubtedly, what is described of this action on the part of Allah, the Exalted, is quite different from that described on the part of His slave, just as the essence of the Creator differs from the essence of the created being.

v) *Eetaa'* (granting, giving): Allah (ﷻ) describes Himself as doing this action, which is giving. He says:

﴿ يُؤْتِي الْحِكْمَةَ مَن يَشَاءُ ... ﴿٢٦٩﴾ ﴾

《He grants *Ḥikmah* [wisdom, knowledge] to whom He wills...》 *(Qur'an 2: 269)*

﴿ ... وَيُؤْتِ كُلَّ ذِي فَضْلٍ فَضْلَهُ ... ﴿٣﴾ ﴾

《...And bestow His abounding Grace to every owner of grace [i.e. the one who helps and serves the needy and deserving, physically and with his wealth, and even with good words]...》 *(Qur'an 11: 3)*

And He (ﷻ) describes His slaves as also giving:

﴿ ... وَآتَيْتُمْ إِحْدَاهُنَّ قِنطَارًا ... ﴿٢٠﴾ ﴾

《...And you have given one of them a *Qinṭaar* [of gold, i.e. a great amount as *Mahr*]...》 *(Qur'an 4: 20)*

﴿ وَآتُوا النِّسَاءَ صَدُقَاتِهِنَّ نِحْلَةً ... ﴿٤﴾ ﴾

《And give to the women [whom you marry] their *Mahr* [obligatory bridal-money given by the husband to his

wife at the time of marriage] with a good heart...﴿
(Qur'an 4: 4)

Undoubtedly, this action Allah ascribed to Himself is different from the action He ascribed to His slaves, just as His essence differs from theirs.

Aṣ-Ṣifaat al-Jaami'ah (All-Encompassing Attributes)

Then *Shaykh* Muhammad al-Ameen ash-Shanqeeṭi (may Allah have mercy on him) discusses *Aṣ-Ṣifaat al-Jaami'ah*, such as *Al-'Aluw* (highness), *Al-'Iẓam* (greatness), *Al-Kibar* (greatness), *Al-Mulk* (sovereignty), *Al-Kibr* (pride), *Al-Jabaroot* (compelling power), *Al-'Izzah* (might), *Al-Quwwah* (strength) and other all-encompassing attributes.

i) - iii) The attributes of *Al-'Aluw* (highness), *Al-Kibar* (greatness) and *Al-'Iẓam* (greatness)

Allah describes Himself as having the attributes of *Al-'Aluw* (highness), *Al-Kibar* (greatness) and *Al-'Iẓam* (greatness). He (ﷻ) says:

﴾... وَلَا يَـُٔودُهُۥ حِفْظُهُمَا ۚ وَهُوَ ٱلْعَلِىُّ ٱلْعَظِيمُ ﴿٢٥٥﴾﴿

﴾...And He feels no fatigue in guarding and preserving them. And He is the Most High, the Most Great.﴿
(Qur'an 2: 255)

And He (ﷻ) said, describing Himself as having the attributes of *Al-'Aluw* (highness) and *Al-Kibar* (greatness):

﴾...إِنَّ ٱللَّهَ كَانَ عَلِيًّا كَبِيرًا ﴿٣٤﴾﴿

﴾...Surely, Allah is Ever Most High, Most Great.﴿
(Qur'an 4: 34)

﴾عَـٰلِمُ ٱلْغَيْبِ وَٱلشَّهَـٰدَةِ ٱلْكَبِيرُ ٱلْمُتَعَالِ ﴿٩﴾﴿

﴿All-Knower of the unseen and the seen, the Most Great, the Most High.﴾ *(Qur'an 13: 9).*

And He (ﷻ) described some of the things He has created as being great:

﴿... فَانفَلَقَ فَكَانَ كُلُّ فِرْقٍ كَالطَّوْدِ الْعَظِيمِ ﴿٦٣﴾﴾

﴿And it parted, and each separate part [of that sea water] became like huge [*'aẓeem*] mountain.﴾ *(Qur'an 26: 63)*

﴿... إِنَّكُمْ لَتَقُولُونَ قَوْلًا عَظِيمًا ﴿٤٠﴾﴾

﴿...Verily, you indeed utter an awful [*'aẓeem*] saying.﴾ *(Qur'an 17: 40)*

﴿... وَلَهَا عَرْشٌ عَظِيمٌ ﴿٢٣﴾﴾

﴿...And she has a great throne.﴾ *(Qur'an 27: 23)*

And He described some of the things He has created as being high:

﴿وَرَفَعْنَاهُ مَكَانًا عَلِيًّا ﴿٥٧﴾﴾

﴿And We raised him to a high station.﴾ *(Qur'an 19: 57)*

﴿... وَجَعَلْنَا لَهُمْ لِسَانَ صِدْقٍ عَلِيًّا ﴿٥٠﴾﴾

﴿...And We granted them lofty honour on the tongue of truth.﴾ *(Qur'an 19: 50)* (Yusuf 'Ali's translation).

And He described some of the things He has created as being great:

﴿... أُولَٰئِكَ لَهُم مَّغْفِرَةٌ وَأَجْرٌ كَبِيرٌ ﴿١١﴾﴾

﴿...Theirs will be forgiveness and a great reward [Paradise].﴾ *(Qur'an 11: 11)*

﴿...بَلْ فَعَلَهُ كَبِيرُهُمْ هَٰذَا ... ﴿٦٣﴾﴾

﴿...Nay, this one, the biggest of them [idols] did it...﴾ *(Qur'an 21: 63)*

Undoubtedly, the nature of these all-encompassing attributes, such as highness and greatness, is different in the case of Allah from their nature as applied to the created beings, just as the essence of the Creator differs from the essence of the created being. There is no comparison between the essence of the Creator and the essence of His creation, just as there is no comparison between the attributes of the Creator and the attributes of His creation.

iv) The attribute of sovereignty

Allah describes Himself with the attribute of sovereignty. He (ﷻ) says:

﴿يُسَبِّحُ لِلَّهِ مَا فِى ٱلسَّمَٰوَٰتِ وَمَا فِى ٱلْأَرْضِ ٱلْمَلِكِ ٱلْقُدُّوسِ ٱلْعَزِيزِ ٱلْحَكِيمِ ۝١﴾

﴿Whatsoever is in the heavens and whatsoever is on the earth glorifies Allah, the King [of everything], the Holy, the All-Mighty, the All-Wise.﴾ *(Qur'an 62: 1)*

﴿فِى مَقْعَدِ صِدْقٍ عِندَ مَلِيكٍ مُّقْتَدِرٍۭ ۝٥٥﴾

﴿In a seat of truth [i.e. Paradise], near the Omnipotent King.﴾ *(Qur'an 54: 55)*

Allah (ﷻ) has also described some of His created beings as possessing sovereignty:

﴿وَقَالَ ٱلْمَلِكُ إِنِّىٓ أَرَىٰ سَبْعَ بَقَرَٰتٍ سِمَانٍ... ۝٤٣﴾

﴿And the king [of Egypt] said: 'Verily, I saw [in a dream] seven fat cows...'﴾ *(Qur'an 12: 43)*

﴿وَقَالَ ٱلْمَلِكُ ٱئْتُونِى بِهِۦ... ۝٥٠﴾

﴾And the king said: 'Bring him to me...'﴿
(Qur'an 12: 50)

﴿... وَكَانَ وَرَآءَهُم مَّلِكٌ يَأْخُذُ كُلَّ سَفِينَةٍ غَصْبًا ۝٧٩﴾

﴾...There was a king behind them who seized every ship by force.﴿ *(Qur'an 18: 79)*

﴿... تُؤْتِي ٱلْمُلْكَ مَن تَشَآءُ وَتَنزِعُ ٱلْمُلْكَ مِمَّن تَشَآءُ... ۝٢٦﴾

﴾...You give the kingdom to whom You will, and You take the kingdom from whom You will,...﴿
(Qur'an 3: 26)

Undoubtedly Allah possesses true Sovereignty in a manner which befits His Perfection and Majesty, whilst His created beings possess sovereignty in a manner that is suited to their transient nature, imperfection and need for Allah.

v), vi) The attributes of compelling power and pride

Allah describes Himself as being the Compeller (*Al-Jabbaar*) and Most Great (*Al-Mutakabbir*):

﴿... ٱلْعَزِيزُ ٱلْجَبَّارُ ٱلْمُتَكَبِّرُ... ۝٢٣﴾

﴾...The All-Mighty [*Al-'Azeez*], the Compeller [*Al-Jabbaar*], the Supreme [*Al-Mutakabbir*]...﴿
(Qur'an 59: 23).

And He (ﷻ) has described some of His creatures as being so,

﴿... كَذَٰلِكَ يَطْبَعُ ٱللَّهُ عَلَىٰ كُلِّ قَلْبِ مُتَكَبِّرٍ جَبَّارٍ ۝٣٥﴾

﴾...Thus does Allah seal up the heart of every arrogant (*mutakabbir*), tyrant (*jabbaar*).﴿ *(Qur'an 40: 35)*

﴿وَإِذَا بَطَشْتُم بَطَشْتُمْ جَبَّارِينَ ۝١٣٠﴾

﴿And when you seize [somebody], seize you [him] as tyrants (*jabbaareen*)?.﴾ *(Qur'an 26: 130)*

﴿ ... أَلَيْسَ فِي جَهَنَّمَ مَثْوًى لِّلْمُتَكَبِّرِينَ ﴿٦٠﴾ ﴾

﴿...Is there not in Hell an abode for the arrogant (*mutakabbireen*)?﴾ *(Qur'an 39: 60)*

﴿ وَاسْتَفْتَحُوا وَخَابَ كُلُّ جَبَّارٍ عَنِيدٍ ﴿١٥﴾ ﴾

﴿And they [the Messengers] sought victory and help [from their Lord (Allah)] and every obstinate, arrogant dictator [*jabbaar*] [who refuses to believe in the Oneness of Allah] was brought to a complete loss and destruction.﴾ *(Qur'an 14: 15)*

Undoubtedly, the nature of these attributes in the case of the Creator is different from that in the case of His created beings, just as the essence of the Creator is different from the essence of His created beings.

vii) The attribute of might (*Al-'Izzah*)

Allah (ﷻ) describes Himself as possessing might (*Al-'Izzah*):

﴿ ... إِنَّ اللَّهَ عَزِيزٌ حَكِيمٌ ﴿٢٢٠﴾ ﴾

﴿...Truly, Allah is All-Mighty [*Al-'Azeez*], All-Wise.﴾ *(Qur'an 2: 220)*

﴿ أَمْ عِندَهُمْ خَزَائِنُ رَحْمَةِ رَبِّكَ الْعَزِيزِ الْوَهَّابِ ﴿٩﴾ ﴾

﴿Or have they the treasures of the Mercy of your Lord, the All-Mighty [*Al-'Azeez*], the Real Bestower?﴾ *(Qur'an 38: 9)*

And Allah (ﷻ) has described some of His created beings as also possessing the attribute of might:

﴿ ... قَالَتِ ٱمْرَأَتُ ٱلْعَزِيزِ ... ۝٥١ ﴾

﴾...The wife of Al-'Azeez said...﴿ *(Qur'an 12: 51)*

﴿ ... وَعَزَّنِى فِى ٱلْخِطَابِ ۝٢٣ ﴾

﴾...And he overpowered me [*'azzani*] in speech.﴿ *(Qur'an 38: 23)*

And the two examples are mentioned together in the *aayah*:

﴿ ... وَلِلَّهِ ٱلْعِزَّةُ وَلِرَسُولِهِۦ وَلِلْمُؤْمِنِينَ ... ۝٨ ﴾

﴾...But honour, power and glory [*'izzah*] belong to Allah, and to His Messenger [Muhammad], and to the believers...﴿ *(Qur'an 63: 8)*

Undoubtedly, these attributes as ascribed to the Creator are different from these attributes as ascribed to His created beings, just as the essence of the Creator differs from the essence of His created beings.

viii) The attribute of strength (*Al-Quwwah*)

Allah (ﷻ) describes Himself as possessing the attribute of strength:

﴿ مَآ أُرِيدُ مِنْهُم مِّن رِّزْقٍ وَمَآ أُرِيدُ أَن يُطْعِمُونِ ۝٥٧ إِنَّ ٱللَّهَ هُوَ ٱلرَّزَّاقُ ذُو ٱلْقُوَّةِ ٱلْمَتِينُ ۝٥٨ ﴾

﴾I seek not any provision from them [i.e. provision for themselves or for My creatures] nor do I ask that they should feed Me [i.e. feed themselves or My creatures]. Verily, Allah is the All-Provider, Owner of Power, the Most Strong.﴿ *(Qur'an 51: 57-58)*

﴿ ... وَلَيَنصُرَنَّ ٱللَّهُ مَن يَنصُرُهُۥٓ ۗ إِنَّ ٱللَّهَ لَقَوِىٌّ عَزِيزٌ ۝٤٠ ﴾

﴾...Verily, Allah will help those who help His [Cause]. Truly, Allah is All-Strong, All-Mighty.﴿ *(Qur'an 22: 40)*

And Allah (ﷻ) describes some of His creatures as being strong, as He says:

﴿ ... وَيَزِدْكُمْ قُوَّةً إِلَىٰ قُوَّتِكُمْ ... ﴿٥٢﴾ ﴾

﴾...And add strength to your strength,...﴿ *(Qur'an 11: 52)*

﴿ ۞ اللَّهُ الَّذِي خَلَقَكُم مِّن ضَعْفٍ ثُمَّ جَعَلَ مِنۢ بَعْدِ ضَعْفٍ قُوَّةً ثُمَّ جَعَلَ مِنۢ بَعْدِ قُوَّةٍ ضَعْفًا ... ﴿٥٤﴾ ﴾

﴾Allah is He Who created you in [a state of] weakness, then gave you strength after weakness, then after strength gave [you] weakness...﴿ *(Qur'an 30: 54)*

And both examples are mentioned together in the *aayah* (verse):

﴿ فَأَمَّا عَادٌ فَاسْتَكْبَرُوا فِي الْأَرْضِ بِغَيْرِ الْحَقِّ وَقَالُوا مَنْ أَشَدُّ مِنَّا قُوَّةً ۖ أَوَلَمْ يَرَوْا أَنَّ اللَّهَ الَّذِي خَلَقَهُمْ هُوَ أَشَدُّ مِنْهُمْ قُوَّةً ۖ وَكَانُوا بِآيَاتِنَا يَجْحَدُونَ ﴿١٥﴾ ﴾

﴾As for 'Aad, they were arrogant in the land without right, and they said: 'Who is mightier than us in strength?' See they not that Allah Who created them was mightier in strength than them. And they used to deny Our *Aayaat* [proofs, evidences, verses, lessons, revelations, etc.]!﴿ *(Qur'an 41: 15)*

The attributes concerning which the scholars of *kalaam* differed

Then the *Shaykh* discusses the attributes concerning which the scholars of *kalaam* differed as to whether they are *Ṣifaat af'aal* or *Ṣifaat ma'na*. What the *Shaykh* confirmed was that they are *Ṣifaat ma'aani*, part of the essence of Allah. These attributes include the following:

i), ii) The attributes of kindness (*Ar-Ra'fah*) and mercy (*Ar-Raḥmah*)

Allah has described Himself as being Kind and Merciful:

﴿...إِنَّ رَبَّكُمْ لَرَءُوفٌ رَّحِيمٌ ﴿٧﴾﴾

﴿...Truly, your Lord is full of kindness, Most Merciful.﴾ *(Qur'an 16: 7)*

And He (سبحانه وتعالى) has described some of His created beings in similar terms. He described our Prophet (ﷺ) as follows:

﴿لَقَدْ جَآءَكُمْ رَسُولٌ مِّنْ أَنفُسِكُمْ عَزِيزٌ عَلَيْهِ مَا عَنِتُّمْ حَرِيصٌ عَلَيْكُم بِٱلْمُؤْمِنِينَ رَءُوفٌ رَّحِيمٌ ﴿١٢٨﴾﴾

﴿Verily, there has come unto you a Messenger [Muhammad] from amongst yourselves. It grieves him that you should receive any injury or difficulty. He [Muhammad] is anxious over you; for the believers [he is] full of pity, kind, and merciful.﴾ *(Qur'an 9: 128)*

iii) The attribute of Forbearance (*Al-Ḥilm*)

Allah (سبحانه وتعالى) has described Himself as Forbearing. He says:

﴿لَيُدْخِلَنَّهُم مُّدْخَلًا يَرْضَوْنَهُۥ وَإِنَّ ٱللَّهَ لَعَلِيمٌ حَلِيمٌ ﴿٥٩﴾﴾

﴿Truly, He will make them enter an entrance with which they shall be well-pleased, and verily, Allah indeed is All-Knowing, Most Forbearing.﴾ *(Qur'an 22: 59)*

﴿... وَٱعْلَمُوٓا۟ أَنَّ ٱللَّهَ يَعْلَمُ مَا فِىٓ أَنفُسِكُمْ فَٱحْذَرُوهُ ۚ وَٱعْلَمُوٓا۟ أَنَّ ٱللَّهَ غَفُورٌ حَلِيمٌ ﴿٢٣٥﴾﴾

﴿...And know that Allah knows what is in your minds, so fear Him. And know that Allah is Oft-Forgiving, Most Forbearing.﴾ *(Qur'an 2: 235)*

﴿ ۞ قَوْلٌ مَّعْرُوفٌ وَمَغْفِرَةٌ خَيْرٌ مِّن صَدَقَةٍ يَتْبَعُهَآ أَذًى ۗ وَٱللَّهُ غَنِىٌّ حَلِيمٌ ﴿٢٦٣﴾ ﴾

﴿Kind words and forgiving of faults are better than *Ṣadaqah* [charity] followed by injury. And Allah is Rich [Free of all needs] and He is Most-Forbearing.﴾
(Qur'an 2: 263)

And He (ﷻ) describes some of His created beings as forbearing:

﴿ فَبَشَّرْنَٰهُ بِغُلَٰمٍ حَلِيمٍ ﴿١٠١﴾ ﴾

﴿So We gave him the glad tidings of a forbearing boy.﴾
(Qur'an 37: 101)

﴿ ... إِنَّ إِبْرَٰهِيمَ لَأَوَّٰهٌ حَلِيمٌ ﴿١١٤﴾ ﴾

﴿...Verily, Ibraaheem was *Awwah* [one who invokes Allah with humility, glorifies Him and remembers Him much] and was forbearing.﴾ *(Qur'an 9: 114)*

iv) The attribute of forgiveness:
Allah (ﷻ) describes Himself as forgiving:

﴿ ... إِنَّ ٱللَّهَ غَفُورٌ رَّحِيمٌ ﴿١٧٣﴾ ﴾

﴿...Truly, Allah is Oft-Forgiving, Most Merciful.﴾
(Qur'an 2: 173)

﴿ ... فَيَغْفِرُ لِمَن يَشَآءُ وَيُعَذِّبُ مَن يَشَآءُ ۗ ... ﴿٢٨٤﴾ ﴾

﴿...Then He forgives whom He wills and punishes whom He wills...﴾ *(Qur'an 2: 284)*

And He (ﷻ) describes some of His created beings as forgiving:

﴿ وَلَمَن صَبَرَ وَغَفَرَ إِنَّ ذَٰلِكَ لَمِنْ عَزْمِ ٱلْأُمُورِ ﴿٤٣﴾ ﴾

﴾And verily, whosoever shows patience and forgives, that would truly be from the things recommended by Allah.﴿ *(Qur'an 42: 43)*

﴿ قَوْلٌ مَّعْرُوفٌ وَمَغْفِرَةٌ ... ﴿٢٦٣﴾ ﴾

﴾Kind words and forgiving of faults...﴿

(Qur'an 2: 263)

﴿ قُل لِّلَّذِينَ ءَامَنُوا۟ يَغْفِرُوا۟ لِلَّذِينَ لَا يَرْجُونَ أَيَّامَ ٱللَّهِ ... ﴿١٤﴾ ﴾

﴾Say [O' Muhammad] to the believers to forgive those who [harm them and] hope not for the Days of Allah [i.e. His Recompense]...﴿ *(Qur'an 45: 14)*

Undoubtedly, these attributes as ascribed to the Creator of the heavens and the earth are true, in a manner that is befitting to His Perfection and Majesty, and it is not permissible to deny any of them for fear of *tashbeeh* or likening Allah to His creation. And these attributes as applied to His creation are true, in a manner that suits their transient state, imperfection and need for Allah.

The situation of those who deny the attributes of Perfection and Majesty

After the *Shaykh* discussed the shortcomings in the methodology used by the scholars of *kalaam* (scholasticism), and explained in detail the Qur'anic methodology of faith which shows the right approach and lights the way, he concludes by saying:

"Whatever maybe the case, it is not permissible for anyone to try to be too clever concerning any attribute that Allah has affirmed for Himself and to deny this attribute out of insolence toward the Lord of the heavens and the earth, claiming that this attribute with which Allah has praised Himself does not befit Him, so he denies it, then he produces his own made-up attributes of perfection. This is utter madness and delusion, which no one would suggest except those whose eyes Allah has sealed."

The attribute of *istiwaa* (rising above the Throne) is an attribute of perfection, not imperfection

In order to illustrate the seriousness of the offence committed by the scholars of *kalaam* against the attributes of the Creator, *Shaykh* Ash-Shanqeeṭi (may Allah have mercy on him) gave the example of one of the greatest attributes, *istiwaa* (rising above the Throne). He said: "This is the attribute of *istiwaa*, concerning which people have indulged in too many arguments. Many people have denied it on the basis of philosophy and logic, and argumentative evidence aimed at proving the truth to be false and the false to be true. Thousands of those who claim to be Muslims have had the audacity to deny this attribute of the Lord of the heavens and the earth on the basis of logic.

For example, they say: 'If He had risen above His Throne, then He would be like His creation in some way, but He is not like His creation, therefor He did not rise above His Throne.' This is a false conclusion, because it is clearly contrary to the Qur'an.

The *Shaykh* (may Allah have mercy on him) explained that the attribute of *istiwaa* is an attribute of Perfection and Majesty, by which the Lord of the heavens and the earth praises Himself. The proof that it is an attribute of Perfection and Majesty is that whenever it is mentioned in the Qur'an, it is in the context of other great attributes which indicate the Majesty and Perfection of Allah. Then he quotes the texts in which this attribute is mentioned in order to prove that what he is saying is correct.

1) The first *soorah* (chapter), according to the order in which the *soorahs* (chapters) appear, in which Allah mentions the attribute of *istiwaa* is *Soorah al-A'raaf*, where He (ﷻ) says:

﴿ إِنَّ رَبَّكُمُ ٱللَّهُ ٱلَّذِى خَلَقَ ٱلسَّمَٰوَٰتِ وَٱلْأَرْضَ فِى سِتَّةِ أَيَّامٍ ثُمَّ
ٱسْتَوَىٰ عَلَى ٱلْعَرْشِ يُغْشِى ٱلَّيْلَ ٱلنَّهَارَ يَطْلُبُهُۥ حَثِيثًا وَٱلشَّمْسَ وَٱلْقَمَرَ
وَٱلنُّجُومَ مُسَخَّرَٰتٍۭ بِأَمْرِهِۦٓ ۗ أَلَا لَهُ ٱلْخَلْقُ وَٱلْأَمْرُ ۗ تَبَارَكَ ٱللَّهُ رَبُّ ٱلْعَٰلَمِينَ
﴿٥٤﴾ ﴾

﴿Indeed, your Lord is Allah, Who created the heavens and the earth in Six Days, and then He rose over [*Istawaa*] the Throne [really in a manner that suits His Majesty]. He brings the night as a cover over the day, seeking it rapidly, and [He created] the sun, the moon, the stars subjected to His Command. Surely, His is the creation and commandment. Blessed is Allah, the Lord of the *'Aalameen* [mankind, jinn and all that exists]!﴾ *(Qur'an 7: 54)*

So how can anyone deny any of these attributes which point to His Majesty and Perfection?

2) The second place is in *Soorah Yoonus*, where Allah (ﷻ) says:

﴿ إِنَّ رَبَّكُمُ ٱللَّهُ ٱلَّذِى خَلَقَ ٱلسَّمَٰوَٰتِ وَٱلْأَرْضَ فِى سِتَّةِ أَيَّامٍ ثُمَّ ٱسْتَوَىٰ عَلَى
ٱلْعَرْشِ ۖ يُدَبِّرُ ٱلْأَمْرَ ۖ مَا مِن شَفِيعٍ إِلَّا مِنۢ بَعْدِ إِذْنِهِۦ ۚ ذَٰلِكُمُ ٱللَّهُ رَبُّكُمْ
فَٱعْبُدُوهُ ۚ أَفَلَا تَذَكَّرُونَ ﴿٣﴾ إِلَيْهِ مَرْجِعُكُمْ جَمِيعًا ۖ وَعْدَ ٱللَّهِ حَقًّا ۚ إِنَّهُۥ
يَبْدَؤُا۟ ٱلْخَلْقَ ثُمَّ يُعِيدُهُۥ لِيَجْزِىَ ٱلَّذِينَ ءَامَنُوا۟ وَعَمِلُوا۟ ٱلصَّٰلِحَٰتِ بِٱلْقِسْطِ ۚ وَٱلَّذِينَ
كَفَرُوا۟ لَهُمْ شَرَابٌ مِّنْ حَمِيمٍ وَعَذَابٌ أَلِيمٌۢ بِمَا كَانُوا۟ يَكْفُرُونَ ﴿٤﴾
هُوَ ٱلَّذِى جَعَلَ ٱلشَّمْسَ ضِيَآءً وَٱلْقَمَرَ نُورًا وَقَدَّرَهُۥ مَنَازِلَ لِتَعْلَمُوا۟ عَدَدَ
ٱلسِّنِينَ وَٱلْحِسَابَ ۚ مَا خَلَقَ ٱللَّهُ ذَٰلِكَ إِلَّا بِٱلْحَقِّ ۚ يُفَصِّلُ ٱلْءَايَٰتِ لِقَوْمٍ
يَعْلَمُونَ ﴿٥﴾ إِنَّ فِى ٱخْتِلَٰفِ ٱلَّيْلِ وَٱلنَّهَارِ وَمَا خَلَقَ ٱللَّهُ فِى ٱلسَّمَٰوَٰتِ
وَٱلْأَرْضِ لَءَايَٰتٍ لِّقَوْمٍ يَتَّقُونَ ﴿٦﴾ ﴾

﴿Surely, your Lord is Allah Who created the heavens and the earth in six Days and then rose over [*Istawaa*] the Throne [really in a manner that suits His Majesty], disposing the affair of all things. No intercessor [can plead with Him] except after His Leave. That is Allah, your Lord; so worship Him [Alone]. Then, will you not remember? To Him is the return of all of you. The Promise of Allah is true. It is He Who begins the creation and then will repeat it, that He may reward with justice those who believed and did deeds of righteousness. But those who disbelieved will have a drink of boiling fluids and painful torment because they used to disbelieve. It is He Who made the sun a shining thing and the moon as a light and measured out for it stages that you might know the number of years and the reckoning. Allah did not create this but in truth. He explains the *Aayaat* in detail for people who have knowledge. Verily, in the alternation of the night and the day and in all that Allah has created in the heavens and the earth are *Aayaat* for those people who keep their duty to Allah, and fear Him much.﴾ *(Qur'an 10: 3-6)*

So how can anyone deny any of these attributes which point to His Majesty and Perfection?

3) The third place is in *Soorah ar-Ra'd*, where Allah (ﷻ) says:

﴿ ٱللَّهُ ٱلَّذِى رَفَعَ ٱلسَّمَٰوَٰتِ بِغَيْرِ عَمَدٍ تَرَوْنَهَا ۖ ثُمَّ ٱسْتَوَىٰ عَلَى ٱلْعَرْشِ ۖ وَسَخَّرَ ٱلشَّمْسَ وَٱلْقَمَرَ ۖ كُلٌّ يَجْرِى لِأَجَلٍ مُّسَمًّى ۚ يُدَبِّرُ ٱلْأَمْرَ يُفَصِّلُ ٱلْءَايَٰتِ لَعَلَّكُم بِلِقَآءِ رَبِّكُمْ تُوقِنُونَ ﴿٢﴾ وَهُوَ ٱلَّذِى مَدَّ ٱلْأَرْضَ وَجَعَلَ فِيهَا رَوَٰسِىَ وَأَنْهَٰرًا ۖ وَمِن كُلِّ ٱلثَّمَرَٰتِ جَعَلَ فِيهَا زَوْجَيْنِ ٱثْنَيْنِ ۖ يُغْشِى ٱلَّيْلَ ٱلنَّهَارَ ۚ إِنَّ فِى ذَٰلِكَ لَءَايَٰتٍ لِّقَوْمٍ يَتَفَكَّرُونَ ﴿٣﴾ وَفِى ٱلْأَرْضِ قِطَعٌ مُّتَجَٰوِرَٰتٌ وَجَنَّٰتٌ مِّنْ أَعْنَٰبٍ وَزَرْعٌ وَنَخِيلٌ صِنْوَانٌ وَغَيْرُ صِنْوَانٍ يُسْقَىٰ بِمَآءٍ وَٰحِدٍ وَنُفَضِّلُ بَعْضَهَا عَلَىٰ بَعْضٍ فِى ٱلْأُكُلِ ۚ إِنَّ فِى ذَٰلِكَ لَءَايَٰتٍ لِّقَوْمٍ يَعْقِلُونَ ﴿٤﴾ ﴾

﴾Allah is He Who raised the heavens without any pillars that you can see. Then, He rose above [*Istawaa*] the Throne [really in a manner that suits His Majesty]. He has subjected the sun and the moon [to continue going round], each running [its course] for a term appointed. He manages and regulates all affairs; He explains the *Aayaat* [proofs, evidences, verses, lessons, signs, revelations, etc.] in detail, that you may believe with certainty in the Meeting with your Lord. And it is He Who spread out the earth, and placed therein firm mountains and rivers and of every kind of fruits He made *Zawjayn Ithnayn* [two in pairs - may mean two kinds or it may mean: of two varieties, e.g. black and white, sweet and sour, small and big]. He brings the night as a cover over the day. Verily, in these things, there are *Aayaat* [proofs, evidences, lessons, signs, etc.] for people who reflect. And in the earth are neighbouring tracts, and gardens of vines, and green crops [fields], and date palms, growing into two or three from a single stem root, or otherwise [one stem root for every palm], watered with the same water; yet some of them We make more excellent than others to eat. Verily, in these things there are *Aayaat* [proofs, evidences, lessons, signs] for the people who understand.﴿ *(Qur'an 13: 2-4)*

So how can anyone deny any of these attributes which point to His Majesty and Perfection?

4) The fourth place is in *Soorah Ṭa-Ha*:

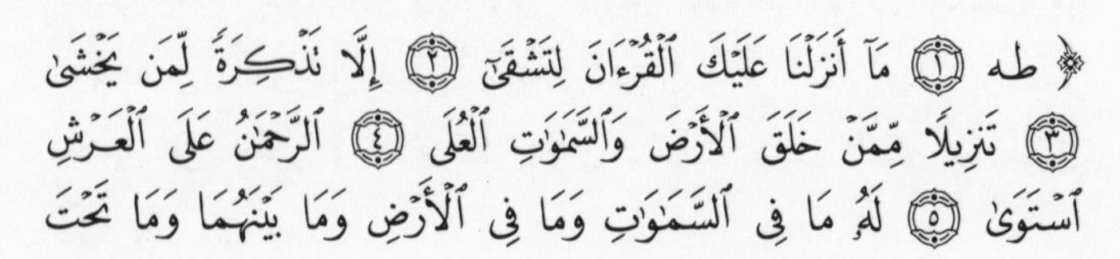

ٱلثَّرَىٰ ﴿٦﴾ وَإِن تَجْهَرْ بِٱلْقَوْلِ فَإِنَّهُۥ يَعْلَمُ ٱلسِّرَّ وَأَخْفَى ﴿٧﴾ ٱللَّهُ لَآ إِلَٰهَ إِلَّا هُوَ لَهُ ٱلْأَسْمَآءُ ٱلْحُسْنَىٰ ﴿٨﴾ ﴾

﴿*Ṭa-Ha*.[127] We have not sent down the Qur'an unto you [O' Muhammad] to cause you distress, but only as a Reminder to those who fear [Allah]. A Revelation from Him [Allah] Who has created the earth and high heavens. The Most Gracious [Allah] rose over [*Istawaa*] the [Mighty] Throne [in a manner that suits His Majesty]. To Him belongs all that is in the heavens and all that is on the earth, and all that is between them, and all that is under the soil. And if you [O' Muhammad] speak [the invocation] aloud, then verily, He knows the secret and that which is yet more hidden. Allah! *Laa ilaah illa Huwa* [none has the right to be worshipped but He]! To Him belong the Best Names.﴾

(Qur'an 20: 1-8)

So how can anyone deny any of these attributes which point to His Majesty and Perfection?

5) The fifth place is in *Soorah al-Furqaan*, where Allah (ﷻ) says:

﴿ وَتَوَكَّلْ عَلَى ٱلْحَىِّ ٱلَّذِى لَا يَمُوتُ وَسَبِّحْ بِحَمْدِهِۦ ۚ وَكَفَىٰ بِهِۦ بِذُنُوبِ عِبَادِهِۦ خَبِيرًا ﴿٥٨﴾ ٱلَّذِى خَلَقَ ٱلسَّمَٰوَٰتِ وَٱلْأَرْضَ وَمَا بَيْنَهُمَا فِى سِتَّةِ أَيَّامٍ ثُمَّ ٱسْتَوَىٰ عَلَى ٱلْعَرْشِ ۚ ٱلرَّحْمَٰنُ فَسْـَٔلْ بِهِۦ خَبِيرًا ﴿٥٩﴾ ﴾

﴿And put your trust [O' Muhammad] in the Ever Living One Who dies not, and glorify His Praises, and Sufficient is He as the All-Knower of the sins of His slaves, Who created the heavens and the earth and all that is between them in six Days. Then He rose over

---

[127] These letters are one of the miracles of the Qur'an, and none but Allah (Alone) knows their meanings.

[*Istawa*] the Throne [in a manner that suits His Majesty]. The Most Gracious [Allah]! Ask Him [O' Prophet Muhammad, concerning His Qualities: His rising over His Throne, His creations], as He is *Al-Khabeer* [The All-Knower of everything, i.e. Allah].》

(Qur'an 25: 58-59)

So how can anyone deny any of these attributes which point to His Majesty and Perfection?

6) The sixth place is in *Soorah as-Sajdah*, where Allah (ﷻ) says:

﴿ أَمْ يَقُولُونَ افْتَرَاهُ ۚ بَلْ هُوَ الْحَقُّ مِن رَّبِّكَ لِتُنذِرَ قَوْمًا مَّا أَتَاهُم مِّن نَّذِيرٍ مِّن قَبْلِكَ لَعَلَّهُمْ يَهْتَدُونَ ﴿٣﴾ اللَّهُ الَّذِي خَلَقَ السَّمَاوَاتِ وَالْأَرْضَ وَمَا بَيْنَهُمَا فِي سِتَّةِ أَيَّامٍ ثُمَّ اسْتَوَىٰ عَلَى الْعَرْشِ ۖ مَا لَكُم مِّن دُونِهِ مِن وَلِيٍّ وَلَا شَفِيعٍ ۚ أَفَلَا تَتَذَكَّرُونَ ﴿٤﴾ يُدَبِّرُ الْأَمْرَ مِنَ السَّمَاءِ إِلَى الْأَرْضِ ثُمَّ يَعْرُجُ إِلَيْهِ فِي يَوْمٍ كَانَ مِقْدَارُهُ أَلْفَ سَنَةٍ مِّمَّا تَعُدُّونَ ﴿٥﴾ ذَٰلِكَ عَالِمُ الْغَيْبِ وَالشَّهَادَةِ الْعَزِيزُ الرَّحِيمُ ﴿٦﴾ الَّذِي أَحْسَنَ كُلَّ شَيْءٍ خَلَقَهُ ۖ وَبَدَأَ خَلْقَ الْإِنسَانِ مِن طِينٍ ﴿٧﴾ ثُمَّ جَعَلَ نَسْلَهُ مِن سُلَالَةٍ مِّن مَّاءٍ مَّهِينٍ ﴿٨﴾ ثُمَّ سَوَّاهُ وَنَفَخَ فِيهِ مِن رُّوحِهِ ۖ وَجَعَلَ لَكُمُ السَّمْعَ وَالْأَبْصَارَ وَالْأَفْئِدَةَ ۚ قَلِيلًا مَّا تَشْكُرُونَ ﴿٩﴾ ﴾

《Or say they: 'He [Muhammad) has fabricated it?' Nay, it is the truth from your Lord, so that you may warn a people to whom no warner has come before you [O' Muhammad], in order that they may be guided. Allah it is He Who has created the heavens and the earth, and all that is between them in six Days. Then He rose over [*Istawaa*] the Throne [in a manner that suits His Majesty]. You [mankind] have none, besides Him, as a *Wali* [protector or helper] or an intercessor. Will you not then remember [or receive admonition]? He manages and regulates [every] affair from the heavens to the

> earth; then it [affair] will go up to Him, in one Day, the space whereof is a thousand years of your reckoning [i.e. reckoning of our present world's time]. That is He, the All-Knower of the unseen and the seen, the All-Mighty, the Most Merciful. Who made everything He has created good and He began the creation of man from clay. Then He made his offspring from semen of despised water [male and female sexual discharge]. Then He fashioned him in due proportion, and breathed into him the soul [created by Allah for that person]; and He gave you hearing [ears], sight [eyes] and hearts. Little is the thanks you give!﴿ *(Qur'an 32: 3-9)*

So how can anyone deny any of these attributes which point to His Majesty and Perfection?

7) The seventh place is in *Soorah al-Ḥadeed*, where Allah (ﷻ) says:

> ﴿هُوَ ٱلْأَوَّلُ وَٱلْءَاخِرُ وَٱلظَّـٰهِرُ وَٱلْبَاطِنُ ۖ وَهُوَ بِكُلِّ شَىْءٍ عَلِيمٌ ﴿٣﴾ هُوَ ٱلَّذِى خَلَقَ ٱلسَّمَـٰوَٰتِ وَٱلْأَرْضَ فِى سِتَّةِ أَيَّامٍ ثُمَّ ٱسْتَوَىٰ عَلَى ٱلْعَرْشِ ۚ يَعْلَمُ مَا يَلِجُ فِى ٱلْأَرْضِ وَمَا يَخْرُجُ مِنْهَا وَمَا يَنزِلُ مِنَ ٱلسَّمَآءِ وَمَا يَعْرُجُ فِيهَا ۖ وَهُوَ مَعَكُمْ أَيْنَ مَا كُنتُمْ ۚ وَٱللَّهُ بِمَا تَعْمَلُونَ بَصِيرٌ ﴿٤﴾﴾

> ﴾He is the First [nothing is before Him] and the Last [nothing is after Him], the Most High [nothing is above Him] and the Most Near [nothing is nearer than Him]. And He is the All-Knower of every thing. He it is Who created the heavens and the earth in six Days and then rose over [*Istawaa*] the Throne [in a manner that suits His Majesty]. He knows what goes into the earth and what comes forth from it, and what descends from the heaven and what ascends thereto. And He is with you [by His Knowledge] wheresoever you may be. And Allah is the All-Seer of what you do.﴿ *(Qur'an 57: 3-4)*

The point is that these attributes — which the ignorant think are attributes of imperfection — and dare to claim that the Lord of the heavens and the earth attributed to Himself attributes of imperfection, and as a result of that they deny them or misinterpret them — are in fact mentioned in the context of praising Allah. He has mentioned them in the context of other attributes of Majesty and Perfection. This indicates the ignorance and confusion of those who try to deny the attributes of Allah by misinterpreting them."

6 - IMPORTANT PRINCIPLES CONCERNING THE NAMES AND ATTRIBUTES OF ALLAH

There are a number of important principles and main points to which the scholars draw attention to, we would like to quote in brief below.

The First Principle: What is said about some Attributes applies to all other Attributes too[128]

By means of this principle, the view of many groups may be refuted:

a) Those who affirm some attributes and deny others
They affirm that Allah (ﷻ), has life, knowledge, power, hearing, seeing, speech and a will. They regard these as true attributes. But they dispute concerning Allah's love, pleasure, anger and hatred, and regard them as metaphorical, or they interpret them as being aspects of His will, or as blessings and punishments.

It should be said to these people: there is no difference between what you affirm and what you deny; what is said concerning one of them also applies to the others. If you say that His life and knowledge are like the life and knowledge of His created beings, then you must say the same about His pleasure, love and anger.

---

[128] *Majmoo' al-Fataawa Shaykh al-Islam*, 3/17.

If you say that He has life, knowledge and a will in a manner that befits Him and that do not resemble the lives, knowledge and wills of His created beings, then you must also say the same with regard to His pleasure, love and anger.

If you say that anger means that the blood in the heart is boiling with the desire for revenge, it must also be said that the will is the heart's desire to get something good or ward off something bad. If you say that this is the will of the created being, we say that this is the anger of the created being.

b) Those who affirm the Names but deny the Attributes

They say that He (ﷻ), is alive without life, All-Knowing without knowledge, and so on.

It should be said to these people, there is no difference between affirming His Names and affirming His Attributes. If you say that affirming life, knowledge and power implies likening Allah to His creation (*tashbeeh*) or thinking of Him in physical terms (*tajseem*) - because we do not find anything that has attributes that is not physical - we say in response: the same applies to His Names, for we do not find anything that is called alive, knowledgeable or powerful, but it is physical. If this is the case, then you should deny the names of Allah too. If they say that these names befit His Perfection and Majesty, we say, the same applies to His Attributes.

c) Those who deny both the Names and the Attributes

They claim that they deny them so that they will not liken Allah to His creation. It should be said to them: you deny His knowledge and life just as you deny that He is All-Knowing and Alive, for fear of likening Him to His created beings, but the implication of your ideas is that you are thinking of Allah in terms of non-existence.

The Second Principle:[129] Speaking about the Attributes is like speaking about the Essence of Allah

Allah (ﷻ), has an Essence which does not resemble the essences of His created beings. By the same token, His attributes and actions do not resemble the essence and actions of His created beings.

Therefore, if someone affirms that Allah is a proven reality, with the attributes of perfection which are unmatched by anything else, then he should accept that His hearing, seeing and speech which are also proven to be real, do not resemble the hearing, seeing and speech of His created beings.

If someone were to say: I deny that Allah rose over His Throne, for fear of likening Allah to His created beings, it should be said to him, Deny the existence and essence of Allah then, because they also imply likening Allah to His created beings. If he says, Allah exists in a unique manner, and He has a unique Essence that does not resemble the essence of His created beings, then we say: the same applies to His descending and His rising above His Throne (*istiwaa*).

The Third Principle: The Fact that names may be the same does not imply that the things so named are the same

We know that what Allah (ﷻ), has told us about the milk, honey and wine in Paradise is true, that these are real things which happen to have the same names as things that exist in this world, but they are not like them. The difference between them and their earthly counterparts is known only to Allah. The difference between the Creator and His created beings is far greater than the difference between one created thing and another. Indeed, in this world a number of things may be given the same name, but each of them has

[129] *Majmoo' al-Fataawa Shaykh al-Islam*, 3/25.

its own nature. We may say for example, the leg of a camel, the leg of a journey and the leg of a man; the leg in each of these three phrases has its own meaning.

The Fourth Principle: Allah cannot be described only in terms of negation

Allah (ﷻ), has affirmed certain Names and Attributes for Himself, and has denied certain names and attributes for Himself.

This affirmation and denial of names and attributes is both general and specific. The general affirmation occurs in the context of general praise ascribed to Allah, as indicated in the *aayaat*:

﴿ ٱلْحَمْدُ لِلَّهِ رَبِّ ٱلْعَـٰلَمِينَ ﴿٢﴾ ﴾

﴿All the praises and thanks be to Allah, the Lord of the *'Aalameen* [mankind, jinn and all that exists].﴾

(Qur'an 1: 2)

﴿ ... وَلِلَّهِ ٱلْمَثَلُ ٱلْأَعْلَىٰ ... ﴿٦٠﴾ ﴾

﴿...And for Allah is the highest description...﴾

(Qur'an 16: 60)

The detailed affirmation deals with every name or attribute narrated in the Qur'an and Sunnah.

The general negation denies every fault or shortcoming that could detract from the perfection of Allah, as when He (ﷻ) says:

﴿ ... لَيْسَ كَمِثْلِهِۦ شَىْءٌ ... ﴿١١﴾ ﴾

﴿...There is nothing like Him;...﴾ *(Qur'an 42: 11)*

﴿ ... هَلْ تَعْلَمُ لَهُۥ سَمِيًّا ﴿٦٥﴾ ﴾

﴿...Do you know of any who is similar to Him?﴾

(Qur'an 19: 65)

The specific negation means declaring that Allah is far above each and every one of these faults and shortcomings. So Allah should be declared to be above having a father, a son, a partner, a wife or a rival, and above being ignorant, slumbering, sleeping, doing things for no purpose, etc.

But the Qur'anic method of negating is not to deny anything in absolute terms. So the Qur'an does not deny that Allah has any shortcomings except in the context of praising Him and mentioning His perfection. It does not deny anything absolutely as some of these groups do.[130]

Allah (سُبْحَانَهُ وَتَعَالَى), says:

﴿ ٱللَّهُ لَآ إِلَٰهَ إِلَّا هُوَ ٱلۡحَيُّ ٱلۡقَيُّومُۚ لَا تَأۡخُذُهُۥ سِنَةٞ وَلَا نَوۡمٞۚ لَّهُۥ مَا فِي ٱلسَّمَٰوَٰتِ وَمَا فِي ٱلۡأَرۡضِۗ مَن ذَا ٱلَّذِي يَشۡفَعُ عِندَهُۥٓ إِلَّا بِإِذۡنِهِۦۚ يَعۡلَمُ مَا بَيۡنَ أَيۡدِيهِمۡ وَمَا خَلۡفَهُمۡۖ وَلَا يُحِيطُونَ بِشَيۡءٖ مِّنۡ عِلۡمِهِۦٓ إِلَّا بِمَا شَآءَۚ وَسِعَ كُرۡسِيُّهُ ٱلسَّمَٰوَٰتِ وَٱلۡأَرۡضَۖ وَلَا يَـُٔودُهُۥ حِفۡظُهُمَاۚ وَهُوَ ٱلۡعَلِيُّ ٱلۡعَظِيمُ ﴿٢٥٥﴾ ﴾

﴾Allah! *Laa ilaaha illa Huwa* [none has the right to be worshipped but He], *Al-Ḥayyul-Qayyoom* [the Ever Living, the One Who sustains and protects all that exists]. Neither slumber nor sleep overtakes Him. To Him belongs whatever is in the heavens and whatever is on the earth. Who is he that can intercede with Him except with His Permission? He knows what happens to them [His creatures] in this world, and what will happen to them in the Hereafter. And they will never compass anything of His Knowledge except that which He wills. His *Kursiy* extends over the heavens and the earth, and He feels no fatigue in guarding and preserving them...﴿ *(Qur'an 2: 255)*

---

[130] E.g., *Al-Jahamiyah al-Maḥḍah*. See *Majmoo' al-Fataawa*, 3/39.

Here Allah (ﷻ), denies that He slumbers or sleeps, but the denial of these two implies the affirmation of His life and self-sustainment. One aspect of the perfect nature of His life is that He is not overtaken by slumber (which is the beginning of sleep) or sleep. The phrase ﴿...And He feels no fatigue in guarding and preserving them...﴾ *(Qur'an 2: 255)* implies the perfection of His power, for the meaning is that it does not tire Him out or weigh Him down.

A similar example is the *aayah*:

﴿ ... لَا يَعْزُبُ عَنْهُ مِثْقَالُ ذَرَّةٍ فِى ٱلسَّمَٰوَٰتِ وَلَا فِى ٱلْأَرْضِ ... ﴿٣﴾ ﴾

﴿...Not even the weight of an atom [or a small ant] or less than that or greater escapes His Knowledge in the heavens or in the earth...﴾ *(Qur'an 34: 3).*

The denial that anything may escape His knowledge implies that He, the Exalted, All-Knower, knows every atom (or small ant) in the heavens and on earth.

And Allah (ﷻ), says:

﴿ وَلَقَدْ خَلَقْنَا ٱلسَّمَٰوَٰتِ وَٱلْأَرْضَ وَمَا بَيْنَهُمَا فِى سِتَّةِ أَيَّامٍ وَمَا مَسَّنَا مِن لُّغُوبٍ ﴿٣٨﴾ ﴾

﴿And indeed We created the heavens and the earth and all between them in six Days and nothing of fatigue touched Us.﴾ *(Qur'an 50: 38).*

Denying fatigue (which is tiredness and exhaustion) points to the completeness of His power and strength.

And Allah (ﷻ), says:

﴿ لَّا تُدْرِكُهُ ٱلْأَبْصَٰرُ ... ﴿١٠٣﴾ ﴾

﴿No vision can grasp Him,...﴾ *(Qur'an 6: 103)*

— means, no vision can encompass Him. Even though He will be seen in the Hereafter, because of His greatness, no vision will encompass Him.

Similarly, each time Allah denies something, it implies a positive attribute for which Allah is to be praised.

Allah does not describe Himself in terms of absolute denial, unless it highlights a positive attribute. Thus it becomes clear that those who tend to engage in excessive denial (or what they call negation) are mistaken, because negation does not imply praise or perfection unless it implies a positive affirmation. Absolute denial is absolute nothingness, and absolute nothingness is nothing.

Most of the innovators who deny in absolute terms say: "Allah does not speak, He does not see, He is not high above the universe." Some of them go to extremes and say: "He is neither within the universe nor outside it; He is neither separate from it nor joined to it," and other such nonsense which makes Allah as if He is nothing — Exalted and Glorified be He.

The Fifth Principle: Words which may be true or false

The attributes narrated in the Qur'an and Sunnah are true, and we are obliged to believe in them, even if we do not understand their meaning.

But the things that people say about Allah, not narrated in the Qur'an or Sunnah, and which people dispute about — we neither affirm them nor deny them until we know what the person saying them means.

For example, it may be said to the one who denies that Allah has direction, "What do you mean by direction? If you mean that Allah is within the physical confines of the heaven, and that the heaven contains Him, then it is not permissible for us to say that Allah is in a certain direction. But if you mean that Allah is above His creation and above the heavens, then this is true."

The Sixth Principle: Denial of Attributes caused primarily by anthropomorphic beliefs (*Tashbeeh*)

The principle is explained by *Shaykh* Muhammad al-Ameen ash-Shanqeeṭi (may Allah have mercy on him), who pointed out that the origin of this problem was the fact that hearts are contaminated with the filth of *tashbeeh*. So when a person whose heart is thus contaminated with the filth of *tashbeeh* hears of one of the attributes of perfection by which Allah praises Himself, such as His descent to the first heaven during the last third of the night, or His rising over His throne, or His coming on the Day of Resurrection, and other attributes of Majesty and perfection, the first thing that crosses his mind is that this attribute resembles an attribute of created beings. So his heart is contaminated with the filth of *tashbeeh*, and he does not estimate Allah with an estimation due to Him or venerate Allah as He should be venerated, because the first thing that crosses his mind is that the attribute of the Creator resembles the attribute of His created beings. So first of all his heart is contaminated with the filth of *tashbeeh*, and this evil *tashbeeh* leads him to deny the attribute of the Creator on the basis that it resembles the attributes of His created beings. So he starts with *tashbeeh* (anthropomorphism) and ends up with *ta'ṭeel* (denying the divine attributes altogether), but from the beginning to the end he is insulting the Lord of the Worlds, denying His attributes by claiming that these attributes do not befit Him.

The *Shaykh* mentioned a principle of *uṣool* upon which the scholars are unanimously agreed. It was not permissible for the Prophet (ﷺ) to delay teaching anything once it was needed, especially in the case of *'aqeedah* (creed - matters of belief). If we were to go along with their false argument, that the apparent meaning of the *aayaat* is *kufr* (disbelief), we should note that the Prophet (ﷺ) did not interpret *istiwaa* as meaning controlling or any of these other interpretations.

Had these *aayaat* meant what these interpretations say, the Prophet would have hastened to explain that, because it was not permitted for him to delay explaining things when needed.

The *Shaykh* explained that what the Muslim is obliged to do, when he hears of an attribute which the Creator of the heavens and the earth ascribed to Himself, or which His Messenger (ﷺ) attributed to Him, is to fill his heart with glorification of Allah and be certain that this attribute has reached the utmost in perfection, majesty, honour and highness, in such a manner as to cut off any possible thoughts of *tashbeeh* (anthropomorphism) or resemblance between this attribute and the attributes of His creation. Thus (the believer's) heart glorifies Allah and declares Him to be far above such resemblance, uncontaminated with the filth of *tashbeeh*. Thus his heart will be receptive to faith and belief in the attributes of Allah with which He is to be praised and with which His Prophet praised Him, as Allah (ﷻ), says:

﴿... لَيْسَ كَمِثْلِهِۦ شَىْءٌ ۖ وَهُوَ ٱلسَّمِيعُ ٱلْبَصِيرُ ﴿١١﴾﴾

﴿...There is nothing like Him, and He is the All-Hearer, the All-Seer.﴾ *(Qur'an 42: 11).*

The worst thing is not to glorify Allah, when the first thing that crosses a person's mind is that the attribute of the Creator resembles the attributes of the created being, so that this poor soul is forced to deny the attribute of the Creator on the grounds of this false claim.

The Seventh Principle: The *Aayaat* (Verses) which speak of the Divine Attributes are not Ambiguous

Shaykh Ash-Shanqeeṭi stated that many people describe the *aayaat* which speak of the divine attributes as being ambiguous *aayaat* (*mutashaabih*). In one way this is a mistake, and in another way it could be acceptable, as Imam Maalik ibn Anas said: "*Istiwaa* is not unknown, how is not understandable, asking about it is *bid'ah* and believing in it is obligatory."

Likewise, it may be said about Allah's descent (to the first heaven during the last third of the night): The descent is not unknown, how is not understandable, asking about it is *bid'ah* and believing in it is obligatory. The same applies to all the attributes, because these attributes are known to the Arabs, but in the case of the Creator of the heavens and the earth, they are too perfect, too majestic and too great to resemble any of the attributes of the created beings. Just as the essence of the Creator is real, so too the created beings have their essences, but the essence of the Creator is too perfect and too great to resemble the essences of His creatures in any way.

The Eighth Principle: The Apparent meaning of the Attributes does not imply *Tashbeeh* so there is no need to find a different interpretation

The guideline in the field of *uṣool* is that if a word has only one possible meaning, then it is called *naṣṣ* (a statement), such as the *aayah* (verse),

﴿... تِلْكَ عَشَرَةٌ كَامِلَةٌ ... ﴿١٩٦﴾﴾

﴾...Making ten days in all...﴿ *(Qur'an 2: 196).*

If there are two or more possible meanings, then one of the two possibilities is more apparent than the other, or both are equally apparent.

If both are equally possible then it is called *mujmal* (general, not specific). An example would be the phrase *'adaa al-laṣooṣ al-baariḥah 'ala 'ayn Zayd* (yesterday the thieves attacked the *'ayn* of Zayd). The word *''ayn* could mean the eye of Zayd, which they blinded; or it may mean his spring, which they dammed; or it may mean his gold and silver, which they stole. This is an example of *mujmal* (general meaning). The ruling concerning *mujmal* words or phrases is that we should refrain from interpreting it in a particular way unless there is evidence to specify what is meant.

But if the text is clear and unambiguous, then we should follow it and not turn away from it unless there is proof that it has been abrogated.

If one of the two possible meanings is more apparent, this is called *Az-Zaahir* (the apparent), and its counterpart is called *muḥtamal marjooḥ* (unlikely, possibility). The apparent meaning is the one which should be followed, unless there is evidence to divert us from it. For example, if you say '*ra'aytu asadan*,' the apparent meaning is a savage animal (I saw a lion), but it may refer to a courageous man.

So when we read the *aayaat* which speak of the attributes of Allah, such as ﴾...The Hand of Allah is over their hands...﴿ *(Qur'an 48: 10)* and other similar *aayaat*, is the first thing that strikes our minds that this *aayah* is likening the attributes of Allah to His creation, so that we have to interpret it in order to divert the word away from its apparent meaning? Or is the apparent meaning that comes to mind when we read it that the Lord of the heavens is above resembling His creation in any of His attributes so we accept this *aayah* in that context, declaring Him to be above any such resemblance? The answer to that is that the first thing which should come to the Muslim's mind when he hears of any of the attributes of the Lord of the heavens and the earth is that Allah is completely above any resemblance to His creation.

The correct understanding is to accept the apparent meanings of these *aayaat* (verses), which is to think of the Lord of the heavens and the earth as being far above any resemblance to His creation in any of His attributes. Can any rational person deny that the first thing that crosses the sound mind is that the Creator differs from His creation in His essence and in all His attributes? No, by Allah, no one will dispute this except those who are arrogant.

The Ninth Principle: The Reality of *Ta'weel* [131]

The word *ta'weel* which has tempted people and led thousands of this ummah astray could mean three things:

1) It could mean the way the things develop and end up. This is the meaning in the *aayaat* such as the following:

﴿ ... ذَٰلِكَ خَيْرٌ وَأَحْسَنُ تَأْوِيلًا ﴿٥٩﴾ ﴾

﴾...That is better and more suitable for final determination [*ta'weelan*].﴿ *(Qur'an 4: 59)*

﴿ ... وَلَمَّا يَأْتِهِمْ تَأْوِيلُهُۥ ... ﴿٣٩﴾ ﴾

﴾...Even before the elucidation [*ta'weel*] thereof has reached them...﴿ *(Qur'an 10: 39)*

— Abdullah Yusuf 'Ali's translation, i.e., the way things ultimately turn out.

﴿ ... يَوْمَ يَأْتِى تَأْوِيلُهُۥ يَقُولُ ٱلَّذِينَ نَسُوهُ مِن قَبْلُ ... ﴿٥٣﴾ ﴾

﴾...On the Day the event is finally fulfilled [*ta'weel*], those who neglected it before...﴿ *(Qur'an 7: 53)*

2) *Ta'weel* may mean *tafseer* (interpretation). This is a well known usage, such as Ibn Jareer's comment: the opinion on the *ta'weel* (interpretation) of the *aayah* (verse) is such and such...

3) In the terminology of *uṣool, ta'weel* means: interpreting a word in a way other than the apparent meaning which first springs to mind, on the basis of evidence.

---

[131] I have written a paper on this topic entitled: *At-Ta'weel khuṭooratuhu wa athaaruhu* (Interpretation: its dangers and effects).

According to the scholars of *uṣool*, interpreting a word in a way other than the apparent meaning which first springs to mind is done in three cases:

a) It is interpreted in a way other than the apparent meaning which first springs to mind on the basis of *ṣaheeḥ* (sound) evidence from the Qur'an or Sunnah. This kind of *ta'weel* or interpretation is correct and is acceptable; there is no dispute about it. Examples of this kind include the hadith narrated from the Prophet (ﷺ):

"The neighbour has more right to proximity."[132]

The apparent meaning of this hadith is that the neighbour has the right of pre-emption (concerning decisions on or sales of neighbouring property etc.).

But if we interpret this as referring specifically to a neighbour whose property is contiguous, this is following a meaning that is not immediately apparent. But the *ṣaheeḥ* hadith narrated by Jaabir, "When boundaries are being drawn up and routes are taking shape, there is no right of pre-emption,"[133] proves that what is meant by the neighbour who has more right to proximity is specifically the neighbour whose property is contiguous. This kind of interpreting a word in a way other than the apparent meaning which first springs to mind on the basis of clear evidence from the Qur'an and Sunnah is called *ta'weel ṣaheeḥ* (correct interpretation) or *ta'weel qareeb* (acceptable interpretation).

b) A word is interpreted in a way other than the apparent meaning which first springs to mind because of something which the scholar believes to be evidence, but in fact it is not an evidence. This is called

[132] Aḥmad, Nasaee and Ibn Maajah (*Muntaqa al-Akhbaar*, Pp. 492, hadith no. 3177).

[133] Bukhari, Abu Dawood, Tirmidhi and Aḥmad (*Muntaqa al-Akhbaar*, Pp. 492).

ta'weel ba'eed (far-fetched interpretation), or sometimes it is called *faasid* (corrupt).

An example of this is Abu Ḥaneefah's interpretation of the word 'woman' in the hadith of the Prophet (ﷺ):

> "Any woman who gets married without the permission of her guardian, her marriage is invalid."[134]

His interpretation of this as referring specifically to a slave woman who had a written contract of emancipation, is *ta'weel ba'eed* (a far-fetched interpretation), because the particle *ayy* in the word *ayyumaa* (any) is general in meaning; the suffix *maa* emphasizes the fact that this phrase (*ayyumaa imra'atin* — any woman) is general in meaning, referring to any woman whatsoever. Interpreting this as referring to a specific case (the slave woman who has a written contract of emancipation) is interpreting it in a way other than the apparent meaning which first springs to mind, without any evidence for doing so.

c) With regard to interpreting words or phrases in a way other than the apparent meaning which first springs to mind, without any evidence, this is not called *ta'weel*; in scholarly terminology it is called *la'ib* (playing), because it involves playing with the Book of Allah and the Sunnah of His Messenger (ﷺ). An example of this is the way in which the extreme *Rawaafiḍ* (shi'as) interpret the *aayah*, ﴾...Verily, Allah commands you that you slaughter a cow...﴿ *(Qur'an 2: 67)*. They said, (this refers to) 'Aa'ishah.

This kind of (mis)interpretation also includes interpreting the *aayaat* (verses) which speak of the attributes of Allah, distorting them from their apparent meanings to unlikely meanings for which Allah has

---

[134] Abu Dawood, Tirmidhi, Ibn Maajah and Aḥmad (*Muntaqa al-Akhbaar*, 539, hadith no. 3452).

not revealed any authority, such as when they interpret *istawaa* (rise above) as meaning *istawlaa* (possess, take control). This cannot be included under the heading of *ta'weel*, because there is no evidence for this at all. In the terminology of the scholars of *uṣool*, it is called *la'ib* (playing), because it is playing with the Book of Allah with no evidence and no basis. This kind of interpretation (which is misinterpretation) is not permissible, because it is an assault against the words of the Lord of the Worlds. The basic principle which was known to the scholars among the *salaf* (pious predecessors), is that it is not permissible to change the meaning of anything in the Book of Allah or the Sunnah of His Messenger from the apparent meaning which first springs to mind, unless there is evidence which must be referred to.

7 - THE VIEW OF *AHL AS-SUNNAH WA'L-JAMA'AH* CONCERNING THE ATTRIBUTES OF ALLAH

Ibn Taymiya summed up the view of the righteous *Salaf* (Pious Predecessors) on this topic:

"The basic principle regarding this matter is that Allah is to be described as He has described Himself, and as His Messenger (ﷺ) has described Him, in terms both of affirmation and negation. We affirm for Allah what He has affirmed for Himself, and we deny for Him what He has denied for Himself.

It is known that the method of the *salaf* and *Aaimmah* (the reputed scholars and guides) of this ummah is to affirm the attributes which Allah has affirmed for Himself, without asking how or making comparisons, and without distorting or denying them."[135]

---

[135] *Majmoo' al-Fataawa*, 3/3. The *'aqeedah* (belief, creed) of the *salaf* (Predecessors) has been stated by many scholars, including Ṭaḥaawi, on whose =

Allah (ﷻ) has warned us against deviating from the method of understanding that He explained in His Book with regard to His Names and attributes. He says:

﴿ وَلِلَّهِ ٱلْأَسْمَآءُ ٱلْحُسْنَىٰ فَٱدْعُوهُ بِهَا ۖ وَذَرُوا۟ ٱلَّذِينَ يُلْحِدُونَ فِىٓ أَسْمَـٰٓئِهِۦ ۚ ... ﴿١٨٠﴾ ﴾

﴿And [all] the Most Beautiful Names belong to Allah, so call on Him by them, and leave the company of those who belie or deny [or utter impious speech against] His Names...﴾ *(Qur'an 7: 180).*

The root of the Arabic word *ilḥaad* [*yulḥidoon* - translated here as belie or deny (or utter impious speech against)] means turning away, leaning, deviating or going to extremes. From the same root comes the word *laḥd* (niche in the side of a grave), because it tilts the body of the deceased towards the direction of the *qiblah.*[136]

Allah (ﷻ) declares Himself to be above that which the misguided heretics and *mushrikoon* (idolaters) attribute to Him:

﴿ سُبْحَـٰنَ ٱللَّهِ عَمَّا يَصِفُونَ ﴿١٥٩﴾ ﴾

﴿Glorified be Allah! [He is free] from what they attribute unto Him!﴾ *(Qur'an 37: 159)*

﴿ سُبْحَـٰنَ رَبِّكَ رَبِّ ٱلْعِزَّةِ عَمَّا يَصِفُونَ ﴿١٨٠﴾ ﴾

﴿Glorified be your Lord, the Lord of honour and power!

= *'Aqeedah* a commentary was written by Muhammad ibn Muhammad ibn Abi'l-'Izz al-Ḥanafi, entitled *Sharḥ al-'Aqeedah aṭ-Ṭaḥaawiyah*; Abu'l-Ḥasan al-Ash'ari, *Al-Ibaanah 'an Uṣool ad-Dayaanah*; Aṣ-Ṣaabooni, *'Aqeedat as-Salaf*; and many others. We are following in their footsteps, asking Allah to gather us with them on the Day of Judgement.

[136] *Ma'aarij al-Qubool*, 1/88.

[He is free] from what they attribute unto Him!﴿

(Qur'an 37: 180)

But He (ﷻ) excludes from that the things that His sincere slaves attribute to Him:

﴿ إِلَّا عِبَادَ ٱللَّهِ ٱلْمُخْلَصِينَ ١٦٠ ﴾

﴾Except the slaves of Allah, whom He chooses [for His mercy, i.e. true believers of Islamic Monotheism who do not attribute false things unto Allah].﴿ *(Qur'an 37: 160)*

And in another *aayah* He (ﷻ), greets the Messengers with *salaam* for the soundness of what they say and what they ascribe to Allah (ﷻ):

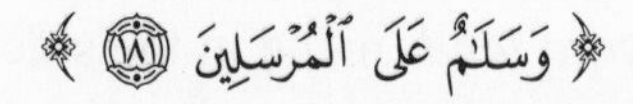

﴾And peace be on the Messengers!﴿ *(Qur'an 37: 181)*

Imam Abu'l-Ḥasan al-Ash'ari's *'Aqeedah* concerning the attributes of Allah

Some of those who do not accept the *madhhab* of *Ahl as-Sunnah* try to stir up feelings against the *Ahl as-Sunnah* by claiming that the *madhhab* (school) of the *Ash'aris* goes against that which we affirm. They claim that their *madhhab* is the *madhhab* of *Ahl as-Sunnah*. We will quote here the *madhhab* which Abu'l-Ḥasan al-Ash'ari narrated from the *Ahl as-Sunnah* and scholars of hadith, at the end of which he stated that he believed in this and followed it.

He gave this statement the title, "This is the report of the views of the scholars of hadith and *Ahl as-Sunnah*." Then he said:

"The summary of the beliefs of *Ahl al-Ḥadeeth wa's-Sunnah* is belief in Allah, His angels, His Books and His Messengers, what came from Allah, and what is narrated by trustworthy sources from the

Messenger of Allah (ﷺ). They do not reject any of that.[137] (And they believe) that Allah is One God, Unique, Eternally Self-Sufficient. There is no god except He, and He does not have a wife or son. And (they believe) that Muhammad (ﷺ) is His slave and Messenger. Paradise is real, Hell is real, the Hour will undoubtedly come and Allah will resurrect those who are in the graves. Allah (ﷻ), is above His Throne, as He says:

﴿ ٱلرَّحْمَٰنُ عَلَى ٱلْعَرْشِ ٱسْتَوَىٰ ﴿٥﴾ ﴾

﴾The Most Gracious [Allah] rose over [*Istawaa*] the [Mighty] Throne [in a manner that suits His Majesty].﴿ *(Qur'an 20: 5)*

He (ﷻ), has two Hands, but we do not ask how, as He says:

﴿ ... لِمَا خَلَقْتُ بِيَدَيَّ ... ﴿٧٥﴾ ﴾

﴾...I have created with Both My Hands...﴿ *(Qur'an 38: 75)*

﴿ ... بَلْ يَدَاهُ مَبْسُوطَتَانِ يُنفِقُ كَيْفَ يَشَآءُ ... ﴿٦٤﴾ ﴾

﴾...Nay, both His Hands are widely outstretched...﴿ *(Qur'an 5: 64).*

And He (ﷻ) has two eyes, but we do not ask how, as He says:

﴿ تَجْرِى بِأَعْيُنِنَا ... ﴿١٤﴾ ﴾

﴾Floating under Our Eyes...﴿ *(Qur'an 54: 14)*

---

[137] Note how he made *ṣaḥeeḥ aḥaadeeth* proof for *'aqeedah*, because he is speaking about issues of *'aqeedah*, not about *aḥkaam* (rulings). So he does not differentiate between *mutawaatir* and *aaḥaad*. The way in which he derives evidence concerning issues of *'aqeedah* in his books proves that what we have stated above is true.

And He (ﷻ) has a Face, as He says:

﴿ وَيَبْقَىٰ وَجْهُ رَبِّكَ ذُو ٱلْجَلَٰلِ وَٱلْإِكْرَامِ ﴿٢٧﴾ ﴾

﴾And the Face of your Lord full of Majesty and Honour will remain forever.﴿ *(Qur'an 55: 27)*

We cannot say that the names of Allah are something other than Allah, as the *Mu'tazilah* and *Khawaarij* said. They (*Ahl al-Ḥadeeth wa's-Sunnah*) said that Allah (ﷻ), has knowledge as He said:

﴿ ... أَنزَلَهُۥ بِعِلْمِهِۦ ... ﴿١٦٦﴾ ﴾

﴾...He has sent it down with His Knowledge...﴿ *(Qur'an 4: 166)*

﴿ ... وَمَا تَحْمِلُ مِنْ أُنثَىٰ وَلَا تَضَعُ إِلَّا بِعِلْمِهِۦ ... ﴿١١﴾ ﴾

﴾...And no female conceives or gives birth but with His Knowledge...﴿ *(Qur'an 35: 11)*

They affirm that Allah can hear and see; they do not deny that as the *Mu'tazilah* do. And they affirm that Allah has power, as He (ﷻ) says:

﴿ ... أَوَلَمْ يَرَوْا أَنَّ ٱللَّهَ ٱلَّذِى خَلَقَهُمْ هُوَ أَشَدُّ مِنْهُمْ قُوَّةً ... ﴿١٥﴾ ﴾

﴾...See they not that Allah Who created them was mightier in strength than them...﴿ *(Qur'an 41: 15)*

They say that the Qur'an is the word of Allah and is not created. The idea that we should not give any opinion on this matter or that the recitation (but not the Qur'an itself) is created, is a *bid'ah* in their view. It cannot be said that the pronunciation of the Qur'an is created and it cannot be said that it is not created.

They believe that people's eyes will see Allah on the Day of Resurrection just as they see the moon at night when it is full. The believers will see Him but the *kaafireen* (disbeleivers) will not, because they are veiled from Allah as He (ﷻ), says:

﴿ كَلَّآ إِنَّهُمْ عَن رَّبِّهِمْ يَوْمَئِذٍ لَّمَحْجُوبُونَ ﴿١٥﴾ ﴾

﴿Nay! Surely they [evil-doers] will be veiled away from seeing their Lord that Day.﴾ *(Qur'an 83: 15).*

And they believe that Moosa (Moses) (عليه السلام) asked Allah to let him see Him in this world, but Allah manifested Himself (appeared) to the mountain and He made it collapse to dust. Thus Allah showed Moosa that he would not see Him in this world, but he would see Him in the Hereafter.

They believe in the *aḥaadeeth* narrated from the Messenger of Allah (ﷺ), saying that Allah descends to the lowest heaven and says "Is there anyone who is seeking forgiveness?" - as is stated in the hadith narrated from the Messenger of Allah. They affirm that Allah will come on the Day of Resurrection as He (ﷻ) says:

﴿ وَجَآءَ رَبُّكَ وَٱلْمَلَكُ صَفًّا صَفًّا ﴿٢٢﴾ ﴾

﴿And your Lord comes with the angels in rows.﴾ *(Qur'an 89: 22)*

(And they affirm) that Allah (ﷻ) is close to His creation in the manner that He wills, as He says:

﴿ ... وَنَحْنُ أَقْرَبُ إِلَيْهِ مِنْ حَبْلِ ٱلْوَرِيدِ ﴿١٦﴾ ﴾

﴿...And We are nearer to him than his jugular vein [by Our Knowledge].﴾ *(Qur'an 50: 16)*

Abu'l-Ḥasan al-Ash'ari concluded his narration from the *Ahl as-Sunnah* and the *Ahl al-Ḥadeeth* by saying:

"This is the summary of what they believe and teach. All that we have quoted of their views is also our view and our opinion. We have no strength except by Allah (ﷻ), He is sufficient for us and the best Disposer of our affairs. His help we seek, in Him we put our trust, and to Him is our final destination."[138]

This quotation makes it quite clear that the belief of Abu'l-Ḥasan al-Ash'ari is identical to the belief of *Ahl as-Sunnah wa'l-Jamaa'ah* concerning the names and attributes of Allah.[139]

---

[138] See *Maqaalaat al-Islamiyeen*, Pp. 290-297. We have quoted only that which has to do with the attributes of Allah; we have not quoted the rest of the beliefs of *Ahl as-Sunnah* and *Ahl al-Ḥadeeth* of which he approved.

[139] I have also written a book describing the belief and methodology of Abu'l-Ḥasan al-Ash'ari.

CHAPTER THREE
THE ONENESS OF ALLAH (*TAWḤEED*)[1]

1 - MEANINGS AND CATEGORIES

Allah (ﷻ) is One in His Essence. There is nothing like unto Him and He has no equal. Exalted be He above having a wife or son.

﴿ قُلْ هُوَ ٱللَّهُ أَحَدٌ ۝١ ٱللَّهُ ٱلصَّمَدُ ۝٢ لَمْ يَلِدْ وَلَمْ يُولَدْ ۝٣ وَلَمْ يَكُن لَّهُۥ كُفُوًا أَحَدٌۢ ۝٤ ﴾

﴿Say [O' Muhammad]: He is Allah, [the] One. *Allah-uṣ-Ṣamad* [Allah — the Self-Sufficient Master, Whom all creatures need, (He neither eats nor drinks)]. He begets not, nor was He begotten. And there is none co-equal or comparable unto Him.﴾ *(Qur'an 112: 1-4)*

Allah (ﷻ) is described with attributes of perfection, and none of His creatures resemble Him in any of His attributes:

﴿ ... لَيْسَ كَمِثْلِهِۦ شَىْءٌ ۖ وَهُوَ ٱلسَّمِيعُ ٱلْبَصِيرُ ۝١١ ﴾

﴿...There is nothing like Him, and He is the All-Hearer, the All-Seer.﴾ *(Qur'an 42: 11)*

---

[1] True *Tawḥeed* is the belief in the Oneness (unity) of Allah, His Oneness in His Essence and Attributes, and worshipping Him alone with no partner or associate. This concept has been distorted. Some people claim that *Tawḥeed* dictates denying the attributes of Allah, because these attributes - or so they say - make the Eternal more than one. Some Ṣufis claim that the *Tawḥeed* to which we refer here is the "*Tawḥeed* for the masses" and that the *Tawḥeed* of the elite is that which is proven through the *ḥaqaa'iq* (mystical "realities"). They even claim that there is a *Tawḥeed* for the elite of the elite. All of that is misguidance.

He (ﷻ), Alone is the Creator, the Giver of life and death, the Sustainer of the heavens and the earth. He is not a believer who does not know with absolute certainty that Allah is Unique in all of that.

It is not Enough merely to Know that Allah is One; This *Tawḥeed* must be Reflected in One's Actions

The theoretical *Tawḥeed* is not sufficient for a person to be counted as a believer. He must also take Allah Alone as his God and object of worship, directing worship to Him alone and none other.

Because the Creator, the Provider, the Bestower of blessings, the Giver of bounty, the Giver of life and death, the One Who bears the attributes of perfection and is far above any shortcomings, is the only One Who is deserving of worship. Everything and everyone else is subject to His Lordship and Divinity, and does not have the power to cause harm or bring benefits to itself, so how can it be worshipped instead of Allah?

The Contradictions of Those who do not Worship Allah Alone

The *kuffaar* (disbelievers), from the *mushrik* (idolaters, polythiests) Arabs and many others, did believe that Allah was the Only Creator, Unique in His provision, power over life and death, and sovereignty. But they refused to worship Him alone to the exclusion of all others. This was an appalling contradiction, for the One Who is Unique in His powers of creation is the only One deserving of worship, submission and glorification. The Qur'an debated at length with the *mushrikeen* and pointed out their contradictions. It explains that what they believed about His being unique in His powers of creation and provision, etc., obliged them to worship Him alone and direct their devotion solely to Him.

2 - *KALIMAAT AT-TAWḤEED* (THE WORDS OF *TAWḤEED*): THEIR MEANINGS, VIRTUES AND CONDITIONS

The word of *Tawḥeed* — *Laa ilaaha illa-Allah* (there is no god except Allah) — sums up and encompasses faith. This phrase is the slogan and basis of Islam.

The meaning of this phrase is: there is no god deserving of worship except Allah. Those who interpret it as meaning that nothing exists except Allah are mistaken, because the meaning of the word *ilaah* is god or object of worship. So according to these people, the meaning would be there is no god that exists except Allah, and this is incorrect, because then it would imply that everything that is worshipped, rightfully or wrongfully, is Allah, which would mean that all that the *mushrikeen* worship, such as the sun, the moon, the stars, etc., is Allah. It is as if they were saying that nothing is worshipped in this manner except Allah — which is the falsest of falsehoods.

The correct meaning is that which we mentioned in the first place: that there is no god deserving of worship except Allah, and Allah Alone.

There are texts which indicate the virtue and great benefits of the phrase *Laa ilaaha illa-Allah*. We have quoted above the texts which indicate that whoever says *Laa ilaaha illa-Allah* sincerely from the heart will enter Paradise. By this statement (these words) a person's wealth and blood are protected, and a person becomes a Muslim.

But uttering this statement (these words) is not enough. This statement will not benefit a person before his Lord unless seven conditions are met:

1) Knowing its Meaning

Allah (ﷻ) says:

﴿ فَٱعْلَمْ أَنَّهُۥ لَآ إِلَٰهَ إِلَّا ٱللَّهُ ... ﴿١٩﴾ ﴾

﴿So know [O' Muhammad] that *Laa ilaaha illa-Allah* [none has the right to be worshipped but Allah],...﴾

(Qur'an 47: 19)

﴿ ... إِلَّا مَن شَهِدَ بِٱلْحَقِّ وَهُمْ يَعْلَمُونَ ﴿٨٦﴾ ﴾

﴿...Except for those who bear witness to the truth knowingly [i.e. believed in the Oneness of Allah, and obeyed His Orders], and they know [the facts about the Oneness of Allah].﴾ *(Qur'an 43: 86)*

It is narrated that 'Uthmaan ibn 'Affaan stated that the Messenger of Allah (ﷺ) said:

"Whoever dies knowing that there is no god except Allah will enter Paradise."[2]

2) Certainty

The one who says it must be absolutely certain about what this statement implies. Faith will not benefit him at all unless he is certain, beyond any shadow of doubt. Allah (سبحانه وتعالى) says:

﴿ إِنَّمَا ٱلْمُؤْمِنُونَ ٱلَّذِينَ ءَامَنُوا۟ بِٱللَّهِ وَرَسُولِهِۦ ثُمَّ لَمْ يَرْتَابُوا۟ ... ﴿١٥﴾ ﴾

﴿Only those are the believers who have believed in Allah and His Messenger, and afterward doubt not...﴾

(Qur'an 49: 15).

The sincerity of their faith is conditional upon their not doubting. It is narrated on the authority of Abu Hurayrah (رضي الله عنه) that the Messenger of Allah (ﷺ) said:

---

[2] Muslim, 1/55, hadith no. 26.

> "I bear witness that there is no god except Allah and that I am the Messenger of Allah. No person meets Allah with this, not doubting it, and is denied Paradise."[3]

It is also narrated that the Messenger of Allah (ﷺ) sent Abu Hurayrah with his shoes, saying:

> "Whoever you meet beyond this wall (of the garden in which he was) who says *Laa ilaaha illa-Allah*, with certainty in his heart, give him the glad tidings of Paradise."[4]

The condition for the person who says it entering Paradise is that he should be certain of it in his heart, with no doubts at all. If the condition is not met, then the reward will not be attained.

3) Acceptance of What is Implied by this Statement

Both verbal acceptance and acceptance in the heart. The Qur'an tells us that Allah punished the disbelievers of the nations who rejected this statement (*kalima*) and were too arrogant to accept it:

﴿ إِنَّهُمْ كَانُوٓا۟ إِذَا قِيلَ لَهُمْ لَآ إِلَٰهَ إِلَّا ٱللَّهُ يَسْتَكْبِرُونَ ﴿٣٥﴾ وَيَقُولُونَ أَئِنَّا لَتَارِكُوٓا۟ ءَالِهَتِنَا لِشَاعِرٍ مَّجْنُونٍۭ ﴿٣٦﴾ ﴾

> ﴿Truly, when it was said to them: *Laa ilaaha illa-Allah* [none has the right to be worshipped but Allah], they puffed themselves up with pride [i.e. denied it]. And [they] said: 'Are we going to abandon our *a'alihah* [gods] for the sake of a mad poet?'﴾ *(Qur'an 37: 35-36)*

So Allah stated that the reason for their punishment was their arrogant refusal to say *Laa ilaaha illa-Allah*, and their disbelief in the one who brought this message.

---

[3] Muslim, 1/57, hadith no. 27.

[4] Ibid, 1/60, hadith no. 31.

4) Submission to What it Implies

Allah (ﷻ), says:

﴿ وَأَنِيبُوٓا۟ إِلَىٰ رَبِّكُمْ وَأَسْلِمُوا۟ لَهُۥ ... ﴿٥٤﴾ ﴾

﴾And turn in repentance and in obedience with true Faith [Islamic Monotheism] to your Lord and submit to Him...﴿ *(Qur'an 39: 54)*

﴿ ۞ وَمَن يُسْلِمْ وَجْهَهُۥٓ إِلَى ٱللَّهِ وَهُوَ مُحْسِنٌ فَقَدِ ٱسْتَمْسَكَ بِٱلْعُرْوَةِ ٱلْوُثْقَىٰ ... ﴿٢٢﴾ ﴾

﴾And whosoever submits his face [himself] to Allah, while he is a *Muḥsin* [good-doer, i.e. performs good deeds totally for Allah's sake without any show-off or to gain praise or fame and does them in accordance with the Sunnah of Allah's Messenger Muhammad], then he has grasped the most trustworthy handhold [*Laa ilaaha illa-Allah* (none has the right to be worshipped but Allah)]...﴿ *(Qur'an 31: 22)*

Submitting one's face means submitting oneself, whilst one is also *Muḥsin* (good-doer) i.e., one who believes only in Allah. The most trustworthy handhold has been interpreted as referring to (the phrase) *Laa ilaaha illa-Allah.*

5) Sincerity

This means saying it sincerely from the heart, with no contradiction between what is said and what is in the heart. Allah (ﷻ), says:

﴿ وَمِنَ ٱلنَّاسِ مَن يَقُولُ ءَامَنَّا بِٱللَّهِ وَبِٱلْيَوْمِ ٱلْـَٔاخِرِ وَمَا هُم بِمُؤْمِنِينَ ﴿٨﴾ يُخَـٰدِعُونَ ٱللَّهَ وَٱلَّذِينَ ءَامَنُوا۟ وَمَا يَخْدَعُونَ إِلَّآ أَنفُسَهُمْ وَمَا يَشْعُرُونَ ﴿٩﴾ ﴾

﴾And of mankind, there are some [hypocrites] who say: 'We believe in Allah and the Last Day,' while in fact they believe not. They [think to] deceive Allah and those who believe, while they only deceive themselves, and perceive [it] not!﴿ *(Qur'an 2: 8-9)*

These are the ones who lie when they speak, and they conceal something other than that which they show openly. Mu'aadh ibn Jabal narrated that the Prophet (ﷺ) said:

"There is no one who bears witness that there is no god except Allah and that Muhammad is the Messenger of Allah, sincerely from the heart, but Allah will deny him to the Fire."[5]

So the condition for salvation from the Fire is that one should say it sincerely from the heart.

6) Purity of Intention (*Ikhlaaṣ*)

This means purifying one's deeds by having the correct intention, free from all contamination of *shirk*. Allah (ﷻ) says:

﴿ أَلَا لِلَّهِ ٱلدِّينُ ٱلْخَالِصُ ... ﴿٣﴾ ﴾

﴾Surely, the religion [i.e. the worship and the obedience] is for Allah only...﴿ *(Qur'an 39: 3)*

﴿ وَمَآ أُمِرُوٓا۟ إِلَّا لِيَعْبُدُوا۟ ٱللَّهَ مُخْلِصِينَ لَهُ ٱلدِّينَ حُنَفَآءَ ... ﴿٥﴾ ﴾

﴾And they were commanded not, but that they should worship Allah, and worship none but Him Alone [abstaining from ascribing partners to Him...﴿

(Qur'an 98: 5)

It is narrated from Abu Hurayrah that the Prophet (ﷺ) said:

---

[5] Bukhari, 1/226, hadith no. 128.

"The most entitled of people to my intercession will be the one who said *Laa ilaaha illa-Allah* sincerely with all his heart and soul."[6]

And it is narrated from 'Utbaan ibn Maalik that the Prophet (ﷺ) said:

"Allah has forbidden to the Fire all those who say *Laa ilaaha illa-Allah*, seeking thereby the Face of Allah."[7]

7) Love

For this statement (*kalima*) and for what it implies and indicates; love for those who act upon it and adhere to its conditions, and hatred for those who go against that. Allah (ﷻ), says:

﴿ وَمِنَ ٱلنَّاسِ مَن يَتَّخِذُ مِن دُونِ ٱللَّهِ أَندَادًا يُحِبُّونَهُمْ كَحُبِّ ٱللَّهِ وَٱلَّذِينَ ءَامَنُوٓا۟ أَشَدُّ حُبًّا لِّلَّهِ ... ﴿١٦٥﴾ ﴾

﴿And of mankind are some who take [for worship] others besides Allah as rivals [to Allah]. They love them as they love Allah. But those who believe, love Allah more [than anything else]...﴾ *(Qur'an 2: 165)*

So Allah (ﷻ), tells us that His believing slaves love Him more (than anything else), because they do not take anything else as rivals to Him. The sign of the slave's love for his Lord is that he gives priority to what He loves, even if it goes against his own desires, and he hates what his Lord hates, even if his desires incline towards it. He befriends those who are the friends of Allah and His Messenger, and he takes as enemies those who are the enemies of Allah and His Messenger. And he follows the Messenger of Allah (ﷺ), walking in his footsteps and accepting his guidance.

---

[6] Bukhari, 1/193, hadith no. 99.

[7] Ibid, 1/519, hadith no. 425.

How the *Salaf* (Pious Predecessors) Referred to Some of These Conditions

Al-Ḥasan al-Baṣri said to Al-Farazdaq — the famous poet — when he was burying his wife: "What have you prepared for a day like this?" He said, "The testimony that there is no god except Allah, for seventy years." Al-Ḥasan said: "That is good preparation, but there are conditions attached to *Laa ilaaha illa-Allah*; beware of slandering chaste women (i.e., in your poetry)."

It was said to Al-Ḥasan al-Baṣri that some people were saying that whoever says *Laa ilaaha illa-Allah* will enter Paradise. He said, "Whoever says *Laa ilaaha illa-Allah* (there is no god except Allah) and fulfils the rights and obligations that this phrase entails, will enter Paradise.

Wahb ibn Munabbih was asked by someone: "Isn't the key to Paradise *Laa ilaaha illa-Allah*?" He said, Yes, but there is no key that does not have teeth; if you use a key that has teeth, you will open the door, otherwise you will not open it.

3 - *'IBAADAH* (WORSHIP)

1) Definition of *'Ibaadah*

***Tawḥeed* can only be achieved through two things**

a) Testimony that Allah is One in His Essence and Attributes.
b) Seeking Him alone and none other, in all acts of worship.

'Ibaadah (worship) is a word which covers all words and actions, inward and outward, that Allah (ﷻ), loves and is pleased with. Outward actions include uttering the *Shahaadatayn* (two testimonies),[8] praying and fasting; inward actions include belief

[8] Witnessing that there is One and only One Allah (ﷻ), and witnessing that Muhammad (ﷺ) is His (last) Messenger.

in Allah, His angels, His Books and His Messengers, and fearing Him and putting one's hopes in Him.

2) The True Worshipper is the One who Alternates between Fear and Hope

True worship is that in which a person alternates between loving Allah and fearing Him, humbling himself before Him, putting his hope in Him and seeking His mercy.

The person whose worship does not stem from love, fear or hope is simply making meaningless movements which are of no significance.

The person who worships out of love but without humility, fear or hope often falls into sin and disobedience. He claims that he loves Allah but he neglects good deeds and commits sins in an audacious manner. A long time ago, some people claimed to love Allah but they did not do good deeds, so Allah (ﷻ) put them to the test by saying:

﴿ قُلْ إِن كُنتُمْ تُحِبُّونَ اللَّهَ فَاتَّبِعُونِي يُحْبِبْكُمُ اللَّهُ ... ﴿٣١﴾ ﴾

﴾Say [O' Muhammad to mankind]: 'If you [really] love Allah, then follow me [i.e. accept Islamic Monotheism, follow the Qur'an and the Sunnah], Allah will love you...﴿ *(Qur'an 3: 31)*

So whoever claims to love Allah but does not follow His Messenger is lying.

Imam Shaafa'i (may Allah have mercy on him) said: If you see a man walking on the water or flying through the air, do not believe him unless you know whether he is following the Messenger of Allah.

Similarly, if there is hope on its own, unaccompanied by fear of Allah, a person may audaciously disobey Allah and feel secure against His Plan:

﴿ ... فَلَا يَأۡمَنُ مَكۡرَ ٱللَّهِ إِلَّا ٱلۡقَوۡمُ ٱلۡخَٰسِرُونَ ﴿٩٩﴾ ﴾

﴾...None feels secure from the Plan of Allah except the people who are the losers.﴿ *(Qur'an 7: 99)*

If fear is not accompanied by hope, a person may think in negative terms of Allah, despairing of His mercy and compassion. Allah (ﷻ), says:

﴿ ... إِنَّهُۥ لَا يَاْيۡـَٔسُ مِن رَّوۡحِ ٱللَّهِ إِلَّا ٱلۡقَوۡمُ ٱلۡكَٰفِرُونَ ﴿٨٧﴾ ﴾

﴾...Certainly no one despairs of Allah's Mercy, except the people who disbelieve.﴿ *(Qur'an 12: 87)*

True worship is that in which a person is in a state between fear and hope:

﴿ ... وَيَرۡجُونَ رَحۡمَتَهُۥ وَيَخَافُونَ عَذَابَهُۥٓۚ ... ﴿٥٧﴾ ﴾

﴾...And they ['Eesa (Jesus), 'Uzair (Ezra), angels and others] hope for His Mercy and fear His Torment...﴿ *(Qur'an 17: 57)*

﴿ أَمَّنۡ هُوَ قَٰنِتٌ ءَانَآءَ ٱلَّيۡلِ سَاجِدٗا وَقَآئِمٗا يَحۡذَرُ ٱلۡأٓخِرَةَ وَيَرۡجُواْ رَحۡمَةَ رَبِّهِۦۗ ... ﴿٩﴾ ﴾

﴾Is one who is obedient to Allah, prostrating himself or standing [in prayer] during the hours of the night, fearing the Hereafter and hoping for the Mercy of his Lord [like one who disbelieves]?...﴿ *(Qur'an 39: 9)*

And he should be in a state between hope and fear, as Allah (ﷻ), said concerning the family of Zakariya (Zachariya) (upon whom be peace):

﴿ ... إِنَّهُمۡ كَانُواْ يُسَٰرِعُونَ فِي ٱلۡخَيۡرَٰتِ وَيَدۡعُونَنَا رَغَبٗا وَرَهَبٗاۖ وَكَانُواْ لَنَا خَٰشِعِينَ ﴿٩٠﴾ ﴾

﴾...Verily, they used to hasten on to do good deeds and they used to call on Us with hope and fear, and used to humble themselves before Us.﴿ *(Qur'an 21: 90)*

The righteous slave will sometimes be filled with hope, so that he almost soars with his longing for Allah (ﷻ), and sometimes will be seized with such fear, that he almost melts with fear of Allah. He persistently seeks the pleasure of Allah, turning to Him out of fear of His punishment, seeking refuge with Him from it, and seeking that which is with Him (i.e. Paradise).

3) The Pillars of *'Ibaadah*

'*Ibaadah* has three pillars or essential components

a) Purity of intention (*ikhlaaṣ*): Whereby a person seeks the Face of his Lord and the Hereafter. The Prophet (ﷺ) said:

> "Actions are but by intention and every man shall have but that which he intended. Thus he whose migration was for Allah and His Messenger, his migration was for Allah and His Messenger, and he whose migration was to achieve some worldly benefit or to take some woman in marriage, his migration was for that for which he migrated."[9]

If there is no purity of intention, good deeds are invalidated.

b) Sincerity (*Ṣidq*): What we mean by sincerity is sincere resolve, whereby a person strives to obey the commands of Allah and avoid that which He has prohibited, to prepare himself to meet Him and to avoid feeling helpless or being too lazy to obey Allah.

---

[9] Bukhari and Muslim. This hadith is so famous that there is no need to mention its isnad. See our book *Maqaaṣid al-Mukallifeen*, Pp. 519, where we discuss its isnads (chain of narrators).

c) Following the Messenger (ﷺ): So a person does not worship Allah except according to what Allah has prescribed and what the Messenger brought. When people worship their Lord without knowledge, this is *bid'ah* against which the Messenger (ﷺ) warned us, and condemned those who do it, and said that doing it is misguidance. He (ﷺ) said:

> "Every newly-invented thing (in religion) is a *bid'ah* and every *bid'ah* is a going astray, and every going astray is in the Fire."

The one who does acts of *bid'ah* will have his action rejected and it will not be accepted from him.

It is narrated in *Ṣaḥeeḥayn* (Bukhari and Muslim) from 'Aa'ishah (may Allah be pleased with her) that the Messenger of Allah (ﷺ) said:

> "Whoever invents something in this matter of ours (i.e., Islam) that is not part of it, will have it rejected." According to a version narrated by Muslim: "Whoever does something that is not part of this matter of ours, will have it rejected."[10]

There is no worship without these pillars

If there is no sincere resolve, there is no worship. In such a case, worship becomes no more than wishful thinking; hardly does a person start to do it but his will dissolves and fades away. As long as there is no purity of intention or following the Messenger (ﷺ), worship is unacceptable to Allah.

---

[10] Attributed by Ibn al-Atheer in *Jaami' al-Uṣool*, 1/289, hadith no. 75 to Bukhari, Muslim and Abu Dawood.

4) Kinds of Worship not Permissible for Anyone Except Allah

The kinds of worship not permissible for anyone except Allah (ﷻ), are of several types:

a) Beliefs

These form the basis of all acts of worship. This means that a person believes that Allah (ﷻ), is the One and Only Lord, Who Alone has the power to create and command, and the power to benefit or harm; He has no partner, and none can intercede with Him except with His permission; and there is none who may be rightfully worshipped except Him.

b) Actions of the heart

This is the kind of worship in the heart, not permitted to be directed to anything or anyone except Allah and Allah alone. Directing worship to anything other than Allah is *shirk*, and such acts are many, e.g., fear and hope, humility, love, turning in repentance, trusting and submitting.

c) Utterance

Such as uttering the word of *Tawḥeed*. It is not sufficient merely to believe in its meaning. It must also be uttered, such as seeking refuge with Allah, seeking His help, calling upon Him, Glorifying and Praising Him, and reciting the Qur'an.

d) Physical actions

Such as Praying, Fasting, doing Ḥajj, sacrificing animals, fulfilling vows, etc.

e) Financial

Such as paying zakah and other kinds of charity, offering *kaffaarah* (expiation), offering sacrifices, and spending on others.

4 - WHAT GOES AGAINST *TAWḤEED*

What goes against *Tawḥeed* and is its opposite is *shirk*. It is said in Arabic *sharaktuhu fi'l-amr* (I became somebody's partner) if one becomes a partner (*shareek*). And Allah (ﷻ) says:

﴿ وَأَشۡرِكۡهُ فِيٓ أَمۡرِي ٣٢ ﴾

> ﴿[Moosa (Moses) said:] 'And let him share my task [*ashrikhu*] [of conveying Allah's Message and Prophethood].'﴾ *(Qur'an 20: 32)*

- meaning, let him be my partner.

Shirk is of two types

According to the terminology of Islamic shari'ah, *shirk* is of two types:

a) *Ash-Shirk al-Akbar* (major *shirk*)

The *mushrik* who is guilty of major *shirk* is the one who believes in someone else as a lord alongside Allah, such as the Christians who regard Allah as the third of three (trinity), or the Magians (Zoroastrians) who attribute good events to the Light and bad events to the Darkness, or the Sabians who believed that the stars and planets controlled what happened on earth. Similar to these are the grave-worshippers who claim that the souls of the *awliya'* ("saints") can control things after their death: they fulfil people's needs, relieve their distress, help those who call upon them, and protect those who seek refuge with them and seek their protection. Another aspect of *Ash-Shirk al-Akbar* is making something or someone god alongside Allah, whether it be an angel, a Messenger, a *wali* ("saint"), the sun, the moon, a rock or a human being, which is worshipped as Allah is worshipped, by praying to it, seeking its help, offering sacrifices to it, making vows to it, and other kinds of worship.

The so-called partner does not have to be regarded as equal to Allah to be counted as *shirk*

The thing that is associated with Allah does not have to be regarded as equal to Allah in all aspects to be counted as *shirk*. According to shari'ah, a person is called a *mushrik* if he believes that anyone or anything is a partner of Allah, even if he regards it as inferior to Allah in terms of power and knowledge, for example.

When Allah (ﷻ) tells us that the *mushrikeen* (polytheists) will say (in Hell, in the Hereafter):

﴿ تَٱللَّهِ إِن كُنَّا لَفِى ضَلَٰلٍ مُّبِينٍ ﴿٩٧﴾ إِذْ نُسَوِّيكُم بِرَبِّ ٱلْعَٰلَمِينَ ﴿٩٨﴾ ﴾

﴾By Allah, we were truly, in a manifest error, When we held you [false gods] as equals [in worship] with the Lord of the *'Aalameen* [mankind, jinn and all that exists].﴿ *(Qur'an 26: 97-98)*

- this refers to equality in love, fear, hope, obedience and submission, not in the power of creation, because they used to believe that Allah alone had the power of creation.

The serious nature of this *shirk*

Ash-Shirk al-Akbar is the most serious of sins, because it cancels good deeds. Allah (ﷻ) says:

﴿ ... وَلَوْ أَشْرَكُوا۟ لَحَبِطَ عَنْهُم مَّا كَانُوا۟ يَعْمَلُونَ ﴿٨٨﴾ ﴾

﴾...But if they had joined in worship others with Allah, all that they used to do would have been of no benefit to them.﴿ *(Qur'an 6: 88)*

And Allah (ﷻ) said to His Messenger (ﷺ):

﴿ وَلَقَدْ أُوحِىَ إِلَيْكَ وَإِلَى ٱلَّذِينَ مِن قَبْلِكَ لَئِنْ أَشْرَكْتَ لَيَحْبَطَنَّ عَمَلُكَ وَلَتَكُونَنَّ مِنَ ٱلْخَٰسِرِينَ ﴿٦٥﴾ ﴾

﴿And indeed it has been revealed to you [O' Muhammad], as it was to those [Allah's Messengers] before you: 'If you join others in worship with Allah, [then] surely, [all] your deeds will be in vain, and you will certainly be among the losers.'﴾ *(Qur'an 39: 65)*

The one who is guilty of *Ash-shirk al-Akbar* (major *shirk*) will abide in Hell for all eternity, and Allah (سُبْحَانَهُ وَتَعَالَى) will not forgive him or admit him to Paradise:

﴿إِنَّ ٱللَّهَ لَا يَغۡفِرُ أَن يُشۡرَكَ بِهِۦ وَيَغۡفِرُ مَا دُونَ ذَٰلِكَ لِمَن يَشَآءُۚ... ﴿٤٨﴾﴾

﴿Verily, Allah forgives not that partners should be set up with Him [in worship], but He forgives except that [anything else] to whom He wills;...﴾ *(Qur'an 4: 48)*

﴿لَقَدۡ كَفَرَ ٱلَّذِينَ قَالُوٓاْ إِنَّ ٱللَّهَ هُوَ ٱلۡمَسِيحُ ٱبۡنُ مَرۡيَمَۖ وَقَالَ ٱلۡمَسِيحُ يَٰبَنِيٓ إِسۡرَٰٓءِيلَ ٱعۡبُدُواْ ٱللَّهَ رَبِّي وَرَبَّكُمۡۖ إِنَّهُۥ مَن يُشۡرِكۡ بِٱللَّهِ فَقَدۡ حَرَّمَ ٱللَّهُ عَلَيۡهِ ٱلۡجَنَّةَ وَمَأۡوَىٰهُ ٱلنَّارُۖ وَمَا لِلظَّٰلِمِينَ مِنۡ أَنصَارٖ ﴿٧٢﴾﴾

﴿Surely, they have disbelieved who say: 'Allah is the Messiah ['Eesa (Jesus)], son of Maryam [Mary].' But the Messiah ['Eesa] said: 'O' Children of Israel! Worship Allah, my Lord and your Lord.' Verily, whosoever sets up partners [in worship] with Allah, then Allah has forbidden Paradise to him, and the Fire will be his abode. And for the *Ẓaalimeen* [polytheists and wrongdoers] there are no helpers.﴾ *(Qur'an 5: 72)*

The greatest crime and the worst sin

It is narrated that 'Abdullah ibn Mas'ood (رضي الله عنه) said: I asked the Messenger of Allah (ﷺ), Which sin is the greatest with Allah? He said,

"That you should claim that Allah has a rival when He has created you." (Bukhari and Muslim)[11]

And Allah (ﷻ) says:

﴿ ... إِنَّ ٱلشِّرْكَ لَظُلْمٌ عَظِيمٌ ﴿١٣﴾ ﴾

﴾...Verily, joining others in worship with Allah is a great *Ẓulm* [wrong] indeed.﴿ *(Qur'an 31: 13)*

﴿ ... وَمَن يُشْرِكْ بِٱللَّهِ فَقَدِ ٱفْتَرَىٰٓ إِثْمًا عَظِيمًا ﴿٤٨﴾ ﴾

﴾...And whoever sets up partners with Allah in worship, he has indeed invented a tremendous sin.﴿ *(Qur'an 4: 48)*

b) *Ash-Shirk al-Aṣghar* (minor *shirk*)

Minor *shirk* is actions such as showing off or doing things for the sake of created beings, and not performing acts of worship purely for the sake of Allah. This means that a person may do things sometimes for the sake of his ego, or for some worldly purpose, or to gain status and power, so he allocates a share of his action to Allah and a share to something or someone other than Him. This kind of *shirk* may involve verbal statements such as swearing by something other than Allah, or by saying "Whatever Allah and you want" or "I have no one to help me except Allah and you."

It may constitute *shirk akbar*, depending on who says it and what he means.

This kind of *shirk* (*ash-shirk al-aṣghar*), even though it does not put a person beyond the pale of Islam, still puts a person in grave danger, because it reduces his reward to a great extent and may cancel out his good deeds altogether. Bukhari and Muslim narrated from Abu

[11] *Mishkaat al-Maṣaabeeḥ*, 1/21, hadith no. 49.

Moosa: "A man came to the Prophet (ﷺ) and said: 'A man who fights in order to get the booty, a man who fights in order to become famous and a man who fights in order to gain a high status - which of them is fighting for the sake of Allah?' The Messenger of Allah (ﷺ) said:

> 'The one who fights in order that the word of Allah may become supreme is the one who is fighting for the sake of Allah.'"[12]

Imam Muslim related: the Messenger (ﷺ) narrated that his Lord (Allah) said:

> "I am so self-sufficient that I am in no need of having an associate. Thus he who does an action for someone else's sake as well as Mine will have that action renounced by Me to him whom he associated with Me."[13]

It is narrated in *Al-Musnad* that the Messenger (ﷺ) said:

> "What I fear the most for you is *ash-shirk al-aṣghar.*" They said, "O' Messenger of Allah, what is *ash-shirk al-aṣghar*?" He said: "Showing off."

In *Shu'ab al-Eemaan*, Al-Bayhaqi added:

> "And Allah will say to them on the Day on which He requites His slaves for their actions: 'Go to those for whom you used to show off in the world, and see whether you can find any reward or anything good with them.'"[14]

---

[12] Bukhari, 6/28, hadith no. 281; Muslim, 3/1512, hadith no. 1904.

[13] Muslim. See *Jaami' al-Uṣool*, 4/545, hadith no. 2651.

[14] *Mishkaat al-Maṣaabeeḥ*, 2/687, hadith no. 5334.

Prohibiting this kind of *shirk*, Allah (ﷻ), revealed the following words:

﴿... فَمَن كَانَ يَرْجُوا۟ لِقَآءَ رَبِّهِۦ فَلْيَعْمَلْ عَمَلًا صَٰلِحًا وَلَا يُشْرِكْ بِعِبَادَةِ رَبِّهِۦٓ أَحَدًۢا ١١٠﴾

﴿...So whoever hopes for the Meeting with his Lord, let him work righteousness and associate none as a partner in the worship of his Lord.﴾ *(Qur'an 18: 110)*

CHAPTER FOUR
A BRIEF HISTORY OF THE CREED — *'AQEEDAH*

1 - DID *'AQEEDAH* DEVELOP WITH THE PASSAGE OF TIME?

Many western scholars believe that man did not come to know religious belief — creed — as it is known today in one step, and that it evolved and developed over the centuries.

It is no wonder that this is suggested by people whom Allah has not blessed with His Book, in which He clearly and unambiguously tells the history of *'aqeedah*; what is strange is that this view is echoed by the so-called Muslim researchers.

For example, 'Abbas Maḥmood al-'Aqqaad says in his book entitled *Allah*[1] — which is a research on the development of belief in God — that man's beliefs evolved, and he states that the evolution of man's religious beliefs was similar to the development of other branches of man's knowledge.

He says: "The earliest human beliefs were appropriate to early human life, as was man's scientific knowledge and handicrafts. Man's early scientific knowledge and handicrafts were not more developed than his early religious beliefs and acts of worship. The elements of truth in one field were not more abundant than the elements of truth in another."

Indeed, he thinks that the development of human religious belief was more complex than the development of his scientific knowledge and handicrafts. He says: "Human efforts to develop religious knowledge

---

[1] Published by *Daar al-Hilal*, Cairo. See Pp. 10.

must have been more complex and taken longer than the attempts to develop scientific knowledge and handicrafts, because the greater the realities of the universe, the more difficult it is to discover and the longer it takes to explore than the realities of those things which may be dealt with sometimes by science and sometimes by handicrafts."

He thinks that the Divine reality did not manifest itself to mankind in one go. He says: "Tracing the origins of religions in the early times of ignorance (*Jaahiliyah*) does not indicate that this sort of religious belief is false or that they believed in something impossible which was not real. All that it demonstrates is that the greater reality is too great to be fully manifested in one time."

Then he starts to quote the views of scholars who have researched the history of religious belief. Some of them say that the reason for the development of religious beliefs was man's weakness in the face of natural phenomena and hostile natural forces and living beings. Some think that religious belief is a state of sickness in individuals and societies, others believe that the origin of religious belief was the worship of totems, as some tribes had adopted animals as totems which they regarded as the ancestor of the tribe; the totem may also have been a tree or a rock which they regarded as sacred. And there are other assumptions which have formed in the minds of western researchers.

Unfortunately, these theories[2] have found their way into the minds of many writers and scholars[3] for several reasons such as the following:

---

[2] One of those who showed an inclination towards these theories is Muṣṭafa Maḥmoud in his book entitled Allah.

[3] I do not know what is this belief that has developed. Is it the deviated belief of the Jews, or the distorted belief of the Christians, or the belief of the philosophers? ... these beliefs represent nothing but ideological deviations; they do not represent sound belief.

i) They thought that early man was created imperfect, and was not qualified to receive full knowledge of the greater realities. Their concept of early man makes him more like an animal than a human being.

ii) They thought that man was guided to religious beliefs by himself, with no teacher or guide to explain it to him. So long as this was the case, his knowledge of Allah would inevitably evolve just as his knowledge of science and manufacturing evolved.

iii) When they researched religions to discover their history, they only studied the deviated or misguided religions, which they took as their field of research and subjected them to study and examinations. How could they find out about reality from these religions which represent human deviation in religious belief?

Only the Qur'an Explains the History of Creed - Religious Beliefs

There is no book on earth which explains the true history of religious belief, except the Book of Allah, which offers abundant knowledge of this topic. Human knowledge cannot attain this level of abundant knowledge for several reasons:

a) What we know of history about five thousand years ago is very little, and what we know of history about ten thousand years ago is even less. Anything earlier than that is considered to be entirely unknown. Hence most of the truth together with human history has been lost.

b) The truths which mankind did inherit have been mixed with a great deal of falsehood; indeed they have been lost in the vast ocean of falsehood, deceit and distortion. This indicates that it is extremely difficult for one person or a group of people to write a true history of modern times, let alone a history that stretches back to the dawn of humanity.

c) Part of the history that has to do with religious beliefs — creed — did not happen on earth, but in the heavens.

Hence the only One Who can give us a true history with no confusion is Allah, Glorified and Exalted be He.

﴿ إِنَّ ٱللَّهَ لَا يَخْفَىٰ عَلَيْهِ شَيْءٌ فِي ٱلْأَرْضِ وَلَا فِي ٱلسَّمَآءِ ۝٥ ﴾

﴿Truly, nothing is hidden from Allah, in the earth or in the heaven.﴾ *(Qur'an 3: 5)*

2 - THE HISTORY OF THE CREED (RELIGIOUS BELIEFS) AS TOLD IN THE NOBLE QUR'AN

Allah (ﷻ) has told us that He created Adam as an integrated, upright and independent creature, then He breathed into him of His spirit and caused him to dwell in His Paradise. He permitted him and his wife to eat whatever they wanted from the Garden, apart from one tree. Then his enemy *Iblees* (Satan) tempted him to eat from that tree. Because he obeyed his enemy and disobeyed his Lord. Allah sent him down from Paradise to the earth, but before sending him down, Allah promised him that He would send down His guidance to him and his progeny, so that man would know his Lord and His way and laws. He promised those who responded, guidance in this world and joy in the Hereafter, and He warned those who remained stubbornly arrogant of a life of hardship in this world and even greater hardship in the Hereafter:

﴿ قُلْنَا ٱهْبِطُوا۟ مِنْهَا جَمِيعًا ۖ فَإِمَّا يَأْتِيَنَّكُم مِّنِّى هُدًى فَمَن تَبِعَ هُدَاىَ فَلَا خَوْفٌ عَلَيْهِمْ وَلَا هُمْ يَحْزَنُونَ ۝٣٨ وَٱلَّذِينَ كَفَرُوا۟ وَكَذَّبُوا۟ بِـَٔايَـٰتِنَآ أُو۟لَـٰٓئِكَ أَصْحَـٰبُ ٱلنَّارِ ۖ هُمْ فِيهَا خَـٰلِدُونَ ۝٣٩ ﴾

﴿We said: 'Get down all of you from this place [the Paradise], then whenever there comes to you Guidance from Me, and whoever follows My Guidance, there shall be no fear on them, nor shall they grieve. But those who disbelieve and belie Our *Aayaat* [proofs, evidences, verses, lessons, signs, revelations, etc.] - such are the dwellers of the Fire. They shall abide therein forever.'﴾

(Qur'an 2: 38-39)

And in *Soorah Ṭa-Ha* Allah (سُبْحَانَهُ وَتَعَالَى) says:

﴿ قَالَ ٱهْبِطَا مِنْهَا جَمِيعًا ۖ بَعْضُكُمْ لِبَعْضٍ عَدُوٌّ ۖ فَإِمَّا يَأْتِيَنَّكُم مِّنِّى هُدًى فَمَنِ ٱتَّبَعَ هُدَاىَ فَلَا يَضِلُّ وَلَا يَشْقَىٰ ﴿١٢٣﴾ وَمَنْ أَعْرَضَ عَن ذِكْرِى فَإِنَّ لَهُۥ مَعِيشَةً ضَنكًا وَنَحْشُرُهُۥ يَوْمَ ٱلْقِيَٰمَةِ أَعْمَىٰ ﴿١٢٤﴾ قَالَ رَبِّ لِمَ حَشَرْتَنِىٓ أَعْمَىٰ وَقَدْ كُنتُ بَصِيرًا ﴿١٢٥﴾ قَالَ كَذَٰلِكَ أَتَتْكَ ءَايَٰتُنَا فَنَسِيتَهَا ۖ وَكَذَٰلِكَ ٱلْيَوْمَ تُنسَىٰ ﴿١٢٦﴾ ﴾

﴾He [Allah] said: 'Get you down [from the Paradise to the earth], both of you, together, some of you are an enemy to some others. Then if there comes to you guidance from Me, then whoever follows My Guidance he shall neither go astray, nor shall be distressed. But whosoever turns away from My Reminder [i.e. neither believes in this Qur'an nor acts on its teachings] verily, for him is a life of hardship, and We shall raise him up blind on the Day of Resurrection. He will say: 'O' my Lord! Why have you raised me up blind, while I had sight [before].' [Allah] will say: 'Like this: Our *Aayaat* [proofs, evidences, verses, lessons, signs, revelations, etc.] came unto you, but you disregarded them [i.e. you left them, did not think deeply in them, and you turned away from them], and so this Day, you will be neglected [in the Hell-fire, away from Allah's Mercy].'﴾

(Qur'an 20: 123-126)

The First Generation of Mankind Believed in *Tawḥeed*

Adam (ﷺ) came down to earth, and from his progeny Allah created a nation which believed in pure *Tawḥeed* (Oneness of Allah), as Allah (ﷻ) says:

﴿ كَانَ ٱلنَّاسُ أُمَّةً وَٰحِدَةً... ﴿٢١٣﴾ ﴾

﴾Mankind were one community...﴿ *(Qur'an 2: 213)*,

- i.e., they all believed in *Tawḥeed* and followed the true religion. Then they differed,

﴿ ... فَبَعَثَ ٱللَّهُ ٱلنَّبِيِّـۧنَ مُبَشِّرِينَ وَمُنذِرِينَ وَأَنزَلَ مَعَهُمُ ٱلْكِتَٰبَ بِٱلْحَقِّ لِيَحْكُمَ بَيْنَ ٱلنَّاسِ فِيمَا ٱخْتَلَفُوا۟ فِيهِ ... ﴿٢١٣﴾ ﴾

﴾...And Allah sent Prophets with glad tidings and warnings, and with them He sent down the Scripture in truth to judge between people in matters wherein they differed...﴿ *(Qur'an 2: 213)*.

According to a hadith narrated by Abu Umaamah, a man asked the Messenger (ﷺ), "O' Messenger of Allah, was Adam a Prophet?" He said,

> "Yes, and he was spoken to by Allah." The man asked, "How long was there between him and Nooḥ (Noah)?" He said, "Ten centuries."

- This is narrated by Abu Ḥaatim ibn Ḥibbaan in his *Ṣaḥeeḥ*. Ibn Katheer said: "This is sound (*ṣaḥeeḥ*) according to the conditions of Muslim, although he did not narrate it."[4]

Bukhari narrated that Ibn 'Abbaas said:

[4] *Al-Bidaayah wa'n-Nihaayah*, 1/101.

> "And between Adam and Nooḥ (Noah) there were ten centuries, all of whom followed Islam."[5]

A century equals one hundred years. On this basis there were one thousand years between Adam and Nooḥ (Noah) (may peace be upon them).

The period between them may have been longer than that, because the comment of Ibn 'Abbaas, that during these ten centuries people followed Islam, does not rule out the possibility that there were also other centuries during which people followed religions other than Islam.

The word century (*qarn*) may also refer to a generation, as Allah (ﷻ) says:

﴿ وَكَمْ أَهْلَكْنَا مِنَ الْقُرُونِ مِنْ بَعْدِ نُوحٍ ... ﴿١٧﴾ ﴾

> ﴾And how many generations [*quroon*] have We destroyed after Nooḥ [Noah]!...﴿ *(Qur'an 17: 17)*

﴿ ثُمَّ أَنْشَأْنَا مِنْ بَعْدِهِمْ قَرْنًا آخَرِينَ ﴿٣١﴾ ﴾

> ﴾Then, after them, We created another generation [*qarnan*].﴿ *(Qur'an 23: 31)*[6]

The First Deviation from Correct *'Aqeedah* (Creed) and the First Messenger

After mankind had been one community, believing in *Tawḥeed* — Oneness of Allah — there arose deviation and confusion. The first deviation came about as the result of exaggerated veneration of righteous people, raising them to the status of gods and worshipping them.

---

[5] *Al-Bidaayah wa'n-Nihaayah*, 1/101.

[6] Ibid.

Bukhari narrated from Ibn Jurayj, he from 'Aṭaa' and he from Ibn 'Abbaas, concerning the *Tafseer* of the *aayah* (verse):

﴿ وَقَالُوا۟ لَا تَذَرُنَّ ءَالِهَتَكُمْ وَلَا تَذَرُنَّ وَدًّا وَلَا سُوَاعًا وَلَا يَغُوثَ وَيَعُوقَ وَنَسْرًا ﴿٢٣﴾ ﴾

﴿And they have said: 'You shall not leave your gods, nor shall you leave *Wadd*, nor *Suwaa'*, nor *Yaghooth*, nor *Ya'ooq*, nor *Nasr* [names of the idols].'﴾ *(Qur'an 71: 23)*

He (Ibn 'Abbaas) said: These were the names of righteous people from among the people of Nooḥ (Noah). When they died, the Satan inspired their people to set up stone altars in the places where they used to sit, and to call these stone altars by their names. So the people did that, but they were not worshipped until those people died and knowledge about them was lost, then they were worshipped.[7]

This was the first deviation from *Tawḥeed* (Oneness of Allah) in human history, so Allah sent to them the first of His Messengers, Nooḥ (Noah), in fulfilment of the promise that He had given to the father of mankind, Adam, to send Messengers and reveal Books to guide mankind.

The evidence that Nooḥ (Noah) (عليه السلام) was the first Messenger to be sent is the hadith about intercession which Muslim has narrated. It says,

> "After going to Adam, the people will come to Nooḥ and will say to him, among other things, 'O' Nooḥ, you are the first of the Messengers sent to the earth, and Allah called you a thankful slave.'"[8]

---

[7] Bukhari, 8/667; hadith no. 4920.

[8] Muslim, 1/185, hadith no. 194.

The texts of the Book of our Lord which we have before us clearly indicate that Nooḥ (Noah) called his people to pure *Tawḥeed*. He said to his people:

﴿... ٱعْبُدُوا۟ ٱللَّهَ مَا لَكُم مِّنْ إِلَٰهٍ غَيْرُهُۥٓ إِنِّىٓ أَخَافُ عَلَيْكُمْ عَذَابَ يَوْمٍ عَظِيمٍ ﴿٥٩﴾﴾

﴾...Worship Allah! You have no other *Ilaah* [God] but Him. [*Laa ilaaha illa-Allah*: none has the right to be worshipped but Allah.] Certainly, I fear for you the torment of a Great Day!﴿ *(Qur'an 7: 59)*

﴿أَن لَّا تَعْبُدُوٓا۟ إِلَّا ٱللَّهَ ۖ إِنِّىٓ أَخَافُ عَلَيْكُمْ عَذَابَ يَوْمٍ أَلِيمٍ ﴿٢٦﴾﴾

﴾That you worship none but Allah; surely, I fear for you the torment of a painful Day.﴿ *(Qur'an 11: 26)*

﴿... يَٰقَوْمِ ٱعْبُدُوا۟ ٱللَّهَ مَا لَكُم مِّنْ إِلَٰهٍ غَيْرُهُۥٓ ۚ أَفَلَا تَتَّقُونَ ﴿٢٣﴾﴾

﴾...O' my people! Worship Allah! You have no other *Ilaah* [God] but Him [Islamic Monotheism]. Will you not then be afraid [of Him, i.e. of His punishment because of worshipping others besides Him]?﴿

(Qur'an 23: 23)

Those who responded to his call for *Tawḥeed* (Oneness of Allah) were the weakest of his people; it was rejected by the leaders and powerful ones, who thought themselves to be clever and intelligent when they arrogantly refused to follow the truth:

﴿قَالَ ٱلْمَلَأُ مِن قَوْمِهِۦٓ إِنَّا لَنَرَىٰكَ فِى ضَلَٰلٍ مُّبِينٍ ﴿٦٠﴾﴾

﴾The leaders of his people said: 'Verily, we see you in plain error.'﴿ *(Qur'an 7: 60).*

The leaders referred to here were the prominent and powerful ones among his people, who said to him:

﴿ ... وَمَا نَرَىٰكَ ٱتَّبَعَكَ إِلَّا ٱلَّذِينَ هُمْ أَرَاذِلُنَا بَادِىَ ٱلرَّأْيِ ... ﴿٢٧﴾ ﴾

﴾...Nor do we see any follow you but the meanest among us and they [too] followed you without thinking...﴿ *(Qur'an 11: 27),*

— i.e., they follow you without thinking deeply or pondering or examining the matter. The thing for which they accused them was the thing for which they should have been praised, for when the truth is made manifest, it does not need to be examined; it needs to be followed.

They found it strange that Allah would send a human Messenger, and said:

﴿ ... مَا نَرَىٰكَ إِلَّا بَشَرًا مِّثْلَنَا ... ﴿٢٧﴾ ﴾

﴾...'We see you but a man like ourselves,'...﴿ *(Qur'an 11: 27)*

﴿ فَقَالَ ٱلْمَلَؤُا۟ ٱلَّذِينَ كَفَرُوا۟ مِن قَوْمِهِۦ مَا هَٰذَآ إِلَّا بَشَرٌ مِّثْلُكُمْ يُرِيدُ أَن يَتَفَضَّلَ عَلَيْكُمْ وَلَوْ شَآءَ ٱللَّهُ لَأَنزَلَ مَلَٰٓئِكَةً... ﴿٢٤﴾ ﴾

﴾But the chiefs of his people who disbelieved said: 'He is no more than a human being like you, he seeks to make himself superior to you. Had Allah willed, He surely, could have sent down angels...'﴿ *(Qur'an 23: 24)*

They asked him to reject the poor and weak who followed him, but he ignored their demand:

﴿ ... وَمَآ أَنَا۠ بِطَارِدِ ٱلَّذِينَ ءَامَنُوٓا۟ ۚ إِنَّهُم مُّلَٰقُوا۟ رَبِّهِمْ وَلَٰكِنِّىٓ أَرَىٰكُمْ قَوْمًا تَجْهَلُونَ ﴿٢٩﴾ ﴾

﴾...I am not going to drive away those who have

believed. Surely, they are going to meet their Lord, but I see that you are a people that are ignorant.﴿
(Qur'an 11: 29)

A long time passed, and the dispute between Nooḥ (Noah) and his people intensified, as Allah (ﷻ) says:

﴿... فَلَبِثَ فِيهِمْ أَلْفَ سَنَةٍ إِلَّا خَمْسِينَ عَامًا... ﴿١٤﴾﴾

﴾...And he stayed among them a thousand years less fifty years...﴿ *(Qur'an 29: 14)*

Then he prayed against them:

﴿وَقَالَ نُوحٌ رَّبِّ لَا تَذَرْ عَلَى ٱلْأَرْضِ مِنَ ٱلْكَٰفِرِينَ دَيَّارًا ﴿٢٦﴾ إِنَّكَ إِن تَذَرْهُمْ يُضِلُّوا۟ عِبَادَكَ وَلَا يَلِدُوٓا۟ إِلَّا فَاجِرًا كَفَّارًا ﴿٢٧﴾﴾

﴾And Nooḥ [Noah] said: 'My Lord! Leave not one of the disbelievers on the earth! If You leave them, they will mislead Your slaves, and they will beget none but wicked disbelievers.'﴿ *(Qur'an 71: 26-27)*

So Allah (ﷻ) destroyed them with the Flood:

﴿وَقَوْمَ نُوحٍ لَّمَّا كَذَّبُوا۟ ٱلرُّسُلَ أَغْرَقْنَٰهُمْ ... ﴿٣٧﴾﴾

﴾And Nooḥ's people, when they denied the Messengers, We drowned them,...﴿ *(Qur'an 25: 37)*

And He, the Exalted and Almighty, saved Nooḥ (Noah) and the believers by His mercy. He cleansed the earth of the evildoers and did not leave anyone there except those who believed in the Oneness of Allah (*Tawḥeed*). When they deviated from *Tawḥeed*, He sent another Messenger:

﴿ثُمَّ أَنشَأْنَا مِنۢ بَعْدِهِمْ قَرْنًا ءَاخَرِينَ ﴿٣١﴾ فَأَرْسَلْنَا فِيهِمْ رَسُولًا مِّنْهُمْ... ﴿٣٢﴾﴾

﴾Then, after them, We created another generation. And

We sent to them a Messenger from among themselves...﴾ *(Qur'an 23: 31-32).*

So he called them to believe in Allah (سُبْحَانَهُ وَتَعَالَى) Alone:

﴿... أَنِ ٱعۡبُدُواْ ٱللَّهَ مَا لَكُم مِّنۡ إِلَٰهٍ غَيۡرُهُۥٓۚ ... ﴿٣٢﴾﴾

﴿...Worship Allah! You have no other *Ilaah* [God] but Him...﴾ *(Qur'an 23: 32).*

So Allah's mercy and care for the children of Adam continued. Every time they went astray and deviated, He sent down His guidance to them, to bring them light in the darkness:

﴿ثُمَّ أَرۡسَلۡنَا رُسُلَنَا تَتۡرَاۖ كُلَّ مَا جَآءَ أُمَّةٗ رَّسُولُهَا كَذَّبُوهُۖ فَأَتۡبَعۡنَا بَعۡضَهُم بَعۡضٗا وَجَعَلۡنَٰهُمۡ أَحَادِيثَۚ فَبُعۡدٗا لِّقَوۡمٖ لَّا يُؤۡمِنُونَ ﴿٤٤﴾﴾

﴿Then We sent Our Messengers in succession. Every time there came to a nation their Messenger, they denied him; so We made them follow one another [to destruction], and We made them as *Aḥaadeeth* [the true stories for mankind to learn a lesson from them]. So away with a people who believe not!﴾ *(Qur'an 23: 44)*

This is the true story of mankind, a long conflict between truth and falsehood, between the Messengers who brought guidance and truth, and the misguided who turned away from *Tawḥeed* and clung to the customs they had learned from their fathers and grandfathers, and to their desires and false beliefs:

﴿أَلَمۡ يَأۡتِكُمۡ نَبَؤُاْ ٱلَّذِينَ مِن قَبۡلِكُمۡ قَوۡمِ نُوحٖ وَعَادٖ وَثَمُودَ وَٱلَّذِينَ مِنۢ بَعۡدِهِمۡ لَا يَعۡلَمُهُمۡ إِلَّا ٱللَّهُۚ جَآءَتۡهُمۡ رُسُلُهُم بِٱلۡبَيِّنَٰتِ فَرَدُّوٓاْ أَيۡدِيَهُمۡ فِيٓ أَفۡوَٰهِهِمۡ وَقَالُوٓاْ إِنَّا كَفَرۡنَا بِمَآ أُرۡسِلۡتُم بِهِۦ وَإِنَّا لَفِي شَكّٖ مِّمَّا تَدۡعُونَنَآ إِلَيۡهِ مُرِيبٖ ﴿٩﴾ ۞ قَالَتۡ رُسُلُهُمۡ أَفِي ٱللَّهِ شَكّٞ فَاطِرِ ٱلسَّمَٰوَٰتِ وَٱلۡأَرۡضِۖ يَدۡعُوكُمۡ لِيَغۡفِرَ لَكُم مِّن ذُنُوبِكُمۡ وَيُؤَخِّرَكُمۡ

إِلَىٰٓ أَجَلٍ مُّسَمًّىۚ قَالُوٓاْ إِنۡ أَنتُمۡ إِلَّا بَشَرٞ مِّثۡلُنَا تُرِيدُونَ أَن تَصُدُّونَا
عَمَّا كَانَ يَعۡبُدُ ءَابَآؤُنَا فَأۡتُونَا بِسُلۡطَٰنٖ مُّبِينٖ ﴿١٠﴾

﴾Has not the news reached you, of those before you, the people of Nooḥ [Noah], and 'Aad, and Thamood? And those after them? None knows them but Allah. To them came their Messengers with clear proofs, but they put their hands in their mouths [biting them from anger] and said: 'Verily, we disbelieve in that with which you have been sent, and we are really in grave doubt as to that to which you invite us [i.e., Islamic Monotheism].' Their Messengers said: 'What! Can there be a doubt about Allah, the Creator of the heavens and the earth? He calls you [to Monotheism and to be obedient to Allah] that He may forgive you of your sins and give you respite for a term appointed.' They said: 'You are no more than human beings like us! You wish to turn us away from what our fathers used to worship. Then bring us a clear authority [i.e., a clear proof of what you say].'﴿

(Qur'an 14: 9-10)

When we ponder the call of the Messengers as detailed by the Qur'an, the following truths will become clear to us:

i) That from the beginning, Allah created man as a complete and integrated creature, for a specific goal, that is, to worship Him, and that He created him with the ability to do that.

ii) That He taught man about Himself from the beginning, and did not leave him to find out about his Lord through his own thoughts and wanderings. He sent many Messengers to man, so that they might convey the Message to all of mankind.

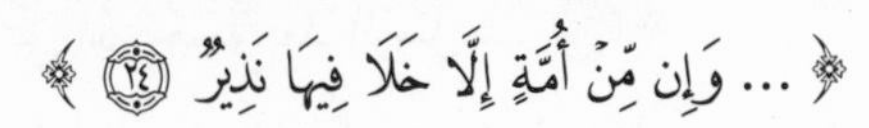

﴾...And there never was a nation but a warner had passed among them.﴿ *(Qur'an 35: 24)*

Hence we do not know the names of all the Messengers who were sent by Allah (ﷻ):

﴿ وَلَقَدْ أَرْسَلْنَا رُسُلًا مِّن قَبْلِكَ مِنْهُم مَّن قَصَصْنَا عَلَيْكَ وَمِنْهُم مَّن لَّمْ نَقْصُصْ عَلَيْكَ ... ﴾ (٧٨)

﴾And, indeed We have sent Messengers before you [O' Muhammad], of some of them We have related to you their story. And of some We have not related to you their story,...﴿ *(Qur'an 40: 78)*

One of the proofs of that is the fact that on the Day of Resurrection, the disbelieving nations will affirm and acknowledge that the Messengers conveyed the call of Allah to them. Allah (ﷻ) says:

﴿ ... كُلَّمَآ أُلْقِيَ فِيهَا فَوْجٌ سَأَلَهُمْ خَزَنَتُهَآ أَلَمْ يَأْتِكُمْ نَذِيرٌ (٨) قَالُوا۟ بَلَىٰ قَدْ جَآءَنَا نَذِيرٌ فَكَذَّبْنَا وَقُلْنَا مَا نَزَّلَ ٱللَّهُ مِن شَىْءٍ إِنْ أَنتُمْ إِلَّا فِى ضَلَٰلٍ كَبِيرٍ (٩) ﴾

﴾...Every time a group is cast therein, its keeper will ask: 'Did no warner come to you?' They will say: 'Yes, indeed a warner did come to us, but we belied him and said: Allah never sent down anything [of Revelation]; you are only in great error.'﴿ *(Qur'an 67: 8-9)*

This succession of Messengers sent throughout history was no more than a mercy from Allah (ﷻ) to His slaves, the fulfilment of His promise to Adam (عليه السلام), the father of humanity, leaving His creation with no excuse:

﴿ ... لِئَلَّا يَكُونَ لِلنَّاسِ عَلَى ٱللَّهِ حُجَّةٌۢ بَعْدَ ٱلرُّسُلِ ... ﴾ (١٦٥)

﴾...In order that mankind should have no plea against

Allah after the [coming of] Messengers...﴾
(Qur'an 4: 165)

﴿ ... وَمَا كُنَّا مُعَذِّبِينَ حَتَّىٰ نَبْعَثَ رَسُولًا ﴿١٥﴾ ﴾

﴾...And We never punish until We have sent a Messenger [to give warning].﴾ *(Qur'an 17: 15)*

iii) The call of the Messengers is one, and the basis and heart of the call of all of them is *Tawḥeed*, to tell mankind of their Lord and God, and to show them the way to worship Him.

iv) The religion of all the Messengers was Islam and they had no other religion:

﴿ وَمَن يَبْتَغِ غَيْرَ ٱلْإِسْلَٰمِ دِينًا فَلَن يُقْبَلَ مِنْهُ وَهُوَ فِى ٱلْءَاخِرَةِ مِنَ ٱلْخَٰسِرِينَ ﴿٨٥﴾ ﴾

﴾And whoever seeks a religion other than Islam, it will never be accepted of him, and in the Hereafter he will be one of the losers.﴾ *(Qur'an 3: 85)*

﴿ ... وَأُمِرْتُ أَنْ أَكُونَ مِنَ ٱلْمُسْلِمِينَ ﴿٧٢﴾ ﴾

﴾[Nooḥ (Noah) said]: ...and I have been commanded to be of the Muslims [i.e. those who submit to Allah's Will].﴾ *(Qur'an 10: 72).*

Allah (ﷻ) said concerning the *Tawraat* (Torah):

﴿ ... يَحْكُمُ بِهَا ٱلنَّبِيُّونَ ٱلَّذِينَ أَسْلَمُوا۟ لِلَّذِينَ هَادُوا۟ ... ﴿٤٤﴾ ﴾

﴾...By which the Prophets, who submitted themselves to Allah's Will, judged for the Jews...﴾ *(Qur'an 5: 44)*

Moosa (Moses) (عليه السلام) said to his people:

﴿ ... إِن كُنتُمْ ءَامَنتُم بِٱللَّهِ فَعَلَيْهِ تَوَكَّلُوٓا۟ إِن كُنتُم مُّسْلِمِينَ ﴿٨٤﴾ ﴾

﴾...If you have believed in Allah, then put your trust in Him if you are Muslims [those who submit to Allah's Will].﴿ *(Qur'an 10: 84)*

Allah (ﷻ) enjoined Islam upon His Close Friend (*Khaleel*) Ibraaheem (Abraham) (عليه السلام), who said:

﴿... أَسْلَمْتُ لِرَبِّ ٱلْعَٰلَمِينَ ﴿١٣١﴾﴾

﴾...I have submitted myself [as a Muslim] to the Lord of the *'Aalameen* [mankind, jinn and all that exists].﴿ *(Qur'an 2: 131)*

﴿وَوَصَّىٰ بِهَآ إِبْرَٰهِـۧمُ بَنِيهِ وَيَعْقُوبُ يَٰبَنِىَّ إِنَّ ٱللَّهَ ٱصْطَفَىٰ لَكُمُ ٱلدِّينَ فَلَا تَمُوتُنَّ إِلَّا وَأَنتُم مُّسْلِمُونَ ﴿١٣٢﴾﴾

﴾And this [submission to Allah, Islam] was enjoined by Ibraaheem upon his sons and by Ya'qoob [Jacob] [saying], 'O' my sons! Allah has chosen for you the [true] religion, then die not except in the Faith of Islam [as Muslims - Islamic Monotheism].'﴿ *(Qur'an 2: 132)*

When Ya'qoob (Jacob) (عليه السلام) asked his sons who they would worship after he died,

﴿... قَالُوا۟ نَعْبُدُ إِلَٰهَكَ وَإِلَٰهَ ءَابَآئِكَ إِبْرَٰهِـۧمَ وَإِسْمَٰعِيلَ وَإِسْحَٰقَ إِلَٰهًا وَٰحِدًا وَنَحْنُ لَهُۥ مُسْلِمُونَ ﴿١٣٣﴾﴾

﴾...They said, 'We shall worship your *Ilaah* [God - Allah] the *Ilaah* [God] of your fathers, Ibraaheem [Abraham], Ismaa'eel [Ishmael], Isḥaaq [Isaac], One *Ilaah* [God], and to Him we submit [in Islam].﴿ *(Qur'an 2: 133)*

And Queen of Sheba said:

﴿... قَالَتْ رَبِّ إِنِّي ظَلَمْتُ نَفْسِي وَأَسْلَمْتُ مَعَ سُلَيْمَانَ لِلَّهِ رَبِّ الْعَالَمِينَ ﴿٤٤﴾﴾

﴾[The queen of Saba' (Sheba) said]: ...'My Lord! Verily, I have wronged myself, and I submit [in Islam, together with Sulaymaan (Solomon)] to Allah, the Lord of the *'Aalameen* [mankind, jinn and all that exists].'﴿ *(Qur'an 27: 44)*

Yusuf (Joseph) (عليه السلام) used to say in his *du'aa'*:

﴿... تَوَفَّنِي مُسْلِمًا وَأَلْحِقْنِي بِالصَّالِحِينَ ﴿١٠١﴾﴾

﴾...Cause me to die as a Muslim [the one submitting to Your Will], and join me with the righteous.﴿ *(Qur'an 12: 101)*

The Messenger (ﷺ) said:

"The Prophets are brothers, their mothers are different but their religion is one."[9]

The variations that we see in their laws does not indicate that their religion varied, because Allah may legislate something for a reason, then legislate something else at another time for another reason. Indeed, this may occur in one shari'ah, as at the beginning Allah decreed that the Muslims should face *Bayt al-Maqdis* (*Al-Quds* - Jerusalem) when praying, then this was abrogated by the command to face *Al-Bayt al-Ḥaraam* (the Sacred House - the Ka'bah in Makkah). At first Islam faced towards *Al-Quds*, then its focal point changed to the Ka'bah. The same applies to all the laws of the Prophets: what came later abrogates what came before. The shari'ah which was revealed to Muhammad (ﷺ) is the final shari'ah which abrogates all laws that came before it.

---

[9] Bukhari, 6/478, hadith no. 3443.

v) The development of religious beliefs throughout the centuries is not the reason for *shirk* and the adoption of gods other than Allah, as *Al-'Aqqaad* and the westerners whom he follows suggest. The reason for that was the deviation of the followers of the Messengers from the Message which the Messengers brought, and their abandonment of that Message.

﴿ وَمَنْ أَعْرَضَ عَن ذِكْرِى فَإِنَّ لَهُۥ مَعِيشَةً ضَنكًا ... ﴿١٢٤﴾ ﴾

﴾But whosoever turns away from My Reminder [i.e. neither believes in this Qur'an nor acts on its teachings] verily, for him is a life of hardship,...﴿ *(Qur'an 20: 124)*

And they followed their own conjectures and desires, ignoring true guidance:

﴿ ... إِن يَتَّبِعُونَ إِلَّا ٱلظَّنَّ وَمَا تَهْوَى ٱلْأَنفُسُ ۖ وَلَقَدْ جَآءَهُم مِّن رَّبِّهِمُ ٱلْهُدَىٰٓ ﴿٢٣﴾ ﴾

﴾...They follow but a guess and that which they themselves desire, whereas there has surely, come to them the guidance from their Lord!﴿ *(Qur'an 53: 23)*

﴿ ... وَلَا تَتَّبِعُوٓا۟ أَهْوَآءَ قَوْمٍ قَدْ ضَلُّوا۟ مِن قَبْلُ وَأَضَلُّوا۟ كَثِيرًا وَضَلُّوا۟ عَن سَوَآءِ ٱلسَّبِيلِ ﴿٧٧﴾ ﴾

﴾...And do not follow the vain desires of people who went astray before and who misled many, and strayed [themselves] from the Right Path.﴿ *(Qur'an 5: 77)*

Allah (ﷻ) says concerning the Jews:

﴿ فَبِمَا نَقْضِهِم مِّيثَٰقَهُمْ لَعَنَّٰهُمْ وَجَعَلْنَا قُلُوبَهُمْ قَٰسِيَةً ۖ يُحَرِّفُونَ ٱلْكَلِمَ عَن مَّوَاضِعِهِۦ ۙ وَنَسُوا۟ حَظًّا مِّمَّا ذُكِّرُوا۟ بِهِۦ ۚ ... ﴿١٣﴾ ﴾

﴿So, because of their breach of their covenant, We cursed them and made their hearts grow hard. They change the words from their [right] places and have abandoned a good part of the Message that was sent to them...﴾ *(Qur'an 5: 13)*

And He (ﷻ) says concerning the Christians:

﴿ وَمِنَ ٱلَّذِينَ قَالُوٓاْ إِنَّا نَصَٰرَىٰٓ أَخَذْنَا مِيثَٰقَهُمْ فَنَسُواْ حَظًّا مِّمَّا ذُكِّرُواْ بِهِۦ فَأَغْرَيْنَا بَيْنَهُمُ ٱلْعَدَاوَةَ وَٱلْبَغْضَآءَ إِلَىٰ يَوْمِ ٱلْقِيَٰمَةِۚ... ﴿١٤﴾ ﴾

﴿And from those who call themselves Christians, We took their covenant, but they have abandoned a good part of the Message that was sent to them. So We planted amongst them enmity and hatred till the Day of Resurrection;...﴾ *(Qur'an 5: 14)*

And He (ﷻ), says, explaining their deviation from the *Tawḥeed* which was enjoined upon them:

﴿ ٱتَّخَذُوٓاْ أَحْبَارَهُمْ وَرُهْبَٰنَهُمْ أَرْبَابًا مِّن دُونِ ٱللَّهِ وَٱلْمَسِيحَ ٱبْنَ مَرْيَمَ وَمَآ أُمِرُوٓاْ إِلَّا لِيَعْبُدُوٓاْ إِلَٰهًا وَٰحِدًاۖ لَّآ إِلَٰهَ إِلَّا هُوَۚ سُبْحَٰنَهُۥ عَمَّا يُشْرِكُونَ ﴿٣١﴾ ﴾

﴿They [Jews and Christians] took their rabbis and their monks to be their lords besides Allah [by obeying them in things which they made lawful or unlawful according to their own desires without being ordered by Allah], and [they also took as their Lord] Messiaḥ, son of Maryam [Mary], while they [Jews and Christians] were commanded [in the *Tawraat* (Torah) and the *Injeel* (Gospel)] to worship none but One *Ilaah* [God - Allah] *Laa ilaaha illa Huwa* [none has the right to be worshipped but He]. Praise and glory be to Him [far above is He] from having the partners they associate [with Him].﴾ *(Qur'an 9: 31)*

Hence the Messengers will disown those who deviated from their path:

﴿ وَإِذْ قَالَ ٱللَّهُ يَٰعِيسَى ٱبْنَ مَرْيَمَ ءَأَنتَ قُلْتَ لِلنَّاسِ ٱتَّخِذُونِي وَأُمِّيَ إِلَٰهَيْنِ مِن دُونِ ٱللَّهِ ۖ قَالَ سُبْحَٰنَكَ مَا يَكُونُ لِيٓ أَنْ أَقُولَ مَا لَيْسَ لِي بِحَقٍّ ۚ إِن كُنتُ قُلْتُهُۥ فَقَدْ عَلِمْتَهُۥ ۚ تَعْلَمُ مَا فِي نَفْسِي وَلَآ أَعْلَمُ مَا فِي نَفْسِكَ ۚ إِنَّكَ أَنتَ عَلَّٰمُ ٱلْغُيُوبِ ﴿١١٦﴾ مَا قُلْتُ لَهُمْ إِلَّا مَآ أَمَرْتَنِي بِهِۦٓ أَنِ ٱعْبُدُوا۟ ٱللَّهَ رَبِّي وَرَبَّكُمْ ۚ ... ﴿١١٧﴾ ﴾

﴾And [remember] when Allah will say [on the Day of Resurrection]: 'O' 'Eesa [Jesus], son of Maryam [Mary]! Did you say unto men: Worship me and my mother as two gods besides Allah?' He will say: 'Glory be to You! It was not for me to say what I had no right [to say]. Had I said such a thing, You would surely have known it. You know what is in my inner-self though I do not know what is in Yours; truly, You, only You, are the All-Knower of all that is hidden [and unseen]. Never did I say to them aught except what You [Allah] did command me to say: 'Worship Allah, my Lord and your Lord.'...'﴾ *(Qur'an 5: 116-117)*

CHAPTER FIVE
CONCEPTS OF GOD AMONG THE MISGUIDED NATIONS

This study is not meant to be a complete history of deviation in religious beliefs. This is impossible, because there are so many varieties of deviation, and what would be the point of such a history when wrongdoing and *kufr* (disbelief) are all of the same nature? Our purpose here is to learn something about the errors into which other nations have fallen, so that we may properly appreciate the tremendous value by which the Islamic *'aqeedah* is distinguished.

Those who understand and recognize falsehood will adhere more strongly to the truth when they follow it. There is the fear that those who follow Islam and do not know about its opposite, which is falsehood, may slip and follow the paths of falsehood. 'Umar ibn al-Khaṭṭab (رضي الله عنه) spoke the truth when he said: "Soon the bonds of Islam will be undone one by one, when there will be people brought up in Islam will know nothing of *Jaahiliyah*." Undoubtedly the one who knows the darkness of night is more able to appreciate the light of day, and good health is the crown on the heads of the healthy, which none acknowledges except those who are sick.

Sayyid Quṭb understood this when he said: "Man cannot know the necessity of this message (Islam), the necessity of freeing himself from the misguided ways in the darkness of which mankind is wandering, the necessity of steadfast, clear certainty in matters of *'aqeedah*... until he has seen the vast extent of that misguidance, until he has wandered in that confusion of beliefs and concepts, philosophies and fables, thoughts and illusions, rituals and traditions, situations and circumstances, which Islam came and found controlling the human consciousness in all places; until he has understood the nature of the jumbled confusion, complexity and human additions that have affected what is left of the heavenly religions, which have become mixed with philosophy, idolatry and fables."

Three examples will suffice us here: first, the beliefs of one of the nations which people regard as one of the civilized nations of ancient times; the second is the deviation of the followers of a heavenly religion from the truth; and the third is the idolatry of the Arabs before the time of the Messenger (ﷺ).

1 - GOD ACCORDING TO THE GREEKS [1]

Researchers consider the Greeks to be one of the civilized nations of the past, so let us look at the religious beliefs of this misguided nation. They claimed that "Zeus" was the chief of their gods. Their image of him was closer to the image of a devil than of a god. He was filled with hatred and enmity, preoccupied with his desires for food and love. He cared nothing for the affairs of gods or men, unless they could help him maintain his hold on power and persist in his tyranny. He got angry with Asclepius, the god of medicine, because he treated the sick, thus depriving Zeus of the taxes on the souls of the dead who moved from the face of the earth to the Underworld.

They claim that he got angry with Prometheus, the god of knowledge and handicrafts, because he taught man how to use fire for manufacturing purposes, and thus man learned how to use power to combat the power of the gods. He ruled that he should be subjected to eternal punishment; he was not content merely to kill him and remove him from the arena of the gods. He sought to invent different ways of punishing him. So he tied him to a remote mountain and sent vultures to eat his liver all day long; when night came his liver was

---

[1] *Haqaa'iq al-Islam wa Abaaṭeel Khuṣoomihi.*

restored in his body, so that the vultures could come back and eat it after the sun came up... this punishment continued, and all intercession and prayers were of no avail.

One of the reasons which the Greek philosopher-poet Hesiod came up with for the god's anger against Prometheus was that the latter had given him a share of food at a banquet of the gods, and he had included too many bones in it, and not enough meat and fat. Zeus thought that Prometheus was trying to act superior, because he was famous among the gods for his vast knowledge and intelligence, for which the great god was not known.

Hesiod, the philosopher-poet, tried his best to exalt Zeus and to give the people an image of him as holy and mighty, as would befit the image of a god after the development of the concept of worship in the ancient Greek religion.

Further, Greek scholars speak of Zeus as having betrayed his wife Hera, as he used to send the god of love to conceal the sun as it rose, lest his jealous wife should come and catch him unawares among his lovers at the throne of Olympus.

It is said that on one occasion she did catch him unawares as he was kissing his drink-bearer Ganymede, the beautiful shepherd whom he had once seen in the fields, so he had kidnapped him and brought him up to heaven. Zeus did not try to conceal his love for his drink-bearer, and he justified his behaviour to his wife by saying that she knew nothing of the delights of the meeting between the nectar of the cup and the nectar of the lips.

This is an example of the misguided beliefs of *shirk* which are produced by myths and illusions, which become fables. The gods of the Greeks were many, who fought with one another and punished one another. Like humans, they ate and drank, and got married. A god might betray his wife, commit sodomy and justify his bad behaviour. What kind of effect would such beliefs have on those who believed in them? What effect would they have on individuals and societies? What values would be affirmed by such deviant, misguided beliefs in *shirk*?

2 - GOD ACCORDING TO THE JEWS [2]

The religion of the Children of Israel — Judaism — is full of both idolatrous concepts and tribalistic hallucinations. Many Messengers came to the Children of Israel — Ya'qoob (Jacob) ibn Isḥaaq (Isaac) ibn Ibraaheem (Abraham) (peace be upon them) — the first of whom was Israa'eel (Israel), bringing the message of pure *Tawḥeed* (Oneness of Allah) which their father Ibraaheem (Abraham) had taught them. Then their greatest Prophet, Moosa (Moses), came to them with the same message of *Tawḥeed*, on which the Mosaic Law was based. But they deviated with the passage of time, and went down to the level of idolatrous concepts which they affirmed in their "holy" books. In the midst of the Torah there are fables and concepts of God which are no higher than the idolatrous concepts of the Greeks and other idolatrous nations who did not receive heavenly guidance and who had no book from Allah.

The belief in *Tawḥeed* which Allah revealed to Ibraaheem (Abraham) (Peace be upon him) was a complete, integrated, clear and pure belief with which he confronted idolatry in a most decisive manner, as the Qur'an describes. Ibraaheem enjoined this belief upon his sons just as Ya'qoob (Jacob) (Peace be upon him) enjoined it upon his sons before he died:

﴿ وَٱتْلُ عَلَيْهِمْ نَبَأَ إِبْرَٰهِيمَ ﴿٦٩﴾ إِذْ قَالَ لِأَبِيهِ وَقَوْمِهِۦ مَا تَعْبُدُونَ ﴿٧٠﴾
قَالُوا۟ نَعْبُدُ أَصْنَامًا فَنَظَلُّ لَهَا عَٰكِفِينَ ﴿٧١﴾ قَالَ هَلْ يَسْمَعُونَكُمْ إِذْ تَدْعُونَ

[2] Adapted from *Khaṣaa'iṣ at-Taṣawwur al-Islami*, by Sayyid Quṭb, Pp. 11.

﴿٧٢﴾ أَوْ يَنفَعُونَكُمْ أَوْ يَضُرُّونَ ﴿٧٣﴾ قَالُوا۟ بَلْ وَجَدْنَآ ءَابَآءَنَا كَذَٰلِكَ يَفْعَلُونَ
﴿٧٤﴾ قَالَ أَفَرَءَيْتُم مَّا كُنتُمْ تَعْبُدُونَ ﴿٧٥﴾ أَنتُمْ وَءَابَآؤُكُمُ ٱلْأَقْدَمُونَ ﴿٧٦﴾
فَإِنَّهُمْ عَدُوٌّ لِّىٓ إِلَّا رَبَّ ٱلْعَٰلَمِينَ ﴿٧٧﴾ ٱلَّذِى خَلَقَنِى فَهُوَ يَهْدِينِ ﴿٧٨﴾ وَٱلَّذِى
هُوَ يُطْعِمُنِى وَيَسْقِينِ ﴿٧٩﴾ وَإِذَا مَرِضْتُ فَهُوَ يَشْفِينِ ﴿٨٠﴾ وَٱلَّذِى يُمِيتُنِى
ثُمَّ يُحْيِينِ ﴿٨١﴾ وَٱلَّذِىٓ أَطْمَعُ أَن يَغْفِرَ لِى خَطِيٓـَٔتِى يَوْمَ ٱلدِّينِ ﴿٨٢﴾ رَبِّ
هَبْ لِى حُكْمًا وَأَلْحِقْنِى بِٱلصَّٰلِحِينَ ﴿٨٣﴾ وَٱجْعَل لِّى لِسَانَ صِدْقٍ فِى
ٱلْءَاخِرِينَ ﴿٨٤﴾ ﴾

﴾And recite to them the story of Ibraaheem [Abraham]. When he said to his father and his people: 'What do you worship?' They said: 'We worship idols, and to them we are ever devoted.' He said: 'Do they hear you, when you call on [them]? Or do they benefit you or do they harm [you]?' They said: '[Nay] but we found our fathers doing so.' He said: 'Do you observe that which you have been worshipping - You and your ancient fathers? Verily, they are enemies to me, save the Lord of the *'Aalameen* [mankind, jinn and all that exists], Who has created me, and it is He Who guides me. And it is He Who feeds me and gives me to drink. And when I am ill, it is He Who cures me. And Who will cause me to die, and then will bring me to life [again]. And Who, I hope, will forgive me my faults on the Day of Recompense [the Day of Resurrection]. My Lord! Bestow *Ḥukm* [religious knowledge, right judgement of the affairs and Prophethood] on me, and join me with the righteous. And grant me an honourable mention in later generations.'﴿ *(Qur'an 26: 69-84)*

﴿ وَمَن يَرْغَبُ عَن مِّلَّةِ إِبْرَٰهِۦمَ إِلَّا مَن سَفِهَ نَفْسَهُۥ ۚ وَلَقَدِ ٱصْطَفَيْنَٰهُ فِى
ٱلدُّنْيَا ۖ وَإِنَّهُۥ فِى ٱلْءَاخِرَةِ لَمِنَ ٱلصَّٰلِحِينَ ﴿١٣٠﴾ إِذْ قَالَ لَهُۥ رَبُّهُۥٓ أَسْلِمْ ۖ قَالَ

أَسْلَمْتُ لِرَبِّ ٱلْعَٰلَمِينَ ﴿١٣١﴾ وَوَصَّىٰ بِهَآ إِبْرَٰهِـۧمُ بَنِيهِ وَيَعْقُوبُ يَٰبَنِىَّ إِنَّ
ٱللَّهَ ٱصْطَفَىٰ لَكُمُ ٱلدِّينَ فَلَا تَمُوتُنَّ إِلَّا وَأَنتُم مُّسْلِمُونَ ﴿١٣٢﴾ أَمْ كُنتُمْ
شُهَدَآءَ إِذْ حَضَرَ يَعْقُوبَ ٱلْمَوْتُ إِذْ قَالَ لِبَنِيهِ مَا تَعْبُدُونَ مِنۢ بَعْدِى
قَالُوا۟ نَعْبُدُ إِلَٰهَكَ وَإِلَٰهَ ءَابَآئِكَ إِبْرَٰهِـۧمَ وَإِسْمَٰعِيلَ وَإِسْحَٰقَ إِلَٰهًا وَٰحِدًا
وَنَحْنُ لَهُۥ مُسْلِمُونَ ﴿١٣٣﴾ ﴾

﴿And who turns away from the religion of Ibraaheem [Abraham] [i.e. Islamic Monotheism] except him who befools himself? Truly, We chose him in this world and verily, in the Hereafter he will be among the righteous. When his Lord said to him, 'Submit [i.e. be a Muslim]!' He said, 'I have submitted myself [as a Muslim] to the Lord of the *'Aalameen* [mankind, jinn and all that exists].' And this [submission to Allah, Islam] was enjoined by Ibraaheem [Abraham] upon his sons and by Ya'qoob [Jacob] [saying], 'O' my sons! Allah has chosen for you the [true] religion, then die not except in the Faith of Islam [as Muslims - Islamic Monotheism].' Or were you witnesses when death approached Ya'qoob? When he said unto his sons, 'What will you worship after me?' They said, 'We shall worship your *Ilaah* [God - Allah] the *Ilaah* [God] of your fathers, Ibraaheem, Ismaa'eel [Ishmael], Isḥaaq [Isaac], One *Ilaah* [God], and to Him we submit [in Islam].'﴾

(Qur'an 2: 130-133)

They turned away from this pure *Tawḥeed* (Oneness of Allah), this clear faith and this belief in the Hereafter, and remained in their state of deviation until Moosa (Moses) came to them with the renewed Message of *Tawḥeed* and Divine transcendence. But they did not adhere to it; rather they strayed from it.

Their deviation began whilst Moosa (Moses) (ﷺ) was still among them, when they worshipped the calf which As-Saamiri made for them from the gold jewellery of the Egyptian women which they had brought with them:

﴿ قَالُوا۟ مَآ أَخْلَفْنَا مَوْعِدَكَ بِمَلْكِنَا وَلَـٰكِنَّا حُمِّلْنَآ أَوْزَارًا مِّن زِينَةِ ٱلْقَوْمِ فَقَذَفْنَـٰهَا فَكَذَٰلِكَ أَلْقَى ٱلسَّامِرِىُّ ﴿٨٧﴾ فَأَخْرَجَ لَهُمْ عِجْلًا جَسَدًا لَّهُۥ خُوَارٌ فَقَالُوا۟ هَـٰذَآ إِلَـٰهُكُمْ وَإِلَـٰهُ مُوسَىٰ فَنَسِىَ ﴿٨٨﴾ ﴾

﴾They said: 'We broke not the promise to you, of our own will, but we were made to carry the weight of the ornaments of the [Pharaoh's] people, then we cast them [into the fire], and that was what As-Saamiri suggested.' Then he took out [of the fire] for them [a statue of] a calf which seemed to low. They said: 'This is your *ilaah* [god], and the *ilaah* [god] of Moosa [Moses], but he [Moosa] has forgotten [his god].'﴿ *(Qur'an 20: 87-88)*

Before that, they had asked Moosa (Moses) to set up an idol for them to worship:

﴿ وَجَـٰوَزْنَا بِبَنِىٓ إِسْرَٰٓءِيلَ ٱلْبَحْرَ فَأَتَوْا۟ عَلَىٰ قَوْمٍ يَعْكُفُونَ عَلَىٰٓ أَصْنَامٍ لَّهُمْ ۚ قَالُوا۟ يَـٰمُوسَى ٱجْعَل لَّنَآ إِلَـٰهًا كَمَا لَهُمْ ءَالِهَةٌ ۚ قَالَ إِنَّكُمْ قَوْمٌ تَجْهَلُونَ ﴿١٣٨﴾ ﴾

﴾And We brought the Children of Israel [with safety] across the sea, and they came upon a people devoted to some of their idols [in worship]. They said: 'O' Moosa [Moses]! Make for us an *ilaah* [a god] as they have *aalihah* [gods].' He said: 'Verily, you are a people who know not [the Majesty and Greatness of Allah and what is obligatory upon you, i.e. to worship none but Allah Alone, the One and the Only God of all that exists].'﴿
(Qur'an 7: 138)

The Qur'an speaks at length about their deviation and false concepts of Allah — Glorified be He — and their *shirk* and idolatry. They attributed a son to Allah —

﴿ وَقَالَتِ ٱلْيَهُودُ عُزَيْرٌ ٱبْنُ ٱللَّهِ ... ﴿٣٠﴾ ﴾

﴾And the Jews say: 'Uzair [Ezra] is the son of Allah...'﴿
(Qur'an 9: 30)

— and they accused Him (Allah) — Glorified be He — of miserliness and poverty:

﴿ وَقَالَتِ ٱلْيَهُودُ يَدُ ٱللَّهِ مَغْلُولَةٌ ۚ غُلَّتْ أَيْدِيهِمْ وَلُعِنُوا۟ بِمَا قَالُوا۟ ۘ بَلْ يَدَاهُ مَبْسُوطَتَانِ يُنفِقُ كَيْفَ يَشَآءُ ... ﴿٦٤﴾ ﴾

﴾The Jews say: 'Allah's Hand is tied up [i.e. He does not give and spend of His Bounty].' Be their hands tied up and be they accursed for what they uttered. Nay, both His Hands are widely outstretched. He spends [of His Bounty] as He wills...﴿ *(Qur'an 5: 64)*

﴿ لَّقَدْ سَمِعَ ٱللَّهُ قَوْلَ ٱلَّذِينَ قَالُوٓا۟ إِنَّ ٱللَّهَ فَقِيرٌ وَنَحْنُ أَغْنِيَآءُ ۘ سَنَكْتُبُ مَا قَالُوا۟ وَقَتْلَهُمُ ٱلْأَنۢبِيَآءَ بِغَيْرِ حَقٍّ ... ﴿١٨١﴾ ﴾

﴾Indeed, Allah has heard the statement of those [Jews] who say: 'Truly, Allah is poor and we are rich!' We shall record what they have said and their killing of the Prophets unjustly...﴿ *(Qur'an 3: 181)*

An example of their tribalistic belief is the notion that their god is a tribal deity who does not judge them by laws of ethics except in their dealing with one another; but when it comes to "strangers" (non-Jews), they will not be brought to account for shameful behaviour towards them.

Another example of their tribalistic attitude was narrated by the Qur'an:

﴿ ۞ وَمِنْ أَهْلِ ٱلْكِتَـٰبِ مَنْ إِن تَأْمَنْهُ بِقِنطَارٍ يُؤَدِّهِۦٓ إِلَيْكَ وَمِنْهُم مَّنْ إِن تَأْمَنْهُ بِدِينَارٍ لَّا يُؤَدِّهِۦٓ إِلَيْكَ إِلَّا مَا دُمْتَ عَلَيْهِ قَآئِمًا ۗ ذَٰلِكَ بِأَنَّهُمْ قَالُوا۟ لَيْسَ عَلَيْنَا فِى ٱلْأُمِّيِّـۧنَ سَبِيلٌ وَيَقُولُونَ عَلَى ٱللَّهِ ٱلْكَذِبَ وَهُمْ يَعْلَمُونَ ﴿٧٥﴾ ﴾

﴾Among the people of the Scripture [Jews and Christians] is he who, if entrusted with a *Qinṭaar* [a great amount of wealth], will readily pay it back; and among them there is he who, if entrusted with a single silver coin, will not repay it unless you constantly stand demanding, because they say: 'There is no blame on us to betray and take the properties of the illiterates [Arabs].' But they tell a lie against Allah while they know it.﴿ *(Qur'an 3: 75)*

Their distorted books contain descriptions of their God which are not much better than the Greeks' descriptions of their idols.

In the third chapter of the Book of Genesis it says:

After Adam committed the sin of eating from the tree (which, as it says in this chapter, was the tree of the knowledge of good and evil), they "heard the sound of the Lord God as he was walking in the garden in the cool of the day. So Adam and his wife hid from the face of the Lord God in the midst of the Garden. The Lord God called out to Adam, saying 'Where are you?' He answered, 'I heard you in the garden, and I was afraid because I was naked, so I hid.' And he said, 'Who told you that you were naked? Have you eaten from the tree that I commanded you not to eat from?...'

And the Lord God said: 'The man has now become like one of us, knowing good and evil. He must not be allowed to reach out his hand

and take also from the tree of life and eat, and live for ever.' So the Lord God banished him from the Garden of Eden to work on the ground from which he had been taken. After he drove the man out, he placed on the east side of the Garden of Eden cherubim and a flaming sword flashing back and forth, to guard the way to the tree of life."[3]

This passage describes God as ignorant, for He does not know where Adam is until he tells Him, and He is walking about as humans walk about. The reason for Adam's expulsion from the Garden is not his disobedience towards his Lord as the Qur'an states, it is because God is afraid that man may eat from the tree of life and thus become immortal! God did not teach man the difference between good and evil, he only learned that after he ate from the tree. All of this is a lie and a fabrication against Allah, may He be Glorified and Exalted.

From what they say it may be understood that the never-ending life of Allah came about only because He ate from the tree of life — Exalted be He above what they say.

Just as they attributed ignorance to God, they also attributed to Him sorrow and regret for what He had done. They say that He regretted creating man because of his great evil and mischief at the time of Nooḥ (Noah):

"The Lord saw how great man's wickedness on earth had become, and that every inclination of the thoughts of his heart was only evil all the time. The Lord was grieved that he had made man on earth, and his heart was filled with pain. So the Lord said: 'I will wipe mankind, whom I have created, from the face of the earth — men and animals, creatures that move along the ground and birds of the air — for I am grieved that I have made them,' But Noah found favour in the eyes of the Lord."[4]

---

[3] Genesis 3:8-11, 22-24 (New International Version) [Translator].

[4] Genesis 6:5-8 (New International Version) [Translator].

Listen to this myth which is narrated in the eleventh chapter of the Book of Genesis:

After the land had been populated by the progeny of Nooḥ (Noah), "the whole world had one language and a common speech. As men moved eastwards, they found a plain in Shinar and settled there. They said to each other, 'Come, let us make bricks and bake them thoroughly.' They used brick instead of stone and tar instead of mortar. Then they said, 'Come, let us build ourselves a city, with a tower that reaches to the heavens, so that we may make a name for ourselves and not be scattered over the face of the whole earth.'

But the Lord came down to see the city and the tower that the men were building. The Lord said, 'If as one people speaking the same language they have begun to do this, then nothing they plan will be impossible for them. Come, let us go down and confuse their language so they will not understand each other.' So the Lord scattered them from there over all the earth, and they stopped building the city. That is why it was called Babel - because there the Lord confused the language of the whole world. From there the Lord scattered them over the face of the whole earth."[5]

What kind of myth is this that falsifies the truth and almost wipes out its features! What kind of God is this portrayed in this myth? This God who fears humans and is afraid of their coming together, so He fights them before they can unite and become strong, and He scatters them throughout the world after confusing their languages.

The Jews attribute evil actions to God, as well as regret for what He has done.

In the Second Book of Samuel, in the twenty-fourth chapter, it says:

---

[5] Genesis 11:1-9 (New International Version) [Translator].

"So the Lord sent a plague on Israel from that morning until the end of the time designated, and seventy thousand of the people from Dan to Beersheba died. When the angel stretched out his hand to destroy Jerusalem, the Lord was grieved because of the calamity and said to the angel who was afflicting the people, 'Enough! Withdraw your hand.'"[6]

Now let us turn from what the Qur'an says about the misguided descriptions that the Jews gave of their Lord, and the distortions and falsifications in the Torah, and look at the *Talmud*, which is the book written by the Jewish scholars and rabbis. For the Jews, this book is even more important than the Torah. If we look at the *Talmud*, we will be stunned by the misguidance into which the Jews have fallen, not only in the matter of religious belief, but in all aspects of the Law.

It is sufficient here to quote only from the book *Al-Kanz al-Marṣood fi Qawaa'id at-Talmud* concerning what the *Talmud* says about the Divine power. For example, they say that God needs to read and learn, and that He jokes and plays. It is said in their *Talmud* that "the day has twelve hours. During the first three, (God) sits and studies the Law. During the second three, He passes judgements. During the third three He feeds (His creatures). And during the last three He sits and plays with a whale, the king of the fish."

Listen to something even worse than that: "God has no other work to do except learning the *Talmud* with the angels." And not only the angels, but also with "Asmodeus" the chief of the demons, in the school of heaven!

What is this whale with which the Lord plays? It is a very big whale, through whose throat a fish three parasangs long (i.e., nine hundred miles) could pass without bothering it. Because it is so huge, God is

---

[6] 2 Samuel 24: 15-16 (New International Version) [Translator].

afraid that if it were to produce offspring, it would destroy the world, so He decided to keep it from its mate, because if He did not do that, they would fill the world and destroy everyone in it. Hence God detained the male by His divine strength, and He killed the female, salted it and prepared it to feed the believers in Paradise.

To these myths which have become part of their religious beliefs, they added the notion that "God did not play with the whale after the destruction of the Temple, and after the destruction of the Temple He did not like to dance with Eve, after He adorned her with clothes and tied up her hair."

May they perish and be doomed! They are saying the same things as those who disbelieved before them, the misguided *mushrik* (Polythiest) nations. According to their beliefs, their god is no different to a human being; He thinks like they do, acts like they do, plays, dances, feels grief, and weeps - for what? For sorrow at the destruction of the Temple of the Jews which Sulaymaan had built for them.

The Temple is a symbol of the glory of the Jews. From the time when the Temple was destroyed, until the present day, the Jews say that God weeps for three-quarters of the night, roaring like a lion and saying, "May I perish! For I have allowed My house to be destroyed and the Temple to be burned, and My children to be scattered."

They go to extremes in their distortions and lies. They say that the essence of God became less — exalted be He far above what they say — because of His grief over the destruction of the Temple. "God filled the space of four heavens after He had filled the heavens and the earth at all times."

They describe the Most High, Most Majestic, as humbling Himself when His servants — by which they mean the Jews, of course — praise Him. "When the Creator hears the people glorifying Him, He bows His head and says. 'How happy is the king when he is praised at the time when he deserves that, but the father who leaves his children in misery does not deserve any praise.'"

﴿... قَـٰتَلَهُمُ ٱللَّهُ أَنَّىٰ يُؤْفَكُونَ ﴿٣٠﴾﴾

﴿...Allah's Curse be on them, how they are deluded away from the truth!﴾ *(Qur'an 9: 30)*

Another of the lies which they have fabricated against the Lord of Glory - glorified and sanctified be He above what they say - is that He strikes His cheeks and weeps, and His tears flow down, all because of the misery of the Jews and what has happened to them: "God regrets leaving the Jews in their miserable state, so much so that He strikes His cheeks and weeps every day, and two tears fall from His eyes into the sea, and the sound of their falling can be heard from one end of the universe to the other. The water of the ocean is disturbed, and sometimes the earth trembles, that is, when earthquakes happen."

They attribute mistakes to Him and say that He admits to and expiates for sin. They claim falsely that the moon was God's mistake and that it said to the Lord (exalted be He above what they say), "You made a mistake when You created me smaller than the sun," and God accepted that and admitted His mistake. He said, "Offer Me a sacrifice through which I will expiate for My sin, for I created the moon smaller than the sun." How could they claim that God would offer expiation - to whom would He offer that expiation?!

The minds which fabricated this lie are very foolish indeed, and the minds which believe this nonsense are no less foolish. Praise be to Allah Who has guided us to the truth and the clear light.

Another aspect of their foolishness is their belief that God was overtaken by recklessness, which happened on the day when He became angry with the Children of Israel, and He swore to deprive them of eternal life. But after His recklessness left Him, He regretted that so He did not carry out that vow, because He had done something unjust.

The matter does not end there, with Him swearing an oath out of ignorance and recklessness, and doing wrong then expiating. They also claim that He needed an expiation to free Him from this vow. It says in their *Talmud*: "When God swore an unlawful oath, He needed someone to free him from this vow. One of the wise men among the Israelites heard God saying, 'Who will free Me from the vow that I swore to Myself?' When the rest of the rabbis heard that he [the wise man] had not freed Him from it, they regarded him as a donkey, because he has not freed God from His vow. Hence they invented an angel between the heavens and the earth, called May, to free God from His vow and oath when needed."[7]

These are a few examples of the false and distorted beliefs of the Jews, which form the basis of their religion. They are no less decadent than the myths of the Greeks and idolators about their idols.

3 - THE ARABS' DEVIATION FROM *TAWḤEED*

The Arabs were following the religion of *Tawḥeed*, the religion of their father Ibraaheem (Abraham). They continued to follow that until four hundred years before the coming of the Prophet (ﷺ), when there appeared among them a leader who was listened to and obeyed, and no one could oppose, and who changed their religion. His name was 'Amr ibn 'Aamir al-Khuzaa'i.

Bukhari narrated from Abu Hurayrah (رضي الله عنه) that the Prophet (ﷺ) said:

> "I saw 'Amr ibn 'Aamir al-Khuzaa'i dragging his intestines in Hell. He was the first one to introduce the

[7] This is just a little of the many things that the Jews have written in their *Talmud.*

> *taboo* of the *saa'ibah* (a she-camel let loose for the sake of the idols, and nothing was allowed to be carried on it)."[8]

Bukhari also narrated from 'Aa'ishah (may Allah be pleased with her) that the Prophet (ﷺ) said:

> "I saw Hell, parts of it consuming other parts, and I saw 'Amr dragging his intestines. He was the first one to introduce the *taboo* of the *saa'ibah*."[9]

This 'Amr changed the religion of the Arabs by calling them to worship idols, and by introducing reprehensible innovations into the religion of Allah, forbidding and permitting things according to his own desires. Among that were the things which Allah (ﷻ), mentioned in His Book:

﴿ مَا جَعَلَ ٱللَّهُ مِنۢ بَحِيرَةٍ وَلَا سَآئِبَةٍ وَلَا وَصِيلَةٍ وَلَا حَامٍ وَلَٰكِنَّ ٱلَّذِينَ كَفَرُوا۟ يَفْتَرُونَ عَلَى ٱللَّهِ ٱلْكَذِبَ وَأَكْثَرُهُمْ لَا يَعْقِلُونَ ﴿١٠٣﴾ ﴾

> ﴾Allah has not instituted things like *Baḥeerah* or a *Saa'ibah* or a *Waṣeelah* or a *Ḥaam* [all these animals were liberated in honour of idols as practiced by pagan Arabs in the pre-Islamic period]. But those who disbelieve invent lies against Allah, and most of them have no understanding.﴿ *(Qur'an 5: 103)*[10]

---

[8] Bukhari, 8/283, hadith no. 4623.

[9] Ibid, hadith no. 4624.

[10] *Baḥeerah*: A she-camel whose ear was slit, then it was let loose. This slit in its ear was a sign to the Arabs who knew from it that she was not to be ridden or used to carry things. This would be done to a she-camel after she produced her fifth offspring, provided that the last calf was a male.

Saa'ibah: This had to do with a man's vow; if what he wanted happened, he would set a she-camel free and it would be like the *baḥeerah* in that no one would use it for his own benefit.

The reports differ as to how 'Amr spread the idols through the Arabian Peninsula. Some say that 'Amr was given dreams by the jinn which showed him where the idols had been buried since the time of Nooḥ (Noah), when the people of Nooḥ had worshipped them. So 'Amr dug them up and distributed them among the Arabs. It is also said that he brought the idols from Syria. When 'Amr saw the Syrians worshipping idols. He asked for an idol. They gave him one which he set up in Makkah.[11]

The reason why the Arabs followed 'Amr ibn Luḥayy was that he had a high position among them. He was the leader of Khuzaa'ah when they took over Makkah and the Ka'bah, after expelling Jurham from Makkah. The Arabs had taken him as a lord; Although he did not introduce any innovation, they adopted it as a law, because he used to feed and clothe the people on the occasion of Ḥajj. At one time he might sacrifice ten thousand camels, and give ten thousand suits of clothing.[12]

It is further said that this 'Amr was the one who called the people to worship *Al-Laat*. He was a man who used to prepare (*latta* - to pound, mix with water, knead) *saweeq* (a kind of mush made with wheat or barley) for the pilgrims on a rock in Aṭ-Ṭaa'if. When he died, 'Amr ibn Luḥayy claimed that he had not died, but had entered the rock on which he used to prepare that food, and he commanded them to worship it.

Waṣeelah: If a she-camel gave birth to a female, the calf would belong to the people, but if it gave birth to a male, the calf would be dedicated to their gods. If she gave birth to twins, one male and one female, they would say that this female *waṣalat akhaahaa* (delivered her brother), so it would be forbidden to slaughter that male.

Ḥaam: A stallion camel that had fathered ten offspring, so they forbade slaughtering or riding him, and he was not to be barred from any grazing area or water.

[11] *As-Seerah an-Nabawiyyah* by Ibn Hishaam, 1/121.

[12] *Al-Bidaayah wa'n-Nihaayah*, 2/187.

It is also said that he was the one who changed the *Talbiyah* which was a declaration of *Tawḥeed* - belief in Allah alone. The *Talbiyah* from the time of Ibraaheem (Abraham) had been "*Labbayk Allahumma labbayk, labbayka laa shareeka laka labbayk* (At Your service, O' Allah, at Your service. At Your service, You have no partner, at Your service)." This continued until the time of 'Amr ibn 'Aamir. Whilst he was circumambulating the Ka'bah and reciting the *Talbiyah*, the *Shayṭaan* (Satan) appeared to him in the form of an old man reciting the *Talbiyah* with him. When he said, "At Your service, You have no partner," the old man said, "except the partner that You have." 'Amr found this odd and said, "What is this?" The old man said, "Say, You own him and whatever he owns - there is nothing wrong with that." So 'Amr said it, and the Arabs followed him.

The Beginning of Deviation

Ibn Isḥaaq tells us how the deviation began among the Arabs, who were the descendents of Ismaa'eel (Ishmael). "It started with them worshipping stones. At first they used to venerate the *Ḥaram* (the sanctuary in Makkah), and they did not go anywhere else until they became too great in number and the place became too crowded. Then they started to move away, looking for more space. But none of them would move away from the *Ḥaram* to another place until he took one of the stones of the *Ḥaram* with him, out of respect for it. Wherever they settled, they would set the stone up and circumambulate it as they used to circumambulate the Ka'bah. This led to their worshipping these stones, then they started worshipping whatever stones they found attractive."[13]

Look at the state they ended up in: it is narrated that Abu Rajaa' al-'Uṭaaridi said: "We used to worship stones during the *Jaahiliyah*. If

---

[13] *As-Seerah* by Ibn Hishaam, 1/122.

we found a stone that we liked better, we would throw (the first one) aside and adopt the new one (as an object of worship). If we couldn't find a stone, we would gather a handful of earth, then milk a sheep over it, then circumambulate it." One of the strange things about the *Jaahiliyah* was that when a man travelled, he would take four stones with him - three for his cooking pot and one to worship.

The Idols of the Arabs

The Arabs adopted idols. Hishaam ibn Muḥammad ibn al-Saa'ib al-Kalbi said: "One of the most ancient of their idols was *Manaat*, erected on the shore of the Red Sea near *Al-Mushallal* in *Qadeed*, between Makkah and Madeenah. All the Arabs used to venerate it. The Aws and Khazraj, and those who settled in Madeenah and Makkah and neighbouring regions used to venerate it and offer sacrifices to it, but none held it in higher esteem than Aws and Khazraj. The veneration of Aws and the Arabs of the regions around Yathrib (Madeenah) reached such an extent that when they went for Ḥajj they would do all the rituals of Ḥajj with the people, but they would not shave their heads; when they left Makkah, they would go to *Manaat* and shave their heads there and stay there for a while. They believed that their Ḥajj was not complete until they had done that.

Manaat belonged to Hudhayl and Khuzaa'ah, so the Messenger of Allah (ﷺ) sent 'Ali (رضي الله عنه) in the year of the conquest (of Makkah) to destroy it.

The Arabs then adopted *Al-Laat* in Aṭ-Ṭaa'if; this idol was more recent than *Manaat*. It was a square rock whose keepers were from Thaqeef. They built (a shrine) over it and Quryash and all the Arabs venerated it. *Zayd al-Laat* and *Taym al-Laat* were named after it. It was on the site where the left-hand minaret of the mosque of Aṭ-Ṭaa'if stands today. It remained like that until the Messenger of Allah (ﷺ) sent Al-Mugheerah ibn Shu'bah and Abu Sufyaan ibn Ḥarb, when Thaqeef embraced Islam. They destroyed it and burned.

But Ibn Jareer narrated in his *Tafseer* of the *aayah* (verse):

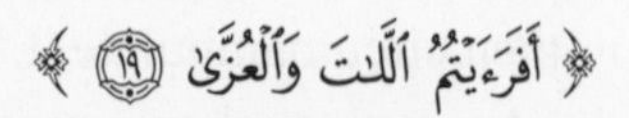

> ﴿Have you then considered *Al-Laat*, and *Al-'Uzzaa* [two idols of the pagan Arabs].﴾ *(Qur'an 53: 19)*

- that Mujaahid said: *Al-Laat* used to prepare (grind, etc.) *saweeq* for the pilgrims; when he died they clung to his grave. Abu'l-Jawzaa' also narrated from Ibn 'Abbaas that he used to prepare *saweeq* for the pilgrims. Bukhari also narrated something similar.

Then they adopted *Al-'Uzzaa*, which was more recent than *Al-Laat*. It was adopted by Ẓaalim ibn Sa'd in the *Nakhlah* valley, above *Dhaat 'Uraq*. They built a house over it, and used to hear voices from it. According to what is narrated by Al-Kalbi from Ibn 'Abbaas, he said: "*Al-'Uzzaa* had a she-devil which used to come to three trees in *Baṭn Nakhlah*."

When the Messenger of Allah (ﷺ) conquered Makkah, he sent Khaalid ibn al-Waleed, and said: "Go to *Baṭn Nakhlah*, where you will find three trees, and cut down the first one." So he went to it and cut it down. When he came back, the Prophet asked him, "Did you see anything?" He said, "No." So the Prophet said, "Cut down the second one." So he cut it down, then he came to the Prophet, who asked him, "Did you see anything" He said, "No." He said, "Go and cut down the third one." So he came to it, and he saw an Ethiopian woman with unkempt hair, placing her hands on her shoulders and gnashing her teeth. Her keeper stood behind her. Khaalid said:

"I disbelieve in you, I do not glorify you. I can see that Allah is humiliating you."

Then he struck her, cleaving her head, and she turned into ashes. Then he cut down the tree and killed the keeper. Then he came to the Prophet (ﷺ) and told him about that. He said,

> "That was *Al-'Uzzaa*, but the Arabs will have no *'Uzzaa* after this."

Al-'Uzzaa belonged to the people of Makkah, in a place near *'Arafaat*; it was a tree at which they would offer sacrifices and make supplications.

Al-Kalbi said in his book *Al-Aṣnaam*: "The Quraysh had idols in and around the Ka'bah, the greatest of which in their sight was Hubal. It was made of red carnelian in the form of a man. When they had a dispute about something or they wanted to travel, they would come to it and cast lots before it."

Also among their idols were *Isaaf* and *Naa'ilah*. Some narrators reported that a man and a woman committed *zina* in the Sacred House, and Allah turned them into two stones. Quraysh placed them by the Ka'bah to be a lesson to the people, but as time passed and the people started to worship idols, they worshipped these two stones too.

When the Messenger (ﷺ) conquered Makkah, he found three hundred and sixty idols around the Ka'bah. He started striking their faces and eyes with his bow, saying,

﴿ وَقُلْ جَآءَ ٱلْحَقُّ وَزَهَقَ ٱلْبَٰطِلُ ۚ إِنَّ ٱلْبَٰطِلَ كَانَ زَهُوقًا ﴿٨١﴾ ﴾

> ﴿Truth has come and *Baaṭil* [falsehood] has vanished. Surely, *Baaṭil* is ever bound to vanish.﴾ *(Qur'an 17: 81)*

And:

﴿ ... جَآءَ ٱلْحَقُّ وَمَا يُبْدِئُ ٱلْبَٰطِلُ وَمَا يُعِيدُ ﴿٤٩﴾ ﴾

> ﴾...*Al-Ḥaqq* [the truth, i.e. the Qur'an and Allah's Revelation] has come, and *Al-Baaṭil* [falsehood - *Iblees* (Satan)] can neither create anything nor resurrect [anything].﴿ *(Qur'an 34: 49).*

The idols fell on their heads, then he issued orders that they should be taken out of the mosque and burned. Something similar is narrated in *Ṣaheeḥayn* (Bukhari and Muslim) from Ibn Mas'ood, but he did not say that they fell on their heads... etc. According to the reports in *Ṣaheeḥayn*, he struck them with a stick that was in his hand.

The worship of idols spread until every house in Makkah had an idol which was worshipped by the household. When anyone wanted to travel, the first thing he would do would be to touch the idol then wipe his hand on himself (for blessing). When he would come back from his journey, this would again be the first thing that he would do.

Ibn Isḥaaq al-Kalbi said: "*Dhu'l-Khalaṣah* [an idol] belonged to Daws, Khath'am and Bajeelah, and the Arabs who lived in their land. It was a white stone carved with the image of a crown, and it had a house (shrine). The Messenger of Allah (ﷺ) said to Jareer ibn 'Abdullah al-Bajali,

> "Will you deal with *Dhu'l-Khalaṣah*?' So he went to it with (people from the tribe of) Aḥmas; Khath'am and Baahilah fought him, but he defeated them and destroyed the house of *Dhu'l-Khalaṣah*, and lit a fire in it."

According to Bukhari and Muslim, it is narrated that Jareer ibn 'Abdullah said: The Messenger of Allah (ﷺ) said to me,

> "Will you deal with *Dhu'l-Khalaṣah*?" There was a house in (the land of) Khath'am which was called the Yemeni Ka'bah. So I set out for *Dhu'l-Khalaṣah* with one hundred and fifty horsemen from Aḥmas. I said, "O'

Messenger of Allah! I cannot ride a horse well." He struck his hand against my chest so hard that I could see the marks of his fingers on my chest and said, "O' Allah! make him steadfast and make him guided and a guide to others." Then he went there and destroyed it [*Dhu'l-Khalaṣah*].

The Deep Darkness at the Time when the Prophet (ﷺ) was sent

Before the Messenger (ﷺ) came, there was nothing left of the heavenly light which the Prophets had brought except the faintest glow which was not enough to guide people or to show them the way revealed by Allah (سبحانه وتعالى), because that way had been lost and mixed with so much falsehood. It says in a hadith that "Allah looked at the people of the earth - before the Prophet was sent - and He hated them, Arabs and non-Arabs alike, except for what was left of the People of the Book."

Historical texts have preserved for us the stories of four wise men of Quraysh who withdrew from the people during one of the festivals of Quraysh celebrating one of their idols. They were Waraqah ibn Nawfal, 'Ubaydullah ibn Jaḥsh, 'Uthmaan ibn al-Ḥuwayrith ibn Asad ibn 'Abd al-'Uzzaa and Zayd ibn 'Amr ibn Nufayl.

They said to one another, "You know, by Allah, that your people are not following anything (any true path), and they have deviated from the religion of their father Ibraaheem (Abraham). What is this stone that we circumambulate, which can neither hear nor see, and can neither cause harm nor bring benefits? O' people! find yourselves a religion, for you are not following anything." So they split up and travelled to different lands, seeking the religion of Ibraaheem.

Waraqah ibn Nawfal followed the Christians, and learned about their books from their scholars, until he gained some knowledge from the People of the Book.

‘Ubaydullah ibn Jaḥsh remained in his state of confusion until he became a Muslim, then he migrated with the Muslims to Abyssinia, with his Muslim wife Umm Ḥabeebah bint Abi Sufyaan. When he reached Abyssinia he became a Christian, and left Islam. He died as a Christian.

‘Uthmaan ibn al-Ḥuwayrith went to Caesar (Qayṣar), the ruler of the Romans, and became a Christian, and was held in high esteem by Caesar.

Zayd did neither become a Jew nor a Christian. He left his people and shunned idols. He avoided dead meat, blood and the meat of animals that had been sacrificed to idols. He spoke out against the practice of burying infant girls alive; he said, “I worship the Lord of Ibraaheem (Abraham)”; and he started to criticize his people for their ways. Bukhari narrated from ‘Abdullah ibn ‘Umar (may Allah be pleased with them both) that the Prophet (ﷺ) met Zayd ibn ‘Amr ibn Nufayl at the bottom of Baldah (a valley to the west of Makkah) before the Revelation came to the Prophet. Some food was offered to the Prophet, but he refused to eat it. Then Zayd said: “I do not eat from what has been sacrificed on your stone altars; I only eat from that over which the name of Allah has been mentioned.” Zayd ibn ‘Amr used to criticize Quraysh for their sacrifices. He said: “Allah created the sheep; He sent down water for it from heaven and caused food to grow for it from the earth, then you slaughter it in a name other than that of Allah” Thus he denounced them and pointed out the enormity of their actions.[14]

Moosa ibn ‘Uqbah said, Saalim ibn ‘Abdullah told me - and I do not know of him narrating it from anyone except Ibn ‘Umar - that Zayd ibn ‘Amr ibn Nufayl went out to Syria asking about a religion he

---

[14] Bukhari, 7/142, hadith no. 3826.

could follow. He met a Jew scholar and asked him about their religion, saying, "Perhaps I will follow your religion. Tell me about it." He said, "You cannot follow our religion unless you take your share of the wrath of Allah." Zayd said, "The anger of Allah is what I am running away from; I can never bear anything of the wrath of Allah, how could I bear it? Can you tell me about any other religion?" The Jew said, "I do not know of any other religion except being a *ḥaneef.*" Zayd said, "What is a *ḥaneef*?" He said, "The religion of Ibraaheem (Abraham). He was neither a Jew nor a Christian, and he worshipped nothing but Allah."

Then Zayd went and met a Christian scholar and asked him about their religion, saying, "Perhaps I will follow your religion. Tell me about it." He said, "You cannot follow our religion unless you take your share of the curse of Allah." Zayd said, "The curse of Allah is what I am running away from; I can never bear anything of the curse and anger of Allah, how could I bear it? Can you tell me about any other religion?" The Christian said, "I do not know of any other religion except being a *ḥaneef.*" Zayd said, "What is a *ḥaneef*?" He said, "The religion of Ibraaheem. He was neither a Jew nor a Christian."

When Zayd heard what they said about Ibraaheem (عليه السلام), he went out, then he raised his hands and said, "O' Allah, bear witness that I am following the religion of Ibraaheem."[15]

Al-Layth said: Hishaam ibn 'Urwah wrote to me, (narrating) from his father, that Asmaa' bint Abi Bakr (may Allah be pleased with her) said: "I saw Zayd ibn 'Amr ibn Nufayl standing leaning back against the Ka'bah, saying, O' Quraysh! By Allah, no one among you is following the religion of Ibraaheem except me. He used to (rescue and) protect girls who were buried alive. He would say to a man who

---

[15] Bukhari, 7/142, hadith no. 3827.

wanted to bury his daughter alive, 'Do not kill her, I will take care of her.' He would take the child, and when she grew up he would say to her father, If you want I will give her to you, or if you want I will take care of her."[16]

The Messenger (ﷺ) was asked about this Zayd, and he said: "He will be gathered as a nation on his own, between me and 'Eesa ibn Maryam." Ibn Katheer said: its isnad is *jayyid ḥasan* (good and approved).

It is narrated from 'Aa'ishah (may Allah be pleased with her) that the Messenger (ﷺ) said:

> "I entered Paradise and I saw two gardens for Zayd ibn 'Amr ibn Nufayl." Ibn Katheer said, this is a *jayyid* isnad (good chain of transmission).

After that intense darkness, Allah (ﷻ), decreed the dawn of Islam, whose light shone upon the people and guided them. To Him be praise and grace.

---

[16] Bukhari, 7/143, hadith no. 3828.

REFERENCES

Abul Ḥasan al-Ash'ari: *Al-Ibaanah, Maṭbooa'at al-Jamey'a al-Islamiah*, Madeenah, Saudi Arabia.

Shaltoot: *Al-Islam Aqeedah wa Sharee'ah*, 9th ed., *Daar Ash-Shurooq*, Cairo, 1397H/1977G.

'Umar S. al-Ashqar: *Asmaa' Allah wa Ṣifatuhu fi Mu'taqad Ahl as-Sunnah wa'l Jama'ah*, 2nd ed. *Daar an Nafa'ais*, Amman, Jordan 1414H/1994G.

Baihaqi: *Al-Asmaa' waṣ-Ṣifaat*, Photo print, Beirut.

'Umar S. al-Ashqar: *Aṣl al-'Itiqaad*, 1st ed. *Daar an-Nafa'ais*, Kuwait, 1410H/1990G.

Raazi: *'Itiqadaat Firaq al-Muslimeen*, *Daar al-Kutub al-'Ilmiah*, Beirut, 1402H/1982G.

Ibn Katheer: *Al-Bidayah wa'n Nihaayah*, 2nd ed., *Maktabah al-Ma'arif*, Beirut, 1394H/1974G.

'Umar S. al-Ashqar: *Taweel Khuṭooratuh wa Athaaruhu* 1st ed. *Daar an-Nafa'ais*, Amman, Jordan, 1412H/1992G.

Qurṭubi: *Tafseer* (*Al-Jame'y li Aḥkaam al-Qur'an*), 2nd Print. *Daar al-Kutub al-'Arabi*, Cairo, 1387H/1967G.

Ibn Ḥajar al-'Asqalani: *Talkheeṣ al-Ḥubayr*, published by Abdullah Hashim al-Yamani, Madeenah, S.A., 1384H/1964G.

Ibn Khuzaymah: *Tawḥeed, Maktaba al-Kulliyaat al-Azhariah*, Cairo.

Zandani: *Tawḥeed*, 1st ed., *Daar al-Khayr*, 1411H/1990G.

Ibn al-Atheer: *Jame'y al-Uṣool fi Aḥadeeth ar-Rasool*, Edited by Abdul Qaadir al-Arnaooṭ, *Maktabah al-Ḥalwani et al.*, 1389H/ 1969G.

Bukhari: *Khalq Af'aal al-'Ibaad*, 1st ed., *Daar as-Salafiyah*, Kuwait, 1405H/1985G.

Naaṣiruddeen al-Albani: *Silsilat al-Aḥaadeeth aṣ-Ṣaḥeeḥah*, 1st ed., *Al-Maktab al-Islami*, Damascus.

Ibn Hisham: *Seerat an-Nabawiyah* along with *Sharḥ* by Abu Dhar al-Khashani, 1st ed., *Maktabah al-Manar*, Jordan, 1409H/1988G.

Muhammad Abi'l 'Izz al-Ḥanafi: *Sharaḥ al-'Aqeedah aṭ-Ṭaḥaawiyah, Al-Maktab al-Islami*, Beirut, 1391H.

Nawawi: *Sharḥ an-Nawawi 'ala Muslim*, *Al-Maṭba'ah al-Miṣriyah wa Maktabataha*, Cairo.

Bukhari: *Al-Jam'ey aṣ-Ṣaḥeeḥ* with *Sharḥ Fatḥ al-Baari*, *Al-Maṭba'ah as-Salafiyah wa Maktabaataha*, Cairo.

Ṣaḥeeḥ al-Jaame'y aṣ-Ṣagheer, 1st ed., *Al-Maktab al-Islami*, Beirut.

Naṣiruddeen al-Albani: *Ṣaḥeeḥ Sunan ibn Maajah*, 2nd Printing, *Maktab at-Tarbiah al-'Arabi li Duwal al-Khaleej*, Riyadh, 1408H/ 1988G.

Abu Dawood: *Ṣaḥeeḥ Sunan*, 1st ed., *Al-Maktab al-Islami*, Beirut, 1409H/1980G.

Naaṣiruddeen al-Albani: *Ṣaḥeeḥ Sunan at-Tirmidhi*, 1st Print, *Maktab at-Tarbiyah al-'Arabi li Duwal al-Khaleej*, Riyadh, 1408H/ 1988G.

Nasaa'i: *Ṣaḥeeḥ Sunan*, 1st ed., *Al-Maktab al-Islami*, Beirut, 1409H/ 1988G.

Muslim: *Al-Jam'ey aṣ-Ṣaḥeeḥ*, edited by Muhammad Fuad Abdul Baaqi, 1st ed., *Daar Iḥiyah al-Kutub al-'Arabiah*, Egypt, 1375H/ 1956G.

Ibn Ḥajar al-'Asqalani: *Fatḥ al-Baari bi Sharḥ Ṣaḥeeḥ al-Bukhari, Al-Maktabah as-Salafiyah*, Cairo.

Shawkaani: *Fatḥ al-Qadeer al-Jam'ey bayna Fannay ar-Riwayah wa'd Diraayah fi't Tafseer, Daar Iḥiyah at-Torath*, Beirut.

Ibn Taymiyah: *Al-Fatwah al-Ḥamawiyah al-Kubrah*, 4th ed., *Al-Maktabah as-Salafiyah*, Cairo 1410H.

Syed Quṭb: *Fi Ẓilaal al-Qur'an, Daar ash-Shurooq*, 1394H/1974G.

Yusuf Khayaaṭ and Nadeem Mar'ashlee (ed): *Lisaan al-'Arab*, 1st ed., *Daar Lisaan al-'Arab*, Beirut.

Safaareeni: *Lawame'y al-Anwaar al-Bahiyah*, State of Qatar.

Ibn Qaasim (ed): *Majmoo' al-Fataawa Shaykh al-Islam ibn Taymiyah*, 1st ed., Govt. of Saudi Arabia, 1381H.

Khaṭeeb at-Tabrezi: *Mishkaat al-Maṣaabeeḥ*, 1st ed., *Al-Maktab al-Islami*, Damascus, 1380H.

Shaykh Ḥafiẓ ibn Aḥmad al-Ḥakami: *Ma'arij al-Qubool*, Daa'irat al-Ifta' Publications, Saudi Arabia.

'Umar S. al-Ashqar: *Mu'taqad al-Eemaan Abi'l Ḥasan al-Ash'ari*, 1st ed., *Daar an-Nafa'ais*, Amman, Jordan, 1414H/1994G.

Abul Ḥasan al-Ash'ari: *Maqalaat al-Islamiyeen, Daar Iḥiyah at-Toraath al-'Arabi*, Beirut.

Ibn Taymiyah: *Muntaqa min Aḥaadeeth al-Aḥkaam, Al-Maṭba'ah as-Salafiyah*, Cairo.

Muhammad al-Ameen ash-Shinqṭi: *Manhaj wa Dirasaat li Aayaat al-Asmaa' wa'ṣ-Ṣifaat*, *Manshooraat al-Jamey'ah al-Islamiah*, Madeenah, 2nd ed. 1388H.

Bayhaqi: *Al-Asmaa' wa'ṣ-Ṣifaat*, Photoprinting, Beirut.

Ibn al-Qayyim: *Aṣ-Ṣawa'iq al-Mursalah*, *Maṭba'a al-Imaam*, Cairo.

Adh-Dhabi: *Makhtaṣar al-'Ulu*, summary by Al-Albaani, *Al-Maktab al-Islami*, 2nd ed. 1412H/1991C.

Ibraheem Anees et al: *M'ujam al-Waseeṭ*, *Daar Iḥya' at-Toraath al-'Arabi*, Beirut, 2nd edition.

'Aqqaad: *Kitaab-Allah*, *Daar al-Halaal*, Cairo.

Shawkaani: *Fawaai'd al-Majmoo'ah*, *Maṭba'a as-Sunnah al-Muḥammdia*, Cairo.

Imam Shaafa'i: *Ar-Risalah*, *Daar al-Fikr*, Beirut.

Muhammad Ḥasan Ḥamaṣi: *Naḥlah Tasabbaḥallah*, *Daar ar-Rasheed*, Damascus, 2nd ed. 1977C.

Darimi: *Radd ad-Daarisee 'Ala al-Mareesi*, *Daar al-Kutub al-'Ilmiya*, Beirut.

Muhammad Khaleel al-Haras: *Sharḥ al-'Aqeedah al-Waasṭiyah*, *Manshooraat al-Jaame'a al-Islamia*, Madeenah, 4th ed.

Abu 'Ubayd al-Qaasim ibn Salaam: *Eemaan*, edited by Al-Albaani in the anthology under the name "*Min Kunooz as-Sunnah - Rasaail Arb'a*". *Al-Maṭba'a al-'Umoomiyah*, Damascus.

GLOSSARY

'Aalameen	عالمين	:	The Worlds; the Universe, Mankind, jinn and all that exist.
'Amal	عمل	:	Action, deeds.
'Aqaa'id	عقائد	:	Sing. *'Aqeedah*. belief, faith, creed.
Ai'mmah	أئمة	:	Sing. Imam. Leading jurists and scholars of Islam, like Imam Abu Ḥaneefah, Maalik, Shafi'i, Ḥanbal, Bukhari, Muslim, Ibn Taymiyah etc.
Aalihah	آلهة	:	Sing. *Ilaah*. gods.
Aayaat	آيات	:	Sing. *Aayah*. Verses of the Qur'an, signs; proof.
Abraar	ابرار	:	Righteous, pious.
Ad-Dawaab	الدواب	:	Moving (living) creatures, beasts.
Al-'Aleem	العليم	:	All-Knowing; an attribute of Allah.
Al-'Azeez	العزيز	:	The Almighty; an attribute of Allah.
Al-Awwal	الأول	:	The First; an attribute of Allah.
Aẓ-Ẓaahir	الظاهر	:	The Apparent; an attribute of Allah.
Aaḥaad	آحاد	:	A term in hadith discipline, a narration of hadith by less than *mutawaatir*, i.e. by three, two or one person at each/ any stage of reporting.

Aḥkaam	أحكام	:	Sing. *Ḥukm*. Ruling; ordainments.
Ahl al-Kalaam	أهل الكلام	:	Scholastics, Islamic philosophers.
Al-Ḥaafiẓ	ألحافظ	:	The Protector; an attribute of Allah; Also a man who memorizes whole of the Qur'an.
Al-Ḥakeem	الحكيم	:	The All-Wise, an attribute of Allah.
Al-Ḥannan	الحنان	:	The Compassionate; an attribute of Allah.
Al-Ḥayy al-Qayyoom	الحي القيوم	:	The Ever living; the One Who sustains and protects all that exists; an attribute of Allah.
Al-Jabbaar	الجبار	:	The Compeller; an attribute of Allah.
Al-Kareem	الكريم	:	The Most Generous; an attribute of Allah.
Al-Khaafiḍ	الخافض	:	The Abaser; an attribute of Allah.
Al-Khabeer	الخبير	:	The All-Aware; an attribute of Allah.
Al-Laghw	اللغو	:	Dirty, false, evil, vain talk, falsehood, and all that Allah has forbidden.
Al-Lawḥ al-Maḥfooẓ	اللوح المحفوظ	:	The Book of Decrees with Allah; the Preserved Tablet.
Al-Maani'	المانع	:	The Withholder, an attribute of Allah.
Al-Malik	الملك	:	The King; an attribute of Allah.

Al-Mannaan	المنان	:	The Gracious; an attribute of Allah.
Al-Masaakeen	المساكين	:	Sing. *Miskeen*. the Poor.
Al-Mu'min	المؤمن	:	The Giver of security; an attribute of Allah.
Al-Mudhill	المذل	:	The Dishonourer; an attribute of Allah.
Al-Muhaymin	المهيمن	:	The Watcher over His Creatures; an attribute of Allah.
Al-Muḥsinoon	المحسنون	:	Sing. *Muḥsin*. Pious, Righteous, the good-doers.
Al-Muḥṣee	المحصي	:	The Reckoner, an attribute of Allah.
Al-Muntaqim	المنتقم	:	The Avenger; an attribute of Allah.
Al-Mureed	المريد	:	The One Who Wills; an attribute of Allah..
Al-Mutakabbir	المتكبر	:	Most Great, the Greatest; an attribute of Allah.
Al-Muttaqoon	المتقون	:	Sing. *Muttaqi*. The pious, Righteous.
Al-Qaabiḍ	القابض	:	The Seizer, an attribute of Allah.
Al-Qaḍaa' wal-Qadar	القضاء والقدر	:	Divine Will and Predestination.
Al-Qadar	القدر	:	Divine Pre-Ordainments.
Al-Qadeer	القدير	:	The Able, an attribute of Allah.
Al-Quddoos	القدوس	:	The Holy, an attribute of Allah.
Ar-Raḥmaan	الرحمن	:	The Most Beneficent, an attribute of Allah.

Ar-Raḥeem	الرحيم	:	The Most Merciful, an attribute of Allah.
Ar-Razzaaq	الرزاق	:	The All-Provider, Sustainer; an attribute of Allah.
Ar-Raḥmah	الرحمة	:	The Mercy.
Ash-Shaheed	الشهيد	:	The Witness.
Aṣ-Ṣaani'	الصانع	:	The Maker, an attribute of Allah.
As-Salaam	السلام	:	The One Free from all defects; an attribute of Allah.
As-Samee'	السميع	:	All-Hearing; an attribute of Allah.
Awwah	اواه	:	One who invokes Allah with humility, glorifies Him and remembers Him much.
Az-Zaari'	الزارع	:	The Grower.
Baḥeerah	بحيرة	:	A she-camel whose ear was slit.
Baaṭil	باطل	:	False, Wrong.
Bid'ah	بدعة	:	Reprehensible innovation in religion, heresy.
Ḍa'eef	ضعيف	:	Weak; also a term in hadith discipline for a narration whose original narrator is missing or some narrators missing in the chain etc. This type of hadith is termed as weak.
Faasiqoon	فاسقون	:	Sing. *Faasiq*. Rebellious, disobedient to Allah, Sinner.
Fatrah	فترة	:	Interval between two Prophets,

			when no divine message reached.
Fiqh	فقه	:	Islamic jurisprudence.
Fitnah	فتنة	:	Trial, affliction.
Fiṭrah	فطرة	:	Human instinct; nature.
Fuqahaa'	فقهاء	:	Sing. *Faqeeḥ*. Scholars of Islamic jurisprudence.
Haam	هام	:	A stallion camel that fathered ten offspring.
Ḥadd	حد	:	Pl. *Ḥudood*. Islamic penal code; Divinely set limit between *ḥalaal* and *ḥaraam*; specific punishment.
Ḥajj	حج	:	Pilgrimage to Makkah in *Dhul-Ḥijja*; one of the five pillars of Islam.
Ḥalaal	حلال	:	Legal (from Islamic point of view).
Ḥaraam	حرام	:	Forbidden in Islam.
Ḥaneef	حنيف	:	The religion of Prophet Ibraheem, Belief in One Allah.
Ḥaqaa'iq	حقائق	:	Sing. *Ḥaqeeqah*. Truth, reality; Mystical "realities."
Iblees	ابليس	:	Satan, Devil, (Lucifer).
Ijmaa'	اجماع	:	The Consensus of opinion of the Companions / Islamic Jurists on an issue from Islamic point of view.
'Ilm al-Kalaam	علم الكلام	:	Scholastism, Science of Divinity in Islam (Islamic Philosophy).
Jaahiliyah	جاهلية	:	Pre-Islamic period, non Islamic.

Jihad	جهاد	:	Struggle, striving, battle for the supremacy of the words of Allah.
Kaffaarah	كفارة	:	Expiation.
Kaafir	كافر	:	Disbeliever, denier of truth, opposing Islam.
Khaleel	خليل	:	Very close friend, a title of the Prophet Ibraheem (Abraham).
Khuṭbah	خطبة	:	Sermon, address, speech.
Laa-Adriyyah	لا ادريه	:	Lit: Not knowing; School of philosophers affirming uncertainty of ultimate cause as god; agnosticism.
Laḥd	لحد	:	Niche in the side of a grave.
Madhhab	مذهب	:	School of thought (in jurisprudence).
Mahr	مهر	:	Obligatory bridal money given by the husband to his wife at the time of marriage, dowry.
Makrooh	مكروه	:	Abominable.
Matn	متن	:	Text.
Mawḍoo'	موضوع	:	A hadith terminology, Fabricated narration of a hadith.
Mufsidoon	مفسدون	:	Sing: *Mufsid*; Mischief-makers.
Munqaṭi'	منقطع	:	A hadith term meaning broken; a kind of Ḍa'eef hadith wherein narrator/s is/ are missing in one or more chain.

Mutawaatir	متواتر	:	Lit. Continuous: a hadith term meaning a large number of narrators have narrated a particular hadith at all level and through various channels.
Nutfah	نطفة	:	Male and female semen drops.
Najwaa	نجوى	:	Secret counsel.
Naṣṣ	نص	:	Source, a statement, text, Qur'an and Sunnah.
Qaaḍi	قاضي	:	A judge; A Shari'ah judge.
Qareen	قرين	:	Jinn companion.
Qiblah	قبله	:	Ka'bah: Direction to which Muslims face while praying.
Qinṭaar	قنطار	:	A great amount; weight of a hundred pound, quintal.
Rabb	رب	:	Lord and Master, Sustainer, Protector, Supporter, Nourisher, and Guardian, Sovereign and Ruler, He who controls and directs, Divine name of Allah.
Ribaa	ربا	:	Interest, usury.
Rooḥ	روح	:	Soul; spirit.
Saa'ibah	سائبه	:	A she-camel let loose for the sake of the idols, and nothing was allowed to be carried on it.
Ṣadaqah	صدقة	:	Charity: obligatory and/or optional.
Ṣaḥaabah	صحابه	:	Sing. *Ṣaḥaabi*. The Companions of

			the Prophet.
Ṣaḥeeḥ	صحيح	:	Sound and authentic, a hadith term used for authentic statement of (and about) the Prophet. All the narrators are pious and possess excellent memory and the chain is continuous. It is also used for compilations of hadith like *Ṣaḥeeḥ* Bukhari, *Ṣaḥeeḥ* Muslim etc.
Ṣalaah	صلاة	:	Prayer: obligatory and/or optional.
Saweeq	سويق	:	A kind of mush-made with wheat or barley.
Shari'ah	شريعه	:	Islamic law.
Shirk	شرك	:	Polytheism, associating others to Allah with divine powers.
Shuhada'	شهداء	:	Sing. *Shaheed*. Martyrs for the cause of Allah.
Ṣifaat al-Af'aal	صفات الأفعال	:	Attributes describing some of Allah's actions.
Aṣ-Ṣifaat al-Jaami'ah	الصفات الجامعة	:	All encompassing and comprehensive attributes.
Ṣifaat Nafsiyah	صفات نفسية	:	Attributes referring to "emotions" e.g., love, hate, etc.
Ṣubḥ	صبح	:	*Fajr*, Dawn.
Sunni	سني	:	*Ahl as-Sunnah*, people following the Sunnah of the Prophet.
Ta'ṭeel	تعطيل	:	Denying all attributes of Allah.
Ta'weel Ba'eed	تأويل بعيد	:	Far-fetched interpretation.

Tafseer	تفسير	:	Interpretation of the Qur'an; exegesis.
Tawḥeed	توحيد	:	Belief in the Oneness of Allah.
Uloohiyah	الوهية	:	Divinity.
Wuḍoo'	وضوء	:	Ritual ablution.
Waḥy	وحي	:	Revelation, Divine revelation.
Wajh	وجه	:	Face; for the sake of.
Zaaniyah	زانية	:	Adulteress.
Zakah	زكوة/ زكاة	:	An annual obligatory prescribed charity (or poor due) by a Muslim in possession of riches, merchandise, agricultural produce, livestock, trading goods etc. over a prescribed limit - a certain minimum called *niṣaab*. A pillar of Islam. Rate of payment varies according to the kind of possession. Details to be found in *Fiqh* books. Way of distribution to be found in the Qur'an 9:60.
Zina	زنا	:	Adultery, fornication.

INDEX OF THE QUR'AN

INDEX OF HADITH

	Kitaab Mawaqeet aṣ-Ṣalaat	521	295
	Kitaab al-Jumu'ah	1053	301
		1113	396
	Kitaab ad-Daa'waat	5927	326
	Kitaab ash-Shirkah	2315	380
	Kitaab al-'Ilm	125	395
	Kitaab ar-Riqaa'iq	6085	396
	Kitaab Bad' al-Waḥy	1	400
	Kitaab ad-Diyyaat	6354	406
Muslim	*Kitaab adh-dhikr wad Du'aa'*	4852	47
		4905	244
		4844	290
		4836	306
	Kitaab al-Eemaan	135	47
		86	52, 63
		81	52
		146	53
		98	53
		91	54
		51	63
		266	250, 295
		263	251, 301
		276	256
		274	279
		24	290
Muslim		110	292
		259	292

	Musnad al-Mukaththaireen min-aṣ-Ṣaḥaaba	3528	307
	Musnad al-Qaba'il	25927	380
Tirmidhi	*Kitaab ad-Daa'waat*	3463	47
		3397	313
		3314	324
	Kitaab al-Adab	2710	61
	Kitaab Tafseer al-Qur'an	3290	147
		2879	95
	Kitaab al-Birr waṣ-Ṣalah	1847	271
	Kitaab an-Nikaaḥ	1021	381
Dawood	*Kitaab al-Adab*	4393	248
	Kitaab al-Adab	4444	248
	Kitaab as-Sunnah	4102	264
	Kitaab al-Aymaan wan Nudhoor	2856	271
	Kitaab aṭ-Ṭibb	3394	189
Nasaa'i	*Kitaab as-Sahw*	1289	248
Ibn Majah	*Kitaab al-Muqaddamah*	185	255
	Kitaab ad-Du'aa'	3846	314

Note: The above given reference nos. of hadith are from the CD programme "Hadith Encyclopedia" by Harf Information Technology.

TRANSLITERATION CHART

أ	a
آ . ى	aa
ب	b
ت	t
ة	h or t (when followed by another Arabic word)
ث	th
ج	j
ح	ḥ
خ	kh
د	d
ذ	dh
ر	r
ز	z
س	s
ش	sh
ص	ṣ
ض	ḍ
ط	ṭ

ظ	ẓ
ع	‘
غ	gh
ف	f
ق	q
ك	k
ل	l
م	m
ن	n
هـ - ه - ـه	h
و	w
و (as vowel)	oo
ي	y
ي (as vowel)	ee
ء	’ (Omitted in initial position)

َ	Fatḥah	a
ِ	Kasra	i
ُ	Ḍammah	u
ّ	Shaddah	Double letter
ْ	Sukoon	Absence of vowel

SYMBOLS' DIRECTORY

(ﷻ) : *Subḥaanahu wa Ta'aala* - "The Exalted."

(ﷺ) : *Ṣalla-Allahu 'Alayhi wa Sallam* -
"Blessings and Peace be upon him."

(عليه السلام) : *'Alayhis-Salaam* - "May Peace be upon him."

(رضي الله عنه) : *Raḍi-Allahu 'Anhu* - "May Allah be pleased with him."